On this order, the hatches of the three Panzers closed.
. . . The guns' barrels were wound down to firing elevation. Anti-tank shells were loaded on the move. . . . Several Shermans were spotted rolling at a dangerous distance
towards us through the orchard of a farm. We had driven
right in front of their barrels and were showing them our
vulnerable flanks.

'Enemy tanks from the left—9 o'clock—200—open fire!'
This was all the chief of 8 [SS Panzer Company], who was
also the commander of the point Panzer, could do. Nothing
else was required. The months-long drills and battle experience of the crews now proved themselves. The driver jerked
the Panzer to the left, bringing it into the firing position.
The closest enemy tank had been hit. Within a minute or
so, four or five Shermans were burning. Only the last one
. . . brought sweat to the commander's brow. It had only
just been spotted as it was already swinging its barrel towards us.

'Enemy tank hard left—10 o'clock—100!' Then came a
blow, a flash of fire from the breech of the gun, the case
dropped into the sack, the enemy tank exploded!

*To all who fought with honour in Normandy in 1944—
many of them deserved better commanders.*

STEEL INFERNO

I SS PANZER CORPS IN NORMANDY

by
Michael Reynolds

The story of the 1st and 12th SS Panzer Division in the 1944 Normandy campaign

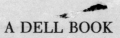

A DELL BOOK

Published by
Dell Publishing
a division of
Bantam Doubleday Dell Publishing Group, Inc.
1540 Broadway
New York, New York 10036

ISBN: 0-440-22596-5

Reprinted by arrangement with Sarpedon Publishers

Printed in the United States of America

Published simultaneously in Canada

August 1998

10 9 8 7 6 5 4 3 2

OPM

Contents

Contents

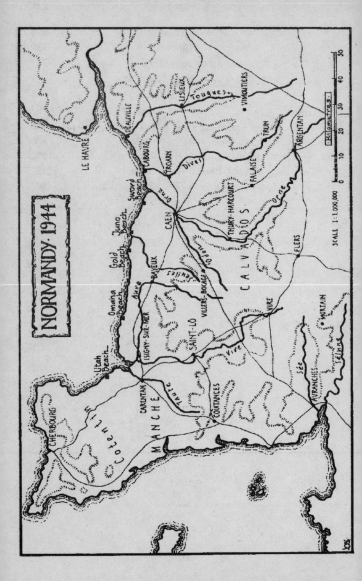

List of Maps

List of Plates

1. On the occasion of the 1936 Berlin Olympics, Theodor (Teddy) Wisch heads the Leibstandarte SS Adolf Hitler Guard of Honour. Seven years later he was the commander of the 1st SS Panzer Division LAH.
2. Hitlerjugend recruiting poster 1943.
3. Kurt Meyer, Fritz Witt and Sepp Dietrich with Field Marshal von Rundstedt, early 1944.
4. Sepp Dietrich, commander I SS Panzer Corps, with Field Marshal Erwin Rommel, commander Army Group B.
5. Lieutenant General Omar Bradley, commander First US Army, General Sir Bernard Montgomery, commander 21st Army Group and Lieutenant General Miles Dempsey, commander Second British Army.
6. Wilhelm Mohnke, Walter Ewert, Kurt Meyer, Dr Besuden and Teddy Wisch, 28th May 1943.
7. Near Kharkov 28th May 1943—officers of the LAH celebrate Dietrich's birthday—front row: Kurt Meyer, Hugo Kraas, Sepp Dietrich, Albert Frey, Weiser, Rudolf Sandig, Bernhard (Papa) Krause, Schönberger (Hubert Meyer behind Sandig).
8. Teddy Wisch, commander of the 1st SS Panzer Division LAH.
9. Kurt Meyer (Panzermeyer), commander 25th SS Panzer-Grenadier Regiment HJ on D-Day and 12th SS Panzer Division HJ from 16th June until 6th September 1944.
10. Panzermeyer driving Fritz Witt, his Divisional commander, on a reconnaissance in Normandy in early June 1944. The Regimental Medical Officer mounts the pillion. It is difficult to imagine equivalent Allied officers doing the same thing.
11. Max Wünsche, commander 12th SS Panzer Regiment HJ.
12. Wünsche, slightly wounded on 9th June, with the injured Rudolf von Ribbentrop, commander 3rd Company 1st SS

The majority of these photographs are from the author's personal collection and in many cases their precise origin is unknown. They have been obtained over the years from friends in numerous countries, and from various German, British, Canadian and United States National Archives and Collections. Those obtained more recently through the Polish Institute and Sikorski Museum (PISM) in London are indicated. The author extends his gratitude to all those who have made possible the publication of this particular set of photographs.

Acknowledgments

I am grateful to a number of people and organisations without whose help this book would not have been written. Firstly, to my publisher Jamie Wilson, who has become a valued friend. Having been bold enough to publish my first book, he then encouraged me to write this one.

Next, I would like to thank an American—Jay Karamales. Once again he has taken my hand-drawn maps and charts and turned them into the excellent end-products which appear in this book; just as importantly, he obtained for me much invaluable information from the US National Archives. His own book, *Against the Panzers,* co-authored with Allyn R. Vannoy was published last year by McFarland; it contains further details of the Mortain counter-attack which will be of great interest to American readers.

On the subject of archival material I am very grateful to Viscount Montgomery of Alamein for allowing me to quote from his father's private letters and to the Montgomery Collections Committee of the Trustees of the Imperial War Museum in London for permission to quote from the Montgomery Papers. My thanks must also go to the willing staff at the Public Record Office at Kew, in particular Mike Rogers, to John Harding of the British Army Historical Branch, and to Krzysztof Barbarski and the staff of the Polish Institute and Sikorski Museum in London.

I am particularly indebted to John Fedorowicz and Michael Olive, President and Vice-President respectively, of J. J. Fedorowicz Publishing Inc of Winnipeg, Canada, for permission to use material from the Fedorowicz books specified in the Bibliography. Their agreement was of great importance for the satisfactory completion of this book.

Jeff Dugdale and Mike Wood are recognised experts on 1944 German Orders of Battle and unit equipment holdings. They generously agreed to share their knowledge with me, for which I am much indebted.

The following translated German, French and Polish documents for me—Vic Lawson and his wife Lotte, Marie-France Grégoire, Michael Young, Stanislaw Grabowski and John Suchcitz—I am most grateful.

Frank Warnock, an American, kindly loaned me two documents which were essential to painting the picture of COBRA and the Mortain counter-attack. He was wounded with the 117th Infantry Regiment in Normandy and later won the Distinguished Service Cross in the Battle of the Bulge. Sadly, he died whilst I was writing this book. I hope, and think, he would have enjoyed reading it. We never met but we corresponded regularly and I feel I knew him well.

My thanks are due to Zbigniew Mieczkowski who kindly invited me to join some twenty-five veterans of the 1st Polish Armoured Division at their remembrance services in Normandy in 1996. He, Stanislaw Grabowski and John Suchcitz could not have been more patient in showing me where various actions happened, or more helpful in providing me with documents, translations and photographs.

Canadian historian and author, Don Graves, generously made his personal collection of German and Canadian documents available to me, which greatly helped my understanding of certain parts of the battle. I am indebted to him. His own book, *South Albertas: A Canadian Regiment at War,* is due to be published this year; it describes Canadian participation in the Falaise Pocket fighting in more detail and will be of particular interest to Canadian readers.

During several visits to France to see where each action took place, I stayed with Mike and Rosemary Chilcott at their charming Manoir Au Pont Rouge, near Bayeux. Mike is an expert on Normandy and I thank him for his views on various aspects of the battle.

My old Sandhurst colleague and great friend, Brigadier Tony Baxter, corrected my typescript and advised me how to present certain aspects of this book. And another retired member of the Armed Forces, Bill Sumpter, gave me invaluable help with my computer software; I wish I had a little of his techni-cal expertise. I am very grateful to both of them.

And lastly I must thank my wife, Anne, for her patience and encouragement—not to mention one or two good ideas!

Sussex, England   MFR
July 1997

Introduction

'Nations and peoples are largely the stories they feed themselves. If they tell themselves stories that are lies, they will suffer the future consequences of those lies. If they tell themselves stories that face their own truths, they will free their histories for future flowerings'—Ben Okri.

After the publication of my first book, *The Devil's Adjutant—Jochen Peiper, Panzer Leader,* a number of people, including some who had fought against the Germans in the Second World War, wrote to tell me that although they could never forget or forgive the outrages and atrocities committed by some members of Hitler's Wehrmacht, particularly the Waffen-SS, they had to admire their military achievements and astounding resilience. One retired senior British officer wrote:

> Despite all their defeats and casualties they always seemed to have an endless supply of platoon leaders and battalion commanders. Sadly this was not always the case with our own army as John Keegan noted in his book, *Six Armies in Normandy.* I would be interested to know how the Germans were able to pull out good leaders at the moment of crisis. They also were better than allied armies at blending a wide variety of units and arms of the service into one group and then fighting like tigers! Is there anything our army can learn from them?

These thoughts led me to look again at some of the more remarkable achievements and actions of the German Army and at the extraordinary casualty rates they seemed to be able to sustain without a collapse of morale. I looked in particular at the Normandy campaign in the summer of 1944, when the Germans were engaged against the Armed Forces of not just one nation but four. The result is this book which deliberately focuses on the two particular Waffen-SS Divisions designated by Hitler in the summer of 1943 to form his new I SS Panzer Corps and which, between them, fought in every major battle in Normandy. They were the 1st SS Panzer-Grenadier Division Leibstandarte Adolf Hitler and 12th SS Panzer-Grenadier Division Hitlerjugend. Both were later redesignated as Panzer Divisions.

Although other formations such as 21st Panzer and Panzer Lehr were placed under the command of I SS Panzer Corps during the battle of Normandy, this book will describe only the actions of the designated Divisions of the Corps and the 101st SS Heavy Panzer Battalion which was an integral part of it—only those units whose members were entitled to wear Hitler's name on their sleeves and the 'Dietrich' emblem on their vehicles. This book will not therefore discuss or describe the strategic aspects of the Battle of Normandy—more than enough books have already done so. Rather, it will trace the tactical battle as it affected the fighting soldier. I hope it will help to explain both the strengths and weaknesses of the Waffen-SS, and that future soldiers may learn from the agonies endured by their forbears, of whichever nation, in Normandy in 1944. I hope too that the reader will judge it to be balanced and unbiased.

Shortly after starting this book I happened to pick up an old copy of the *House Journal of the British Army;* it contained an article suggesting that historians too often indulge in revisionist thinking and writing and are, in the calm of academe, too quick to criticise past military commanders and suggest that their soldiers were badly trained and equipped and often poorly motivated. I realise that this book may well open me to such criticisms, but I believe it right and proper to attempt to chronicle military campaigns correctly, to expose any myths that have arisen and point out obvious mistakes and omissions. Whilst the aim of any military campaign must be to defeat the enemy, it cannot be wrong to assess later the cost involved and draw appropriate lessons. The history of amphibious landings, beginning with Gallipoli, is a case in point—it was as well the Allies had learned the necessary lessons for Normandy.

During my own military career I fought alongside American

and Canadian troops in Korea, even accompanying a US infantry company on one operation. Later on I served for two years as an exchange officer with the Canadian army in Canada, sixteen intermittent years in Germany and for three years amongst Americans, albeit in Germany; I also had the great privilege of commanding American, Canadian and German as well as British soldiers during my three years as commander of NATO's International Mobile Force in the 1980s. I have therefore had a unique opportunity to study the strengths and weaknesses, in both human and material terms, of these armies and their soldiers, and to compare them with those of their 1944 predecessors. I am thankful that in any future war we are likely to be all on the same side.

Senior Dramatis Personae

GERMAN

Gerd von Rundstedt, Field Marshal	CinC West until 2nd July
Hans von Kluge, Field Marshal	CinC West 2nd July to 17th August
Walter Model, Field Marshal	CinC West 17th August to end of campaign
Erwin Rommel, Field Marshal	Commander Army Group 'B' until 17th July
Geyr von Schweppenburg, General	Commander Panzer Group West until 2nd July
Friedrich Dollmann, General	Commander 7th Army until 28th June
Paul Hausser, SS General	Commander II SS Panzer Corps until 28th June, then Commander 7th Army
Heinrich Eberbach, General	Commander Panzer Group West from 2nd July, 5th Panzer Army from 5th August and Panzer Group Eberbach from 9th August
Sepp Dietrich, SS General	Commander I SS Panzer Corps until 9th August, then Commander 5th Panzer Army

ALLIED

Dwight D. Eisenhower, General	Supreme Commander Allied Expeditionary Force
Sir Bernard Montgomery, General	Commander 21st Army Group
Omar Bradley, General	Commander First US Army

	until 31st July, then Commander 12th US Army Group
George Patton, General	Commander Third US Army
Courtney Hodges, Lieutenant General	Commander First US Army from 1st August
Miles Dempsey, Lieutenant General	Commander Second British Army
Henry Crerar, Lieutenant General	Commander First Canadian Army
John Crocker, Lieutenant General	Commander I British Corps
Guy Simonds, Lieutenant General	Commander II Canadian Corps
Sir Richard O'Connor, Lieutenant General	Commander VIII British Corps
Gerard Bucknall, Lieutenant General	Commander XXX British Corps

Prologue

By the beginning of June 1941, Hitler controlled Europe from the North Cape to the Pyrenees and from the English Channel and North Sea coasts to the borders of the Soviet Union and Turkey. Only the British Empire and Commonwealth remained at war with Germany and Italy. Exactly three years later the Americans, British and Canadians had assembled the necessary forces to embark on their crusade to destroy the Third Reich from the west, whilst Stalin's armies advanced relentlessly from the east.

Shortly after midnight on 6th June 1944 a small glider-borne force of some 200 men from the British 6th Airlanding Brigade seized the bridges over the Caen Canal and Orne river at Ranville. It was the first action in the Allied invasion of Normandy. By 0240 hours 1,200 transport aircraft and 700 gliders had delivered nearly 24,000 American and British paratroopers to the flanks of the planned 80km beachhead.

Offshore in rough seas, nine Allied battleships, twenty-three cruisers and seventy-three destroyers stood ready to commence their bombardment of the German defences and a further thirty-one destroyers and seventy-one corvettes were protecting nearly 6,500 converted liners, merchantmen and tank landing craft with the 150,000 soldiers and 800 tanks due to be put ashore before the day was ended.

Onshore, in the immediate invasion area, five unsuspecting German infantry divisions and one parachute regiment were positioned behind the so-called 'Atlantic Wall'. Many of the German commanders responsible for the defence of the Channel coast were not even present in their Headquarters. The only armour within immediate striking distance of the coast was the famous 21st Panzer Division, but it could not be released for action without the personal permission of the Commander of Army Group 'B'—Field Marshal Erwin Rommel, and he was nearly 1000km away near Ulm in Germany.

The Allied naval bombardment began just before 0530 hours and at 0620 hours 1,600 Allied heavy and medium bombers completed their missions against the coastal defences and infrastructure. Ten minutes later the first American troops waded ashore at UTAH beach and at 0725 hours British mine-clearing tanks touched SWORD beach on the eastern flank. Fighters and fighter-bombers of the Allied Tactical Air Forces roared overhead in support of what was to be the largest and most complex amphibious operation in the history of warfare.

Without command of the sea or air, even for limited periods, the only German formations with any hope of defeating the Allied invasion were the six Panzer divisions based in northern France and Belgium. Two of these were unique in that they were the only divisions in the German army to bear Hitler's own name—one, the 12th SS Panzer Division Hitlerjugend, was untested but would soon earn for itself an awesome reputation; the other, the 1st SS Panzer Division Leibstandarte Adolf Hitler, had fought almost continuously since September 1939 and was probably the most feared of all the Waffen-SS divisions. Together they had been designated by the Führer to form his I SS Panzer Corps Leibstandarte. Despite the odds against them by this stage of the war, the members of this unique Corps were still confident of victory—as one arrogant Waffen-SS Regimental commander put it on the night of the Allied landings, 'Little fish! We'll throw them back into the sea in the morning.'

What follows is the story of their attempt to do so and of the battles which led to their destruction.

1 | Origins

The origin of the I SS Panzer Corps Leibstandarte (Bodyguard) lay in the Headquarters Guard formed at the beginning of 1933 to supplement Adolf Hitler's existing personal protection force. The Führer appointed Sepp Dietrich, an intimate associate and a former personal bodyguard, to command this new unit and in order to man it all SS units were asked to provide three dependable young men who were to be under 25, at least 1.8m tall, in good health, without criminal records and to have joined the SS before 30th January 1933.[1] By the end of February 1933 Dietrich had selected 117 men for the SS-Stabswache Berlin, as the force was initially called, and they assembled on 17th March in the Kaiserin Augusta Victoria Kaserne on Friesenstrasse, near the Chancellery. They were indeed a select group of men—of the 117, three became divisional commanders, at least eight became regimental commanders, fifteen became battalion commanders and over thirty became company commanders, all within the framework of the Waffen-SS.[2] Significantly, two of them—Theodor (Teddy) Wisch and Fritz Witt—would be commanding the two SS Panzer Divisions which formed I SS Panzer Corps in Normandy at the end of June 1944; another, Wilhelm Mohnke, would be commanding a regiment in the same campaign and Dietrich himself would be the Corps Commander.

A Prussian State Police battalion, also stationed in the Friesenstrasse Kaserne, provided administrative support and basic instruction for the new Guard. In April it was retitled SS-Sonderkommando Berlin and moved into the famous Lichterfelde Kaserne, opened by Kaiser Wilhelm I in 1873 as an officer cadet school for the Prussian Army. Its first public appearance was as an Honour Guard to Hitler on 8th April at the Sports Palace in Berlin, where he addressed a

Sturmabteilung (SA) rally, and shortly afterwards the first twelve-man guard under Wilhelm Mohnke took post at the Reichs Chancellery. Ironically, twelve years later Mohnke was again commander of the Chancellery Guard, but this time as an SS major general, with Hitler dead and the Soviets at the very gates of the building.

The remainder of 1933 saw the new Guard expand rapidly, but strict entrance regulations were imposed. Some of the requirements were extreme—no filled teeth, well proportioned bodies with no disparity between body and legs and lower leg and thigh, and proof of ancestry back to 1800 for soldiers and 1750 for officers.

Two separate training units, also known as SS-Sonderkommando, were set up at Jüterbog and Zossen, and a music corps and cavalry unit were established. In July a detachment under the command of Teddy Wisch mounted guard at Hitler's summer retreat at the Berghof above Berchtesgaden.[3] This indicated that the Führer saw the SS-Sonderkommando Berlin as a personal guard and not merely as a force for guarding the Reichs Chancellery.

On 9th November, after the three SS-Sonderkommandos had been amalgamated into one unit, all 835 men swore an oath of allegiance to the Führer in a torchlight ceremony held in front of the hallowed Feldherrnhalle War Memorial in Munich.[4] 'Adolf Hitler' banners were presented to the new unit which was renamed Die Leibstandarte Adolf Hitler, although the letters 'SS' were inserted shortly afterwards and the title usually abbreviated to LSSAH. In recognition of their unique status the men wore the Führer's name on their cuff bands.

The new Guard was reorganised into two battalions, the first with two guard companies and a machine gun company and the second with two guard companies and a motor company. As well as providing a large presence at the Reichs Chancellery, guards were also mounted at Berlin's three airports, SS Headquarters, the Treasury, Ministry of Food and the private residences of Himmler and the chief of the Security Service, the notorious Reinhard Heydrich.

On 30th June 1934 the Leibstandarte took part in the infamous 'Night of the Long Knives', when Hitler finally took action against Ernst Röhm, the Chief of Staff of the SA, and other senior members of the organisation which had helped him to power and been purposely designed for political indoctrination and strong-arm activities. Six members of the Guard, led by Sepp Dietrich himself, executed six SA men in Munich, and in the Lichterfelde Kaserne in Berlin three more senior members of the SA were shot dead by eight Leibstandarte NCOs and the Drum Major. The following day a further eleven were killed. It is perhaps noteworthy that in the semi-official History[5] of the Leibstandarte it is stressed that as far as Dietrich personally was concerned it was unimaginable that Hitler could ever give him an illegal order. If the Führer said the men were guilty of high treason then that was sufficient and he was merely carrying out a legal sentence. It also has to be said that many more than the twenty mentioned above died during the 'Night of the Long Knives' and the day following it.

During 1933–4 the Nazis organised a number of political action squads throughout major German towns and cities and these gradually merged into what became known as the SS-Verfügungstruppe (SS-VT). By April 1935 these Special Purpose Troops, as they can best be described, consisted of the Leibstandarte SS Adolf Hitler, with a strength now of over 2,500, and two other Standarten or Regiments—the Germania and the Deutschland. Two officer training schools had also been established at Bad Tölz and Braunschweig.

The expansion of the Bodyguard continued during 1935 and on 1st March it led the Army in its peaceful occupation of the Saarland.[6] Life in the Leibstandarte at this time was extremely pleasant, if at times a little boring. It was after all a Guard unit with all that implies, though providing Honour Guards such as that at the 1936 Winter Olympics obviously had its compensations. (The Leibstandarte can be seen in many of the archival films of Hitler's Germany being shown on television throughout the world as this book is being written. Those soldiers wearing black uniforms with white accoutrements are members of the Guard). Being known as the 'asphalt soldiers' to their compatriots in the Army certainly did not worry the swaggering occupants of the Lichterfelde Kaserne. They were close to their hypnotic leader and revelled in the many State occasions, like those in Austria in 1938 following the Anschluss, and on Hitler's 50th birthday in 1939 when he opened the new 7km long Tiergartenstrasse in Berlin by driving its entire length—his Bodyguard, in their striking black uniforms with white accoutrements, shining high boots and cuff titles bearing the name of the man who had already mesmerized the nation, stood as Honour Guard at the beginning and end of this magnificent boulevard.[7] In fairness, however, it must be said that whilst a substantial element of the LSSAH always provided the necessary ceremonial guards, the remainder of the force was undergoing normal military training as a potential combat formation. Many exaggerated stories have been told about the toughness of this training, including the ludicrous one that a recruit was required to stand still whilst a grenade was exploded on his helmet. In reality training was very similar to that carried out in the army but with more emphasis on sport.

Surprisingly perhaps, there was a remarkable degree of informality within and between ranks in the Leibstandarte, and members addressed one another as 'Kamerad' when off duty; as time went on first names were frequently used. Much emphasis was placed on honour and trust, even to the extent of forbidding locks on personal wardrobes. The motto of the unit was 'My loyalty is my honour'. The fact that all officers served in the ranks before commissioning did much to foster the feeling of kinship.

In March 1938 a motorised battalion of the Leibstandarte accompanied German troops when they marched into Austria.[8] Four months later a fourth SS-VT Regiment, Der Führer, was formed in Vienna and in the same month Hitler decreed that all the SS-VT Standarten would form part of the Army in time of war.[9] Thus, by 1943, the Leibstandarte had become the 1st SS Panzer Division Leibstandarte, the Deutschland and Der Führer Standarten had formed the 2nd SS Panzer Division Das Reich (DR) and the Germania had become part of the 5th SS Panzer Division Wiking.

In October 1938 the Bodyguard took part in the occupation of the Sudetenland.[10] There is no truth in the story that it was involved in the notorious 'Kristallnacht' the following month, which saw the first open intimidation of the Jewish population.

By the time the Second World War (WWII) started in September 1939 the LSSAH was a full Regiment with three infantry battalions, an artillery battalion and anti-tank, reconnaissance, motor-cycle, heavy infantry gun, engineer and signals sub units. A fourth 'Wach' Battalion had been formed in December 1939 for guard and ceremonial duties. It should be made clear, however, that the LSSAH was completely separate from both the Allegemeine, or general, SS and the Totenkopf Standarten which had been formed by Theodor Eicke for concentration camp duties and from which grew the 3rd SS Totenkopf Division (T-Div). This is not to say that there were no reinforcements from these elements as the war progressed. Similarly, if a member of the Leibstandarte became unfit for combat he was fully eligible for transfer to the non-combatant parts of the SS.

In order to understand better the organisation which was to sustain unbelievable casualties in Russia and Normandy and yet still continue to fight, it is necessary to look at the principles which Hitler laid down for the Waffen-SS (known until March 1940 as the SS-VT). These were set out in August 1940[11] and can be summarised as follows:

1. The Greater German Reich will, in its final form, encompass many different peoples, some of which will be unwilling members. It will therefore be necessary to establish a national force which has complete authority to execute the authority of the State within its borders.

2. This mission can only be fulfilled by a force which has within its ranks men of the best German blood and which identifies itself with the basic philosophy which underpins the Greater German Reich. This force, due to pride in its racial and philosophical purity, will never fraternize with those who might undermine the basic concept of the German State.

3. This force must be organised on military lines.

4. The German people have already seen, by the glorious events of the present war and by Nazi education, the advan-

tages of a military system; they realise that previous German State police forces, in 1848 and 1918, have been ineffective and that unless this new State force serves at the Front and suffers casualties just like any other unit of the Wehrmacht [Armed Forces], it will not be respected. After returning from the Front members of this force will possess the necessary authority to carry out their duties.

5. This use of the Waffen-SS at home is in the full interests of the Wehrmacht, which with its universal conscription, must never be allowed to raise its weapons against German citizens. The Wehrmacht is to be dedicated exclusively and solely for deployment against the external enemies of the Reich.

6. In order to ensure the quality of the Waffen-SS is maintained, its numbers must be limited.

Whilst it is unlikely that the men of the Leibstandarte had any detailed knowledge of this secret directive, there is no doubt that they knew they were part of an elite organisation which was quite separate from the Army and the Police. They were at the pinnacle of the hysteria which swept the entire German nation in the 1930s with its notion of a 'Master Race', and they soon began to think of themselves as the real successors to the Teutonic knights of old. They were flattered to be told that they were 'the future aristocratic spine of the German nation' and they did not question Himmler's words when he said, 'We march according to eternal laws. We are on the way to a distant future. We don't just want to fight better than past generations, we want to produce the future generations to ensure the eternal life of the German people.' As will be seen, this sense of ethical superiority undoubtedly contributed to the ability of the Waffen-SS to continue in combat long after others would have capitulated and it remained with many of its members even after the collapse of everything for which they had been fighting.

One of the more remarkable things about the Leibstandarte when it went to war in 1939 was that within its ranks were the future Corps commander, Sepp Dietrich, two future divisional commanders, Teddy Wisch and Kurt Meyer, three future regimental commanders, Mohnke, Sandig and Frey, three future battalion commanders, Becker, Max Hansen and Ullerich and a future divisional operations officer, Hubert Meyer, of the I SS Panzer Corps which would fight in Normandy five years later. Fritz Witt, another divisional commander, had been transferred temporarily to the SS Deutschland Standarte, but Wilhelm Bittrich, the subsequent commander of II SS Panzer Corps in Normandy, was also in the Regiment at this time. And just to add more flavour, two of the most famous Waffen-SS officers of WWII were also members of the Leibstandarte in 1939, but they were detached—Max Wünsche as an Adjutant to Adolf Hitler and Jochen Peiper as an Adjutant to Heinrich Himmler. They too would play a prominent part in Normandy battles.

The Leibstandarte crossed the border into Poland on 1st September 1939 and took part in the first highly successful Blitzkrieg (lightning war) operation of the war. It suffered just over 400 casualties[12] in a campaign which lasted less than a month. The Army considered these casualties, like those of other SS-VT units, to be unnecessarily high and an indication of poor training.

Although guard elements of the LSSAH remained in Berlin and at Berchtesgaden throughout the war, the fighting components never again returned to the Lichterfelde Kaserne. They moved first to secure the Protectorate of Bohemia and Moravia and then in November to the Bad Ems-Nassau region near Koblenz. It was at this time that the SS-V Division, comprising the Deutschland, Germania and Der Führer Standarten, was formed, together with the SS Totenkopf Division from Eicke's Totenkopfverbände. Himmler also managed to put together an SS Polizei Division. The LSSAH, however, because of its special status, remained quite separate within the SS-VT.

On 23rd December 1939 Hitler joined his Bodyguard Regiment for their Christmas celebrations in the Spa hotel at Bad Ems.[13] Every member received a Christmas cake, a bottle of wine and tobacco and after choral renderings and humorous sketches, the Führer made a speech to 'his' Standarte. In it he said, 'As long as I have the honour to stand at the spearhead of this battle, it is for you, the men of my Leibstandarte, an honour to be the spearhead of this battle.'

In the early part of 1940 the LSSAH was expanded into a fully independent Motorised Infantry Regiment and a Sturmgeschütz (assault gun) battery was added to its establishment; this can be described as the Leibstandarte's first Panzer (tank) unit.

On 10th May the LSSAH crossed the border into Holland and by the 15th the campaign had been successfully completed, at a cost to the Regiment of five dead and seven wounded.[14] Two more future Normandy regimental commanders, Wünsche and Steineck, and four future battalion commanders, Bremer, Scappini, Weidenhaupt and Steinert, had taken part in the operation.

The Bodyguard then moved to join in the equally successful Blitzkrieg invasion of France. By now Jochen Peiper had returned temporarily from his duties with Himmler to earn his spurs as a company commander and, in the process, the Iron Cross both 2nd and 1st class. He would be commanding a Panzer Regiment in Normandy.

It was during this short campaign that the LSSAH had its first clash with the British Army which, the unofficial History says, 'fought with great courage and gave us tough resistance.'[15] At this time an event occurred which is pertinent to our story. On 28th May at Wormhoudt, near Dunkirk, some eighty to ninety British soldiers of the 48th Division died in suspicious circumstances at the hands of the LSSAH. Wilhelm Mohnke, then a battalion commander and a future Normandy regimental commander, has been named in more than one book, and even in the British Parliament, as the officer responsible for this atrocity. In an attempt to look a little further into this matter the author asked, in 1994, to see a particular file in the British Public Record Office at Kew, near London. It contains papers received from the British member of the SHAEF Court of Enquiry (Lieutenant Colonel Scotland) into alleged WWII atrocities in the European theatre of operations. He was told that it was 'closed' and was handed the following statement:

This crime was thoroughly investigated after the war but a number of people, including Mohnke, were not in British hands and despite considerable efforts, it did not prove possible to bring anyone to trial. The case was reopened in 1988 by the German authorities at the request of one of the survivors who had discovered that Mohnke had returned from Russian captivity and was alive in Germany. The British records of the post-war war crimes investigations were closed but were made available to the German Prosecutor, who came to this country to further his investigations. . . . He has now concluded that there is insufficient evidence to bring charges against Mohnke.

An appeal to the Prime Minister, John Major, to see the file brought the following response from his representative:

These papers will remain closed for the time being because they form part of a small collection of files that may be relevant to ongoing German investigations into alleged atrocities on the Channel Islands.

Two years later, as this book is being written, the situation has not changed. The author has been told that the file will remain closed until the year 2024. It is of interest that Mohnke was in fact released by the Russians on 10th October 1955 and has been living quite openly in the western part of Germany ever since.

Following the conclusion of the French campaign, in which it suffered a further 501 casualties, the LSSAH was stationed in Metz; and it was there that it was presented by Himmler, on behalf of Hitler, with the Banner of the Führer—in British terminology, its Regimental Colour. The banner was a replica of the pennant flown from the Führer's official car and at the Reichs Chancellery to signify his presence—again a practice used by the British monarch. On scarlet silk, it carried a black swastika on a white field surrounded by a gold oak-leaf wreath and flanked by four golden German eagles.

In April 1941 the Leibstandarte took part in the operations in Yugoslavia and Greece. Four more future Normandy battalion commanders, Prinz, Krause, Olboeter and Knittel were now serving within its ranks.

The Regiment was initially held in reserve in the Balkan campaign and did not cross into Yugoslavia until 7th April; however, a Yugoslav air attack the day before[16] badly wounded SS Major Wilhelm Mohnke who was commanding one of the four Kamfpgruppen (Battlegroups) of the Regiment—he lost a foot.

The organisation of the LSSAH for the highly successful campaign in Greece shows just how far German military thinking had progressed by this early stage of the war; each fighting element was a mixture of all arms—infantry, light and heavy gun, anti-tank and Flak (anti-aircraft) units, artillery and engineers. When one couples this imaginative grouping with the fact that ground troops could call for immediate air support through air force liaison personnel co-located with the attacking columns, one begins to understand the reasons for the success of Blitzkrieg. It is also of interest that there is evidence,[17] even at Regimental level, of the Germans using radio interception as early as 1941 to follow British movements in the Greek campaign.

On 10th April the Leibstandarte had its second clash with British troops, this time some armoured cars; and perhaps more significantly, it suffered its first attack from the Royal Air Force[18]—a force which was to cause it many casualties and great disruption in Normandy three years later.

The outstanding success of the LSSAH in capturing the Klidi Pass into Greece from the 6th Australian Division, withstanding a counter-attack by the British 1st Armoured Brigade, and its subsequent operations at the Klissura Pass, contributed greatly to the successful conclusion of this short campaign and did much for the Regiment's reputation and that of its Commander, Sepp Dietrich. One prisoner taken during the fighting was a British cavalryman named Sir George Kennard; he paid an unusual compliment to the Leibstandarte:

Over the entire fighting they had been brave, chivalrous and, towards the end, they would go out of their way, at considerable risk to themselves, to take prisoners rather than lives.[19]

This view contrasts strongly with that of members of the British 48th Division who had encountered the LSSAH in May 1940 in France. And such behaviour was certainly not repeated in the campaign it was about to undertake in the East.

On 8th May, after a victory parade in Athens and a short rest in the Larissa area, the Leibstandarte was ordered to Bohemia to prepare for Operation BARBAROSSA—the attack on the Soviet Union. On Hitler's order it was reorganised into a division and titled SS-Division Leibstandarte SS Adolf Hitler. However, it was usually known as the 'LAH' after the letters worn on the uniform shoulder straps.

The clash between Hitler's Third Reich and Stalin's Soviet Empire was militarily significant for two reasons—its scale and its savagery. Geographically it was the largest land campaign of the war; its savagery was hardly surprising in view of the fact that it was a struggle between two autocratic political systems which were each determined to eradicate the other. Neither side tolerated dissent and their military arms rarely offered or expected mercy.

The early successes of the German Blitzkrieg operation in Russia are legendary—by mid July 1941, less than a month after crossing the border, Hitler's armies were nearing Leningrad in the north and Kiev in the south. In the centre Smolensk, only 200 miles from Moscow, had been captured. It appeared that the war in the East would end shortly in total victory.

The Leibstandarte, owing to its latest restructuring, was unable to take part in the initial advances and was not committed until 2nd July; then, as part of von Rundstedt's Army Group South, it took part in the bitter fighting to secure the right bank of the Dnieper river and the pursuit of the Soviet Army along the Sea of Azov. By 21st November III Panzer Corps, of which the LAH was now part, had secured Rostov on the Don river. In three days the Corps had captured 10,000 prisoners, 159 artillery pieces, fifty-six tanks and two armoured trains.[20] But by now the dreaded Russian winter had come to the rescue of its peoples and the Leibstandarte was exhausted. It had lost 5,281 officers and men out of a total of 9,994[21] and its average infantry company numbered only sixty-six men out of an establishment of just under 200. Only 15% of its vehicles were roadworthy—it was clearly time to go on to the defensive. But the LAH had definitely won its spurs and all talk of 'asphalt soldiers' had long ceased. On the contrary, the Bodyguard was well on its way to a new title, 'The Führer's Fire Brigade'. On 26th December 1941, the Corps Commander, General von Mackensen, wrote to the Reichführer-SS as follows:

> I can assure you that the Leibstandarte is held in high regard, not only by the officers but also by its fellow comrades in the Heer [Army]. Every unit wants to have the Leibstandarte as its adjacent unit, both in the attack and in defence. The unit's internal discipline, its refreshing eagerness, its cheerful enthusiasm, its unshakable calmness in crisis no matter how great, and its toughness are examples to us all. Its members' feeling for their fellow soldiers, I would like to emphasize, is exemplary and unsurpassed. . . . This truly is an elite unit.[22]

The average age of its soldiers was 19.35 years.

In July 1942, after a year in Russia, it was decided to rest the LAH and expand it into a full Panzer-Grenadier Division. It was transferred to France and took part in a ceremonial parade through Paris in front of Field Marshal von Rundstedt. Between August and December the restructuring took place in the Evreux region, west of Paris. A Sturmgeschütz (Assault Gun) Battalion had already been added before it left Russia, but now two Panzer-Grenadier Regiments, each with three battalions, Flak, infantry gun and anti-tank companies, an Artillery Regiment of four battalions, a Flak Battalion with six batteries, and most important of all, a Panzer Regiment of two medium tank battalions, one heavy (Tiger I) company and a Panzer engineer company, were formed.[23] This gave the Division a strength of nearly 21,000. There was, however, a penalty—the rigid entry regulations finally had to be relaxed and 'ethnic Germans', those of German ancestry living outside the borders of the Reich itself, had to be admitted.

In October the Division moved to Normandy and was thus able to see the ground over which it would do battle in 1944; but then, in January 1943, the 1st SS Panzer-Grenadier Division LAH entrained for the Ukraine where it was urgently needed to help stem the Russian winter offensive. It was to be part of SS General Hausser's SS Panzer Corps. This had been originally set up in May 1942 at Bergen-Belsen in northern Germany, but its Divisions, the LAH, Das Reich and Totenkopf did not come fully under command until January 1943. The task of the SS Corps was the defence of the Donetz river and the city of Kharkov. During desperately savage fighting the city was, to Hitler's fury, evacuated; but then, on 14th March, after a terrible struggle it was recaptured—by the Leibstandarte. Hitler awarded Sepp Dietrich 'Swords' to his Knight's Cross for this action.

By 27th March, when a period of rest was ordered following the capture of Belgorod and the restoration of the German line on the Donetz, the LAH had lost 167 officers and 4,373 men—44% of its fighting strength.[24] But the fighting in Kharkov also brought accusations of major atrocities by Dietrich's men. As late as 1976 the Soviets produced charges[25] alleging that some 300 wounded Russian soldiers had died when the Leibstandarte had burned down a hospital in Kharkov and that a further 400 or more officers had been shot in their beds in an army isolation hospital. These claims were never substantiated but there can be little doubt that the savagery of the fighting resulted in both sides committing numerous acts of barbarism. The Leibstandarte History features a photograph[26] taken as early as 3rd July 1941 showing the graves of a whole German bicycle company which it says was 'bestially murdered' near Olyka and goes on, in another volume, to highlight a number of examples of the mutilation of German dead and allege that some of these mutilations were inflicted before death.

The rest period lasted until the end of June and was used not only for leave, which the Führer had reinstated after the recapture of Kharkov, but for re-equipping and yet another restructuring. This was occasioned by some astounding news which Dietrich brought back with him when he returned from receiving his 'Swords' from Hitler on 21st March in Berlin. After ten years in command of the Leibstandarte, he was to leave and take command of a new I SS Panzer Corps Leibstandarte, which was to take precedence over Hausser's SS Panzer Corps. The latter would consequently be demoted to become II SS Panzer Corps. Just as astounding was the news that all the senior officers in this new Headquarters were to be found from the Leibstandarte and, perhaps most astonishing of all, that a new SS Division was to be formed from the Hitlerjugend organisation, while all its regimental, battalion and most of the company commanders were also to come from the LAH! This radical change and expansion had been decided upon by Hitler, after representations by Himmler and probably Gottlob Berger, Chief of the SS Central Office, the previous February. Apart from Himmler's wish to increase the number of SS troops, there was anyway an urgent need to create more divisions for the army as a whole.

One would have expected that any division in any army, on being asked to staff a new Corps Headquarters and at the same time to provide cadres for a new division, would have been returned to its home country for a prolonged period of reorganisation and training—not so with the Waffen-SS—quite the contrary. Dietrich handed over command of the LAH on 4th June to Teddy Wisch and on 5th July the Division was launched into the largest armoured battle of the war—Kursk. During April and May the battle casualties and transfers had been made good. The replacements, however, included 2,500 Luftwaffe personnel[27] who had not even volunteered for army, let alone Waffen-SS service, and there were also a number of non volunteers from Waffen-SS replacement units. The purity of the LAH was again being diluted. But incredibly all these 'Yankalongs', as they were known, were soon transformed into worthy and enthusiastic members of the Division. It was an incredible feat, but then the Leibstandarte was an incredible organisation. In only ten years it had developed a spirit and fighting reputation second to none. In this short period it had achieved what most armies and regiments strive for but take decades and even centuries to attain; moreover, it had gone even further and formed something never before achieved in any army: a division of all arms—infantry, armour, artillery, engineers etc, but with the same badge, spirit and sense of 'family' as a regiment. To this was added the advanced military thinking current in the Wehrmacht generally at this time, thinking which had developed the tactics of Blitzkrieg, produced the necessary equipment to practise it and maintained a cooperation on the battlefield between different ground elements, and even between air and ground elements, unknown to other nations.

How did the LAH create and maintain its remarkable spirit? The fact that it was the Guard unit of the national leader must be one factor, constant active service another. The Leibstandarte spent over five and a half years at war and from July 1941 enjoyed only ten months away from front-line service—even then it was based in occupied countries and often faced resistance forces. Perhaps the sense of elitism and an awareness of being quite separate from, and 'above' the rest of the Werhmacht and Police played a part? But there was something else which gave the LAH its unique character. A hint of it appeared in von Mackensen's letter of December 1941. The LAH, and other premier Waffen-SS divisions like Das Reich, had developed their own philosophy of soldiering. It glorified fighting for fighting's sake. Its members had little regard for life, either their own or that of anyone else. This, to modern Western thinking, alien attitude is well described by a Leibstandarte SS captain:

> It was those defensive battles in Russia which I shall always remember for the sheer beauty of the fighting, rather than the victorious advances. Many of us died horribly, some even as cowards, but for those who lived, even for a short period out there, it was well worth all the dreadful suffering and danger. After a time we reached a point where we were not concerned for ourselves or even for Germany, but lived entirely for the next clash, the next engagement with the enemy. There was a tremendous sense of 'being', an exhilarating feeling that every nerve in the body was alive to the fight.

This type of thinking and philosophy inevitably permeated to the members of the new I SS Panzer Corps; they would be a strange mixture of leaders, hardened and tempered in the crucible of the Eastern Front, and fanatical young soldiers who had been thoroughly indoctrinated in Nazi thinking through their membership of the Hitlerjugend organisation. It was to be a potent combination.

NOTES

1. Bavarian State Archives. 2. Lehmann, *The Leibstandarte I*, p. 1. 3. Ibid., p. 9. 4. Ibid., p. 14. 5. Ibid., p. 28. 6. Ibid., p. 36. 7. Ibid., p. 81. 8. Ibid., p. 67. 9. Ibid., p. 70. 10. Ibid., p. 72. 11. Ibid., p. 251. 12. Ibid., p. 122. 13. Ibid., p. 125. 14. Ibid., p. 139. 15. Ibid., p. 148. 16. Ibid., p. 201. 17. Ibid., p. 208. 18. Ibid., p. 203. 19. Messenger, *Hitler's Gladiator*, p. 94. 20. Lehmann, *The Leibstandarte II*, p. 169. 21. Ibid., p. 186. 22. Ibid., p. 199. 23. Ibid., pp. 300–308. 24. Lehmann, *The Leibstandarte III*, p. 194. 25. Ibid., p. 185. 26. Lehmann, *Die Leibstandarte im Bild*, p. 123. 27. Lehmann, *The Leibstandarte III*, p. 196.

2 Formation

Hitler's decision to form both a Corps headquarters and a new SS division based on cadres from the 1st SS Panzer-Grenadier Division LSSAH inevitably had a profound effect on the Leibstandarte. Not least was the loss of its greatly admired and, by now, very experienced commander. Dietrich's military ability has been much criticised in post-war years due to oft-repeated remarks like those of von Rundstedt who called him 'decent but stupid'[1] and Bittrich who recalled, 'I once spent an hour and a half trying to explain a situation to Sepp Dietrich with the aid of a map. It was quite useless. He understood nothing at all.'[2] Whilst Hitler certainly exaggerated when he described Dietrich as 'a phenomenon in a class like Frundsberg, Zeithen and Seydlitz,'[3] he was undoubtedly correct when he called him 'cunning, energetic and brutal' and went on to say 'For the German people Sepp Dietrich is a national institution.' He was certainly that to his men, whom he referred to as his 'boys'; and it is not without significance that the badge of the Leibstandarte, later to be incorporated into that of both the Hitlerjugend Division and I SS Panzer Corps, was a skeleton key—'Dietrich' is German for skeleton key.

Max Wünsche, a former Adjutant to Hitler and distin-guished senior officer in the LAH, was close to Dietrich in France in 1940 and his Adjutant in the Balkan campaign of 1941. Referring to Greece he said:

> If our men had not been motivated and if Sepp Dietrich had not been at the right places at the right times during the decisive phases, with his orders and decisions, the campaign would have gone a different way.[4]

Rudolf Lehmann, one of Dietrich's principle staff officers from early 1941, wrote of him:

> To be sure our old commander (whom we called Obersepp among ourselves) was no strategic genius. But he was a first-class leader of soldiers and of men. As commanding general . . . he would not be using this gift, and knowing that caused him pain. His forte did not lie in formulating a complete tactical evaluation. But he had an extraordinary sense of a growing crisis and for finding the favourable mo-ment for action. His rare and brief speeches to his men contained no flashes of brilliance, but were palpably heart-felt. And the men took them to heart. His brilliance was in his amazing presence. Anyone who experienced it can only recall with wonder and admiration how he, in the darkest night of a crisis, with everything pushing us back, would face the waves of retreating men, his collar pulled up, his hands shoved in his pockets up to the elbows. Uttering sounds incomprehensible, but full of recognisable rage, he could not only bring the men to stop, but even to turn around and head back in. Unforgettable too, was his warn-ing to unit leaders of any rank as they set off to battle: 'Bring my boys back!'[5]

This then was the man who had been selected by Hitler to command his new Bodyguard Corps. It remained to be seen whether he was capable of handling such a complex and large formation. The former WWI sergeant-major with an Iron Cross 1st Class, had certainly come a long way—on 23rd June 1943, shortly after leaving the LAH, he was promoted to the unique rank of SS Obergruppenführer (lieutenant general) und Panzergeneral der Waffen-SS.

The new Divisional Commander was SS Brigadier Teddy Wisch, one of the original 117-man SS-Stabswache Berlin. He was to prove a worthy successor.

Between the end of March and the end of June 1943 five SS lieutenant-colonels, one SS major, three SS captains and three SS lieutenants were removed from the Divisional staff and posted to the new ISS Panzer Corps Headquarters.[6] They were all experienced men. But whilst it is relatively easy to replace staff officers, it is difficult to find first class combat leaders at short notice. The removal of the commanders of both the Division's Panzer-Grenadier Regiments, the commander and entire 1st SS Panzer Battalion, the commander and one of the companies of the Reconnaissance Battalion, a company commander from the Sturmgeschütz Battalion, the Regimental Commander and an entire Battalion from the Artillery Regiment, the Battalion Commander and a battery commander from the Flak Battalion and company commanders from the signals and supply units[7]—all this caused, needless to say, a major crisis. The following, most of whom were to fight in Normandy, replaced them: Frey to command 1st SS Panzer-Grenadier Regiment, Kraas to the 2nd, Schiller and Becker to Panzer-Grenadier battalions, Mertsch and de Vries to the artillery, Knittel to the Reconnaissance and Ullerich to the Flak Battalions.[8] The loss of Wünsche and the 1st SS Panzer Battalion could not be made good and the LAH entered Operation ZITADELLE, the battle of Kursk, with only one Panzer Battalion.[9]

The need for major reinforcements to be drafted into the combat elements of the Division was no less of a problem. When Dietrich heard that 2,500 of them were to come from the Luftwaffe, he flew to Göring's Headquarters and negotiated for them to include not just senior NCOs, as originally intended, but 25% sergeants and 25% junior ranks.[10] On arrival, few volunteered for the fighting parts of the Division, preferring naturally enough, to take their places in the support elements. Dietrich was disgusted but accepted that, as volunteers for the Luftwaffe who had been unceremoniously 'dumped' into the premier fighting Division of the Waffen-SS with little or no training, they had been badly treated. The way these and other reinforcements from Waffen-SS replacement units were quickly welded into the LAH has already been described.

The gigantic battle of Kursk was finally halted on 13th July. By then the Leibstandarte had lost over a third of its armour and suffered 2,753 casualties including 474 killed.[11]

One of the reasons given for Hitler's decision to call off the Kursk offensive was the Allied invasion of Sicily and his worry about his southern flank. Consequently at the end of July, the LAH handed over its remaining tanks to the Das Reich and Totenkopf Divisions and moved to northern Italy. It then spent the first part of August disarming the Italian army in the Po river valley, following the collapse of Mussolini's fascist dictatorship, before undertaking the defence of northern Italy and Croatia. During this period the 1st SS Panzer Battalion, equipped with Panthers, rejoined the Division. It was also during this time in Italy that more accusations of brutality were made against the LAH. Jochen Peiper, commanding the 3rd SS (Armoured) Panzer-Grenadier Battalion, and two of his officers were accused of killing Italian civilians in the small town of Boves after the kidnapping of two of his NCOs by persons unknown. Peiper had allegedly taken the whole of his SS Panzer-Grenadier Battalion to the rescue and shelled the town with 150mm infantry guns, killing thirty-four residents. Needless to say he got his men back; but in a Stuttgart court in 1968, the Italian authorities charged him with murder. The Court found that 'there was insufficient suspicion of criminal activity on the part of any of the accused to warrant prosecution'.[12] In the same year, however, the Osnabrück Assize Court convicted five ex-members of the Leibstandarte for the murder, or aiding and abetting with the murder, of Jews living in several towns along Lake Maggiore in northern Italy.[13] This had occurred at the same time as the Boves affair. Although these proceedings were also dropped because the prosecution had exceeded the Statute of Limitations, the reputation of the LAH was again tarnished.

After a few more weeks in the relatively peaceful surroundings of northern Italy, it was time for the 1st SS Panzer Division LSSAH, as it was retitled on 22nd October 1943,[14] to return to the Ukraine for another six months' bitter fighting. But once more it was to be weakened in order to form the new I SS Panzer Corps—in October, just before leaving for the front, its Sturmgeschütz Battalion and one of its medical companies were transferred to the 12th SS Panzer-Grenadier Division HJ.[15]

The winter campaign was harder than ever. The Division even had to fight its way out of its detraining stations. In the weeks which followed the LAH took part in many desperate actions to stem the Soviet advance and by 28th February 1944 it had been reduced to little more than a Kampfgruppe (KG), with only three tanks and four armoured assault guns operational.[16] Two weeks later, after retreating into Galicia, the Division had ceased to exist as such—its combat strength was forty-one officers and 1,188 NCOs and men.[17]

Field Marshal von Manstein wrote:

> Our forces had finally reached the point of exhaustion. The German divisions . . . were literally burnt out. . . . The fighting had eaten away at the very core of the fighting units. How could we wage effective counter-attacks, for example, when an entire Panzerkorps had only twenty-four Panzers ready for battle?[18]

On 18th April when the pathetic remnants of the 1st SS Panzer Division left the Eastern Front, Sandig's 2nd SS Panzer-Grenadier Regiment, the only part of the LAH for which firm figures are available but which was typical of the Division, had suffered 869 casualties out of a fighting strength of 2,296—418 men were dead. A further 1,388 had been wounded but had remained with the Regiment.[19] The few remaining veterans of the Division would once more become the nucleus around which a new Leibstandarte would have to be built.

In the meantime the Commander of the I SS Panzer Corps had been enjoying a fairly quiet time. Dietrich had activated his new Headquarters on 26th July 1943 at the Lichterfelde Kaserne in Berlin.[20] The formation staff of the Hitlerjugend (HJ) Division, under SS Brigadier Fritz Witt, had established its offices there the previous month. Dietrich selected Colonel Fritz Kraemer as his Chief of Staff. Kraemer had graduated from the Berlin War Academy in 1934, served on the staff of a Panzer division until the end of 1942 and then become the senior administrative officer of I Panzer Corps. He was an ideal choice, although this selection would lead him to stand trial alongside Dietrich at Dachau in 1946, charged with war crimes.

During its time in Italy the LAH had operated under the command of Hausser's II SS Panzer Corps, since Dietrich's I SS Panzer Corps Headquarters was still forming. The latter set up in Merano, just south of the Brenner Pass and was given the relatively simple task of area security.

After returning from Italy in October, Dietrich found himself with a Corps Headquarters but only one formation to command and that, the 12th SS Panzer Division HJ, was carrying out basic training in Belgium and consequently non-operational. His other Division, the LAH, was still fighting in the Ukraine and he would not see it for another six months, and even then it would not be under his operational command. In December Dietrich set up his Corps Headquarters in Brussels; it remained there until the beginning of April when it moved to Septeuil to the west of Paris. It comprised an artillery headquarters under SS Colonel Staudinger, a signals battalion, a military police company and a security company.

The formation of the Hitlerjugend Division was in many ways unique. A Führer Order dated 24th June 1943 said that an SS Panzer-Grenadier Division Hitlerjugend was to be raised at the troop training area Beverloo, south-east of Antwerp and gave the date of formation as 1st June 1943. This title was amended on 30th October to 12th SS Panzer Division Hitlerjugend. The major commanders in the new Division were highly experienced and had all proved their personal courage in battle. SS Major General Fritz Witt, the Divisional commander, had been one of the original 117 members of the Stabswache Berlin of March 1933. He was born in Höhenlimburg in May 1908 and had won an early Knight's Cross for bravery during the French campaign in 1940. He was the first commander of 1st SS Panzer-Grenadier Regiment LAH and added Oak Leaves to his Knight's Cross for service in Russia in 1943. Witt was greatly admired by both officers and men.

The commander of the 12th SS Panzer Regiment was Max Wünsche, a pre-war Adjutant to Adolf Hitler. Handsome, blue eyed and fair haired, Wünsche was everyone's idea of a typical SS officer. He had been commissioned into the LSSAH, along with Jochen Peiper, in April 1936 and had soon won recognition on the battlefield. He was wounded and won two Iron Crosses in France in 1940; later he was awarded the German Cross in Gold and the Knight's Cross for his actions in Russia. He was another outstanding leader.

The commanders of the two SS Panzer-Grenadier Regiments of the Hitlerjugend Division were Kurt Meyer and Wilhelm Mohnke. Kurt 'Panzermeyer', who would command the Division when Witt was killed very early on in the Normandy Campaign, is one of the best known Waffen-SS officers. The illegitimate son of a labourer and World War I sergeant-major, Meyer became a policeman before being accepted into the Leibstandarte in May 1934. Being only 1.75m in height and having to wear a raised orthopedic left shoe as a result of a serious leg injury, he was fortunate to be allowed to join, but his enthusiasm and police experience and rank were deciding factors. Meyer found the Leibstandarte a natural home and by 1937 he was an SS captain and commanding a motor-cycle rifle company. He fought in Poland and France, where he earned an Iron Cross 1st Class, but it was in Greece in 1941 that he had made his name as the commander of the LAH's Reconnaissance Detachment and was awarded the Knight's Cross. This was followed in 1943 by Oak Leaves for his bravery in Russia. A natural and brilliant soldier, Meyer was destined to become Nazi Germany's youngest general at the age of 34 and to be branded a war criminal in 1945.

Wilhelm Mohnke, commander of the 26th SS Panzer-Grenadier Regiment was another original member of the 1933 Bodyguard; recall that he mounted the first Reichs Chancellery Guard in April that year. He took command of an SS infantry battalion in France in 1940 when his commanding officer was wounded, and it was during this period that his name became linked with the war crime against British soldiers at

Wormhoudt. Readers will also recall that Mohnke lost a foot during an air attack in Yugoslavia in 1941. As a result of this injury he was sent to command the LAH Replacement Battalion in Berlin in March 1942, but a year later, with the formation of the Hitlerjugend Division, he saw his chance to return to operational service and was given command of one of its Regiments. Mohnke was the only senior commander in either the LAH or HJ who did not already wear the Knight's Cross.

Finally we come to SS Major Gerhard Bremer, the commander of the Division's SS Reconnaissance Battalion. In France in 1940 he had been in the same battalion of the Leibstandarte as Kurt Meyer, Jochen Peiper, Max Hansen, Hugo Kraas and Max Wünsche. When he was awarded the Knight's Cross in 1941 he was one of the youngest officers in the Regiment to wear this coveted medal. He went on to fight in all the LAH's campaigns in Russia before being transferred to the HJ in 1943. It is of interest that after the war Wehrmacht General Heinrich Eberbach, of whom we shall hear much more and who knew the Hitlerjugend Division well, described Witt, Meyer and Wünsche as Waffen-SS idealists but Mohnke and Bremer as bullies and brawlers.

The 12th SS Panzer Division was unique in WWII in that it was formed, in the main, from Hitler youths born in the first half of the year 1926—this means that the youngest of the 10,000 young men who reported to Lichterfelde Kaserne in Berlin in July 1943 should have been at least seventeen years old, and they should all have been over eighteen by the time they fought in Normandy a year later. This is an important point because it has become a post-war myth that some members of 12th SS were little more than children. A captured nominal roll of the 1st SS Panzer-Grenadier Battalion of the 25th Regiment HJ serving in Normandy in July 1944 shows that 65% of its personnel were eighteen, 17% nineteen and the remainder over twenty.[21] It is also worth pointing out that during WWII Great Britain called up its young men at the age of eighteen and there are plenty of eighteen-year-olds in British military cemeteries throughout the world—the author himself was eighteen and one month when he was enlisted in 1948 and over 65% of his platoon in the Korean war were only eighteen or nineteen years old. What made the HJ Division different was that it was *based* on eighteen-year-olds.

In the eyes of Hitler and Himmler the new Division was to be a symbol of the willingness of German youth to sacrifice itself to the achievement of final victory; it was therefore essential that all the new recruits were volunteers. This created some initial problems because in many cases parents, teachers and industrialists were reluctant to see young men go off to war before they had finished their education and apprenticeships; this meant the timetable for the establishment of the Division could not be met. Potential recruits had to be a minimum height of 1.7m for infantry units and 1.68m for Panzer, signals and reconnaissance units, provided they already had special skills. Despite these difficulties and restrictions the HJ Division was 5,718 soldiers over-strength by early April 1944. There was, however, still a desperate shortage of officers and NCOs—over 2,000; and this despite the very strong injection of experienced officers and NCOs from the Leibstandarte during 1943, as described in the previous chapter. This shortfall led to more than fifty non-SS officers being transferred in from the Army. The fact that the Division was over-strength, whilst the 1st SS Panzer Division was desperately short after being bled white in Russia, made it necessary to transfer 2,055 men, including thirteen officers, from the HJ to the LAH in May 1944.

The build-up of 12th SS was also plagued by shortages in equipment, fuel and ammunition. At the beginning of January 1944 it had only forty tanks and a third of the SPWs and reconnaissance vehicles needed for an SS Panzer division, while many of its trucks were worn-out, captured Italian vehicles.

The training of the young members of the HJ Division differed from that in the rest of the Army. From 1942 onwards all Hitler youths received 160 hours pre-military training, which included small bore shooting and fieldcraft; this provided them with a reasonable foundation for the full military training they were to receive in Belgium and France, but it differed little from that carried out in the cadet corps of most British public schools at that time. Where it did differ markedly was in motivation—the Germans were highly indoctrinated in Nazi thinking and its ethnic philosophies.

The training priorities laid down by the Divisional commander, Fritz Witt, were: physical fitness, character training and weapon training—in that order. But since initially there were not nearly enough Waffen-SS camouflaged uniforms to go round, many of the youngsters found themselves doing their training in home clothes or Hitler Youth uniform. Smoking and drinking alcohol was forbidden, as was visiting brothels—in fact any relationship with girls was prohibited for those under eighteen; however, it is interesting to note that the only soldiers in Normandy not to have short hair were those of the Hitlerjugend.

The Division was spread over a wide area of Belgium centred on Beverloo, but with the Panzer Regiment in a French training area at Mailly-le-Camp; in January 1944 this moved to Hasselt to join the rest of the Division.

Kurt Meyer, in his book *Grenadiers,* has given a detailed description of the methods used in training the young recruits of the Hitlerjugend Division:

As the youngsters were still developing, the principles and forms of education had to be somewhat different from those which a unit used to train and educate older recruits. Many established principles of military training were replaced with new ones which, when all is said and done, had their origin in the German youth movement which came into being at the turn of the century [and continued after Hitler came to power with amendments to accommodate Nazi thinking].

There was no dominant superior relationship [no] recognising only orders and unconditional obedience. The relationship between officers, NCOs and other ranks was that between older experienced and younger comrades. The officers' authority existed in the fact that they were the champions and close friends of the young soldiers. They strove for the close relationship of the parental home in so far as was possible in the circumstances of war.

The boys were educated to a sense of responsibility, a

sense of community, a willingness to make sacrifices, deci-
siveness, self control, camaraderie, and perception. The
leadership of the division was of the conviction that the
boys would achieve more if they recognised and approved of
the sense of their prospective employment and activity. It
was therefore natural practice to develop all orders consis-
tently out of a detailed assessment of the situation. During
their training square bashing was frowned upon. March-
pasts and similar exercises were not practised. Everything
focused on training for battle and this took place under the
most realistic battle conditions possible. Physical toughen-
ing was achieved through sport; route marches were disap-
proved of as being unnecessary and harmful. General von
Geyr [Schweppenburg] stimulated the development of a
progressive training in marksmanship. This took place exclusively in the countryside. Target exercises in barracks
ceased completely.

Other aspects of training and motivation which were unusual in the Division were a strong emphasis on night training
and hand-to-hand combat and, perhaps most surprisingly, the
fact that Panzer crews and officers, on the initiative of Max
Wünsche their commander, worked between eight to fourteen
days in the MAN tank production factory in Nürnberg.[22]
On 1st April 1944 the 12th SS Panzer Division HJ began its
move to Normandy where it continued its training but, because of the Allied air threat, this took place mainly at night.
On 1st June 1944 Fritz Witt was able to report 'The Division is
ready for offensive actions';[23] this was despite the fact that the
Panzerjäger Battalion had no Jagdpanzer IVs and the Werfer
Battalion no tractors. But there was no doubt that Witt's Division had extremely high morale. As one eighteen-year-old
wrote:

> We knew that we were quick, agile, and confident. We
> trusted our officers and NCOs who had been hardened in
> battle. We had known them since the beginning of the
> training. During combat training with live ammunition we
> had enjoyed seeing them in the mud together with us, with
> steel helmet and sub machine-gun.[24]

Meanwhile the senior partner in I SS Panzer Corps, the 1st SS Panzer Division LSSAH, had returned from Galicia and moved into the billets of the HJ in Belgium. It was complete by 25th April 1944 with its Headquarters in Turnhout and units in surrounding towns like Hasselt and Herentals. The Divisional Commander, SS Major General Teddy Wisch, took a month's leave on medical grounds while his Chief of Staff, Rudolf Lehmann, assumed temporary command; subsequently, he became seriously ill and had to be replaced by SS Lieutenant Colonel Grensing on 26th May.

On arrival in Belgium an order was issued for the LAH to form commando groups of one officer and twenty-four NCOs and men, for anti-airborne and general security duties. The main task was, however, the reception of new equipment and the training of new soldiers. The former task was made easier by a Führer order dated 3rd May[25] which required the requisition of weapons for his Leibstandarte Division, but even this high priority could not produce new tanks and other important equipment until the second half of the month. Much of it came directly from the factory. Even then a desperate shortage of fuel, unsuitable terrain and the serious need for security against the activities of the Belgian 'White Army' (partisans), made driver training virtually impossible and other types of training extremely difficult. The claim by the Chief of Staff of I SS Panzer Corps, SS Major General Fritz Kraemer, that plenty of fuel was made available by OKW for combined arms training,[26] was certainly not reflected at Divisional level. It is of interest that the 'White Army' managed to detect and report to London the exact locations of sixty-one of the LAH's tanks as of 1st June. This was despite the fact that, to protect them from air attack, the tanks were scattered in small packets of about five or six throughout the area in villages and towns such as Hamont, Hasselt, Lummen and Zwartberg.[27]

The training of the new men, 'Young Marchers' as they were called, by the 'Old Hares', as the experienced men were known, was intensive. Many of the eighteen-year-olds came from the Leibstandarte Replacement Battalion, via the Hitlerjugend Division's training camp at Beverloo, as already described. While senior officers attended map and signals exercises, carried out 'tactical exercises without troops' and played war games,[28] the young recruits worked hard for the honour of wearing SS runes. They idolized their superiors like Wisch, Peiper, Frey and Max Hansen, whose exploits they had heard about from the day they joined the Waffen-SS. But draftees from disbanded Luftwaffe units and the navy naturally took longer to become effective parts of the machine and many were destined to learn the art of war the hard way—in the battle of Normandy. The 1st SS Panzer Division, despite being at more or less full strength when it was ordered to help defeat the Allied landings in Normandy, would in other armies have been considered unfit for operations. Over half its men had been with the Division for less than a month and the major equipments they would use had, in most cases, been in their hands for an even shorter period—indeed, as we shall see, when the Division started its move on 9th June, some important sub units were ineffective and had to be left behind. A rear party was established to receive the missing vehicles and weapons.[29] Training at any level above that of company had been impossible. The 1st SS Panzer Division of June 1944 was only a shadow of the LAH which had fought the Soviets in the previous winter campaign and it would have to rely more than ever on its battle-hardened officers and NCOs, the majority of whom had already been fighting for nearly five years.

They were indeed a remarkable group of men. Recall that Teddy Wisch, the Divisional commander, had joined the original Führer bodyguard in 1933. He served in every Honour Guard during the years 1934–1939, commanded a company in the Polish campaign, was an SS Brigadier and a Panzer-Grenadier Regimental commander in Russia at the age of thirty-five and had already been awarded the Iron Cross 1st and 2nd Class, Knight's Cross with Oak Leaves and the German Cross in Gold. Although he did not display Dietrich's charisma, he certainly had the confidence and admiration of his officers and men.

The commander of 1st SS Panzer Regiment, Jochen Peiper, has been called the 'Siegfried' of the Waffen-SS. A good-looking and dashing leader, Peiper had made his name in Russia where he won the Knight's Cross with Oak Leaves, German

Cross in Gold, and even the Close Combat Badge in Silver which meant he had been in close combat a minimum of thirty times. Peiper's men idolised him. He was twenty-nine.

SS Lieutenant Colonel Albert Frey, commanding the 1st SS Panzer-Grenadier Regiment, had joined the LAH in time for the invasion of Poland and had taken part in all its campaigns; in December 1943 he had been the 359th soldier to receive Oak Leaves to his Knight's Cross. Max Hansen, a Panzer-Grenadier battalion commander, had already been wounded eight times! He had joined in 1934 and was one of the first training officers at the Jüterbog Depot. He never left the LAH and fought in every one of its campaigns, winning the Knight's Cross and Oak Leaves. Rudolf Sandig, commanding the 2nd SS Panzer-Grenadier Regiment, had also been at the Jüterbog Training Depot, where he was one of the twelve 'Lances' as the sergeant-majors there were known. Another Knight's Cross holder, he was renowned as a hard and unsympathetic trainer. Gustav Knittel had been wounded when a reconnaissance platoon commander during the first campaign in France in May 1940; he was now the commanding officer of the 1st SS Reconnaissance Battalion with a Knight's Cross earned in Russia. Other wearers of this prized medal were Heinrich Heimann, commander of the 1st SS Stürmgeschütz Battalion, Herbert Kuhlmann commanding the 1st SS Panzer Battalion, Werner Wolff who had been Peiper's Adjutant and was now commanding the 7th SS Panzer Company and Paul Guhl who had taken over the 3rd SS (Armoured) Panzer-Grenadier Battalion from Jochen Peiper. The survival rate of these men had been, and would continue to be, astonishing.

NOTES

1. Shulman, *Defeat in the West*, p. 120. 2. Messenger, *Hitler's Gladiator*, p. 71. 3. Ibid., p. 105. 4. Ibid., p. 94. 5. Lehmann, *The Leibstandarte III*, p. 199. 6. Ibid., p. 194. 7. Ibid., p. 195. 8. Ibid., p. 196. 9. Ibid., p. 198. 10. Ibid., p. 196. 11. Ibid., p. 249. 12. Ibid., p. 293. 13. Ibid., p. 294. 14. Lehmann, *The Leibstandarte II*, p. 300. 15. Lehmann, *The Leibstandarte III*, p. 196. 16. Lehmann & Tiemann, *The Leibstandarte IV/I*, p. 51. 17. Ibid., p. 75. 18. Manstein, *Verlorene Siege*, p. 601. 19. Lehmann & Tiemann op. cit., pp. 95–96. 20. Lehmann, *The Leibstandarte II*, p. 310. 21. First Cdn Army Int Summary No 46 dated 14 Aug 44. 22. Meyer, Hubert, *The History of the 12th SS Panzer Division Hitlerjugend*, p. 7. 23. Ibid., p. 9. 24. Meyer, Hubert, op. cit., p. 19. 25. Lehmann & Tiemann, op. cit., p. 98. 26.

Kraemer, *I SS Panzer Corps in the West*, MS C-024, IWM, London, AL 2727/1–2. **27**. Documents dated June 1944 in Centre de Documentation Historique, Ministère de la Défense Nationale, Brussels. **28**. Kraemer, op. cit. **29**. Lehmann & Tiemann, op. cit., p. 115.

3 │ The Machines of War

In order to exploit to the full the well proven tactics of Blitzkrieg, the Germans had designed, developed and produced highly advanced equipment. In virtually every sphere they were ahead of the Allies and it is therefore important, before considering the battle of Normandy and without going into too much technical detail, to look at the 1944 weaponry available to both sides.

In the case of tanks there is no doubt that the Germans were superior in every category. The Mark (Mk) IV was numerically the most important German tank in WWII. It weighed 25 tons and mounted a high velocity 75mm gun and two 7.92mm machine guns. In terms of armament even this relatively "light" tank was superior to the American Sherman and British Cromwell it met in Normandy. The Panther was almost certainly the best tank produced by any nation in WWII. With three 7.92mm machine guns and again a high velocity 75mm gun, it weighed 45 tons. The Tiger I, with which I SS Panzer Corps' 101st SS Heavy Panzer Battalion was equipped, weighed a massive 57 tons and mounted the famous 88mm gun and three 7.92mm machine guns. Its frontal armour was 100mm thick. Despite its slow maximum speed, 38kph, and slow turret traverse, it had by 1944 already earned the awesome reputation which the German propaganda machine had intended. Although a few Tiger IIs, or Tiger Royals as they were known, did appear in Normandy, they were not with I SS Panzer Corps. All German tanks used petrol rather than diesel (which was reserved mainly for submarines), had a crew of five: commander, driver, gunner, loader and radio operator, and an average range of about 200km. All types carried about 80 rounds of main armament ammunition.

Facing this impressive array of German tanks, the Allies had Shermans, Cromwells, Churchills and Stuarts. They were provided on a lavish scale but had little to recommend them. The M4 Sherman was the standard medium tank of the American, Canadian, Polish and two-thirds of the British armoured units in Normandy. With its crew of five, it mounted a low-velocity, short-barrelled 75mm gun, had only 50mm of frontal armour and weighed just over 30 tons. It was highly vulnerable to all German tanks and the infantry Panzerfaust, and soon earned for itself the dreadful nickname 'The Ronson Lighter', due to its habit of catching fire after being hit. It was, however, superbly reliable and had a high rate of fire. The British mounted their high velocity 17-pounder (pdr) gun on the Sherman chassis and called it the Firefly; it was much more effective than the 75mm Sherman but only four tanks in each squadron (company) were so equipped. Needless to say they soon became prime targets for German tank and anti-tank guns. The British Cromwells and Churchills were also under-armed with low velocity 75mm guns, although the Cromwell was reliable and fast, 60kph, in contrast to the heavy, well armoured and pedantic, 20kph Churchill, the only redeeming feature of which seems to be the fact that its frontal armour was thicker than a Tiger I's. By equipping their armoured reconnaissance units with Cromwells, the British in effect added an extra medium tank battalion to their armoured divisions. The American M3 Stuart light tank, with a 37mm gun, was virtually useless other than for liaison, light reconnaissance and escort duties.

It is a sad fact that all Allied tanks could easily be knocked out by any German tank at any range out to 1000m, and often more, whilst it took a lucky hit on the tracks, optics or gun for Allied gunners to disable a German tank; in most cases the Tiger was invulnerable, even at very short ranges, to anything other than a Firefly or rocket-firing aircraft. Blame for this scandalous under-gunning of Allies tanks must lie with the generals and national leaders who either did not understand or were not sufficiently interested in the technology of tank design and weaponry. Allied intelligence and technical staffs were fully aware of the advances made in German tank gun performance and the overall superiority of their tanks; at the end of the campaign in Sicily in August 1943 General Mont-

gomery himself had written to the Vice Chief of the Imperial
General Staff in London:

> It is gun power that counts in battle. . . . We must produce
> a tank with a gun as primary armament which is superior to
> the present 88mm of the enemy.

But he knew this was an impossibility in the time available
before the invasion of the European mainland. Despite this
knowledge, in a major speech in London on 24th March 1944,
he stated:

> It is obvious that the armies must be properly equipped,
> and be supplied with the best possible weapons and equip-
> ment. We need not look far back in history to see what
> happens when this is NOT done. And in this respect it must
> forever rebound to our shame that we sent our soldiers into
> this most modern war with weapons and equipment that
> were quite inadequate; we have only ourselves to blame for
> the disasters that early overtook us in the field. Surely we
> must never let this happen again; nor will we.[1]

In a speech which called on the nation 'to inspire the Army
going forth to battle with the greatness of its cause' (Monty's
words), one could hardly expect him to admit that Allied
tanks were inferior to the enemy's; on the other hand, he
inevitably risked losing the confidence of his men by saying
they would never again be sent to fight with anything other
than the best possible.

Prime Minister Winston Churchill wrote in Montgomery's
autograph book on 19th May 1944:

> I record my confidence that all will be well and that the
> organisation and *equipment* [author's emphasis] of the
> Army will be worthy of the valour of the soldiers and the
> genius of their chief.[2]

Even with his knowledge of the shortcomings of Allied
tanks and after the early setbacks in Normandy, Montgomery
still tried to give an impression that all was well. He wrote to
Field Marshal Sir Alan Brooke, the British Chief of Staff, on
27th June 1944:

It will generally be found that when the equipment at our disposal is used properly, and the tactics are good, we have no difficulty in defeating the Germans.

It is, however, a little surprising that in an official 21st Army Group pamphlet, signed by Montgomery himself and dated December 1944, he says:

The weight of any tank should not exceed about 45 tons. *Having selected the best possible gun* [author's emphasis] as a primary weapon, and designed an engine with sufficient horsepower to give the required speed, then armour should be fitted: up to the maximum weight allowed.[3]

He could not have given a better description of a Panther. But of course, directions of this kind were too late and anyway there was little point in making them to his own soldiers who were powerless to improve matters—Allied tank crews had already paid the price.

In the same way it was far too late and of little use General Eisenhower complaining to the US War Department on 3rd July[4] that his anti-tank weapons and Shermans were incapable of taking on Panthers and Tigers. The writing had been on the wall for more than two years after a captured German 88mm had been shipped across the Atlantic for investigation by technical staffs.[5]

The situation was very different on the German side where generals like Guderian, Rommel, and even Sepp Dietrich, took a close personal interest in the weapons available to their men and were listened to by the designers. And it is perhaps highly significant that Hitler himself constantly interfered in the development of both the Panther and the Tiger; indeed it was he who insisted on the 88mm gun being mounted on the latter and who personally attended the trials of the first prototypes at Rastenburg on 20th April 1942.[6] Even the views of junior fighting soldiers were listened to and sometimes quickly accepted and put into operation. When a young HJ officer, Karl-Wilhelm Krause, had the idea of mounting a four-barrelled 20mm anti-aircraft gun on a Mk IV tank chassis in the summer of 1944, he was immediately supported by his superiors and the resulting weapon system proved highly successful in both an air and ground role. Hitler was so impressed that he ordered all Panzer units to be equipped with what became known as the Wirbelwind as soon as possible. The fact that Krause had been a pre-war Adjutant to the Führer may have had something to do with its early adoption—be that as it may, it was a first class weapon system.

German Puma armoured cars, with their 50mm guns and speed of 80kph, were also far superior to American M8 Greyhounds with their 37mm guns and British Humbers with 2 pdrs.

The German half-track, Sd Kfg 251, and American M3 half-track were, on the other hand, roughly equivalent. The German SPW, as it was known, was a splendid vehicle. In its basic mode as an infantry carrier it held a commander, driver and ten men and mounted two 7.92mm machine guns, one fitted in a shield on the front and the other on a pintle mount at the rear. The major variants were a command vehicle, mortar carrier, engineer equipment vehicle carrying a small assault bridge and inflatable rubber boats, an ambulance, 75mm anti-tank vehicle, platoon commander's vehicle mounting a 37mm gun and a final version with a 20mm anti-aircraft weapon. It weighed about 9 (old) tons, had a 200km range and 6 to 14.5mm of armour. Its only snags were its open top and relatively narrow tracks, which reduced its cross-country performance. The US M3 was very similar but with far fewer variants.

In the assault gun and armoured anti-tank gun sphere the Germans also enjoyed superiority. The 1st SS Panzer Division was equipped with the very effective StuG III (Sturmgeschütz), which was really a turretless tank with a limited traverse, high velocity 75mm gun—the same as the one mounted in the Mk IV tank; the HJ's two Panzerjäger companies had to wait until mid July for their new Jagdpanzer IVs (tank hunters). They were much superior to StuGs, with a more powerful 75mm gun mounted on a Mark IV tank chassis. Less than a third of the US anti-tank units were equipped with the inferior American equivalent, the M-10 with a 3-inch gun, and only two had the M-36 with its 90mm gun. The majority of the Allied anti-tank guns, or Tank Destroyers (TDs) as the Americans called them, were towed and therefore quite unsuitable for the offensive operations planned for Normandy. Both sides had towed 75mm or 3-inch anti-tank guns and for once, the British, with their new discarding sabot ammunition for their 6 and 17 pdrs, had weapons with comparable performances to the Germans. It was not so in the case of infantry anti-tank weapons—the German Panzerfaust could penetrate 160mm of armour at 80m, but the US 2.36-inch bazooka could not pierce the frontal armour of any German tank and the British PIAT (Projector Infantry Anti-Tank), although effective up to 100m, was heavy, cumbersome and difficult to fire.

Turning now to artillery, it has to be said that this was the outstanding and most effective arm possessed by the Allies. The British 25 pdr and American 105mm guns lacked killing power but they produced excellent suppressive fire; and although the majority of the Allied guns were towed, they possessed medium and heavy guns in profusion in calibres from 90mm, through 155mm, up to 8-inch. The Germans had self-propelled and towed 105mm and 150mm guns and of course their renowned, very high velocity, towed 88mm was highly effective as an anti-aircraft, anti-tank or conventional artillery piece. Their 100mm Kanone had a range of nearly 25km. And in one field they had a unique and terrifying monopoly—multi-barrelled rocket projectors—Nebelwerfers. They came in three sizes, 150mm, 210mm and 300mm, firing out to 5500m, 7500m, and 9000m respectively.

The SS Panzer-Grenadiers of I SS Panzer Corps were armed with extremely effective machine guns, with very high cyclic rates of fire which completely out-classed anything in use by the Allies. The best known are the MP 38 and MP 40 submachine guns and the 7.92mm MG 42. This latter gun, when used with a bipod or tripod, had ranges of 600m and 2000m respectively, firing 1,200 rounds a minute. Mortars were 80mm and 120mm with ranges of 2400m and 6000m. Battalions were also equipped with towed 75mm infantry light guns; these had a rate of fire of up to 12 rounds a minute and a range of 4500m. Also within each SS Panzer-Grenadier Regiment was a heavy infantry gun company with six 150mm SP guns. They fired out to 5km and gave an infantry commander his own artillery. And finally the German 'potato-masher' grenade, with its long wooden handle, could be thrown much further than the American or British hand grenade—to the Allied infantryman it seemed that the lessons of World War I had been forgotten.

Lastly we come to aircraft, and here the Allies enjoyed clear advantages. Although the Germans led the field in the development of jet propulsion, very few of the revolutionary Me 262s had been produced (only thirty-two were operational in August 1944)[7] and by June 1944 the Allies had achieved almost total air superiority. They were therefore able to cripple German supply lines and movements in daylight; and they had the tank-busting Typhoons and Tempests of the Royal Air Force which were to do so much damage to the Panzer divisions—the Germans had no equivalent.

These then were the tools possessed by each side. The important difference was that the Germans had great confidence in theirs, whereas many personnel in the Allied armies, particularly infantrymen and tank crews, did not.

NOTES

1. Montgomery, *The Memoirs of Field Marshal Montgomery*, p. 227. **2.** Ibid., p. 250. **3.** Montgomery, *The Armoured Division in Battle*, p. 2. **4.** Hastings, *Overlord, D-Day and The Battle for Normandy, 1944*, p. 221. **5.** Ibid., p. 227. **6.** Lefèvre, *Panzers in Normandy Then and Now*, pp. 28–29, 34–36. **7.** Wilmot, *The Struggle for Europe*, p. 443.

4 | Organisation[1] and Tactics

In June 1944 the structures of the 1st and 12th SS Panzer Divisions differed, and neither accorded with the organisations laid down by the Army High Command (OKH). This was due mainly to shortages of equipment; but a lack of senior and experienced officers and NCOs meant that, although overall numbers might approximate to planned figures, many positions of authority were filled by soldiers of junior rank or even no rank at all. It is also important to understand that both divisional commanders made arbitrary changes in their structures without informing the Inspector General of Armoured Forces.[2]

The LAH numbered over 19,500 on 1st June but it was 208 officers and 2,234 NCOs below establishment.[3] On 1st July, three days after it began to arrive in the Normandy battle area, the Division's strength had risen to 22,262 but was still 182 officers and 1,398 NCOs short.[4] The HJ Division numbered 20,540 on 1st June and was 144 officers and 2,192 NCOs short.[5] Both divisions had a 'bayonet', or combat, strength of about 12,000. This figure of about 56% of total strength compares very favourably with an American armoured division which numbered just under 11,000 men and produced a combat strength of no more than 5,000 or 45%; or a British or Canadian armoured division of slightly less than 15,000 men and a combat strength of about 7000 or 47%. The British Official History quotes a figure of 56%, but there are of course many ways of counting combat strength—this author uses a very simple one and accepts that it may not find favour with all readers: those men who, due to their employment, might actually see an enemy soldier (other than a prisoner), or a manned enemy vehicle.

When considering the organisations of the LAH and HJ Divisions in June 1944, readers should be wary of misleading and inaccurate statements which appear in some of the books on this subject. One well known 'authority' writes that Waffen-SS Panzer-Grenadier Regiments were equipped with Hummel 150mm and Wespe 105mm artillery pieces and talks of all battalions being mounted in SPWs. Nothing could be further from the truth. Hummel and Wespe were only to be found in the Divisional Panzer Artillery Regiment, while only one Panzer-Grenadier battalion in both the 1st and 12th SS Panzer Divisions, the one designated 'armoured', was mounted in SPWs—the other five Panzer-Grenadier battalions were carried in trucks. The generally held belief that German infantry were able to move cross-country in tracked vehicles whilst Allied infantry had to walk is a complete myth. Another writer, quite correctly, says that the LAH's Panzer Regiment included a Tiger tank company and that its Panzer-Grenadier Regiments had integral Reconnaissance and Panzerjäger com-

panies. Both these statements are true up to the early summer
of 1944, but in April of that year the Tiger company personnel
were transferred to the 101st SS Heavy Panzer Battalion and in
May the Reconnaissance and Panzerjäger companies were disbanded.[6] In a similar way many writers credit SS Panzer-Grenadier battalions with having five companies each; true, but
only until May 1944, when their Machine Gun companies
were disbanded.

The four major combat elements of a Panzer Division were
the Panzer Regiment, the two Panzer-Grenadier Regiments
and the Panzer Reconnaissance Battalion. With regard to
tanks, in June 1944 the 1st and 12th SS Panzer Divisions each
had a Panzer Regiment of two Panzer Battalions; the
authorised tank strength of each Regiment was seventy-nine
Panthers and 101 Mk IVs. However, on 1st July after arriving
in Normandy, the LAH had sixty-seven Panthers and 103 Mk
IVs.[7] The HJ Division, already in Normandy on D-Day, had
seventy-nine Panthers and ninety-six Mk IVs.[8] The 101st SS
Heavy Panzer Battalion of I SS Panzer Corps was at full
strength on D-Day with thirty-seven Tiger Is combat ready
and eight under short-term repair.

British and Canadian armoured divisions and the majority
of their independent armoured brigades were, not surprisingly, fully up to strength and combat ready on D-Day and
had the same number of medium tanks as a theoretical German SS Panzer division—186. If one adds the British division's integral armoured reconnaissance regiment (battalion),
which was equipped with medium tanks, the total increases to
246. In terms of numbers they were therefore very much
stronger than their German equivalents.

The term 'regiment' can cause confusion because it has different meanings in different armies. To the Americans and
Germans a 'regiment' was normally a semi-permanent grouping of three battalion-sized units, the exception being a German Panzer Regiment which in 1944 had only two tank
battalions. For the British and Canadians however, a 'regiment'—for example, an armoured, artillery or engineer regiment, or the Regina Rifle Regiment—was a unit of only
battalion size. Similar confusion can occur over 'squadrons'

and 'troops' in relation to armoured and reconnaissance units. In the American army a 'squadron' was battalion-sized and a 'troop' company-sized, whereas in the British and Canadian armies they were company and platoon-sized respectively.

American armoured divisions, although numerically weaker in manpower, had three as opposed to two tank battalions and were equipped with eighty-three light and 168 medium tanks.

The Panzer-Grenadier Regiments of the two Waffen-SS Divisions, which numbered about 3,500 men each in twelve combat companies, were more or less manned as planned, despite the shortage of experienced officers and senior NCOs. But at the beginning of June the LAH was still desperately short of SPWs for its armoured Panzer-Grenadier Battalion; and a similar shortage of vehicles and weapons dictated that its Reconnaissance Battalion had two companies incorrectly equipped with jeep-like Volkswagens, and the 1st SS Panzer Artillery Regiment was missing one battery of 105mm guns and another of 150mm.[9] The HJ Division was in a much better state. True, its new Jagdpanzer IVs had yet to arrive and it had an 80% shortfall in cross-country capable vehicles. But this, and some relatively minor deficiencies in specialist vehicles such as recovery tanks, artillery tractors, and armoured cars for its Reconnaissance Battalion,[10] did not prevent the Division being considered 'ready for offensive operations'.

The basic organisations of both the LAH on 1st July and the HJ Division on 6th June 1944 are shown at Appendices 1 to 6.

Although American, British and Canadian armoured divisions had more tanks than the designated SS Panzer Divisions of I SS Panzer Corps, this advantage was in many ways negated by a numerical inferiority in Allied infantrymen. The Waffen-SS Divisions each had twenty-four companies of Panzer-Grenadiers, totalling about 7,000 men, compared with nineteen companies of 3,400 men in a British or Canadian armoured division and only nine rifle companies of 3,000 men in an American armoured division. And to the German figure has to be added the engineer companies to be found within the Panzer Division—engineers in the German army were known as 'Pioniere' (pioneers) and were specially trained in street and

house fighting and often took on an infantry role. The reason
for this difference in infantry strengths was that, without de-
tracting from the importance of tanks, the Germans had
learned in the bitter fighting of the Eastern Front the need for
an adequate number of infantrymen to accompany their tanks
closely. The Allies had still to learn this painful lesson. Whilst
it is true that they had plenty of infantry divisions (there were
to be twenty-seven in France by the time the river Seine was
crossed) these were neither designed nor structured for the
mobile offensive operations which were planned for the Normandy campaign.

Before leaving the subject of infantry and Panzer-Grenadier
battalions, let us look at the question of machine guns—ex-
cluding sub machine guns—and mortars on each side. The
Americans had many more machine guns in the armoured
infantry battalions of their armoured division than the Germans—859 as opposed to 655 (the British came a poor third
with only 305). But when one compares the 1,200 rounds-a-
minute rate of fire of the German MG 42s with the American
or British equivalent of 500 at best, one can understand why
the German small arms ammunition scale for a rifle company
was nearly three times that of its American equivalent—56,000
to 21,000[11]—and why so many Allied infantrymen were reluctant to advance in open country in Normandy. Mortars provided another startling difference—the two SS Divisions had
around sixty medium and heavy mortars each, compared with
the twenty-four of the American, British and Canadian
armoured divisions. Moreover, the Allies had nothing comparable to the multi-barrelled Nebelwerfers of the German brigades and divisions.

In terms of artillery the LAH[12] had, on reaching the battlefield, twenty-three 105mm, seventeen 150mm, and four
100mm guns, plus seventeen 88mm and nine 37mm anti-aircraft weapons which could also be used in a ground role. On
1st June 1944 the HJ[13] had twenty-one 105mm, ten 150mm,
twelve 88mm and nine 37mm guns. To these impressive figures one has to add the six 150mm infantry heavy guns of the
Panzer-Grenadier Regiments and approximately forty-two
Werfers, already mentioned, of the two SS Panzer Werfer Bat-

talions. Nevertheless, as a means of redressing the imbalance in divisional artillery, the Allies could support the forty-eight to fifty-four field guns and howitzers of each of their armoured divisions with a plethora of readily available corps artillery units and devastatingly effective naval guns—at least until the breakout from the Normandy bridgehead. I SS Panzer Corps, on the other hand, could muster a mere two batteries of 175mm and one battery of 100mm guns, which together formed the 101st SS Heavy Artillery Battalion.

The organisations of American, British, Canadian and Polish armoured divisions are shown in Appendices 7 and 8.

Before leaving this section on organisations, we must look at Allied infantry divisions, for these far outnumbered their armoured counterparts and provided a powerful enemy to both the LAH and HJ Divisions. An American infantry division numbered approximately 16,000 men, of which about 9,000 were divided equally between three infantry regiments. The latter each had their own howitzer and anti-tank companies. The division was supported by four artillery battalions with forty-eight guns and an engineer battalion; although not organic, a tank battalion with fifty-four Shermans, a tank destroyer battalion with thirty-six anti-tank guns and an anti-aircraft battalion normally operated with the infantry division. The detailed organisation is shown at Appendix 9.

British and Canadian infantry divisions were similarly organised with about 18,000 men, of which roughly 8,000 were in the three infantry brigades; divisions had integral anti-tank and anti-aircraft regiments (battalions) and a machine gun battalion; although they had only three artillery regiments (battalions), these totalled seventy-two 25pdrs; there was no dedicated tank unit. The basic organisation is shown at Appendix 10.

Let us turn now to the tactical deployment of these men and weapon systems. The tactic of Blitzkrieg, so favoured by the Germans, has already been mentioned. In essence it called for integrated groups of tanks, infantry, artillery and engineers, supported by aircraft dedicated to ground attack and operating in conditions of at least local air superiority, to penetrate enemy defences as rapidly and violently as possible in a series of shock actions on a comparatively narrow front. Frontal attacks were normal and little heed was paid to flanks. The leading formations did not waste time mopping up enemy units which had been bypassed; this was left to follow-up forces. It had proved a battle-winning tactic from September 1939 until May 1944. Even the defeats in Russia had been mitigated by its use. Unfortunately for I SS Panzer Corps and the other German divisions involved in the battle for Normandy, one ingredient essential for the successful practice of Blitzkrieg would be missing—air superiority. Nevertheless, good training in weapon handling, marksmanship, fieldcraft, camouflage and night operations, coupled with physical toughness, self control, and a sense of camaraderie which produced a willingness to make sacrifices—all these factors still created a very formidable fighting machine.

Route marching, square bashing and frequent inspections, so favoured in the British and Canadian armies, were not to be found in the German training programmes; instead the emphasis was on training for battle with a liberal use of live ammunition. Advanced tactics were taught, such as allowing enemy leading elements to bypass one's own hidden positions from which one could then engage second and even third echelon attacking troops; this type of innovative thinking made great demands on the German troops, particularly in terms of personal discipline, but it had a devastating effect on the Allies. The fostering of a close relationship between officers, NCOs and soldiers was strongly emphasised and it is perhaps noteworthy that when talking to German veterans, one rarely encounters the constant criticisms of officers one hears from Allied soldiers. Why is this? One reason is certainly professional competence; another, perhaps the continual sharing of danger and hardship which the Germans had endured throughout the campaigns in Russia. Allied experiences in North Africa and the first months in Italy were not comparable.

In terms of tactics and communications the Allies had a lot to learn. Cooperation between tanks and infantry was in its infancy in comparison with the Germans; indeed, in many cases there was a positive mistrust between the two arms in the

Allied armies. Armoured units often complained that their infantry support was missing when they most needed it—for example, in very close country or in towns and villages, and this led to constant demands that the infantry should 'lead the way'. Such demands were not unreasonable when, as happened on more than one occasion, a tank was requested to deal with a troublesome Tiger or Panther in a village street when it was in fact safer and more realistic for the infantry to deal with it themselves. The attitude of many tank officers can be summed up by the comment, 'all infantry brigadiers look the same—middle aged, rather grim, slow thinkers and without any sense of humour.' On the other side of the coin, the disappearance of the tanks to the rear at night 'for maintenance' did little to endear them to the infantrymen, who failed to understand why the crews needed 'a good rest and a meal' while they had to endure the discomfort of a slit trench with nothing between them and the enemy. But whereas the tank crews could see the miseries being suffered by the foot soldiers, the latter had little comprehension of the stench, heat and claustrophobic atmosphere overwhelming those confined for hours on end in their steel mastodons.

The majority of Allied infantrymen had never trained closely with armour and had no idea how to communicate with the tanks they could often see only a stone's throw away. For instance, it was not until they arrived in England in late February 1944 that the men of the 30th US Infantry Division 'for the first time. . . . practised in earnest working with tanks'.[14] With approximately 9,000 infantrymen and only seventy tanks using the relatively tiny and over-crowded training areas of southern England and with a mere twelve weeks to go before D-Day, they had left it a bit late. The tank telephone—housed in a simple box on the back of a tank so that someone outside could talk to those inside—was not in service in June 1944 and there was simply not enough room in most Allied tanks for an extra radio set with which to talk to the infantry. Also, many infantry officers were loath to 'lose' a combat soldier by making him carry a special radio for communication with tanks. Indeed, many British infantry officers could not even use a radio effectively—they relied instead on a soldier

specially trained for the purpose. Radio orders, even in
armoured divisions, were the exception rather than the rule.
Instead, the time-consuming and dangerous practice of assembling all one's commanders in one place for the issuing of
orders was the normal routine.

Why were the Allies so far behind the Germans in these vital
aspects of modern warfare? In 1950 the British War Office
issued a document defining the problems of WWII communications. In relation to tanks it said:

> The chief technical problem involved was that of radiating
> sufficient power from inside an armoured box, by means of
> a small rod aerial, in order to compete with the ever-in-
> creasing ranges which were demanded and the unusually
> high level of interference. A second problem of almost equal
> importance was the provision of an adequate power supply
> in the confined space available inside a tank. . . . Another
> major problem was liaison with other arms; those, such as
> the Royal Artillery, who were supporting the tanks and
> those whom the tanks were supporting, such as the infantry.
> The artillery used in support of the tanks of an armoured
> division as a rule had ample opportunity to gain experience,
> but the position was more difficult in the case of field and
> medium regiments which had not had the advantage of the
> same training with armour. The problem of liaison with
> infantry was one which was never satisfactorily solved ex-
> cept by units which had trained together over a long period.
> The main difficulty was the wide divergence in the standard
> of training between the [tank]driver operators and the per-
> sonnel who could be spared in an infantry battalion to man
> the more forward wireless sets. The problem was solved, to
> some extent, by having the communication troop's nine
> scout cars fitted with wireless, which enabled liaison officers
> to be sent to other units and come in on the. . . . net
> without any disturbance. Or by the two commanders being
> actually together. But officers were not always available and,
> when they could not be found, the problem arose as to
> whether the infantry should come in on the tank net or
> whether a separate net should be established. A point which

sometimes arose was the natural reluctance of infantry company commanders to have additional, or any, vehicles at their headquarters.[15]

The same document makes further specific, if rather surprising, comments on the problems in the infantry:

There was also a very natural disinclination to increase the weight to be carried and to decrease the bayonet strength of the companies by giving them more wireless sets to carry. There was also a school of thought among officers of long experience which held that junior leaders should be encouraged to act on their own initiative and not be tied to their next senior by a wireless link when engaged in mobile operations. Senior officers, it was argued, should go forward and see for themselves or be content with such information as could be sent back by runner or liaison officer.[16]

The tactics being taught at the time were just as archaic. British instructions, dated May 1943, for cooperation between tanks and infantry in a deliberate attack of the kind being planned for Normandy, stated:

The maximum frontage for a squadron [company] of [average 19] tanks will seldom exceed 300 yards. A squadron so attacking will usually be in two waves. It follows that a division attacking with two infantry battalions and two tank battalions up will normally operate on a frontage not exceeding 1,200 yards. Tanks of a troop [platoon] will be at such a distance from each other as will enable control to be effected. The character of the ground will have a great effect in deciding this matter. In certain circumstances the tanks of a troop may be as close to each other as 20 yards, but such density is exceptional, and is only applicable when the ground affords cover and renders proximity essential.[17]

It would appear that the author of this instruction, 'prepared under the direction of The Chief of the Imperial General Staff' was under the impression that unless tanks could see each other they would be unable to communicate.

It also has to be said that in many Allied infantry units the state of training was abysmal. Nearly 150 years before WWII, Sir John Moore had taught British infantrymen the art of skirmishing and, at Waterloo, the Duke of Wellington had demonstrated the essential value of a reverse slope position. Sir Arthur Bryant in his book, *The Great Duke*, summed up British skirmishing in the Peninsular war:

> A rifleman in battle was the instrument of an orchestra in which every change of position, whether of individual or unit, was protected by coordinated fire, directed at the precise spot from which any interference with that movement might come.

In many infantry units all this had been long forgotten. Men advanced at a walking pace behind rolling barrages of artillery fire, just as they had in World War I, or in the company of tanks with which they could not communicate and which often left them far behind. The only difference between Wellington's infantry at Waterloo and Montgomery's in Normandy was that the former's moved rather quicker and closer together. Indeed, in one battle on 18th June, a Waffen-SS officer described British infantry moving behind their tanks 'strolling, hands in pockets, rifles slung on their shoulders, cigarettes between their lips'. And when a Royal Scots Fusilier officer discovered German soldiers dug in on a reverse slope during an attack on 26th June, he seemed to consider it unfair practice—'something we had never envisaged!'

. To be fair, General Montgomery tried very hard to improve all arms cooperation and instil what he called 'operational eagerness.'[18] But whatever his wishes or directions, in most cases they came too late; on 2nd August he wrote to the British Director of Military Operations in London:

> The old desert [North Africa campaign] divisions are apt to look over their shoulder, and wonder if all is OK behind, or if the flanks are secure, and so on. 7 Armd Div is like that. They want a new General, who will drive them headlong into, and through, gaps torn in the enemy defence—not worrying about flanks or anything.[19]

He was of course asking the British to adopt the tactics of Blitzkrieg. But, sadly, the lessons of the past few years had not been learned and the advances in technology and tactics which had been steadily appearing since the mid-1930s had been largely ignored. The price was paid in casualties.

NOTES

1. The following sources were consulted on organisational details: **A.** Ellis, C. *Tanks of World War 2.;* **B.** Ellis, L. *Victory in the West, Vol I, The Battle of Normandy.* **C.** Davies, *German Army Handbook 1939–45.* **D.** Hewitt, *Work Horse of the Western Front.* **E.** Lehmann & Tiemann, *The Leibstandarte IV/I.* **F.** Lucas & Cooper, *Hitler's Elite, Leibstandarte SS.* **G.** Quarrie, *Hitler's Samurai, The Waffen-SS in Action.* **H.** US War Department *Field Manual FM 101–10,* and very importantly, the personal archives of Jeff Dugdale and Mike Wood. 2. Meyer, Hubert, *The History of the 12th SS Panzer Division Hitlerjugend,* p. 3. 3. LAH Meldung dated 1 Jun 44. 4. LAH Meldung dated 1 Jul 44. 5. HJ Meldung dated 1 Jun 44. 6. Lehmann & Tiemann, op. cit., pp. 304, 307, 311. 7. LAH Meldung dated 1 Jun 44. It is difficult to be precise about vehicle and weapon numbers on any given date after 6th June; new and repaired items were constantly being fed forward to units which were incurring losses. 8. HJ Meldung dated 1 Jun 44 but see note 7 above. 9. Lehmann & Tiemann, op. cit., pp. 319–321 but see note 7 above. 10. Meyer, Hubert, op. cit., p. 9. 11. Hastings, *Overlord, D-Day and the Battle for Normandy 1944,* p. 42. 12. LAH Gliederung dated 1 Jul 44 but see note 7 above. 13. HJ Gliederung dated 1 Jun 44 but see note 7 above. 14. Hewitt, op. cit., p. 8. 15. Gravely, *The Second World War 1939–1945. Signal Communications 3.* pp. 446–7. 16. Ibid., p. 454. 17. War Office, Army Training Instruction No. 2. *The Co-operation of Infantry and Tanks,* 1943, p. 15. 18. Montgomery, *The Memoirs of Field Marshal Montgomery,* p. 243. 19. Recollections of Gen Sir Frank Simpson, recorded by Eugene Wason for Sir Denis Hamilton, 1978.

5 *The Setting*

There was no agreed German strategy for countering an Allied invasion of western Europe in the summer of 1944. The arguments between Field Marshal von Rundstedt, CinC West, and General Ceyr von Schweppenburg, Commander Panzer Group West, on the one hand, and Field Marshal Erwin Rommel, Commander Army Group 'B' on the other, are well known and have been described in most books written about the Normandy campaign. Von Rundstedt was senior to Rommel but he did not have Hitler's confidence and could not overrule the latter's views.

Rommel, with his experience of Allied air power, wanted all available tank forces positioned as close as possible to likely landing areas. He knew the Luftwaffe would be incapable of protecting his armoured columns moving to battle areas in daylight and that the very short summer hours of darkness would be insufficient for any long distance movement. He reasoned that the Germans would therefore lose the battle of the build-up. Von Rundstedt and von Schweppenburg, correct in theory but wrong in the circumstances pertaining at the time, wanted to hold the armour well back from the coasts and out of range of powerful naval guns, until they could see where the main threat was developing and then launch coordinated counter-thrusts against it. The result of all this argument was a disastrous compromise.

To compound matters further, the command system designed to put the strategy into operation was complicated and also inefficient. This was in some ways deliberate on the part of Hitler who, as well as mistrusting his army generals, wished to retain supreme command and have the opportunity to intervene at all levels. He therefore operated on a principle of 'divide and rule'. The German chain of command is shown at Appendix 11.

Von Rundstedt, as CinC West, with his Headquarters at St Germain just outside Paris, had two Army Groups under his command: 'B' commanded by Rommel, responsible for France north of the Loire, Belgium and Holland, and 'G' under Blaskowitz, responsible for France south of the Loire. We need not concern ourselves with Army Group 'G'.

Rommel, with his luxurious Headquarters in the Château La Roche-Guyon near Vernon on the Seine, had two Armies under his command: the Seventh, covering from the river Loire to the river Orne in Normandy and the Fifteenth covering from there to Holland. This was relatively tidy, but when it came to the Panzer forces the picture was very different. The argument over where to position these forces led inevitably to a split command structure and this was to affect dramatically Sepp Dietrich's I SS Panzer Corps, over which Rommel was

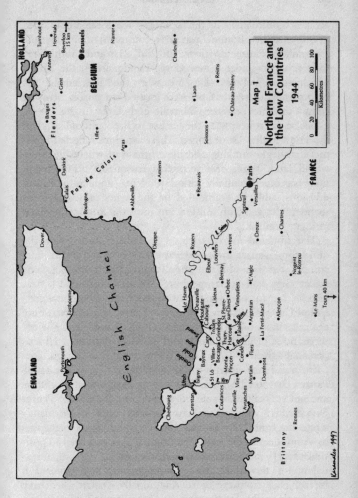

Map 1
**Northern France and
the Low Countries**
1944

Kilometres
0   20   40   60   80   100

given no control, despite the fact that it was located in his area of responsibility. Rommel was given command of only half the six available Panzer divisions: the 2nd, 21st and 116th. They were grouped under a new Corps Headquarters, the XLVII, which was in fact just taking over when the Allies landed. Not surprisingly, these divisions were located reasonably near the coast—the 2nd between Abbeville and Arras in the Pas de Calais, the 21st nearest to the sea just to the south of Caen and the 116th to the east of Rouen. These locations reflected Rommel's strategic thinking and his estimate of where the Allies would land. While this seemed a reasonable arrangement, there was one potentially critical problem—none of the Panzer divisions could be committed by the Army or Corps commanders charged with resisting any invasion. Rommel retained ultimate control.

The situation for Dietrich's I SS Panzer Corps, with the other three Panzer divisions, was even worse and much more complicated. For administration, supply and training it came under Geyr von Schweppenburg's Panzer Group West, near Lisieux, but for operations it was under the operational control of CinC West (von Rundstedt). There was, however, once again a vitally important restriction on its use—as OKW reserve, none of its divisions could be released without Hitler's personal agreement! And, as if this was not bad enough, Dietrich found himself with a widely scattered Corps. The 1st SS Panzer Division LAH was in northern Belgium, still refitting and not yet really ready for operations, and the 12th SS Panzer Division HJ was spread across a huge area of Normandy stretching from Louviers near the Seine and Dreux in the east to Vimoutiers in the west. The original plan had been to position the HJ in the immediate vicinity of Lisieux but, fortunately for the Allies, von Schweppenburg had ordered it further back from the coast. Additionally, Dietrich had been made responsible for the training of the Panzer Lehr Division. Panzer Lehr had started life as a demonstration unit but by May 1944 it was one of the strongest divisions in the German army. It was located well to the south, in the area of Illiers and Nogent-le-Rotrou, between Chartres and Le Mans.

The net result of all this over-control and divided strategy was that there was neither a strong immediate armoured reserve in Normandy nor a strong strategic reserve. Not surprisingly Dietrich had moved his Headquarters to Septeuil, just west of Paris, where he was more centrally located and nearer to his operational superior, von Rundstedt.

What was the attitude of the ordinary German soldier in Normandy in June 1944? Naturally it varied from unit to unit and from formation to formation. Many of those who had been conscripted into static or low calibre infantry divisions had only one real aim and that was to survive the war; more than a few had been medically down-graded. Similarly, enemy soldiers captured in the Russian campaign, who had subsequently 'volunteered' for service with the Germans, could hardly be expected to want to die for the Third Reich. The men of the Waffen-SS were a totally different matter— they still believed in their Führer and the destiny he had planned for them and they were more than ready to fight hard, or even die, for him. But whether volunteer or conscript, there were three highly motivating factors affecting the German soldier. First, he knew he would soon be in action and therefore everything he was doing was real and had a positive purpose. Second, the Allied demand for unconditional surrender gave him little choice other than to fight on—this was particularly true of the Waffen-SS who knew they could expect little mercy if Germany lost the war; and third, the 'Morgenthau Plan', named after the adviser to President Roosevelt who initiated it. This called for the division of Germany into a few deindustrialized, agrarian states, with the aim of preventing that country from ever again threatening world peace. The Germans learned of its existence in May 1944 and needless to say Goebbels used it to stiffen the nation's resolve.

And then there was the question of weaponry. As already mentioned the German soldier had faith in his weapons, and with good reason. Despite all the losses in Russia and the Allied bombing campaign, there was still no serious shortage of equipment. By December 1943 arms and ammunition output was 150% higher than it had been in February 1942.[1] The United States Strategic Bombing Report states:

In general, despite the retreats and losses in the latter part of
1943, the German army was better equipped with weapons
at the beginning of 1944 than at the start of the Russian
war.

Just two examples will suffice:[2] in December 1942 German
industry produced in one month 523 field and medium artillery pieces and 760 tanks. In July 1944 the figures had risen to
1,554 and 1,669 respectively.

German knowledge of Allied overall strategy and strengths
was reasonably good but when it came to precise intentions,
such as when and where they might land in western Europe, it
was extremely poor. The little intelligence which was collected
by the Abwehr, run by Admiral Canaris for the OKW, and
Himmler's Security Service (the SD), was often contradictory
and usually wrongly interpreted. An essential indicator, such
as the artificial floating harbour known as 'Mulberry', was not
even detected. From the few reports they did receive, the Germans estimated that about fifty-five to sixty divisions had been
assembled in England for the forthcoming invasion. This was
reasonably accurate but they were misled into believing that
most of these were located in the south-east of the country.
With such poor intelligence to guide them, the men responsible for the defence of France and the Low Countries were
forced to fall back on military judgement alone. Von Rundstedt believed the main landing would come in the Pas de
Calais:

> In the first place an attack from Dover against Calais would
> be using the shortest sea route to the Continent. Secondly,
> the V-1 and V-2 [German rocket weapons] sites were lo-
> cated in this area. Thirdly, this was the shortest route to the
> Ruhr and the heart of industrial Germany, and once a suc-
> cessful landing had been made it would take only four days
> to reach the Rhine. Fourthly, such an operation would sever
> the forces in Northern France from those along the Medi-
> terranean coast.[3]

The OKW staff believed the assault would come either in
the Pas de Calais, or more probably in the zone between the

Seine and the Somme, around Le Havre and Abbeville. Only Hitler, relying on his intuition, got it right! But it has to be said that Allied deception operations were highly successful and it is not surprising that von Rundstedt and the higher German staffs got it wrong. As late as 5th June Rommel's weekly situation report to von Rundstedt stated:

> Systematic continuation and intensification of enemy air-raids and more intensive mine-laying in own harbours. . . . indicates an advance in enemy's preparations for invasion. Concentration of air attacks on coastal defences between Dunkirk and Dieppe and on the Seine-Oise bridges confirms *presumption* [author's emphasis] as to Schwerpunkt of large-scale landing. . . . Since 1.6.44 increased transmissions of enemy radio of warning messages to French resistance organisation, [but] judging from experience to date, [this is] not explicable as an indication of invasion being imminent. . . . Air reconnaissance showed no great increase of landing craft in Dover area. Other harbours of England's south coast NOT visited by reconnaissance aircraft.[4]

Inevitably, the result of all this speculation was that in the end the Germans had no real intelligence of when or where the assault would come, which explains why many of their commanders were absent from their places of duty when it did. Rommel, responsible for the whole invasion coast, was at home in Herrlingen near Ulm, in order to be with his wife on her birthday (6th June!) and at the same time visit Hitler at the Berghof, and most of the Seventh Army's divisional commanders responsible for the Normandy coast, had been called to Rennes by General Friedrich Dollmann for an anti-invasion exercise. The whereabouts of Sepp Dietrich is uncertain—he was either in Belgium visiting Wisch and the Leibstandarte or had just returned from there to Septeuil. Only von Rundstedt and Geyr von Schweppenburg were in the right place; the former could not deploy the Hitlerjugend or Panzer Lehr Divisions without OKW (Hitler) authority and the latter had no operational command.

Now let us look at the setting as far as the Allies were concerned. Their strategy, after not a little argument, was agreed. The first priority was the defeat of Hitler's Reich and the main effort was to be made on the Normandy coast. General Dwight D. Eisenhower had been appointed Supreme Commander Western Europe, with a British airman as his Deputy and an American Chief of Staff. The British were given command of both the Allied Naval and Air Expeditionary Forces and, most important of all as far as this story is concerned, General Sir Bernard Montgomery was given command of all ground forces in the initial stages of the campaign. He had two Armies—Lieutenant General Omar Bradley's First US Army and Lieutenant General Miles Dempsey's second British Army, which on D-Day included the 3rd Canadian Infantry Division and 2nd Canadian Armoured Brigade. It was planned that Eisenhower himself would assume command of all land forces as soon as General George Patton's Third US Army became operational in France. At this time Bradley would take command of the US 12th Army Group and Lieutenant General Courtney H. Hodges replace him at First US Army. It was foreseen that Canadian Lieutenant General Henry Crerar's First Canadian Army would be activated at about the same time, giving Montgomery another Army for his 21st Army Group. Although nominally 'Canadian', Crerar's Army included I British Corps and the 1st Polish Armoured Division. The Allied chain of command on 6th June 1944 is shown at Appendix 12.

Montgomery's overall plan for the Normandy campaign, and indeed it was *his* plan, is well known and there is no need to go into it in any great detail. Following airborne landings at each end of the proposed beachhead, four Allied corps would land on five beaches; it was intended that they would penetrate to an average depth of about 10km on D-Day and capture the towns of Isigny, Bayeux and Caen. Montgomery then planned to hold Caen and the high ground immediately to its south whilst by D+9 an American and a British corps would secure the line of the high ground running from St Lô through Caumont to Villers-Bocage. It was also hoped that another US corps would capture the major port of Cherbourg in the same time frame. From this firm base Bradley's American 12th

Army Group, with Patton's Third Army operative, would expand south, and by D+50 the lodgement area would comprise the Brittany ports and France north of the Loire and east to the line Deauville-Tours. If all went well the Allies would be established along the river Seine by D+90. This then was the plan outlined by Montgomery in front of King George VI, Prime Minister Churchill, General Eisenhower and all senior commanders in St Paul's School, London on 15th May. All who attended were left in no doubt about Monty's intentions. General Omar Bradley wrote later:

> The British and Canadian armies were to decoy the enemy reserves and draw them to their front on the extreme eastern edge of the Allied beachhead. Thus while Monty taunted the enemy at Caen, we were to make our break on the long roundabout road to Paris. When reckoned in terms of national pride, this British decoy mission became a sacrificial one, for while we tramped around the outside flank, the British were to sit in place and pin down Germans. Yet strategically it fitted into a logical division of labors, for it was toward Caen that the enemy reserves would race once the alarm was sounded.[5]

But Monty ended his presentation with the following statement:

> We must blast our way on shore and get a lodgement before the enemy can bring up sufficient reserves to turn us out. Armoured columns must penetrate deep inland, and quickly, on D-Day; this will upset the enemy's plans and tend to hold him off while we build up strength. We must gain space rapidly and peg out claims well inland. . . . once we get control of the main enemy lateral Granville-Vire-Argentan-Falaise-Caen and have the area enclosed in it firmly in our possession, then we will have the lodgement area we want and can begin to expand.[6]

This early mention of Argentan and Falaise and some of Montgomery's later statements and directions gave rise to many arguments and acrimonious discussions concerning this plan, both during the Normandy campaign and in post-war years. Nevertheless, the fact remains that the Allies were on the Seine by D+90 and the German army in France was broken.

There is, however, one aspect of Allied strategy which needs further discussion since it impacted so strongly on the German forces in general and the Panzer forces in particular—air power. Eisenhower, with Montgomery's full support, had insisted that even the Allied Strategic Air Forces of Harris and Spaatz should be switched from their directed task of crippling German industry to a mission of paralysing rail communications in the invasion area. Inevitably this policy would result in casualties to the French population, but Eisenhower's arguments finally won the day and in March 1944 the Combined Chiefs of Staff placed both Air Forces under his operational control. This meant that the whole weight of Allied air power could be used to prevent, disrupt and destroy German armoured reserves as they tried to reach the battlefield. The Allies flew 10,585 strategic and tactical air sorties on D-Day alone and with over 5,000 fighters to provide cover, against only 119 serviceable German fighters on the Channel front, there was little danger of interference from the enemy.[7]

Despite the risk of over-generalizing we must now consider the morale of the Allied armies. Inevitably this varied, not only between units but also between nationalities. The Americans were untried in battle but displayed a cockiness and confidence which epitomised their 'New World' and irritated their compatriots of the 'Old'. They were unpopular with many of their British fellow servicemen who, often in a very arrogant way, considered them amateurish and unprofessional. Supercilious remarks such as, 'where have you been for the last three years?' did little for Anglo-American relations! Even the way the Americans marched was different, as was the music to which they marched—neither was considered particularly 'military' by the British or the Canadians. Whatever the truth, many British officers privately echoed the sentiments expressed by General Sir Harold Alexander when he wrote from Tunisia about the Americans:

> They simply do not know their job as soldiers and this is the case from the highest to the lowest, from the general to the

private soldier. Perhaps the weakest link of all is the junior leader, who just does not lead, with the result that their men don't really fight.[8]

Much of the criticism stemmed from envy—envy of uniforms which were tailored and included shirts with collars and ties for all ranks, envy of less discipline and more freedom, envy of equipment which did not require polishing, and above all, envy over pay. A British private soldier, even with three years' service, was paid only £55 a year in 1944; an American private first class, with the same length of service earned £200 ($778); a British second lieutenant £200, an American £447 ($1800); a British lieutenant colonel £785, an American £868 ($3500).[9] The pay differentials between the ranks in each army are also of interest and tell a story in themselves—the British lieutenant colonel earned 14.25 times the pay of a private, an American only 4.5 times.

It has often been said that the US Army was nothing more than a very large group of civilians in uniform—so it was, but then so were the British and Canadian Armies in 1944; and just as the Americans had problems with incompetent officers (five divisional commanders were sacked in Normandy alone) so the British could not hide the fact that they too faced similar difficulties. Numerous senior officers had been removed since the outbreak of war and, as this book will record, more were to go in the forthcoming campaign.

The same applied to the Canadians. With an Army raised almost entirely from part-time Militia forces and a small population, it was unavoidable that many of its commanders were inexperienced and sometimes owed their positions more to their place in society or commerce than to military ability.

The Americans naturally found the British and their way of life puzzling—no ice or refrigerators, no showers, warm beer, driving on the left, the perils of English pronunciation and so on; keeping warm was a major problem with no central heating in army camps and little or none even in the private houses in which some of them were billeted and others invited. But some things were familiar and comforting—the language, distances measured in miles, even if nobody knew what

a 'block' was, and of course, girls! But since it was the Japanese
who had attacked America and not the Germans, many of the
GIs wondered why they were in Europe at all, and this confusion was compounded by their lack of knowledge of European
history and geography. The fact that a surprising number were
of German origin did not help matters. In the 'Midland' region of the USA (Pennsylvania, New Jersey, Delaware and
Maryland), people of German origin formed up to 70% of the
population in some towns.[10]

The Americans were in fact reasonably well trained. As an
example, the 30th US Infantry Division,[11] part of the National
Guard, was called into active Federal service at Fort Jackson,
South Carolina on 16th September 1940. The chance of America going to war seemed remote but training began in earnest
and, after six months' basic training, the men took part in
divisional and corps manoeuvres at Fort Bragg and in Tennessee. Innumerable reorganisations followed, many involving
manpower turnover, before the 30th, 'Old Hickory', took its
final form at the beginning of 1943. Training followed an established pattern—thirteen weeks individual training followed
by thirteen weeks sub-unit training. In September the Division
spent over two months in the 2nd Army manoeuvre area,
again in Tennessee, where they participated in exercises with
two other infantry divisions and an armoured division. By the
time they embarked for England in February 1944 (the first
US troops landed in the United Kingdom in January 1942 and
by June that year 55,000 had arrived), many men had already
spent a considerable time in uniform and knew their jobs as
well as most of their British and Canadian counterparts, and
better than some.

But just as there were tensions between the soldiers of the
different Allied armies, so there were tensions within these
armies. The men of the US 1st and 9th Infantry Divisions were
bitterly resentful at being brought back from Sicily to prepare
for the invasion of Normandy, particularly those of the 1st
who were to take part in the initial landings. They felt they
had already done their duty and that it was the turn of others.
The same could be said of the British divisions which had
already fought through North Africa, Sicily and the early

stages of the Italian campaign. But both Bradley and Montgomery felt that if their missions were to be successful, they needed the experience and leavening influence of these men. Complaints of this kind never occurred in the Waffen-SS—its members expected to be moved to the most important and dangerous centres of fighting.

US military doctrine differed from that of the British and Canadian Armies which, with good reason, were very casualty conscious. It had remained unchanged since being initiated by General Ulysses S. Grant in the American Civil War, and can be summarised as: 'Find 'em, fix 'em, destroy 'em!' It was well suited for the forthcoming campaign.

The British Army destined to fight in Normandy comprised three divisions which had seen considerable action in the Middle East and the equivalent of a dozen which had never heard a shot fired in anger. Needless to say the former adopted a rather patronising attitude towards the latter and this arrogance gave rise to numerous incidents of ill-discipline. When weekend leave was cancelled shortly before D-Day, the men of one British armoured regiment announced that they had no intention of staying in camp and only a 'pep' talk from Montgomery himself ended what amounted to nothing less than a mutiny.[12] On the other hand, those who had been training for months, and in some cases years, in the British Isles were often bored and stale. Whilst those in the more elite units were eager to 'do their bit', the majority, just like the Americans, Canadians and Germans, were civilians in uniform whose main aim was to survive the war—they had no 'love' for army life and saw little point in the constant parades, drill and long marches. In the main they were over-trained at unit level but almost totally untrained in large scale, combined arms, operations.

Even experienced divisions such as the famous 'Desert Rats', which had achieved a relatively high level of infantry-tank co-operation during the fighting in North Africa and Italy, stayed in their 'compartments' during the short period they had for re-training after arriving home from Italy in January 1944. There was only one Divisional exercise and, as one officer in the infantry brigade of the 7th Armoured Division told the author, 'We never even expected to *see* [author's emphasis] tanks in our training.' The fact that they were stationed in a totally unsuitable part of England for the sort of fighting they would see in the 'bocage' countryside of France, and at the same time made to take over totally unfamiliar British Cromwell tanks, did little to improve their battleworthiness. They had been required to leave in Italy the American Shermans with which they had fought their way from Alamein to Tunis. Sergeant Bobby Bramwell of the 4th County of London Yeomanry described his reactions:

> They [Cromwells] were atrocious tanks, fast enough but thin-skinned and somewhat undergunned. . . . Our training in Norfolk largely consisted of cleaning our new tanks and firing and calibrating the guns. We did no tactical training that I can recall. I was commanding a Firefly tank in 3 Troop, a Sherman tank with a 17 pdr gun—very good kit.[13]

It is therefore hardly surprising that commanders in Normandy were soon complaining about a lack of initiative and flexibility by British units and an unwillingness by many to show any aggressiveness. Few had appreciated that in both the 'bocage' countryside south of Bayeux and open terrain covered with small hamlets to the south-east of Caen, the need for really close cooperation between tanks and infantry would be essential for success. The German understanding of this need, particularly in the Waffen-SS formations, would allow them, time after time and even when desperately outnumbered, to engage and delay the Allies successfully.

Finally, it has to be said that the British regimental system which divides men into relatively small compartments and emphasizes a regimental, as opposed to an army, way of doing things, militated against the strong divisional spirit which was a major strength of the Waffen-SS system. It also led to one or two officers in some of the armoured brigades adopting a jingoistic attitude which actually disdained professionalism, resulting occasionally in disaster. Even senior infantry officers were not immune to the suggestion that war was still something of a 'game' to be played by gentlemen—a battalion commander wrote:

We went to bed [10th June] hoping our vehicles would arrive during the night and that we could relieve the 50th Division. . . . [they] must have had quite their share of the game by now.

Such sentiments and remarks were incomprehensible to most of the soldiers. Montgomery, who saw himself as the ultimate professional, fell into the same trap when he ended his St Paul's School presentation with the words, 'Good luck to each one of you. And good hunting on the mainland of Europe.' Admittedly he was using the vernacular of the time but it still betrayed the cavalier attitude of many officers of the period. On the other hand, the emphasis on regimental loyalty and long, glorious histories—even if sometimes a little exaggerated—gave British regiments an inner strength which made them steadfast in adversity and dangerous adversaries—particularly in defence.

The Canadian Army preparing to take part in the Normandy invasion differed in one important aspect from the American and British—every man had volunteered for overseas service. This policy was deliberate on the part of the Canadian government following unfortunate experiences in World War I. The policy had two effects: first, motivation was high; second, there was a serious shortage of reinforcements available to replace battle or other casualties. The shortage of reinforcements had in turn two serious consequences—a man who had been highly trained in a specialist role could hardly be spared to replace a basic infantryman and, as the campaign progressed, this produced serious undermanning in front-line units; and the army on the battlefield felt increasingly that their sacrifices were being made in isolation from the rest of their nation.

Bitter memories of the disastrous raid on Dieppe in 1942, when over 3,000 of the 5,000 Canadian troops taking part became casualties, also affected morale. There was a mistrust of British generals and a need to avenge that painful defeat. And then, as in the First World War, there was the problem of the French Canadians. Although they provided fifteen of the seventy-five infantry battalions in the Canadian Army in 1944, they could only find enough volunteers to send four of them overseas at full strength. Needless to say these men felt the reputation of French Canada lay on their sholders and they fought accordingly. But many of the problems the Canadian Army faced would only appear as the campaign progressed, and morale on 6th June was generally very high and its men were, on the whole, well trained and keen to get to grips with the enemy.

The soldiers of the 1st Polish Armoured Division were also volunteers. After a courageous but unsuccessful defence of their homeland in September 1939, many Polish soldiers and civilians made their way to Syria and France via Romania and Hungary and the Baltic States. By May 1940 some 84,500 Poles were under arms in those countries. An infantry brigade was sent, as part of an Allied force, to help defend Norway and two full infantry divisions, two partly organised infantry divisions and an armoured cavalry brigade formed part of the armies defending France. However, in the face of a second Blitzkrieg by the seemingly invincible Wehrmacht, the remnants of these divisions, like the British Expeditionary Force, were forced to evacuate Continental Europe during June. Only 24,000 reached Great Britain. From this small core, later reinforced by volunteers from Polish communities all over the world, General Sikorski, their CinC and Prime Minister of a Government in exile, had by April 1942 built and equipped a fine Armoured Division. In General Stanislaw Maczek he found the right leader; one of his best known sayings was, 'The Polish soldier fights for the freedom of other nations but dies only for Poland.' The members of his Division, having waited four years for a chance to exact revenge on their conquerors, harboured a bitter hatred for the Germans. It was fortunate that many Poles who had been impressed into the Wehrmacht after Germany annexed the western Polish provinces in 1939, changed sides soon after capture and were able to replace casualties.

Just how much did the Allies know about their enemy on the eve of the invasion? Until April the intelligence staffs had been delighted to note that all German reinforcements to the

West Wall were going to the Fifteenth Army, north of the Seine.

The Germans did not seem to recognise any serious threat between Le Havre and Cherbourg. In May however, intelligence agencies began to pick up heavy rail traffic between the Seine and Loire and most significantly saw both the 21st Panzer and Panzer Lehr Divisions move into the Caen and Le Mans areas. With 12th SS Panzer Division HJ spread between Louviers and Vimoutiers and the 116th Panzer astride the Seine, west of Paris, this appeared to indicate that the Germans had learned of the intended landings in Normandy and had placed their armoured reserves accordingly. There was more bad news to come. In mid May an infantry division and parachute regiment took up positions at the base of the Cotentin Peninsula—exactly where it was planned to drop two US airborne divisions, and at the same time the 5th German Parachute Division moved to Rennes. It seemed certain that the Germans had discovered the Allied plan. In fact it was nothing more than Hitler's intuition; and a closer look at overall German dispositions revealed that of the sixty divisions available to von Rundstedt, only eighteen were between the Seine and the Loire. Allied intelligence was good and deception plans pointing to the main invasion being in the Pas de Calais region were proving successful. But there were still eight German divisions, two of them armoured, positioned to oppose the landings on D-Day and 12th SS Panzer would be one of them; a further four divisions were available to come into play by D+2.

We must now look at the ground over which the Battle of Normandy was fought and begin by defining 'bocage'. Although 'bocage' exists all over France, and Brittany is full of it, the part we are concerned with is that in Calvados and La Manche. In 1944 this 'bocage' was nearly 80km in depth and lay to the west and south-west of Caen between the Orne and Vire rivers. The more northerly part, extending for some 30km, consisted of irregular small fields, usually little more than 100 square metres in size, separated by high earth banks, on top of which grew dense bushes and trees. Running along these banks were sunken tracks, often overgrown and some so narrow that once in them tanks could not turn or even traverse their guns. Such country resembled a giant, irregular chess board or gigantic shrubbery and was of course ideal for defence and counter-attack. Troops and even vehicles could be moved within it relatively easily without detection, even in daylight. And then, to the south-west of a line drawn roughly from Falaise to St Lô, lies a larger and even wilder part of the 'bocage' known, for reasons obvious to anyone who visits the area, as the Suisse Normande. Here the ground rises to a large plateau about 300m high, dominated by Mont Pinçon (365m), 30km south-west of Caen.

Many streams, running generally north through steep narrow valleys, intersect the Norman countryside and on either side of the 'bocage' the Germans had created severe obstacles by flooding—on the eastern flank along the river Dives between Cabourg and Troarn, and in the west in the estuary of the Vire. Since the war much of the 'bocage' has been opened up, but it can still be seen in its original form in a number of places. Between the 'bocage' and the sea the ground is undulating but fairly flat and open.

And now we must correct a myth which has grown up since the war. It leads us to believe that the British and Canadians spent most of their time fighting in the 'bocage', whilst the Americans fought mainly in open country and were thus more easily able to break out. The truth is very different. Whilst it is certainly true that parts of the Second British Army fought in and eventually through the 'bocage', it was in fact the Americans who were always required in Monty's plan to fight their way *through* it (author's emphasis). As he put it in his 15th May briefing at St Paul's School, 'once *through* [author's emphasis] the difficult 'bocage' country' [the Americans] were to 'thrust rapidly towards Rennes', seal off the Brittany peninsula, and wheel round towards Paris and the Seine, pivoting on the right flank of the British Second Army. But although the Allied bridgehead had been consolidated and the important port of Cherbourg captured by the end of June, there was still a vital need for more space for the troops necessary to launch the crucial breakout offensive. A further belt of 'bocage', 10 to 16km deep, had still to be penetrated. This meant that the Americans had to fight through an area of 'bocage' almost twice the size of that in which the British found themselves. It took four US corps, ultimately employing twelve divisions, to do it—little wonder that in the 'Battle of the Hedgerows', as the Americans called it, and by the time the breakout had been achieved, they had suffered over 30% more casualties than the British and Canadians.

The eastern part of the battlefield, where large numbers of British, Canadians and Poles were to take their share of the suffering, was in the main made up of open, rolling country with large cornfields, broken by occasional clumps of trees or small woods. Intensively cultivated, this area was full of small hamlets, the houses and walls of which were built of strong Caen stone. This undulating, featureless countryside runs south and south-east from Caen in what is known as the Caen-Falaise Plain. Similarly, 8km to the south-west of Caen, which is geographically more than twice as large today as it was in 1944, the ground rises to a height of 112m and from here, as from many parts of the Caen-Falaise plain, one can see for miles.

It was in the more open country that the Germans would naturally concentrate their armour, including the 1st and 12th SS Panzer Divisions.

NOTES

1. Wilmot, *The Struggle for Europe,* p. 150. 2. Ibid., p. 150. 3. Shulman, *Defeat in the West,* pp. 111–112. 4. Wilmot, op. cit. p. 229. 5. Bradley, *A Soldier's Story.* 6. Wilmot, op. cit. p. 216. 7. Ibid., pp. 288–9. 8. Nicolson, *Alex,* p. 211. 9. *Royal Warrant for the Pay, Appointment, Promotion, and Non-Effective Pay of the Army 1940,* HMSO, London; and Ganoe & Lundberg, *The History of the United States Army,* Appendix C. Official exchange rate 1944: $4.03 to £1. 10. *New Encyclopaedia Brittannica, Macropaedia,* Vol 29, p. 191. 11. Hewitt, *Workhorse of the Western Front,* pp. 5–6. 12. Maj Joe Lever, BM 22 Armd Bde, to author October 1995. 13. Neillands, *The Desert Rats,* p. 221.

6 | 6th June—D-Day

At 0230 hours on the 6th of June General Blumentritt, von Rundstedt's Chief of Staff, in response to a request from Army Group 'B', issued an order on his own initiative for 12th SS

Panzer Division to make a reconnaissance into the area east of the Dives river and to the north-east of Troarn. It read:

> The 12th SS Panzer Division, without diminishing its role as OKW reserve, will immediately commence reconnaissance in the direction of 711th Infantry Division. . . . and watch its own sector for a possible air landing.'

The HJ had already been alerted by Dietrich's Chief of Staff, Fritz Kraemer, and the 25th SS Panzer-Grenadier Regiment, on Kurt Meyer's own initiative, had sent out probing patrols in the direction of Caen from its assembly area which ran from Bernay through Orbec to Vimoutiers. At about 0400 hours, in accordance with Blumentritt's orders, Witt told Bremer's SS Reconnaissance Battalion to find out what was happening in the coastal sectors from the mouth of the Seine to Bayeux.

At 0445 hours, Blumentritt asked General Jodl at OKW to release the Panzer divisions of the Strategic Reserve to his commander but the request was turned down. The High Command was still not convinced that the Allied airborne landings were anything more than a feint.

Shortly after 0500 hours the 12th SS Panzer Division HJ under its commander Fritz Witt was attached to Rommel's Army Group 'B', which in turn placed it under General Erich Marck's LXXXIV Corps at St Lô. Witt had visited Marcks and his divisions as part of his reconnaissances during May and had a high regard for the abilities of this veteran who had lost a leg on the Eastern Front.

At 0545 hours CinC West agreed to an Army Group 'B' request for 12th SS to concentrate around Lisieux. This was not in accordance with any of HJ's existing plans and consequently no routes or assembly areas had been prepared for such a move. When Fritz Witt and his commanders received the order they were horrified; the assembly area was very restricted in size and lay too far to the east of the known landings, and the cross-roads at Lisieux were an obvious target for Allied air attacks. Complaints to Kraemer at I SS Panzer Corps were to no avail and the move began at about 1000 hours, led by a motorized SS Panzer-Grenadier battalion of the 25th Regiment. Witt grouped the 2nd SS Panzer Battalion of SS Major

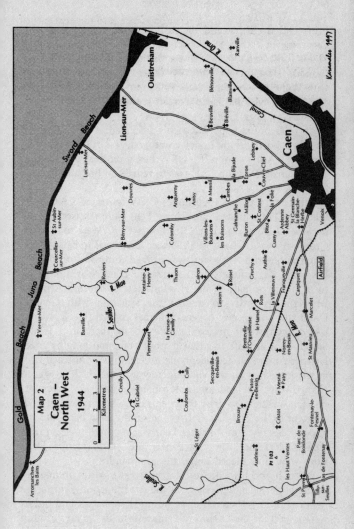

Map 2
Caen –
North West
1944

Kilometres
0 1 2 3 4 5

Gold Beach
Juno Beach
Sword Beach

Arromanches-les-Bains
Ver-sur-Mer
Courseulles-sur-Mer
St Aubin-sur-Mer
Luc-sur-Mer
Lion-sur-Mer
Ouistreham

Banville
Reviers
Bény-sur-Mer
Douvres
Anguerny
Ansy
Beuville
Bénouville
Ranville

Pierrepont
Fontaine-Henry
Colomby
Villons-les-Buissons
les Buissons
le Mesnil
Cambes
la Bijude
Biéville
Blainville

Creully
la Fresne Camilly
Thaon
Caron
Galmanche
Buron
Epron
Lébisey

St Gabriel
Cully
Lasson
Rosel
Gruchy
Authie
Maloo
St Contest
la Folie
Couvre-Chef

Coulombs
Secqueville-en-Bessin
Bretteville l'Orgueilleuse
le Hamel
Rots
la Villeneuve
Franqueville
Cussy
Ardenne Abbey
St Germain-la-Blanche-Herbe
Caen

St Léger
Brouay
Putot-en-Bessin
le Mesnil-Patry
Norrey-en-Bessin
St Mauvieu
Marcelet
Carpiquet
Airfield
Venoix

Audrieu
Cristot
Parc de Boislonde
Fontenay-le-Pesnel
Pt 103

St Pierre
Tilly-sur-Seulles
les Haut Ventes

R. Mue
R. Seulles
R. Orne
Canal

Kossendes 1997

Prinz and the Prinz and the 3rd SS Artillery Battalion with
Panzermeyer's 25th SS Panzer-Grenadier Regiment, and SS
Major Jürgensen's 1st SS Panzer Battalion, the 12th SS Panzer
Pioneer Battalion and the two other SS artillery Battalions
with Wilhelm Mohnke's 26th SS Panzer-Grenadier Regiment.
The Main Divisional Headquarters remained for the time be-
ing at Acon near Tillières-sur-Avre.

At 1400 hours Sepp Dietrich's I SS Panzer Corps, which
now had no divisions under command, was subordinated to
Rommel's Army Group 'B'. OKW had given instructions that
1st SS Panzer Division LAH was to remain in Belgium in strategic reserve.

Between 1430 and 1500 hours OKW informed CinC West
that both Hitlerjugend and Panzer Lehr were released for use
by Seventh Army, and at 1507 hours CinC West told Army
Group 'B' that Dietrich's I SS Panzer Corps was to be subordinated to Seventh Army and was to take command of the two
Divisions. According to Fritz Kraemer,[2] Dietrich was required
to report personally to the Headquarters of Seventh Army at
Le Mans in order to discuss the situation with General
Dollmann and receive orders. Kraemer replied that it was far
too dangerous for his commander to fly there in a Fiesler
Storch light aircraft and that it would take too long by road.
He therefore requested telephone orders, to be confirmed later
in writing. Dietrich was subsequently told that 12th SS was to
change direction and assemble on both sides of Evrecy. Its
mission was then 'to drive the enemy, who has broken through
adjacent to the 21st Panzer Division on the west, back into the
sea and destroy him'.[3] Panzer Lehr was required to secure the
area of Flers-Vire. The 21st Panzer and 716th Infantry Divisions were duly placed under his command.

Dietrich and his Chief of Staff met Fritz Witt, commander
of the Hitlerjugend Division, at the road junction 5km to the
north of St Pierre-sur-Dives at around 1600 hours, and orders
were issued for the Division to concentrate in the area around
Evrecy and to be prepared to counter-attack. It was approximately 1700 hours by the time Witt's Headquarters received
this order and 1740 before Meyer's 25th SS Panzer-Grenadier
Regimental Group was given its new destination. By then it

had already arrived in the Lisieux area—in fact it had been there since 1300 hours. Had it been told to go to Evrecy in the first place it could have been there by about 1500 hours and been ready to launch an attack into the Allied bridgehead by not later than 1800 hours. This could have presented a serious threat to Second British Army. As it was it took until 2100 hours to cross the river Orne and till 2300 hours before the 1st SS Panzer-Grenadier Battalion was able to take up a position near Noyers, to the south-west of Caen. The rest of the Group was to take all night to concentrate in the assembly area. Mohnke's 26th SS Panzer-Grenadier Group, following up with Jürgensen's Panthers and the other units, had an even bigger problem. SS Lieutenant Colonel Bernhard Krause's 1st SS Panzer-Grenadier Battalion needed to cover 190km from its start point and its leading elements would not cross the Orne till late on the 7th; the whole Regimental Group would not be complete in the assembly area until the night of 7th–8th June and even then there would be elements missing due to fuel shortages—Jürgensen's forty-eight Panthers required some 8,000 gallons of fuel after their journey to the battle area. But Allied air power was having a devastating effect on German logistics and movement, and the supplies which the HJ Division was expecting to find in the Evrecy area had already been severely depleted. Meyer's graphic description of his own movement to the battle area gives some idea of conditions on 6th June, although it should be remembered that he was still a committed Nazi when he wrote these words long after the war:

On the Caen-Falaise road we meet French refugees, a bus is ablaze. Heart-rending cries carry towards us. We cannot help, the door is jammed and bars the way to freedom. Mangled bodies hang out of the broken windows, barring the way. What horror! Why these burning civilians? But we must clear the congestion! We must not stop! We must press ever onwards to gain ground. The woods attract us like magnets, more and more fighter planes are above us. We are haunted relentlessly but cannot afford to take cover. The march must go on!

A string of Spitfires is attacking the last platoon of the

15th Company. Rockets and other weapons are reaping a grizzly harvest. The platoon is driving down a sunken road, evasion is not possible. An old French woman comes running towards us shouting, 'Murder! Murder!' A Grenadier is lying on the road, a jet of blood shooting from his throat, an artery has been shot through, he dies in our arms. The ammunition in an amphibious vehicle explodes with a loud bang, the blast shoots flames high into the sky, the vehicle is torn to pieces. In a couple of minutes the rubble is pushed aside, there is no stopping, on—always on!

Darkness arrives. The 15th [Reconnaissance] Company has crossed the Caen—Villers-Bocage road. I'm waiting impatiently for I Battalion. The constant air attacks have slowed speed dramatically. Finally Waldmüller reports the battalion's [arrival], and I'm informed that the air attacks have not caused excessive losses. At about 2300 hours an ordnance officer from the 21st Panzer Division reaches me. This division is fighting near Troarn and north of Caen. The divisional commander, Lt General Feuchtinger, is expecting me at the 716th Infantry Division's tactical headquarters. I leave immediately. Low flying German bombers are flying across the road. They are met with intense defensive fire as soon as they reach the area of the invasion fleet, a few lorries are burning on the road. It is a bizarre journey.

Caen is a sea of flames. Harassed people are wandering through the rubble, streets are blocked, burning smoke is rolling through the town. Venerable churches are converted into heaps of rubble, the work of generations is now a sea of ashes and rubble. Seen from a military point of view, the destruction of Caen is a major mistake.[4]

Meyer also wrote:

Caen, the town from which William the Conqueror started his victorious journey across the Channel, has been destroyed. More than 10,000 men and women are lying beneath the smoking rubble. The town has become a vast cemetery.[5]

Headquarters I SS Panzer Corps began its move from

Septeuil at 1600 hours and set up in the woods near Falaise during the night, whilst Witt's Hitlerjugend Headquarters set out at 1800 hours and established itself at les Moutiers-en-Cinglais on the edge of the Forêt de Grimbosq.

At 1655 hours the senior operations officer at Headquarters CinC West confirmed to the Chief of Staff Seventh Army that it was 'the wish of the Supreme Command that the enemy bridgehead be destroyed by the evening of 6 June because there was the danger of strong airborne and sea landings [in the Pas de Calais region].' Not surprisingly he was told this was impossible.[6]

At 2000 hours[7] Dietrich and Kraemer arrived at the Headquarters of 21st Panzer Division in St Pierre-sur-Dives to assess the situation, and no doubt hoping to coordinate the planned counter-attack by the HJ and 21st Panzer Divisions. To their intense irritation they found no Divisional commander and a Chief of Staff who had himself only just returned from Paris. They were told that in the late morning the 21st had been committed in support of the 716th Infantry Division on the coast and that the Divisional commander, Lieutenant General Edgar Feuchtinger, had gone to visit his opposite number in the 716th at Caen. The Headquarters was out of touch with its units, which were operating piecemeal on both sides of the Orne river. And there was worse to come— Feuchtinger had, unbelievably, failed to take a radio with him so there was no way Dietrich could contact him. He was furious. He had been given command of the Division nearly five hours previously but there was still no way in which he could influence or coordinate the use of its eighty-plus Mk IVs and numerous assault guns with the tanks of the 12th SS Panzer Division. This called for a new plan and it was therefore necessary to talk again with Fritz Witt.

In an interview given in August 1945, Lieutenant General Feuchtinger gave his version of what happened on this fateful day:

I first knew that the invasion had begun with a report that parachutists had been dropped near Troarn a little after midnight on 6 June. Since I had been told that I was to make no move until I heard from Rommel's Headquarters, I could do nothing immediately but warn my men to be ready. I waited impatiently all that night for instructions. But not a single order from higher formation was received by me. Realizing that my armoured division was the closest to the scene of operations, I finally decided, at 6.30 in the morning, that I had to take some action. I ordered my tanks to attack the English 6th Airborne Division which had entrenched itself in a bridgehead over the Orne. To me this constituted the most immediate threat to the German position.

Hardly had I made this decision, when at 7 o'clock I received my first intimation that a higher command did still exist. I was told by Army Group 'B' that I was now under the command of Seventh Army. But I received no further orders as to my role. At 9 o'clock I was informed that I would receive any future orders from LXXXIV Infantry Corps [General Erich Marcks], and finally at 10 o'clock I was given my first operational instructions. I was ordered to stop the move of my tanks against the Allied airborne troops, and to turn west and aid the forces protecting Caen [Richter's 716th Infantry Division]. Once over the Orne, I drove north toward the coast. By this time the enemy, consisting of 3 British and 3 Canadian Infantry Divisions, had made astonishing progress and had already occupied a strip of high ground about 10 km from the sea. From here the excellent anti-tank gun fire of the Allies knocked out eleven of my tanks before I had barely started. However, one battlegroup did manage to by-pass these guns and actually reached the coast at Lion-sur-Mer at about 7 in the evening.

I now expected that some reinforcements would be forthcoming to help me hold my position, but nothing came. . . . I retired to take up a line just north of Caen. By the end of that first day my Division had lost almost 25% of its tanks.[8]

It would appear therefore, that even as late as 1900 hours Feuchtinger had no idea that he had been placed under Dietrich's command.

At midnight Headquarters I SS Panzer Corps finally established formal links with the 12th SS and 21st Panzer Divisions and the battered remnants of the 716th Infantry Division. At about this time Dietrich learned that it was General Dollmann's intention that the newly constituted I SS Panzer Corps should mount a counter-attack into the Allied bridgehead in the sector of the 716th Division using three Panzer Divisions. But there were many problems to be overcome before this could happen. 21st Panzer Division had already been committed to battle by LXXXIV Corps and it would be no easy task to coordinate its use with the 12th SS Panzer Division which had yet to arrive. Dietrich also knew that the Panzer Lehr Division, located over 100km away between Chartres and Le Mans, could not possibly arrive at Thury-Harcourt before first light on the 7th. Its 196 tanks, including eight Tigers, and forty assault guns, were vital for the success of any counter-attack. It was obvious to Dietrich and his Chief of Staff that it would be impossible to launch a coordinated counter-attack before midday on the 7th at the earliest or perhaps as late as the morning of the 8th. General Dollmann was informed by teleprinter message.[9]

12th SS Panzer Division's first major adversary was to be Major General R.F.L. Keller's 3rd Canadian Infantry Division, with the 2nd Canadian Armoured Brigade under command. This force had been set very optimistic objectives for D-Day— 10km of the Bayeux-Caen road, the railway line from Puto-en-Bessin to Carpiquet airport and the airport itself which lies 16km inland from Juno beach where the Division was to land. Needless to say, like its American and British counterparts, the Division failed to reach its D-Day objectives. It was not so much German opposition which stopped the Canadians, for once they were away from the beaches there was little—it was more the congestion on the beaches caused by bad weather. The tanks of Lieutenant McCormick's troop of C Squadron, 6th Armoured Regiment (1st Hussars) did manage to reach the north edge of Secqueville-en-Bessin, but they were miles ahead of their supporting infantry and decided to turn back. Nevertheless the Division had done well, better in fact than any other Allied division; despite some 1,000 casualties, including 335 killed,[10] it had reached a line up to 10km inland and was within sight of Caen. The German 716th Division of General Richter, which comprised many Russian and Polish conscripts and through which the Canadians had fought, had virtually ceased to exist.

And so, by 2115 hours the Canadians were firm.[11] Their 7th Infantry Brigade, with the 1st Hussars in support, was in Banville and Reviers, with forward elements as far south as Cainet, le Fresne-Camilly and Fontaine-Henry; the 8th Infantry Brigade was in Colomby-sur-Thaon and Anguerny with the 10th Armoured Regiment (Fort Garry Horse) in support; and the North Nova Scotia Highlanders from the reserve 9th Infantry Brigade, together with the 27th Armoured Regiment (Sherbrooke Fusiliers), had pushed ahead to reach Villons-les-Buissons where they established a strong defensive position. It was this latter group which would be the first to encounter the youngsters of the Hitlerjugend. After dark the 1st Hussars and the Fort Garry Horse reverted to the command of the 2nd Armoured Brigade and harboured in the areas of Pierrepont and Bény-sur-Mer. Two squadrons of the 1st Hussars had only thirteen tanks left between them and had to be amalgamated.[12]

Another early enemy of 12th SS was the British 9th Infantry Brigade, part of Major General Rennie's 3rd British Infantry Division. Its D-Day objective was the area between St Contest and Bitot, but congestion on the beaches and a mortar bomb wounding the Brigade commander during his first 'O' Group ashore made the early landing and quick deployment of this reserve Brigade impossible. During the late afternoon it was used to help in the Lion-sur-Mer area and with the airborne forces on the Allied eastern flank. This resulted in a large gap developing between the British and Canadian 3rd Divisions.

Kurt Meyer reported as instructed to the tactical Headquarters of General Richter's 716th Infantry Division at midnight. He described it as dug deep into the earth in a sandpit on the north side of Caen, [at la Folie, 3km north of Caen] with wounded men from the 716th Infantry and 21st Panzer Divisions lying in the corridors, groaning in pain as doctors and orderlies tended them and loaded them into ambulances. General Richter said later that on arrival the SS officer had told him:

> I have been on my way to you for about eight hours; I lay a good four hours in roadside ditches because of air attacks. The Division's marching columns are suffering serious losses in men and material.[13]

Lieutenant General Feuchtinger of 21st Panzer and a liaison group from the Panzer Lehr Division were also waiting for Meyer and a discussion took place on the possibilities of a coordinated attack by the three Panzer Divisions on 7th June.

The officers from Panzer Lehr made it clear that there was no chance of their Division arriving in time and Feuchtinger was pessimistic about the chances of success with anything less than three divisions. The fact that he could not communicate with his own Headquarters at St Pierre-sur-Dives could not have helped matters. He gave the following account of this meeting with Meyer to Milton Shulman, then a major in the Canadian Army, in August 1945:

> About midnight, Kurt Meyer arrived at my Headquarters. He was to take over on my left and we were to carry out a combined operation the next morning. I explained the situation to Meyer and warned him about the strength of the enemy. Meyer studied the map, turned to me with a confident air and said, 'Little fish! We'll throw them back into the sea in the morning.' We decided to drive towards Douvres and 12 SS was to take up assembly positions during the night.[14]

Between them Meyer and Feuchtinger had about 160 tanks and five battalions of Panzer-Grenadiers available for the counter-attack and, with a large gap between the British and Canadian 3rd Divisions in the Douvres area, there was every chance of success if only these forces could be refuelled and coordinated in time.

Meyer's own Tactical Headquarters was located in a café about 4km to the west of Caen at St Germain-la-Blanche-Herbe. Liaison officers had instructed his unit commanders to report to him there as soon as possible, but as Meyer was about to leave Richter's Headquarters he received a telephone call from his own Divisional Commander, calling from Feuchtinger's Headquarters at St Pierre-sur-Dives. Witt asked for a situation report and then, having already discussed matters with Dietrich, said:

> The situation necessitates speedy action. First of all, the enemy has to be denied Caen and the Carpiquet airfield. It can be assumed that the enemy has already brought his units to order and that they have been readied for defence in so far as they have not deployed for further attacks. Therefore it would be wrong to throw our Divisional units into battle as soon as they arrive. We can only consider a coordinated attack with the 21st Panzer Division. So the Division is to attack the enemy along with the 21st Panzer Division and throw them into the sea. H-Hour for the attack is 7th June at midday.[15]

He could not tell Meyer when Mohnke's Regimental Group with Jürgensen's Panthers might arrive. Meyer briefed Feuchtinger and both officers left to join their respective Headquarters.

The first indication that 1st SS Panzer Division Leibstandarte in Turnhout received of the Allied landings was in the afternoon of 6th June when the Chief of Staff, SS Lieutenant Colonel Grensing, was told by OKW to put the Division at two and a half hours notice to move.[16] The codeword for any move was 'Blücher'. It will be recalled that the major problem facing the Division was that it was not really operational. Orders were issued to improvise and make use of only those vehicles which would increase combat potential. OKW was well aware of the operational state of the Division and this knowledge, coupled with an intelligence assessment which indicated that the Normandy landings were probably a diversion and that the main assault was still to come in the Pas de Calais, led the High Command, (and no doubt Hitler himself was consulted), to keep the LAH where it was—at least for the time being.

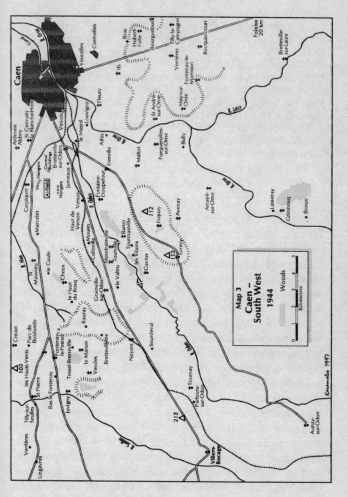

Map 3
Caen –
South West
1944

Kilometres

Woods

Lovendre 1997

Caen

Canal to Sea

R. Orne

Cormelles
Vaucelles
Bras
Hubert-Folie
Bourguébus
Tilly-la-Campagne
Rocquancourt
Bretteville-sur-Laize
Falaise 20 km

Iris
Verrières
Fontenay-le-Marmion
Maysur-Orne
St André-sur-Orne
R. Laize
Fleury
Louvigny
Athis
le Mesnil
St Germain
la Blanche-Herbe
Ardenne Abbey
Venois

Bully
Fleuguerolles-sur-Orne
Maltot
Eterville
Central Railway
Bretteville-sur-Odon
Fontaine-Étoupefour
Jumeaux
R. Odon
Airfield
Hangars
Hangars
Haut de Venois
Vespo

Carpiquet
Marcelet
le Gaule
Cheux
le Haut du Bosq
Rauray
Mouen
Colleville
Grainville-sur-Odon
Mondrainville
Tourville
le Valtru
les Vilains
Gavrus
Baron
Tourmauville
Esquay
Avenay
Amayé-sur-Orne
112
113
Évrecy

Lasseray
Grimbosq
Brieux

Cristot
Parc de Boislonde
St Mauvieu
R. Mue

les Hauts-Vents
Tessel-Bretteville
le Manoir
Bretteville
Vendes
Fontenay-le-Pesnel
Jovigny
102

Verrières
Tilly-sur-Seulles
St Pierre
Bas le Fontenay
Lingèvres

Sourdeval
Noyers
Tournay
Parfouru-sur-Odon
R. Odon

213
Aunay-sur-Odon

Villers-Bocage

R. Seulles

NOTES

1. Meyer, Hubert, *The History of the 12th SS Panzer Division Hitler-jugend*, p. 28. **2.** Kraemer, *I SS Panzer Corps in the West*, MC C—024, IWM, London, AL 2727/1–2. **3.** Meyer, Hubert, op. cit., p. 33. **4.** Meyer, Kurt, *Grenadiers*, p. 118. **5.** Ibid., p. 117. **6.** 7th Army War Diary, 6 Jun 44. **7.** Kraemer, op. cit. **8.** Shulman, *Defeat in the West*, p. 119. **9.** Kraemer, op. cit. **10.** Stacey, *Official History of the Canadian Army in the Second World War, The Victory Campaign, Vol III*, p. 650. **11.** 3rd Cdn Inf Div War Diary, 6 Jun 44. **12.** 6th Armd Regt War Diary, 6 Jun 44. **13.** *Interview with Lt-Gen Wilhelm Richter*, OCMH. MS # B-621. **14.** Shulman, op. cit., p. 121. **15.** Meyer, Kurt, op. cit., p. 120. **16.** Lehmann & Tiemann, *The Leibstandarte IV/I*, p. 113.

7 | *7th June—First Clash*

Early on the morning of 7th June SS Major General Fritz Witt, commander 12th SS Panzer Division, confirmed the telephone orders he had given to Kurt Meyer during the night. The formal operation order, issued from the new Divisional Headquarters location in the Venoix quarter of Caen, stated that the HJ would 'attack the disembarked enemy together with 21st Panzer Division and throw him back into the sea'. The objective was the Channel coast and the boundary between the two Divisions was to be the railway line from Caen to Luc-sur-Mer. H-Hour was delayed, for reasons which will become obvious, from 1200 to 1600 hours and great emphasis was laid on the fact that Carpiquet airport was to be denied to the enemy at all costs. Witt's problem was that many of the essential elements for this counter-attack had not yet arrived—in particular the tanks. It was 1000 hours before about fifty Mk IV tanks of SS Major Karl-Heinz Prinz's 2nd SS Panzer Battalion arrived; the other forty or so were not expected until later in the day or even after dark. The forty-eight combat ready Panthers of SS Major Arnold Jürgensen's 1st SS Panzer Battalion were stranded east of the Orne without fuel and Wilhelm Mohnke's 26th SS Panzer-Grenadier Regiment and the SS Pioneer and other artillery battalions had still to cross the Odon. Until these additional forces could take up their positions on Meyer's left flank there could be no Divisional attack. It was necessary therefore for Meyer's 25th SS Panzer-Grenadier Regiment to adopt temporary defensive positions.

Recall that Meyer had ordered a reconnaissance to the north-west of Caen late on 6th June; at 0100 hours on 7th June it reported that Carpiquet, Rots and Buron were clear of the enemy, the latter being held by minor units of Richter's 716th Infantry Division, but that Villons-les-Buissons was occupied by enemy forces (the Canadian Sherbrooke Fusilier tanks and the North Nova Scotia Highlanders)[2]. Meyer deployed his forces accordingly and made sure they occupied the ground vital to the defence of the area—'vital ground' as it is known to the military. His 1st SS Panzer-Grenadier Battalion and 16th SS Panzer Pioneer Company took up positions around Epron and la Folie, due north of Caen and on the Divisional right flank next to 21st Panzer Division. There was, however, a 3km gap between the two Divisions. Meyer's 2nd SS Panzer-Grenadier Battalion was based on St Contest and Bitot. This area had been the D-Day objective of the British 9th Infantry Brigade which, it will be remembered after a delayed landing and other problems, had been diverted to unforeseen tasks and there was therefore a large gap between the British and Canadian 3rd Divisions. The Canadian left flank was dangerously exposed and, as we shall see, this was to have disastrous results. Meyer planned for SS Lieutenant Colonel Karl-Heinz Milius's 3rd SS Panzer-Grenadier Battalion, which had yet to arrive, to occupy positions south-east of Franqueville, astride the Caen-Bayeux road. After camouflaging their trucks and leaving them south of Caen, each battalion marched to its defensive positions with a platoon of heavy infantry guns and Flak guns attached.

Meyer set up his own forward Command Post[3] in the ruined Ardenne Abbey, 3km outside Caen between St Germain-la-Blanche-Herbe and Authie; with thick stone walls, two church towers and further walls surrounding a large orchard, it made an ideal Headquarters location from which to control the forthcoming battle. SS Lieutenant Colonel Max Wünsche, commander of the HJ's 12th SS Panzer Regiment, and SS Major Karl Bartling, commanding the 3rd SS Panzer (Heavy) Artillery Battalion, also located their Command Posts in the Abbey, thus ensuring full coordination between tanks, Panzer-Grenadiers and supporting artillery. When Prinz's Mk IVs arrived, some time after 1000 hours, five of the 8th Company tanks were located with the 1st SS Panzer-Grenadier Battalion, the 6th and 7th Companies on either side of the Abbey, the 5th Company on the reverse slope south of Franqueville and the 9th Company kept in reserve behind the 5th.[4] According to Hans Siegel, the commander of the 8th Company, the total Panzer strength was no more than thirty.

The towers of the Abbey church were soon occupied by artillery observers who could direct the Divisional and Corps guns located around Caen, whilst the Division's Werfer Battalion took up a position on the north side of the city. Three tank companies of Colonel Oppeln Bronikowski's 22nd Panzer Regiment and two Panzer-Grenadier battalions, all part of 21st Panzer Division, were already in their starting positions near Blainville and Bieville, west of the Orne, and it was planned that they would advance as soon as Meyer's tanks and Panzer-Grenadiers came into line. It was now just a matter of waiting for the rest of 12th SS to catch up and of getting ready for H-Hour at 1600 hours.

What was the position on the Canadian and British side? Brigadier Harry Foster, commanding the 7th Canadian Infantry Brigade, gave orders at 0130 hours. The advance was to be continued at 0600 hours with the same objectives as D-Day. At 0855 hours, having found little or no opposition, the Winnipegs and Reginas were told to go flat out for their final objectives and by midday Putot, Bretteville-l'Orgueilleuse and Norrey were secured. The 7th Brigade then dug-in. Although there was no opposition to its south, there was no attempt to take advantage of this superb opportunity to outflank the German forces, particularly those major elements of the 12th SS and 21st Panzer Divisions to the north of Carpiquet airport and the city of Caen. The problem was that the 2nd Canadian Armoured Brigade, under Divisional command, was seen as a counter-penetration force and not, as it would have been in the German Army, as an exploitation force. Whilst the infantry reached their objectives and dug-in, most of the 1st Hussar and Fort Garry tanks sat idly in their concentration area at

Pierrepont. The only action taken by Brigadier Foster, late on the afternoon of 7th June, was to send a squadron of the 1st Hussars and an infantry company of Canadian Scottish to fill in a gap at Cairon between his Brigade and the 9th Infantry Brigade—6km *behind* his forward positions.

The 8th Canadian Infantry Brigade also had a relatively easy day on 7th June. Two battalions spent their time mopping up pockets of resistance in Colomby-sur-Thaon and Anguerny, whilst the third tried to clear two radar stations west of Douvres; these were located in concrete bunkers and the Canadians made little headway. At the end of the day the task was handed over to the British 51st (Highland) Division.

7th June was a very different day for some of the men of the 9th Canadian and 9th British Infantry Brigades. At 0745 hours the Canadian infantry and tanks began their advance from Villons-les-Buissons with Stuart reconnaissance tanks in the lead. Their objective was Carpiquet airport. The Stuarts were followed by C Company of Lieutenant Colonel Petch's North Nova Scotia Highlanders in carriers and, behind this vanguard, the other three companies followed, mounted on the Shermans of Lieutenant Colonel Mel Gordon's Sherbrooke Fusiliers. The scene was set for a Canadian disaster.

Buron was reached at 1150 hours and whilst the Shermans halted a kilometre to its south-west and opened fire on Authie, C Company advanced again and entered Authie at 1300 hours. By this time the Stuart light tanks had reached Franqueville, A and B Companies of the Highlanders had dismounted halfway between Buron and Authie and the Shermans were continuing their advance towards Authie. It was at this moment, with the Canadian Battlegroup fully extended, beyond the range of its supporting artillery and with its flank exposed, that the tanks and SS Panzer-Grenadiers of the Hitlerjugend went into action. From his position high in a tower of the Ardenne Abbey, Kurt Meyer had a magnificent overview of the whole open and gently undulating area. He gives a graphic account of the ensuing moments in his book *Grenadiers:*

An enemy tank is pushing through the orchards of St Contest! Now it stops. The commander opens the hatch and examines the terrain. Is he blind? Has he not yet realised that he is only 200m from the 2nd Battalion's Grenadiers and that the barrels of our anti-tank guns are aimed at him? Obviously not. He calmly lights a cigarette and blinks at its smoke. Not a single shot is fired. The Battalion maintains excellent fire discipline. Now it is clear. The tank has moved out to protect the flank. Enemy tanks are rolling towards Authie from Buron. My God! What an opportunity! The tanks are driving right across 2nd Battalion's front! [And the 6th and 7th SS Panzer Company fronts]. . . . I give orders to all battalions, the artillery and the available tanks. 'Do not shoot! Open fire on my order only!'. . . . The enemy commander seems to see only the airfield, it is directly in front of him. . . . [he] does not seem to realise that his destruction awaits him beyond the reverse slope. As his tanks cross the Caen-Bayeux road he will run into the 2nd Battalion's waiting tank company. Only a few metres separate the iron monsters from each other. . . . Wünsche, commander of the Panzer Regiment, quietly transmits the enemy tank movements. . . . I am thinking of Guderian's principle and the Divisional attack order [H-Hour 1600 hours] but, in this situation, I must use my own initiative. The 26th Regiment is still east of the Orne and the 1st SS Panzer Battalion cannot move because of the lack of fuel and is 30km east of the Orne. . . . Decision: when the leading enemy tanks pass Franqueville, the 25th Regiment will attack with the tank company waiting on the reverse slope. Once the [3rd] Battalion has reached Authie the other [2nd] Battalion will then join the battle. Objective: the coast.

The commander of the 21st Panzer Division is briefed on the situation and asked for support [but see later in this Chapter]. . . . The enemy spearhead pushes past Franqueville and starts across the road. I give the signal for the attack to Wünsche and can just hear his order, 'Achtung Panzer—marsche!'. . . . The enemy tank at the head of the spearhead smokes and I watch the crew bailing out. More tanks are torn to pieces with loud explosions. Suddenly, one Panzer IV starts to burn, [in this initial clash three Mk IVs were knocked out[5] a blast of flame shoots out of the hatches. Canadian infantry tries to reach Authie and continue the battle from there, but in vain. The 3rd Battalion's Grenadiers are very determined, they do not want the Panzers to be first—they want to enter Authie. They have hardly reached it, when the 1st and 2nd Battalions' attack begins [1500 hours[6]. The enemy has now been struck deep in the flank. We take Franqueville and Authie by this swift attack. St Contest and Buron must fall now.

C Company, North Nova Scotia Highlanders in Authie was soon overrun by the Mk IVs of the 6th SS Panzer Company and Milius' 3rd SS Panzer-Grenadiers, which then went on to attack A Company of the Highlanders which had been withdrawn by Lieutenant Colonel Petch to slightly higher ground to the south-east of Gruchy. After some fierce fighting it too was overrun. There then followed a clash between the Shermans of the Sherbrooke Fusiliers and Mk IVs of the 2nd SS Panzer Battalion to the south of Buron with losses to both sides. Although Lieutenant Colonel Gordon asked for help from his superior and the Fort Garry tanks were alerted at 1430 hours, the commander of 2nd Armoured Brigade, Brigadier Wyman, decided after a personal reconnaissance, that the 'situation was in hand' and no help was provided.[7]

By late afternoon Buron had fallen to the HJ and soon afterwards Brigadier Cunningham authorised the survivors of his leading Battlegroup to fall back on les Buissons, where the other units of his Brigade had formed what the Canadians termed a 'fortress'.[8] Neither of the other two Battalions of the 9th Infantry Brigade were committed in support of their comrades. In both cases it would seem that, unlike Panzermeyer who was constantly well forward with his leading elements and able to keep up with the situation, the Canadian commanders were too far back and unaware of what was really happening. In fairness it has to be added that Major General Keller, the Canadian Divisional commander, should have intervened to control the battle and coordinate the actions of the 7th and 9th Infantry Brigades, but it seems he too was unaware of both the possibilities and problems. It is hardly surprising therefore that his own Division's War Diary for the day gives a totally misleading picture of events:

> The 9th Infantry Brigade encountered tanks and infantry in the area of Authie. The attack was repulsed but it was decided to withdraw to more favourable ground around Villons-les-Buissons.

It has to be said that, although the Canadians fought hard and bravely, proper cooperation between infantry and armour 'left something to be desired' and the passage of information from front to rear was poor.[9]

As we have heard in Meyer's account, when the tanks of the 5th and 6th SS Panzer Companies and Grenadiers of Milius' 3rd Battalion came level with the other two SS Panzer-Grenadier Battalions and 7th and 8th SS Panzer Companies, at about 1500 hours, they too joined in the counter-attack. Just to the north of St Contest three Shermans were encountered and the commanding officer of the 2nd SS Panzer-Grenadier Battalion, Scappini, was killed, his head taken off by a tank shell. Kurt Meyer, who had come forward on a motor-cycle to assess the situation, appointed SS Captain Schrott to command the Battalion. Mk IVs of the 7th SS Panzer Company drove off the Shermans and Mâlon and Galmanche were soon captured. Meanwhile at 1615 hours the 1st SS Panzer-Grenadier Battalion of SS Major Waldmüller, together with Werner's 16th SS Pioneer Company and the five Mk IVs of the 8th SS Panzer Company, began their advance with Anguerny as their objective. They soon clashed with British troops in and around Cambes. The men of the 2nd Battalion, Royal Ulster Rifles (RUR), after assembling in the woods north-east of le Mesnil at 1400 hours, had begun their own attack southwards towards Caen, supported by Shermans of the 1st East Riding Yeomanry. The Shermans and Mk IVs engaged each other on the completely flat ground to the west of Cambes and all five German tanks were either knocked out or immobilised. SS Panzer-Grenadiers claimed to have knocked out three Shermans using Panzerfausts. Despite their tank losses the Germans proved too strong for the Ulster riflemen who, after receiving thirty-six casualties[10] retreated back to le Mesnil, where the 1st Battalion, King's Own Scottish Borderers (KOSB) was in position.[11] But by now the Allied artillery had come into range and this, coupled with heavy and highly accurate naval gunfire, began to take its toll of the Germans—the SS Panzer-Grenadiers in particular. Both sides were by now becoming exhausted. And, perhaps even more importantly for the Germans, Kurt Meyer had seen some very worrying Allied movements on the western flank and a singular lack of corresponding German movements on the eastern flank. To quote from his book *Grenadiers* again:

Whilst with the 1st Battalion, I notice, with some trepidation, that the 21st Panzer Division is not supporting the attack and that its tanks are stationary near Couvre Chef [Bieville and Blainville]. The Regiment's right flank is thus exposed and the enemy tanks are probing the 1st Battalions's flank. . . . Only the Reconnaissance Company of the 26th Regiment has arrived in the battle area. The battalions are delayed by air attacks. We can thus hardly count on any more of the Regiment being deployed. The 12th SS Reconnaissance Battalion still has no contact with the enemy on the Division's left flank; it reconnoitres in the direction of Bayeux [it had in fact had minor skirmishes with forward elements of the 69th Infantry Brigade, part of the British 50th Infantry Division, in the area north and north-west of Audrieu]. . . . we notice much enemy movement west of the Muc [usually spelt Mue]. Tank forces are pushing ahead towards Bretteville. . . . Filled with tension, I observe the dust clouds west of the Muc. Tank after tank is rolling over the high ground towards Bretteville. [This was the 7th Canadian Infantry Brigade.] There are no German troops in that sector that can stop the enemy's advance. Enemy tank forces are thus rolling right into the 26th SS Panzer-Grenadier Regiment's area of deployment if they continue their advance along the Caen-Bayeux road. As fate would have it, there are only a few scattered infantrymen of the 716th Infantry Division in Bretteville itself. The way is open deep into our flank. . . . the 25th Regiment's attack has to be stopped immediately.

Meyer's criticism that 21st Panzer Division failed to support his counterattack continued even after the war. But in an interview with Milton Shulman in August 1945, Feuchtinger, the Divisional commander, said:

Artillery fire was so great that a proper coordination of this attack was impossible. Meyer did make a short spurt with some fifty tanks, but was driven back. He never reached the start-line from which our combined attack was to begin. Allied anti-tank guns prevented him from getting into proper position.[12]

Not unreasonably Meyer strongly refuted these statements but it is perhaps understandable that Feuchtinger was reluctant to attack earlier than the designated H-Hour of 1600 hours. Meyer was undoubtedly a dynamic commander but his habit of riding around the battlefield on a motor-cycle resulted in his being out of touch with his Divisional commander for considerable periods, and moreover sending a despatch rider to tell the commander of the 22nd Panzer Regiment that he was attacking three hours early would, to say the very least, have caused some concern in that officer's mind. In any case there was no intention of 21st Panzer beginning its attack until Meyer's men had come into line and that did not happen until 1615 hours. It would seem that, just as there was a failure of coordination on the Canadian side, so Meyer, Witt and Feuchtinger failed to get their act together at this important time.

As darkness fell on 7th June Meyer's men were holding a defensive line in an arc from Cambes to Franqueville. His 1st SS Panzer-Grenadier Battalion was in Cambes, 2nd Battalion in Galmanche, 3rd in Buron, and Prinz's Mk IVs, with the SS Pioneer, Flak and Reconnaissance Companies, were holding Meyer's vulnerable western flank, from Gruchy to Authie and Franqueville. Two 88mm batteries of the Division's 12th SS Flak Battalion moved in to support this flank during the early hours of 8th June.

It had been a costly day for both sides. The North Nova Scotia Highlanders received 242 casualties with eighty-four killed and another 128 taken prisoner; the Sherbrooke Fusiliers lost twenty-one tanks with seven more damaged and suffered sixty casualties with twenty-six killed.[13] 12th SS lost nine Mk IVs with others damaged (the Canadians claimed thirty-one including eleven Tigers and eighteen anti-tank guns)[14], and suffered over 300 casualties including at least seventy-three dead.[15] But this had been no fast-moving tank battle. The infantry of both sides had fought on their feet and the whole action, which lasted less than six hours, had taken place over an area of only twenty-four square kilometres. It had, however, seen Panzermeyer's men blooded. Their fire discipline, camouflage and shooting had all been of the highest order (only forty rounds of anti-tank ammunition had been fired)[16] and they had halted the Canadian and British advances towards Carpiquet and Caen; it would take another month for the Allies to recapture the ground won by the HJ on this fateful day—a day which ended with the Canadians still having 115 combat ready tanks,[17] the vast majority of which had not fired a shot.

7th June had been a very frustrating day for Sepp Dietrich. Although Kurt Meyer's immediate counter-attack had been successful, it had been limited in nature and there had been no overall Corps counter-stroke. After visiting General Richter's Headquarters in Caen, Dietrich realised that the 716th Infantry Division had ceased to exist as a fighting force; but more serious from Dietrich's point of view was the delayed arrival of the rest of 12th SS in the combat area and the non-arrival of the Panzer Lehr Division. When Fritz Bayerlein, its commander, arrived at the new Corps Headquarters location at Amayé-sur-Orne in the late afternoon, he brought disturbing news. The bridge at Thury-Harcourt had been destroyed by Allied bombers and this, together with the continual air attacks on his columns, meant that his Division could not possibly arrive before the early hours of 8th June.

This in turn meant that a serious gap was developing between I SS Panzer Corps and Marcks's LXXXIV Corps to its west. Dietrich reasoned that if he did not mount a counter-stroke on 8th June, using both HJ and Panzer Lehr, the situation would become critical. He issued the necessary orders to Bayerlein and also gave orders for the Tigers of the Corps

101st SS Heavy Panzer Battalion to move out of Beauvais[18] with an intended assembly area around Bretteville-sur-Odon. Veterans of the 101st say the move began in fact at about 0300 hours on the 7th but in either case the Tigers could not possibly arrive for several days.

Panzer Lehr's move had been fraught with problems. At 0230 hours on 6th June Bayerlein's Panther Battalion was being loaded on to railway flats in preparation for a move to Poland! He cancelled this strategic move on his own responsibility. In the *Saturday Evening Post* of 20th October 1945, Bayerlein gave his account of events on 6th and 7th June:

> At two o'clock in the morning of 6 June, I was alerted. The invasion fleet was coming across the Channel. I was told to begin moving north that afternoon at five o'clock. This was too early. Air attacks had been severe in daylight and everyone knew that everything that could fly would support the invasion. My request for a delay until twilight was refused.
>
> We moved as ordered and immediately came under an air attack. I lost twenty or thirty vehicles by nightfall. . . . At daylight, General Dollmann, commander of Seventh Army, gave me a direct order to proceed and there was nothing else to do. . . . By the end of the day I had lost forty trucks carrying fuel and ninety others. Five of my tanks were knocked out and eighty-four halftracks, prime-movers and self-propelled guns. These were serious losses for a Division not yet in action.

Bayerlein's orderly officer, Captain Hartdegen, takes up the story in Paul Carell's book *Invasion—They're Coming!*:

> General Bayerlein, his driver, Corporal Kartheus, and I were waiting for the vanguard of 901st Panzer-Grenadier Regiment at Condé-sur-Noireau, 50km south of Caen. . . . The little town. . . . had been reduced to a smouldering heap of ruins. The road bridge, too, had been destroyed by bombs. . . . The Panzer Lehr had been placed under I SS Panzer Corps. All night long we had been looking for the battle Headquarters of Sepp Dietrich, the Corps commander, to find out what his plans were and to get our

orders. But we could not find it. Not till the late afternoon of 7 June did we discover it in a small wood north of Thury-Harcourt. Dietrich ordered Bayerlein to get one combat group each into the areas of Norrey and Brouay, on the Caen-Bayeux railway line, by the morning of June 8. From there we were to launch an attack on a broad front together with the 12th SS Panzer Division HJ.

At last, towards the evening, we found vanguards of our Division near Thury-Harcourt. The Grenadiers had arrived first. The tanks were still a long way behind.

General Bayerlein discussed the situation with the regimental commanders and towards 2200 hours we drove to our battle Headquarters at Proussy. . . . The sector from Caumont to Villers-Bocage was a road of death.

Also on this critical day, although unknown to Dietrich, Rommel had ordered the transfer of I SS Panzer Corps from Dollmann's Seventh Army to General Geyr von Schweppenburg's Panzer Group West. The order was to take effect the following day, and would place Dietrich under the watchful eye of a very senior Panzer commander.

NOTES

1. Meyer, Kurt, *Grenadiers,* p. 119. 2. 27th Armd Regt War Diary, 7 Jun 44. 3. Meyer, Kurt, op. cit., p. 121. 4. Meyer, Hubert, *The History of the 12th SS Panzer Division Hitlerjugend,* p. 41. 5. Ibid., p. 42. 6. Ibid., p. 43. 7. 2nd Cdn Armd Bde War Diary, 7 Jun 44. 8. N Nova Scotia Hldrs War Diary, 7 Jun 44. 9. Stacey, *Official History of the Canadian Army in the Second World War, Vol III, The Victory Campaign,* p. 133. 10. 2 RUR War Diary, 7 Jun 44. 11. 3rd Inf Div War Diary, 7 Jun 44. 12. Shulman, *Defeat in the West,* p. 121. 13. Stacey, op. cit., p. 132. 14. 2nd Cdn Armd Bde War Diary, 7 Jun 44. 15. Meyer, Hubert, op. cit., p. 45. 16. Ibid. 17. 2nd Cdn Armd Bde War Diary, 7 Jun 44. 18. Kraemer, *I SS Panzer Corps in the West,* MS C—024 IWM London, AL 2727/1–2.

8 | *8th to 10th June—The Bridgehead Battles*

8TH JUNE

Sepp Dietrich, having recognised the urgent need to launch a major counter-attack against the British and Canadian bridgehead, decided to do so whether or not the Panzer Lehr Division arrived in time to join in. Accordingly he ordered an

attack along the general axis of the Caen to Douvres road with
12th SS on the left and 21st Panzer Division on the right.
H-Hour was fixed for 1000 hours on 8th June.[1] However, the
telephone journal of the German Seventh Army shows that
this order, to attack north and north-east from the area of
Caen, was countermanded at 0810 hours:

> Field Marshal Rommel interrupts and orders I SS Panzer
> Corps to initiate a point of main effort on the left as quickly
> as possible, using all three divisions [12th SS, Panzer Lehr
> and 21st Panzer]. Direction of attack—north and north-
> west of Caen, in the direction of the coast.[2]

The emphasis and main artillery support was therefore
switched to the HJ sector and General Bayerlein's Panzer Lehr
Division was ordered to move in on the left flank of this attack
as it arrived in the operational area.[3] Despite these rather
grandiose orders, Dietrich was well aware that Feuchtinger's
21st Panzer Division was already locked in a defensive battle
with the British 3rd Infantry Division and, being deployed
astride the Orne, was in no position to launch any sort of
major counter-attack. He knew also that only the leading elements of Panzer Lehr had arrived in the area of Fontenay-le-
Pesnel and Tilly-sur-Seulles during the night 7th June and that
this Division too would be in no condition to launch a fully
coordinated attack on the morning of the 8th. It seemed that
Fritz Witt's 12th SS Panzer Division HJ would be very much
on its own. But Witt's Division was also incomplete.
Panzermeyer's 25th SS Panzer-Grenadier Regiment, with
about half of Prinz's Mk IV tanks, had been forced on to the
defensive after its successful, but relatively local, counter-attack
against the Canadian 9th Infantry Brigade the previous day,
and only the 1st Battalion of Mohnke's 26th Regiment had
arrived in the Cheux area in the late afternoon of the 7th. The
rest of the Regiment would not arrive in its assembly area,
centred around Fontenay, until after dark and the remainder
of the Division's tanks were still awaiting fuel on the wrong
side of the Orne.

Major General Keller, commanding the 3rd Canadian Infantry Division, held a conference at 1100 hours on the morning

of 8th June. His orders for the day were simple but optimistic, for by the time he gave them one of his brigades was already under attack. He told the 7th and 8th Brigades to hold their present positions but the 9th was to attack again to capture Buron; it was to be given the support of the entire Divisional artillery.

Brigadier Foster's 7th Canadian Infantry Brigade was firmly holding the positions it had reached the day before. The Winnipegs were in Putot-en-Bessin, Reginas in Bretteville-l'Orgueilleuse and 1st Canadian Scottish in reserve in Secqueville-en-Bessin. There were no tanks in direct support.

In order for 12th SS to launch a Divisional counter-attack in accordance with Dietrich's orders, it was necessary for SS Lieutenant Colonel Wilhelm Mohnke's 26th SS Panzer-Grenadier Regiment to come into line with Meyer's reinforced 25th Regiment and thus protect his exposed western flank. Therefore, despite the lack of tank support, Mohnke ordered his battalions to attack before dawn on the 8th. Krause's 1st Battalion was directed on Norrey and Siebken's 2nd Battalion on Putot; Olboeter's 3rd (SPW) Battalion was told to secure the left flank of the Regiment by seizing Brouay and to link up with Bremer's 12th SS Reconnaissance Battalion in the Audrieu area; the latter was screening both the left flank of I SS Panzer Corps and the HJ, the western boundary of which ran from Fontenay-le-Pesnel, past the west edge of Brouay to the coast at Ver-sur-Mer; unknowingly, it was also giving protection to Panzer Lehr as it moved north into line. It is not surprising that Bremer had been directed to the Audrieu position—from Point 103 near Haut d'Audrieu, one can see the spires of Bayeux and the ground beyond the Seulles to the south of there. However, it seems that no one in 12th SS were aware that, as well as the Panzer Lehr Reconnaissance Battalion, a Panzer-Grenadier battalion of that Division had also moved into the area during the night.

Although Krause's 1st SS Panzer-Grenadier Battalion arrived in its assembly area at Cheux in good time to launch its assault on Norrey at 0300 hours, the 2nd Battalion had to attack off the line of march without pausing to adopt a proper attack formation. The 3rd Battalion, after arriving at

Fontenay-le-Pesnel at about midnight, left its SPWs there and marched forward in the early hours of the morning. On arrival in Cristot, the commanding officer called his company commanders together in a small wood just to the north of the village, to receive orders. During this briefing artillery fire hit the group and the two company commanders destined to lead the attack towards Brouay were wounded. After allocating the six 75mm equipped SPWs of the 12th SS (Heavy) Company to support them, Olboeter ordered their successors to seize Brouay and go firm there. The remainder of the Battalion remained in Cristot.

The attack on Norrey by Krause's 1st SS Panzer-Grenadiers did not go well. They advanced across open fields in the dark at 0300 hours, but the company of the Regina Rifles defending the village fought doggedly. The rest of the Regina Rifles were strongly entrenched in Bretteville-l'Orgueilleuse. Supporting artillery fire proved too effective and by 1100 hours Krause was forced to halt the attack with the loss of five killed and twenty wounded.[4]

SS Major Bernhard Siebken's 2nd SS Panzer-Grenadier Battalion did not arrive in time to coordinate its attack on Putot with that of the 1st Battalion on Norrey. Recall that it had to attack off the line of march; its leading platoons, also advancing across open ground, encountered the enemy as soon as they tried to cross the railway line south of the village at about 0630 hours. Lieutenant Colonel Meldram's Royal Winnipeg Rifles had three companies on the line of the railway and D Company and Battalion Headquarters just to the east of Putot. But Siebken's young soldiers fought with tenacity and by 1330 hours A, B and C Companies of the Winnipegs were surrounded and cut off. The unit War Diary complains that no supporting armour reached the Battalion. But reports that the right half of the Battalion had been 'sliced off by enemy armour' can be discounted. The only German 'armour' in the area were the 75mm equipped SPWs of the 3rd Battalion attacking Brouay on the right flank. The remnants of the three Winnipeg companies managed to get out of Putot under the cover of smoke and join their comrades of D Company to the east of the village; they had suffered appalling casualties—256, of which 105 were dead.

Siebken's men then advanced to their second objective, the Route Nationale 13 running from Bayeux to Caen. But there they encountered Stuart reconnaissance tanks of the British 24th Lancers (24L) operating with the 231st Infantry Brigade, and part of the 50th (Northumbrian) Division. This Division, after occupying Bayeux, was pushing forward with the aim of seizing the high ground in the area of Villers-Bocage, 20km to the south of the city. Its intermediate objective was Tilly-sur-Seulles—a name that would remain forever in the memories of many British soldiers. The 24L Reconnaissance Troop was advancing south-east down the main Route Nationale 13 when it ran into the 6th SS Panzer-Grenadier Company of Siebken's Battalion. It had already lost one tank to the HJ's SS Reconnaissance Battalion near St Leger and this clash with the SS Panzer-Grenadiers, coupled with intense artillery fire, forced it to withdraw back to the area of Loucelles where infantrymen of the 1st Dorset Battalion were positioned.

Meanwhile, at approximately 0800 hours, the 10th and 11th SS Panzer-Grenadier Companies and six 75mm equipped SPWs of the 12th Company of Olboeter's 3rd Battalion, had moved towards Brouay. When the 11th Company reached the village, which lies in low ground, they were amazed to find some elements of a battalion of Panzer Lehr already in situ. The 10th Company, moving on the left, reached the wooded area to the south-west of Brouay about noon. They were shocked to find only the remnants of the Panzer Lehr unit—it had been decimated by artillery. As one German NCO described the scene:

> Here we encountered the most terrible images of the war. The enemy had virtually cut to pieces units of the Panzer Lehr Division with heavy weapons. SPWs and equipment had been ripped apart; next to them on the ground, and even hanging in the trees, were body parts of dead comrades. A terrible silence covered all.[5]

At the end of the day the 3rd SS Panzer-Grenadier Battalion, having lost only six killed and eight wounded,[6] went firm on the line of the railway which dissects Brouay as far east as the railway bridge.

The unit of Panzer Lehr in Brouay was the leading element of the Division, the 1st Panzer-Grenadier Battalion of Colonel Gutmann's 902nd Regiment. It had arrived in the Fontenay area during the night and then advanced to Brouay where, with the assistance of the 12th SS Reconnaissance Battalion, it repulsed light tanks of the British 61st Reconnaissance Regiment. After that it suffered terribly, as we have seen, from artillery and naval gunfire. The latter was a new and extremely unpleasant experience for most of the Germans fighting in Normandy. The 12-in and 14-in guns of the three US battleships and 15-in and 16-in guns of the four British battleships and two monitors (shallow draught bombardment vessels mounting two 15-in guns) could reach out 25km and the 4.5-in and 6-in guns of the Allied cruisers and destroyers demonstrated an accuracy and rate of fire which surprised even those who had fought in Russia. A single British cruiser, HMS *Belfast*, fired 1,996 shells in the period D-Day to 14th June.

Inevitably, the events of the day had forced the Canadian 3rd Infantry Division to cancel its planned attack on Buron by the 9th Infantry Brigade and to pull in the 7th Brigade's company/squadron group at Cairon.

Brigadier Foster, commanding the 7th Canadian Infantry Brigade, was determined to recapture Putot. At 1700 hours he told Lieutenant Colonel Cabeldu's 1st Battalion Canadian Scottish and a squadron of 1st Hussar tanks, supported by two artillery regiments, to retake the village. H-Hour was set for 2030 hours. The attack was successful and by 2130 hours the Canadians were mopping up, Siebken's Grenadiers having been forced back to the line of the railway. It had cost the Canadians 125 casualties, of which forty-five were fatal.[7] The SS Battalion had lost nineteen dead, fifty-eight wounded and twenty-one missing.[8]

During the afternoon of 8th June Rommel visited the Headquarters of Panzer Group West in the Château at la Caine and I SS Panzer Corps at Amayé-sur-Orne. He confirmed that Dietrich was now under Schweppenburg's command and was fully briefed on the situation. He then moved on to the Command Post of Fritz Bayerlein's Panzer Lehr Division at Cheux, only 5km behind the battle lines, where he arrived at 1905 hours. Bayerlein had been wounded and his driver killed during an air attack that morning, but despite this, Rommel's old Chief of Staff from the North African Desert was at his Headquarters. To his surprise Rommel told him to forget any idea of attacking due north together with 12th SS, but instead to move his Division during the night westwards to the Tilly area; on the following morning he was to attack on the axis of the Tilly to Bayeux road with the mission of recapturing Bayeux.

All the senior German commanders, including Kurt Meyer who had been visited by Fritz Witt at the Ardenne Abbey during the afternoon,[9] were therefore fully aware of Rommel's intentions and of what needed to be done that night and the next day. And it would have been obvious to all of them that a prerequisite for any further attack by 12th SS was the need to seize the vital ground, currently held by the Canadians, between Meyer's and Mohnke's Regiments. The most westerly of Meyer's troops were at Franqueville and Authie and the most easterly of Mohnke's in St Mauvieu (now called St Manvieu). The requirement was to secure the line of the railway as a jump-off point for any future drive towards the coast, and this involved capturing Bretteville, Norrey and Rots. Witt ordered Mohnke to take Norrey, in conjunction with an attack by Panzermeyer on Rots and Bretteville; for this latter task Meyer was given the forty or so Panthers of Jürgensen's 1st SS Panzer Battalion and the 2nd SS (105mm) Wespe Battery of SS Lieutenant Timmerbeil; Meyer provided his own 15th SS Reconnaissance Company under SS Captain von Büttner as infantry. A night attack commencing at dusk (2200 hours) was ordered because of the air threat, and also to surprise the enemy.

SS Major Gerd Bremer's 12th SS Reconnaissance Battalion, with its Headquarters in Audrieu, had been defending the western edge of 1 SS Panzer Corps' sector all day and during this time most of Bayerlein's Panzer Lehr Division, with the important exceptions of its Panzer Regiment and Panzerjäger Battalion, had assembled there. However, commencing at 2000 hours, extremely heavy fire from both artillery and naval guns lasting for over two hours, together with a successful probe towards St Pierre by tanks of the British 8th Armoured Brigade, operating with the 1st Dorset and 2nd Devon Battalions of the 50th (British) Infantry Division, forced Bremer to withdraw his companies. By about 2130 hours they were on a line running from south of Brouay, to the western edge of Cristot, to the western edge of les Hauts Vents, and to about 500m north-east of St Pierre. Bremer, a Knight's Cross holder, was himself wounded by shrapnel and handed over command to SS Captain von Reitzenstein.

Meyer's attack more or less coincided with that of the Canadian Scottish against Putot, but by H-Hour only two of the hoped for Panther companies had arrived, the 1st commanded by SS Captain Berlin and the 4th commanded by one of Hitler's former Adjutants, Hans Pfeiffer. Since Jürgensen himself had not arrived in time for the attack, Max Wünsche, commander 12th SS Panzer Regiment, accompanied it in his command Panther. Kurt Meyer commanded in his inimitable way from a motor-cycle! His own flamboyant description of the attack in his book *Grenadiers*, which in places sounds like a, 'Ride of the Valkyries', gives a graphic idea of what it was like:

> The tank commanders are briefed in detail; the company and platoon commanders have examined the ground during the afternoon and know every fold. The tank companies stand ready to move in a wedge-shaped formation.
>
> The Reconnaissance Company's Grenadiers are climbing on to their vehicles [the Panthers]; I drive from tank to tank, calling out to the boys. The company commander, von Büttner, my Adjutant for many years, suddenly reminds me of a promise which I gave the 15th Company during battle training at Beverloo in Belgium. At that time, I had called out to the Company, 'Boys, the Reconnaissance Company is always the spearhead of the Regiment, so you bear a lot of responsibility. I promise you that I will be in your ranks to witness your baptism of fire'. . . . Helmut Belke arrives with a motor-cycle combination. He has been permanently at my side. . . . since 1939. . . . In the side-car is Dr Stift [Regimental dentist]. I jump on the pillion. . . . On our

right tank engines are roaring and the Grenadiers are all now mounted. . .

The tanks are rolling ahead at full speed. . . . The engine is our strongest weapon. . . . the first houses of Rots appear. . . . We are sitting on a volcano, but Helmut drives on indefatigably. We are now barely clinging to the bike so as to be able to get off the road as quickly as possible. We wait for the tanks at the entrance to the village. They arrive in a few minutes; the first group of the Reconnaissance Company dismounts and advances as infantry. The village is clear and we push quickly through.

The Panthers. . . . again form wedge formation. Two Panthers are roaring down the road towards Bretteville. The rest push ahead on both sides of the road. In the darkness I can now only see the red-hot exhaust pipes. . . . Crack! Crack! The two Panthers at the head are firing round after round. . . . down the road to clear it for us, clanking into the village at full speed. . . . This is the way we fought in the East, but will these surprise tactics achieve the same for us here?

All the tanks are now firing into the village, enemy machine gun fire responds. . . . We stop on the right of the road and work our way forward along the ditch. I stumble over a dead Canadian. . . . As we move I hear somebody groaning. . . . More Panthers with Grenadiers mounted on them are pushing into the village. . . . I reach the wounded man. . . . My God, it's von Büttner. . . . shot in the stomach. Büttner recognises me and squeezes my hand; as an old front line soldier he knows that this is his last battle. . . . I hear a sound from the other side of the road, a shadow runs across the road. Friend or foe? Belke shoots as he dives and hits a Canadian in the head; Belke falls at the edge of the ditch. My companion of so many years does not stand up; he has also fought his last battle. . . .

Grenadiers are storming past us. . . . Tears are running down my face, the old comrades become fewer and fewer. I jump on the motor-cycle so as to make contact with the Company again. A few minutes later I am in flames, the fuel

tank is shot through and burning like a torch; the Grenadiers drag me off and smother the flames with earth. . . .

There is firing in all directions in the village. We have
reached the centre but the leading tank has been hit. The
Regina Rifles' battle Headquarters has been overrun. The
surprise attack is successful but where is 26th Regiment's
infantry? We cannot hold out here on our own; we are too
weak to capture all of Bretteville. With heavy heart I decide
to withdraw the troops at dawn to the high ground east of
Rots.

It was indeed a bloody fight. With the help of the anti-tank
guns of the 3rd Anti-tank Regiment, Royal Canadian Artillery,
firing the new armour-piercing (discarding sabot) ammunition, the Reginas had withstood the violent attack. The shock
tactics which had been so successful for the Germans in Russia, had failed against the well disciplined Canadian troops.
Their commanding officer, Lieutenant Colonel Matheson, gave
his version of events:

Altogether twenty-two Panthers circled about Battalion HQ
and A Company's position during the night, and it is hard
to picture the confusion which existed. Contact with all but
D Company was lost. Fires and flames lit up the area and
the enemy several times appeared to be convinced that opposition had ceased . . . a German officer drove his Volkswagen [reconnaissance vehicle] up before Battalion HQ,
dismounted and gazed about for a few seconds, until an
excited PIAT [infantry anti-tank weapon] gunner let fly
with a bomb, which hit him squarely.[10]

It is interesting that this last incident, which is timed at 0030
hours, has been crossed out in the unit War Diary!

One of the drivers in the 4th SS Panzer Company adds his
impressions:

My company advanced to the village along the road, the
Panzers staggered one behind the other. We, of the 4th Platoon, were on the right side of the road which led to the
village. I saw a church straight ahead of me. We were taking
heavy anti-tank fire, some houses were in flames. I can still

today hear the commander Pfeiffer yell, 'Set the houses on fire so that we can see something!' The Panzer ahead of me took a direct hit.[11]

Pfeiffer's own Panther was hit and burst into flames, and altogether six Panthers were lost—five, according to the Canadians, in the vicinity of the Regina's Command Post for the loss of seven of their own carriers.[12]

SS Second Lieutenant Fuss, a platoon commander in the 15th SS Reconnaissance Company who was later killed, tells what it was like for his men:

We were surprised by the violent anti-tank fire. A great number of anti-tank guns seemed to be in positions along the edge of town. Canadian infantry was in position in the trenches to the left and right of the tree-lined road running north-east to Bretteville. They peppered the mounted Grenadiers with wild rifle fire. . . . von Büttner had died. . . . Panzermeyer then sent out two assault teams. . . . I reached the church with only six men after a lot of violent shooting. . . . I fired the arranged signal flares [indicating that no enemy tanks had been seen] and withdrew with my six men into the interior of the church since we were getting fire from all sides. There I awaited the arrival of the Panzers. They did not show up.[13]

The attack on Norrey by the 1st SS Panzer-Grenadier Battalion also failed—recall that it had already failed earlier in the day. Max Wünsche, who was slightly wounded during the fighting, drove his command Panther to the village but found none of Krause's men there and had to withdraw after receiving heavy fire. Meyer later attributed the failure of the whole attack to the fact that the Canadians continued to hold Norrey and thus prevented a link-up between his tanks and Mohnke's infantry.[14] But the Canadians had fought superbly, and this is all the more surprising when one considers that they had no armoured support in the battle. Although the Germans had attacked with tanks in the dark, the War Diary of the Reginas states, rather blandly, 'We were informed that tank support would arrive at dawn.' The attempt to take Bretteville and

Norrey cost the Germans dear—Krause's Battalion suffered sixty-one casualties including twelve dead, and the Meyer-Wünsche KG suffered ninety-one, with thirty-one dead.[15] This meant that, by the morning of D+3, the HJ Division had suffered 725 recorded casualties, of which 186 were fatal. Nevertheless, it had played a vital part in halting the Allied advance on Caen. On 8th June Montgomery wrote to the British Director of Military Operations in London:

> The Germans are doing everything they can to hold on to Caen. I have decided not to have a lot of casualties by butting up against the place; so I have ordered Second Army to keep up a good pressure at Caen, and to make its main effort towards Villers-Bocage and Evrecy and thence S.E. towards Falaise.

Meanwhile, 400km away in Belgium, the 1st SS Panzer Division LAH spent the 8th of June busily trying to make ready its combat and supply vehicles for the move which it expected at any moment.

It will be remembered that 1st SS Panzer Corps' 101st SS Heavy Panzer Battalion began its move from Beauvais to Normandy on 7th June. Its route lay west to Gournay-en-Bray and thence south-west to les Andelys. However, because the lower Seine bridges were all destroyed, it then had to be routed south-east via Paris to Versailles where, during the night of 8th June, it was caught in an air attack which damaged a number of its Tiger Is. It still had 250km to go to reach the battle area, via Dreux, l'Aigle and Argentan.

9TH JUNE

The 9th of June saw an important change of emphasis for Army Group 'B' as well as Second British Army. Late in the morning General Geyr von Schweppenburg, Commander Panzer Group West, paid a visit to Kurt Meyer's Headquarters at the Ardenne Abbey and was fully briefed on the situation in that sector. According to Meyer,[16] Schweppenburg told him of his plan to attack due north during the night of 10th June using all three divisions of I SS Panzer Corps. Meyer concurred with enthusiasm. As von Schweppenburg was leaving he witnessed the start of a local tank attack which Meyer had ordered on his own initiative against the long-suffering D Company of the Regina Rifles in Norrey. It began at 1300 hours and was carried out by a single SS Panzer Company, the 3rd, commanded by SS Captain Lüddemann since its normal commander, von Ribbentrop, the son of the Reichs Foreign Minister and holder of the Knight's Cross for his performance in Russia, had been wounded in an earlier air attack. The 3rd Company had arrived late on the previous evening and not in time for the unsuccessful attack on Bretteville. Quite why Meyer ordered this attack by a single company is unclear— maybe he was still smarting from his rebuff at Bretteville or maybe he genuinely believed, having discussed matters with von Schweppenburg, that it was important to secure Norrey as a prelude for the planned attack on the 10th. Whatever the reason, the scene was set for a German disaster.

The twelve Panthers advanced at speed, as if in an old fashioned cavalry charge. They had no infantry with them and no cover and they were totally unaware that the tanks promised to the Reginas had arrived at 0515 hours. SS Sergeant Morawetz described the attack:

There were almost no fighter-bombers in the air, which was usual for noon-time. . . . We reached completely flat and level terrain, meadows and fields. Half left ahead of us lay Norrey. . . . The whole Company drove as a body, at high speed and without any stops, in a broad front. . . . after a muffled bang and a swaying, as if the track had been ripped off, the vehicle came to a stop. It was quiet inside the vehicle. I thought we had driven onto a mine. When I looked to the left. . . . I happened to see the turret being torn off the Panzer driving on the left flank. At the same moment, after another minor explosion, my vehicle began to burn . . . Paul Veith, the gunner sitting in front of me. . . . did not move. . . . I jumped out. . . . Then I saw flames coming out of the open hatch as if from a blowtorch. . . . to my left, along the same line as my vehicle, other burning Panzers. . . . the crews. . . . were burned without exception in their faces and hands. In the meantime we had noticed that the whole area was under infantry fire.[17]

The history of the 3rd SS Panzer Company adds to the picture:

After bailing out, the wounded, mostly more or less seriously burned, tried first to reach the cover of the railroad embankment. Initially they were prevented from getting there by an enemy machine gun which had taken up position in the linesman's cottage on the road Norrey-Bretteville. Only after Sergeant Hermani had removed this obstacle with a few hand grenades did the situation become more bearable. While the whole sector was under concentrated enemy fire, some of it from ships' guns, the wounded dragged themselves along the rail line back to the starting point of the attack.[18]

Seven Panthers failed to return from what can best be described as the 'raid'; two soldiers were definitely killed, seventeen officers and men wounded, most of them badly burned, and fourteen members of the Company were missing—most of them probably killed.[19] Max Wünsche, who had just returned from receiving medical treatment near Caen when he saw the burning tanks, later wrote, 'I could have cried with rage and sorrow.'[20] It is strange that this incident does not even rate a mention in the Canadian Official History or the Regina's War Diary.

During the 9th of June the British continued their push south towards St Pierre from Point 103, just south of Audrieu. The 8th Battalion Durham Light Infantry (DLI) and 24L tanks captured the village by 1845 hours but a battalion of Panzer Lehr continued to hold the Seulles bridge and after a sharp counter-attack the British were forced to withdraw to the northern outskirts by last light.[21] Even so this thrust posed a threat to the flank of the HJ's 12th SS Reconnaissance Battalion at les Hauts Vents and so the last Panther company to arrive in sector, the 2nd of SS Lieutenant Helmut Gaede, was attached to the Battalion and positioned accordingly.

Following Schweppenburg's visit to Meyer's Command Post

there was a change of inter-divisional and regimental boundaries. It must be assumed that these were agreed after detailed discussions between Schweppenburg, Dietrich, Witt and Bayerlein. As a result Panzer Lehr took over west of the Mue stream, and Witt's eastern boundary with 21st Panzer Division was confirmed as the railway line running from Caen to Luc-sur-Mer. Within the HJ, Mohnke's 26th SS Panzer-Grenadier Regiment, having been relieved of responsibility for Cristot and le Mesnil-Patry, took over from the Mue stream east to Franqueville where Meyer's men were established. But the problem of Norrey still influenced German thinking—they firmly believed that it had to be secured before any future counter-attack could be launched in that area.

With all three of Dietrich's divisions now heavily committed, it was obvious to Rommel that it was time for a pause. He knew that if he was to launch a properly coordinated counter-stroke he needed to extract his Panzer divisions from their current defensive posture, replace them with infantry divisions and prepare them for their proper role. Montgomery's strategy of sucking in the German armoured divisions in a piecemeal manner had worked only too well and so, at 1730 hours, Rommel issued a new instruction. It is recorded in the telephone log of Seventh Army:

There should be a return to the defensive in the sector between the Vire and the Orne and the counter-attack should be postponed until all preparations have been completed.

He had decided to await the arrival of II Parachute Corps from Brittany and there could be no question now of launching von Schweppenburg's intended attack as early as the night of 10th June.

But just as Rommel was amending his plans, so was Montgomery. Although he had decided only the day before that his main effort was to be on the western side of Caen towards Villers-Bocage and Evrecy, he wrote on 9th June to his Chief of Staff, Freddie de Guingand, saying that the 7th (British) Armoured Division was to be:

Launched tomorrow southwards through Bayeux to secure
Villers-Bocage and Noyers and then Evrecy;

but that in addition and at the same time, he would:

Pass 51 Highland Division across R. Orne through 6 Airborne Division, to attack southwards east of Caen towards
Cagny.

It was clear that he now planned an encirclement of Caen;
and to trap the German forces defending the city he also
planned:

To put down 1st Airborne Division somewhere south of
Caen as a big air hook, and to link up with it from Evrecy
and Cagny.

He went on to say:

If the Germans wish to be offensive and drive in our lodgement area between Caen and Bayeux, the best way to defeat
them is to be offensive ourselves and the plan given will
checkmate the enemy completely if we can pull it off.[22]

Montgomery had precisely anticipated General von Schweppenburg's plan but, as Rommel knew, that plan had no chance
of being implemented in the timescale envisaged.

On Friday morning 9th June, German intelligence, as a result of a radio interception, reported to OKW that the Allies
would make a landing in the Pas de Calais area the following
morning. The radio message was in fact a clever decoy, but it
worked, and 1st SS Panzer Division LAH was ordered to move
to a new assembly area east of Bruges that night. SS Major
General Teddy Wisch, the Divisional commander, was given
the mission of launching an immediate counter-attack against
any enemy landings at the mouth of the Scheldt river. A sec-
ondary mission was to take action against any enemy airborne
landings.

The LAH completed its move during the night of 9th June
and at daybreak was established in the area of Ursel,
Maldegem, Aardenburg, Oostburg, Terneuzen, Zelzate and

Eeklo (all between Bruges and Antwerp), with its SPW Panzer-Grenadier Battalion covering the Leopold canal between Kabrijke and Ijzendijke. It was placed under the tactical control of General Neumann's LXXXIX Corps.

Since the LAH was still short of some of its vehicles and weapons, a rear party stayed behind in the Turnhout area to receive them.

10TH JUNE

The 10th of June was a bad day for I SS Panzer Corps. Rommel visited Dietrich at his new Headquarters at Baron-sur-Odon and was fully briefed. After the visit Rommel noted in a report:

> Unit commanders, especially Sepp Dietrich, report the enemy has complete control over the battle area and up to 100 km behind the front. . . . Sepp Dietrich informed me enemy armoured divisions carry on the battle at a range of up to 3000m with maximum expenditure of ammunition and splendidly supported by the enemy air force.[23]

The only good news which Rommel brought on this day when the British began their push towards Villers-Bocage, was that in order to fill the dangerous gap which was developing between Dietrich's Corps and Marck's LXXXIV Corps to its west, XLVII Panzer Corps with two Panzer Divisions would be committed on Panzer Lehr's left flank.[24]

Rommel later talked with von Schweppenburg. The War Diary of Panzer Group West notes:

> After discussion with Field Marshal Rommel, the planned attack by I SS Panzer Corps during the night 10/11 June will not take place. Reasons are lack of forces and enemy reinforcements.[25]

The German frontline at this stage ran from Troarn in the east, through Bieville to Cambes, Buron, Franqueville, Carpiquet, and thence on to le Mesnil-Patry, Cristot and Tilly.

In accordance with Montgomery's orders the British 22nd Armoured Brigade, part of the 7th Armoured Division, with the help of the 56th Independent Infantry Brigade, advanced towards Tilly-sur-Seulles on the morning of 10th June. By the end of the day Panzer Lehr had halted the combined British force, after considerable casualties, on the line Verrières-Tilly.

It will be recalled that the problem of Norrey was still concerning various commanders in the HJ. Accordingly, and having no way of knowing that the attack planned for 10th June was about to be postponed, the 12th SS Panzer Pioneer Battalion of SS Major Siegfried Müller, which had at last caught up, was attached to Mohnke's Regiment and ordered to capture Norrey. The attack was launched on foot from the positions held by Krause's 1st SS Panzer-Grenadier Battalion just before dawn on 10th June, and was, yet again, a disaster.

The battle lasted all day and cost the SS Pioneers eighty casualties, of which twenty-eight were killed, including the commander of the 1st Company, Lieutenant Otto Toll, a holder of the Knight's Cross.[26] The Canadian defence of Norrey and Bretteville over the period 8th to 10th June must surely go down as one of the finest small unit actions of WWII.

On this day too, a tragedy occurred for von Schweppenburg. At 0439 hours, as a result of an ULTRA intercept, the following message was received by 21st Army Group Headquarters, 'Command Post of Panzer Group West in the evening of 9th June in la Caine.' Beginning at 2030 hours 10th June four squadrons of rocket-firing Typhoons, followed by seventy-one medium bombers, struck and destroyed the Headquarters; Schweppenburg was wounded and his Chief of Staff and sixteen others were killed. Amongst the dead was Dietrich's liaison officer, SS Captain Wilhelm Beck, who had won the Knight's Cross in Russia. This devastating attack led to the transfer of I SS Panzer Corps back to Dollmann's Seventh Army, and to Dietrich becoming once again the senior commander in the Caen area.

The first phase of the battle of Normandy was now coming to an end. The Leibstandarte and 101st SS Heavy Panzer Battalion had yet to be committed, but the Hitlerjugend had been heavily involved. Precise casualty figures are impossible to obtain but, by the morning of 11th June, they already numbered approximately 900 personnel, of which about 220 were dead;

and twenty-five tanks had been lost—13%, and not 20% as quoted by Dietrich's Chief of Staff in 1945.[27]

NOTES

1. Kraemer, *I SS Panzer Corps in the West*, MS C-024, IWM London, AL 2727–2. 2. 7th Army Telephone Log, 8 Jun 44. 3. Kraemer, op. cit. 4. Meyer, Hubert, *History of the 12th SS Panzer Division Hitlerjugend*, p. 50. 5. Ibid., p. 52. 6. Ibid. 7. Stacey, *Official History of the Canadian Army in the Second World War, Vol III, The Victory Campaign*, p. 136. 8. Meyer, Hubert, op. cit., p. 51. 9. Meyer, Kurt, *Grenadiers*, p. 125. 10. Stacey, op. cit., p. 137. 11. Meyer, Hubert, op. cit., p. 55. 12. Regina Rifles War Diary, 9 Jun 44. 13. Meyer, Hubert, op. cit., p. 55. 14. Stacey, op. cit., p. 137. 15. Meyer, Hubert, op. cit., p. 57. 16. Meyer, Kurt, op. cit., p. 127. 17. Meyer, Hubert, op. cit., pp. 58–59. 18. Ibid., p. 59. 19. Ibid. 20. Ibid. 21. 24L & 50 Inf Div War Diaries, 9 Jun 44. 22. Demi-official correspondence of CinC 21st Army Group, PRO London. 23. Messenger, *Hitler's Gladiator*, p. 126. 24. Ibid. 25. Meyer, Hubert, op. cit., p. 65. 26. Ibid., p. 61. 27. Kraemer, op. cit.

9 | 11th June—Impasse

Recall that the Allied advance towards Villers-Bocage on 10th June by the 22nd Armoured and 56th Independent Infantry Brigades, under the command of the British 7th Armoured Division, had been halted on the line Verrières-Tilly. On 11th June the 69th Infantry Brigade, supported by tanks of the 8th Armoured Brigade, was ordered to attack on the east side of the Seulles river to capture Cristot, with the aim of bringing the 50th Infantry Division into line with the 7th Armoured and supporting its further advance. It will be remembered that troops of the same 69th (British) Infantry Brigade had penetrated as far south as St Pierre on 8th June, forcing the HJ SS Reconnaissance Battalion to make some local withdrawals; but it still held an outpost line from the Seulles river west of Fontenay, through Fontenay-le-Pesnel itself and north to Cristot, and it was supported by tanks.

On this same day, 11th June, General Dempsey was warned by Allied intelligence sources that the Germans were concentrating for a counter-attack out of the Caen area; little did he realise that Rommel, with Dietrich's concurrence, had already decided to delay this attack. In view of this information and in order to help the British push towards Villers-Bocage, Demp-

sey ordered Lieutenant General John Crocker, commanding I
Corps, to launch a concurrent attack with his Canadian
troops. He also told Crocker to concentrate his armour on the
high ground south of Douvres where it could counter the
expected German attack. This concentration of armour was
known to Dietrich because the German radar station at
Douvres, which was still holding out against all attempts to
capture it, reported during the morning of the 11th,[1] 'Contin-
uous movement, heavy and medium tanks, towards south-
west. More than eighty tanks counted in one hour.' And at
2045 hours it reported, 'Urgent. In Anguerny area assembly of
up to now 200 medium enemy tanks with transport echelon
facing south.' These reports were not exaggerated. Montgomery had written to his Chief of Staff:

> We are VERY strong now astride the road Caen-Bayeux
> about the junction of 3 Div and 3 Canadian Div, and if the
> enemy attacks he should be seen off: I have 400 tanks there.[2]

All this, coupled with air attacks on Caen itself, convinced
Dietrich that something big was about to happen.

11th June was a busy day for Major General Keller, commander of the 3rd Canadian Infantry Division. He still had a
dangerous gap between his 7th and 9th Infantry Brigades and
to close it he knew he had to clear the Hitlerjugend from the
Mue valley. When the British No 46 Royal Marine Commando
was placed under his command, he gave it to the Canadian 8th
Infantry Brigade with orders to clear the valley as far as Rots.
Starting from Thaon, the Marines and A Squadron of the Canadian Fort Garry Horse secured the villages of Cairon, Lasson and Rosel without too much difficulty, but at le Hamel
and Rots they ran into Krause's 1st SS Panzer-Grenadier Company and Jürgensen's 4th SS Panther Company; in addition
the Divisional Escort Company had taken up positions in the
Château park and at la Villeneuve. As a consequence the congested Mue valley and all the ground to the north-east were
under observation. More Canadian tanks and a reinforcing
company from Le Régiment de la Chaudière were called in but
it took until 2200 hours and some very bitter fighting before
the area was cleared and the SS had withdrawn to la Villeneuve

and Franqueville. The operation cost the Marines sixty-one casualties, including seventeen killed[3] and the Chaudières, who took over Rots, reported burying 122 SS dead[4]—the Germans only admitted the loss of sixty-seven men in this battle.[5] The balance may well have been unburied dead from previous encounters in the area. One Panther was destroyed at around 1800 hours in the square at Rots and the Fort Garrys lost six Shermans.[6]

SS Senior Sergeant Wohlgemut, commander of an anti-tank gun detachment, described the intensity of the fighting:

There was heavy fighting in the streets [Rots]. The street surface was literally covered with dead and wounded. They were mostly English. Suddenly a Panther showed up to support us. It was a terrible scene as the Panther, crushing the dead and wounded, made its way to the intersection. There was no escape on the narrow street, framed by houses and walls. With the Panzer's support we started a counter-attack. Soon after, a shout came, 'Tanks from behind!' Our Panzer was in a difficult situation. It could not turn around in the narrow street. So it backed up to a spot where it could at least swing the turret by 180 degrees. . . . Suddenly a Sherman showed up ahead. Our Panzer crew must have spotted it, since the engine was gunned up into a howl in an attempt to gain the edge of the town where the turret could be traversed. They did not make it, our Panther was knocked out. . . . As I heard later, SS Captain Pfeiffer, [commander 4th SS Panzer Company and a former Adjutant to Adolf Hitler] was reported to have been killed in this Panzer.[7]

Kurt Meyer, on his motor-bike as usual, narrowly escaped being shot up by a pair of Shermans during this battle. He had been visiting units and was between St Mauvieu and Rots. In his book *Grenadiers,* he described a visit made during the day to his Regimental medical station:

I again find a lot of wounded. The constant arrival of wounded, without any battle taking place, [his 25th SS Panzer-Grenadier was not involved in any direct fighting on

11th June] makes us all think. The conduct of operations is
such that the Panzer divisions are being decimated by naval
gunfire and low flying aircraft without being able to fight. It
can't go on like this any more! The Panzer divisions must
regain freedom of movement.

General Crocker had received Dempsey's order for an attack
by his I Corps in support of XXX Corps at 1700 hours on 10th
June. It is not known when Major General Keller was told
about it but it must have come as a nasty shock because the
Canadians had not been planning to mount their main attack
against the Cheux area until the 12th at the earliest. To compound matters further, Crocker's orders seem to have taken an
inordinately long time to reach the commanders concerned. It
was 1100 hours on the 11th before Brigadier Wyman, commanding the 2nd Canadian Armoured Brigade, held his 'O'
(Orders) Group.[8] At 1200 hours the Headquarters log of I
Corps noted, '3 Cdn Div told to keep 50 [British]Div fully
informed about progress of 2 Cdn Armd Bde which will help
69 Bde.' It is obvious that the Canadian attack was not, and in
the time available could not be, properly coordinated with that
of the British 69th Brigade and, not surprisingly, both attacks
failed.

Early on the morning of the 11th, Fritz Witt visited the
Headquarters of his Divisional SS Reconnaissance Battalion at
Rauray. He took the lightly wounded commanding officer of
the Battalion with him and Gerd Bremer re-assumed command. They were both shocked by what they found. The reconnaissance companies had been much reduced in strength
by enemy artillery, naval gunfire and air attacks and many of
the company and platoon commanders had become casualties.

At 1430 hours the 50th (British) Infantry Division began its
attack on the east side of the Seulles. The 6th and 7th (Infantry) Battalions of the Green Howards advanced towards les
Hauts Vents and the area to the south of Cristot respectively,
the 6th being supported by tanks from the 4th/7th Royal Dra-
goon Guards (4/7 DG). 8 DLI was already holding St Pierre
and was to be relieved by the 5th East Yorkshire Battalion.

The 6th Green Howards moved through Audrieu at 1600

hours and, after leaving le Haut d'Audrieu at about 1830, advanced towards Hill 102, just south of Cristot, with tanks of the 4/7 DG. They were soon halted by devastating fire from the machine guns, mortars, and a few anti-tank guns of the much weakened 12th SS Reconnaissance Battalion, quickly followed by an immediate counter-attack by Panthers of the 2nd SS Panzer Company. By the time darkness fell they were back at le Haut d'Audrieu, having taken 250 casualties, including two company commanders; the 4/7 DG lost seven tanks—their War Diary described the action as 'a very sticky time'. The 7th Green Howards did little better. They came under heavy fire from Olboeter's 3rd Armoured SS Panzer-Grenadier Battalion in Brouay as soon as they approached the railway line and were forced to withdraw to their starting positions after dark. The HJ SS Reconnaissance Battalion and its few supporting tanks had held their positions but at a cost—sixty-seven casualties including twenty-seven killed.[9]

Meanwhile the Canadian attack through Norrey, to seize the high ground south of Cheux, had been launched by tanks of the 1st Hussars and infantrymen of the Queen's Own Rifles of Canada just after 1430 hours. The plan was to move via le Mesnil-Patry, bypassing Cheux itself, and for the rest of Wyman's 2nd Armoured Brigade to join the attacking force on the objective. Colonel C. P. Stacey's *Official History of the Canadian Army, Vol III*, describes succinctly what happened:

'B' Squadron of the Hussars led the advance, with men of 'D' Company of the Queen's Own riding on its tanks. This force had not gone far across the level grainfields between Norrey and le Mesnil-Patry when very heavy mortar and machine gun fire came down. The infantry were forced to dismount from the tanks [at Norrey], which pushed on in an attempt to deal with the opposition. Both the tanks and a party of infantry fought their way into le Mesnil-Patry. The situation grew worse as enemy armour, which was at first believed to be British, and anti-tank guns came into action. Lt Col Colwell of the Hussars, who was commanding the advanced group, ordered his force to withdraw to the start line. But 'B' Squadron evidently did not receive the order, and was virtually annihilated. All its officers and all save three NCOs were listed as missing, and only two of its tanks returned. As for 'D' Company of the Queen's Own, it was found to have suffered ninety-six casualties, more than half of whom were missing. The total casualties for the day were eighty for the 1st Hussars and ninety-nine for the Queen's Own Rifles, the fatal casualties being fifty-nine and fifty-five respectively.

Unfortunately for the Canadians they had been detected in their assembly area by the 12th SS Panzer Division's radio interception unit and their attack was expected. The 12th SS Panzer Pioneer Battalion, located just to the north of Cheux, had been briefed to take on the Shermans with Panzerfausts and magnetic mines, and Mohnke, the Regimental commander, had asked SS Major Prinz's Mk IV 2nd SS Panzer Battalion to provide a company to back up his 2nd SS Panzer-Grenadier Battalion positioned one kilometre south of le Mesnil-Patry. SS Lieutenant Siegel of the 8th Company describes vividly what happened to the three Mk IVs with him:

'Ready for action!' On this order, the hatches of the three Panzers closed as by themselves. The guns barrels were wound down to firing elevation. Anti-tank shells were loaded on the move. . . . Several Shermans were spotted rolling at a dangerous distance towards us through the orchard of a farm. We had driven right in front of their barrels and were showing them our vulnerable flanks. 'Enemy tanks from the left—9 o'clock—200—open fire!' This was all the chief of 8 [SS Panzer Company], who was also the commander of the point Panzer, could do. Nothing else was required. The months-long drills and battle experience of the crews now proved themselves. The driver jerked the Panzer to the left, bringing it into the firing position. Even before the fighting compartment ventilation fan, crucial for the survival of the crew, got to full speed, the closest enemy tank had been hit. Within a minute or so, four or five Shermans were burning. Only the last one. . . . brought sweat to the commander's brow. It had only just been spotted as it was already swinging its barrel towards us. 'Enemy tank hard left—10 o'clock—100!'. . . . Then came a blow, a flash of fire from the breech of the gun, the case dropped into the sack, the enemy tank exploded![10]

Meanwhile Prinz himself had gathered other tanks of his Battalion not yet engaged and launched a crushing counter-attack against C Squadron of the Hussars. In total the 1st Hussars lost an astonishing thirty-four Shermans and three Fireflys[11] on this tragic day for Canadian arms. But the Germans had not gone unscathed—three tanks had been knocked out, although one was later repaired. Personnel losses were much more grievous—SS Lieutenant Sauer, whose 2nd SS Panzer-Grenadier Company had been overrun, had been killed along with seventeen others of the 26th Regiment and alto-gether 189 men[12] had been lost during the fighting, slightly more than the Canadians.

And so ended the first phase of the battle for Caen. As already explained, both sides were now expecting major at-tacks in this area, but Montgomery's strategy, and Rommel's relative impotence, dictated that action would switch to other areas—and whilst the Leibstandarte remained uninvolved in Belgium, another important element of I SS Panzer Corps, the 101st SS Heavy Panzer Battalion, was to come into play.

NOTES

1. Douvres Radar Station Radio Log, 11 Jun 44. **2.** Demi-official Correspondence of CinC 21st Army Group, PRO London. **3.** 46 Cdo RM War Diary, 11 Jun 44. **4.** Stacey, *The Official History of the Canadian Army in the Second World War, Vol III, The Victory Campaign*, p. 139. **5.** Meyer, Hubert, *The History of the 12th SS Panzer Division Hitlerjugend*, p. 71. **6.** Fort Garry Horse War Diary, 11 Jun 44. **7.** Meyer, Hubert, op. cit., p. 70. **8.** 2nd Cdn Armd Bde War Diary, 11 Jun 44. **9.** Meyer, Hubert, op. cit., p. 67. **10.** Ibid., p. 68. **11.** 2nd Cdn Armd Bde War Diary, 11 Jun 44. **12.** Meyer, Hubert, op. cit., p. 69.

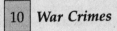

10   *War Crimes*

It would be wrong to chronicle the fighting in Normandy in June 1944 without mentioning the subject of war crimes for, although there has probably never been a military campaign of any length in which prisoners of war were not killed by their captors, the accusations made against the Waffen-SS during the battle for Normandy have been copious.

The vanquished inevitably suffer when any reckoning is made and it was no accident that in the first War Crimes trial held after the war, an attempt was made to establish the responsibility of a senior commander for crimes committed by soldiers under his command. But it is highly significant that it was decided that this principle was to be applicable only to German commanders—Allied officers were exonerated from such responsibility and the Germans were made to learn a painful lesson. When the former Chief of Staff of the Hitlerjugend Division complained about the treatment of disabled comrades in a US prison camp in 1945, he received the following reply from an American officer, 'What do you mean, Geneva Convention? You seem to have forgotten that you lost the war!'

The War Crimes trial mentioned was that of SS Major General Kurt Meyer, the former commander of the 25th SS Panzer-Grenadier Regiment and subsequently of the 12th SS Panzer Division HJ. Meyer was tried at Aurich in Germany. The charge sheet listed five charges including: the killing of twenty-three Canadian prisoners of war at Authie and Buron on 7th June, and eleven prisoners of war at the Ardenne Abbey by troops under his command on the same day; the killing of seven other prisoners at the Abbey either by troops under his command or, as an alternative charge, on his direct orders; and inciting and counselling his troops to deny quarter. It will be recalled that Meyer's Command Post had been located at the Ardenne Abbey.

On 27th December 1945 Meyer was found not guilty of responsibility for the murders at Authie and Buron, nor of ordering the execution of a group of seven prisoners at the Ardenne Abbey. He was, however, found guilty of inciting his troops to deny quarter and of responsibility, as a commander, for the murder of eighteen prisoners who died at the Ardenne Abbey on 7th and 8th June 1944. The President of the Court was—inappropriately even if not illegally—his former adversary of early June 1944 and the commander of many of the men Meyer was accused of killing, none other than Brigadier (now Major General) H. W. Foster, the commander of the 7th Canadian Infantry Brigade. He sentenced Meyer to 'suffer death by being shot'.

In January 1946, the CinC of the Canadian Army in occupied Western Germany, Major General Chris Vokes, commuted Meyer's sentence to life imprisonment. The Canadians were outraged; but Vokes explained his decision as follows:

> When I studied the evidence against Meyer I found it to be a mass of circumstantial evidence. There was certainly the inference to be drawn that he had given the order to have Canadian soldiers executed. But nowhere in the evidence could I find the order to be proved. Not to my satisfaction. There was hearsay evidence. There was nothing direct. So I ordered the execution stayed.[2]

The No 1 Canadian War Crimes Investigation Unit, set up after the war, was headed by Colonel Bruce Macdonald. This Unit was established after the initial findings of the Supreme Headquarters Allied Expeditionary Force (SHAEF) Court of Inquiry, headed by Colonel Paul Tombaugh, US Army, and which included members from Britain and Canada. This Court found that members of the Hitlerjugend Division were responsible for the illegal deaths of sixty-two Allied soldiers, almost all Canadian, between the 7th and 17th June 1944.

After some preliminary investigations, Macdonald believed that more than 134 Canadians had been murdered by the HJ, but he knew he could never bring satisfactory charges for all that number. Nevertheless, he tried hard to develop cases against Wilhelm Mohnke (26th SS Panzer-Grenadier Regiment), Siebken and Schnabel (2nd SS Panzer-Grenadier Battalion, 26th Regiment), Milius (3rd SS Panzer-Grenadier Battalion, 25th Regiment), Müller (12th SS Panzer Pioneer Battalion), Bremer and von Ritzenstein (12th SS Panzer Reconnaissance Battalion), and other less senior members of the HJ Division. But then some of his suspects were found to be dead and the most senior one, Mohnke, was a prisoner of the Russians and out of reach.

No case was ever brought against Milius, Müller or Bremer. In 1946 the Canadian War Crimes Investigation Unit was disbanded and responsibility transferred to the British authorities. Thus, in 1948, ex-SS Major Bernhard Siebken, ex-SS Second Lieutenant Dietrich Schnabel and two former soldiers of the HJ Division were accused before a British Military Court in Hamburg with causing the deaths of three Canadian prisoners of war at le Mesnil-Patry on 9th June 1944. The soldiers were acquitted but both officers were found guilty and hanged at Hameln in West Germany on 20th January 1949.

Whatever the rights and wrongs of what happened to the former members of the 12th SS Panzer Division HJ after the war, there is clear evidence that a minimum of sixty surrendered Canadian prisoners of war were killed in cold blood by men of that Division during the early days of the Normandy campaign. It is also clear that most of those responsible were never brought to justice and that the trial of Kurt Meyer was flawed—General Vokes made this clear when he reviewed the sentence.

On the reverse side of the coin, the Germans alleged that the British and Canadians were also guilty of war crimes. Numerous cases were quoted of Allied officers carrying documents or notes saying that no prisoners were to be taken. To this author's knowledge no evidence of this kind exists today, but in the situation pertaining in 1945–1946, if any such evidence had been produced it would certainly have been ignored or, more likely, destroyed. Meyer himself claimed to have seen a group of German soldiers lying beside a road near the railway at Rots on 9th June, all shot through the head[3] and in another case relevant to I SS Panzer Corps it was alleged that:

The regimental commander of the 130th Panzer Artillery Regiment [Colonel Luxemburger], part of the Panzer Lehr Division, became a British prisoner of war together with a battalion commander, Major Zeissler, Captain Graf Clary-Aldringen, and about six NCOs and men on the morning of 8th June 1944. They were captured by an armoured car patrol of the British Inns of Court Regiment, which had penetrated behind German lines.

After the German officers had refused willingly to act as [human] shields, the badly handicapped Colonel Luxemburger [he had lost an arm in WWI] was fettered by two British officers, beaten unconscious and, covered in blood, tied to a British tank as a shield. . . . Major Zeissler, Captain Graf Clary-Aldringen, and the soldiers were shot by the tanks as they moved off.

Graf Clary was found by members of Siebken's battalion and brought to the battle headquarters. The British tank, on which Colonel Luxemburger was tied as a shield, was hit by a German anti-tank gun. Colonel Luxemburger died two days later in a military hospital.[4]

This story was repeated as evidence by Graf Clary-Aldringen himself in the trial of Siebken and Schnabel. The War Diary of the British Regiment confirms that on the morning of 8th June, patrols of C Squadron ran into Germans near Cristot and:

2 and 6a captured 3 German officers, including a Colonel and 3 [soldiers]. On the way back these were ambushed and lost all vehicles. Lt Yodaiken, Lt Wigram killed, 2 ORs missing; 4 ORs led by Cpl Fowler made way back on foot by compass.

It is perhaps fair to point out that it was impossible to carry extra personnel *inside* a British armoured car and it was therefore not unreasonable to tie a prisoner to the outside of the vehicle to prevent him jumping off whilst on the move. But, even if the allegation was true, it would in no way have excused the shooting of three Canadian soldiers as a reprisal the following day.[5] The Geneva Convention clearly upholds the principle that reprisals may not be taken against prisoners of war but this fact is conveniently ignored by German apologists in this case. The three Canadians concerned were those who died in the 'First Aid Post killings' for which Siebken and Schnabel were hanged in 1949.

The whole subject of surrendered soldiers being killed by their captors has been argued endlessly in the post-war years and it is abundantly clear that war crimes were not, and probably never will be, restricted to one side only. In his admirable book *Overlord, D-Day and the Battle for Normandy 1944*, Max Hastings points out that almost every one of the Allied witnesses he interviewed for his narrative had direct knowledge or even experience of the shooting of German prisoners and that many British and American units shot Waffen-SS prisoners as a matter of routine.

An extreme example of what can happen in the heat of battle is quoted in Tony Foster's *Meeting of Generals*. On page 334 a Canadian sergeant describes how French Canadian soldiers 'slit the throats of most [German] soldiers they found, wounded as well as dead' during the fighting for Carpiquet airfield. The allegation is uncorroborated but would seem to most people to qualify as a war crime. That said, it is this author's firm and perhaps controversial view, that unless a person has been a soldier and experienced the violence of battle and the anger which can arise when he sees his comrades killed or hideously wounded, he is not properly entitled to judge the actions of those accused of such crimes. Nevertheless, there can be no excuse for those who kill or mutilate prisoners away from the heat of battle and such men should always be brought to justice. There are even so, as every soldier knows, occasions when there is little option but to kill prisoners—if they attempt to escape for example, or if there are not enough guards to look after them and they attempt to jeopardize the legitimate actions of their captors. Another aspect which, though unpalatable, needs to be understood, is that once killing starts a blood-lust can sometimes arise amongst inexperienced soldiers. Only well disciplined troops can be brought back under control in such circumstances. Regrettably, many units on both sides in Normandy were not that well disciplined; the case quoted in Tony Foster's book is a good example for it goes on to record that 'the officers of the Regiment had to draw their pistols against their own men to make them come back to reason.'

In conclusion, it has to be said that it is the duty of all nations to bring to justice those who abuse or kill unarmed and surrendered soldiers who have made no attempt to escape or to interfere with the legitimate actions of their captors.

NOTES
   1. Meyer, Hubert, *The History of the 12th SS Panzer Division Hitler-jugend*, p. 329. **2.** Sayer & Botting, *Hitler's Last General, The Case against Wilhelm Mohnke*, p. 182. **3.** Meyer, Kurt, *Grenadiers*, p. 128. **4.** Ibid. **5.** Meyer, Hubert, op. cit., p. 53.

11 | *12th to 14th June—Operation PERCH and the Battle of Villers-Bocage*

12TH JUNE—PRELUDE

Montgomery's plan for encircling Caen was based on a major thrust to the west of Tilly-sur-Seulles leading to the high ground north-east of Villers-Bocage and then east to Evrecy on the far side of the Odon. The strategic importance of this high ground near Villers-Bocage cannot be over-stated—Point 213 can be seen for miles and it dominates the surrounding countryside.

The threat in the Villers-Bocage area posed a major problem for the German commanders, particularly Sepp Dietrich, because the troops earmarked to fill the widening gap between his I SS Panzer Corps just to the west of the Seulles and General Marcks's LXXXIV Corps west of Balleroy had yet to arrive. Marcks had reported to Seventh Army on the 11th[1] that his 352nd Division, 'Now has small combat value and the gap between it and its right flank neighbour [Panzer Lehr] is constantly increasing.' It was planned to fill the gap with the 3rd Parachute and 2nd Panzer Divisions, though the tanks and wheeled vehicles of 2nd Panzer were not expected to arrive before 14th June or be ready for action until the 15th at the earliest. In the meantime the gap would have to be filled by light reconnaissance forces.

General Dollmann's plans for 12th June, as they affected Dietrich, were transmitted to Army Group 'B' as follows:

> I SS Panzer Corps will hold its present line, releasing Panzer forces for the counter-attack. The left wing [Panzer Lehr] will close the gap to 352 Inf Div with reconnaissance units.[2]

Dietrich briefed his commanders on the situation. He told them that he no longer believed a concentrated counter-attack was possible and that he had no reserves left. Misquoting

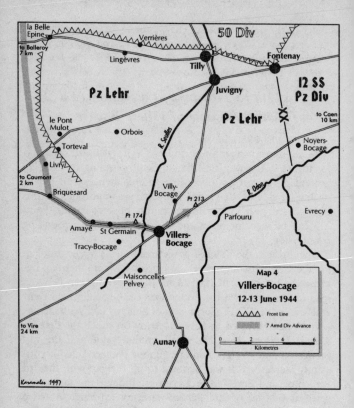

Map 4

Villers-Bocage

12-13 June 1944

△△△△ Front Line

7 Armd Div Advance

0 1 2 3 4 5 6
Kilometres

Frederick the Great he said, 'They want to defend everything. . . . but with what? He who defends everything, defends nothing.'[3]

In fact Dietrich did have one reserve which was about to arrive in sector and play a dramatic part in forthcoming events—the 101st SS Heavy Panzer Battalion—but it would not be available until the 13th.

The crisis came on the 12th of June when the American 1st Infantry Division advanced and captured Caumont on the US left flank. This village stands on a ridge between Villers-Bocage and St Lô and dominates the surrounding area. General Marcks himself was killed on this day in a fighter-bomber attack when leading a group of hastily assembled minor units in a last attempt to defend this vital ground. But it was too late and by nightfall, after an advance of 8km, the Americans entered the village.

The news that the Americans had found a gap to the west of Tilly electrified the British command. Their 7th Armoured Division had failed to penetrate the Panzer Lehr defences at Tilly. Its men, especially those of the 22nd Armoured Brigade, were fighting in a completely new environment and their retraining after the North African desert and Italy, in the fens and heaths of eastern England, had done little to prepare them for the 'bocage.' Chester Wilmot describes the situation perfectly in his book, *The Struggle for Europe*:

> The transition to 'bocage' afflicted the men with claustrophobia. Tank commanders who had always fought with their heads out, were sniped and killed as they drove along apparently peaceful lanes. Crews, who had been accustomed to engage the enemy at half a mile or more, found themselves facing hostile anti-tank guns at a range of 50 yards, or, worse still, dealing with boarding parties who leapt on their tanks from the cover of hedgerows.

It had been no less of a shock for the men of the elite Panzer Lehr Division to find themselves in the 'bocage'; they were, after all, trained for highly mobile, cut-and-thrust type operations in relatively open country. But they were quick to adapt to the new conditions and make the individual tank the hub of

their defence. Each semi-independent Panzer-Grenadier group
was based on a single tank which became their armoured anti-
tank gun and armoured machine gun; and the tank invariably
led local counter-attacks against Allied penetrations. In fairness it has to be said that it was much easier to adapt to the
defence in the 'bocage' than it was to the attack, although the
Germans were always worried that their positions would be
infiltrated, particularly at night.

Infiltration was a tactic almost unknown to the Allies, although rare examples occur later in the battle; Brigadier
Trevor Hart Dyke describes in his short book, *Normandy to
Arnhem*, how on 26th June, when he was commanding the
Hallamshire Battalion in the British 49th Infantry Division, he
persuaded his Brigade Commander to let him try a night infiltration in the Tessel woods sector near Fontenay-le-Pesnel. It
worked—as did a similar operation by the Argylls of Canada
much later in the campaign (see Chapter XXIV).

General Dempsey learned about the American advance on
Caumont at 1145 hours on 12th June when he met the commander of XXX Corps, Lieutenant General Bucknall, at Bayeux railway station. Bucknall told him that his reconnaissance
troops were in contact with the US 1st Infantry Division and
all seemed to be going well. Dempsey wrote in his personal
diary:

> I told him to switch 7 Armd Div from their front immedi-
> ately, to push them thro' behind 11H [Bucknall's Armoured
> Reconnaissance Regiment which had reached Caumont with
> the Americans] and endeavour to get to Villers-Bocage that
> way.[4]

Montgomery sent a message to his Chief of Staff that night:

> Thrust line was switched quickly further to the west and
> Div. . . . reached Bricquessard at 1900 hrs and will move
> on Villers-Bocage and Noyers tomorrow. All this very good
> and Pz Lehr may be in grave danger tomorrow.

As Monty saw it, this move could be a 'turning point in the
battle'.

In view of the obvious threat to his left flank, Dietrich de-

cided to use his only reserve as soon as it arrived and before it
had time for the urgent maintenance and repairs its Tigers so
badly needed. During the move from Beauvais, SS Major Hein
von Westernhagen's 101st SS Heavy Panzer Battalion had suffered badly. As well as the damage suffered in the air attack at
Versailles, the Battalion had been constantly harried from the
air and twenty-seven men had been killed or wounded. Many
tanks had broken down due to the long move on their own
tracks. Even so, whilst the Headquarters and SS Lieutenant
Raasch's decimated 3rd Company remained in the vicinity of
Falaise with only one operational tank, the other two weakened companies were ordered, late on 12th June, to move
across the Orne and Odon and take up reserve positions behind the Panzer Lehr and Hitlerjugend Divisions. The 1st
Company of SS Captain Rolf Möbius, with nine Tigers, was
located behind HJ in the region of Noyers-Bocage, some 9km
north-east of Villers-Bocage, and SS Lieutenant Michael Wittmann's 2nd Company, with only five tanks, was to be found
behind Panzer Lehr, in a small wood directly south of the tiny
hamlet of Montbrocq on the critical Point 213, some 2km
north-east of Villers-Bocage.

By June 1944 Michael Wittmann was already one of the
most famous officers in the Waffen-SS and its greatest Panzer
ace. He had joined the Leibstandarte in 1937. As a sergeant he
commanded an armoured car in Poland and France and he
went on to earn the Iron Cross 2nd Class in Greece. Wittmann
was wounded twice and won the Iron Cross 1st Class in Russia
in 1941, before being sent to an SS Officers' School and commissioned in December 1942. After only one year as a tank
commander in Russia, he was credited with sixty-six tank
'kills' and had been awarded the Knight's Cross. On Hitler's
birthday in 1944 Wittmann was promoted to the rank of SS
Lieutenant and ten days later he received Oak Leaves to his
Knight's Cross. In April 1944 he was given command of the
2nd SS Panzer Company in the 101st SS Heavy Panzer Battalion. He and his gunner, Bobby Woll, had by then been
credited with an astonishing 119 enemy armoured fighting
vehicles destroyed, but Woll, who had also been awarded the
Knight's Cross, had now been given his own Tiger. Recall that

the Panzer and Panzer-Grenadier Regiments of Panzer Lehr were facing north, successfully defending the le Mesnil-Patry—Tilly—Lingèvres—la Belle Epine front, and the Reconnaissance Battalion was covering, as best it could, the left flank of the Division. Contact between the 101st and the Panzer Lehr Reconnaissance Battalion was established through a Battalion liaison officer located initially at Dietrich's Headquarters.

When Major General Bobby Erskine, commander 7th Armoured Division, was given his new orders on 12th June, he had to reorganise his Division for its planned deep probe around the back of Panzer Lehr—Operation PERCH. Although he would be advancing on a very narrow front, with an exposed left flank, he knew that Dietrich's Panzer Divisions were fully committed and that there were no immediate German reserves. An ULTRA decrypt on the 12th indicated that 2nd Panzer was on its way to support Panzer Lehr in the neighbourhood of Villers-Bocage, but it still had some way to go to reach the battle area. The British generals had every reason to expect success the following day—but then, none of them knew about the fourteen newly arrived Tigers.

Erskine decided to lead with his 22nd Armoured Brigade, which for this operation comprised two armoured regiments (battalions)—4th County of London Yeomanry 'Sharpshooters' (4 CLY) and 5th Royal Tank Regiment (5 RTR), one motorised infantry battalion—1st Battalion The Rifle Brigade (1 RB), one SP artillery battalion less a battery—5th Regiment Royal Horse Artillery (5 RHA)—and the 260th Anti-Tank Battery. In order to give the Brigade more infantry for its move through the 'bocage' countryside and, in particular, to help it occupy Villers-Bocage, Erskine took one infantry battalion, 1st/7th Battalion The Queen's Royal Regiment (1/7 Queen's) from his 131st Infantry Brigade and gave it to Brigadier 'Looney' Hinde's 22nd Armoured Brigade. As his nickname may suggest, Hinde was a flamboyant cavalryman, much admired for his personal bravery. The other half of Erskine's Division was Brigadier Michael Ekins's truck-mounted 131st Infantry Brigade, which normally consisted of three battalions of the Queen's Royal Regiment and another towed artillery

Regiment—3 RHA. Ekins, who had been recently appointed to command the Brigade, was a much more pedestrian officer than Hinde and was unknown to his officers and men. To balance the Division and make up for the loss of 1/7 Queen's, Erskine took 22 Brigade's third armoured Regiment, 1st Royal Tank Regiment (1 RTR) and gave it to 131 Brigade. In simple terms, the Armoured Brigade had two tank battalions and two infantry battalions, the Infantry Brigade one tank battalion and two infantry battalions and they were each supported by an artillery battalion.

In addition to these two Brigades, Erskine had an Armoured Reconnaissance Regiment (battalion), the 8th Hussars (8H), of which one squadron (company) was given to 131 Brigade, another told to guard the left rear of the Division near le Pont Mulot, and the remainder given the task of right flank protection under 'Looney' Hinde's command. On top of all this, the XXX Corps Reconnaissance Regiment (battalion), the 11th Hussars in armoured cars, was also given the task of guarding the flanks.

Brigadier Hinde gave his orders at 1500 hours on the 12th. The light tanks of the 8H were to lead, followed by Lieutenant Colonel the Viscount Cranley's 4 CLY with A Company and an anti-tank detachment of 1 RB under command. Their task was to advance, via Livry, to Villers-Bocage and then move on to seize Point 213. 5 RTR, following with another company of 1 RB, was to take the high ground to the south-west of the town at Maisoncelles Pelvey, and the 260th Anti-tank Battery of the Norfolk Yeomanry with its splendid SP 17 pdrs, was to cover the gap between the two groups. 1/7 Queen's was to occupy Villers-Bocage itself. As the operation progressed, Erskine planned for 131 Brigade to move forward and occupy the Livry area.

The advance began at 1600 hours on the 12th and soon ran into a single German anti-tank gun and a few infantrymen near the hamlet of Livry; a Stuart tank was knocked out. It took till 2000 hours to clear this minor opposition and it was then decided to laager for the night and advance again at first light. Hinde said later, in his official report, that he decided to halt because: 'There would be no definite indication to the enemy that our objective was in fact Villers-Bocage'. This decision was the first in a series of errors which led, inexorably, to a British disaster.

Meanwhile at a conference at his Headquarters on 12th June, Hitler ordered that the 1st SS Panzer Division LAH was to be united as quickly as possible with the 12th SS Panzer Division HJ in Normandy, under the command of Headquarters I SS Panzer Corps Leibstandarte.

13TH TO 14TH JUNE—THE BATTLE[5]

The battle of Villers-Bocage has been described in copious detail many times before. Nevertheless, many of the accounts rely heavily on the memoirs of so-called 'eye witnesses' or participants, which are often misleading, inaccurate, or which have become embellished with the passage of time. Even the British *History of the Second World War, Victory in the West, Vol I, The Battle of Normandy* by L. F. Ellis, published by Her Majesty's Stationery Office in 1962, gives a totally distorted account of events on this critical day.

This author has no intention of trying to rehearse the minutiae of the battle, but rather to describe the critical events and to then discuss what went wrong and the repercussions. The 'bottom line' in the battle of Villers-Bocage is that on the morning of 13th June, Michael Wittmann in a single Tiger I, supported only marginally by his other four tanks, brought the 7th Armoured Division to a complete halt. How did this happen?

Hinde's Brigade continued its advance at 0530 hours on 13th June. For reasons unknown, neither the reconnaissance tanks of the 8H nor those of 4 CLY Reconnaissance Troop led the advance; the latter travelled *behind* the leading tanks and infantry.

The order of march of the 22nd Armoured Brigade was: A Squadron 4 CLY and an artillery tank, A Company and an anit-tank detachment of 1 RB mounted in halftracks and carriers, the 4 CLY Reconnaissance Troop, the four Headquarters tanks of 4 CLY and two artillery tanks of 5 RHA, and then B and C Squadrons 4 CLY. Following behind was Hinde's Brigade Tactical Headquarters, an engineer troop, 5 RHA (SP artillery battalion) less a battery, 1 RB less two companies, the truck mounted Battalion of 1/7 Queen's, the 5 RTR Battlegroup with a company of 1 RB, and finally the 260th Anti-tank Battery of the Norfolk Yeomanry.

Moving through Amayé, the 4 CLY Battlegroup reached Villers-Bocage at approximately 0800 hours and continued its advance up the hill towards Point 213, without opposition. On reaching the high ground, the tanks halted where they could look down the long straight road leading towards Caen, less than 20km away. A Company 1 RB and its anti-tank detachment halted nose-to-tail behind them and the men dismounted to stretch their legs and have a cup of tea.

At that moment Michael Wittmann's Tiger emerged from cover on the south side of the road and, after knocking out the rear tank of A Squadron, drove down the infantry column at a range of about 50–80m destroying the RB vehicles as he went. Wittmann said later that he had no time to deploy his other Tigers but ordered them 'not to retreat a step but to hold their ground.'

Christopher Milner, the second-in-command of A Company, described his experiences in George Forty's book, *Desert Rats at War*:

> The enemy attended first of all to the three motor platoons by. . . . trundling back towards Villers, shooting up vehicles and riflemen section by section, with only the company's two 6 pdr anti-tank guns able to offer even a measure of resistance, which I learned afterwards they did with considerable bravery but with little effect.

Wittmann then drove into Villers-Bocage, knocking out three Stuart tanks of the 4 CLY Recce Troop, the four Headquarters tanks, which had halted on the eastern outskirts of the town when Viscount Cranley had gone forward in his scout car to see A Squadron on Point 213, and the two unarmed artillery tanks of 5 RHA (the guns had been removed to make room for extra radios). The Brigade War Diary says that the Headquarters tanks of 4 CLY were knocked out by 0830 hours.

The 4 CLY War Diary records that at 1000 hours A Squadron, on Point 213, reported being surrounded and attacked by Tiger tanks. These were, of course, Wittmann's other four tanks. Half an hour later Viscount Cranley reported that his position was untenable and withdrawal impossible, and at 1035 hours A Squadron's radios went 'dead.'

Whilst all this was happening, Brigadier Hinde's Tactical Headquarters was less than 4km away to the east of Amayé and he himself was somewhere in the forward area in his scout car. At 1000 hours, he gave orders for 1/7 Queen's to enter Villers-Bocage and join B Squadron 4 CLY already in the town. He then left his vehicle and was not seen again until he reappeared at his Headquarters in the afternoon. C Squadron 4 CLY, knowing that the forward units of the Brigade were in trouble, had halted in Tracy-Bocage, 2km to the east, where it was joined by 5 RTR and a company of 1 RB during the morning.

Shortly after 1000 hours Lieutenant Colonel Desmond Gordon (later Major General), commanding 1/7 Queen's and acting on Hinde's orders, told his anti-tank and carrier platoons to move into the town, whilst the rest of the Battalion de-bussed at St Germain and advanced on foot.

Not surprisingly Wittmann now found himself in trouble—he was without infantry support and, as with any tank in a built-up area, highly vulnerable to short range weapons. He said later that he had lost radio contact with his Company and was unable to summon help—'my tanks were out of sight.' His citation for this action says, 'In the centre of the town his tank was immobilized by an enemy heavy anti-tank gun.' Even so, he and his crew managed to bail out and, after a walk of some 7km, Wittmann reached the Headquarters of Panzer Lehr at Orbois, to the north of Villers-Bocage. Again according to his citation:

He reported there to the Ia [Operations officer], turned about with fifteen Panzer IVs from the Panzer Lehr Division and once more headed for Villers-Bocage. His amphibious Volkswagen had caught up with him by that time. In it he drove to the 1st Company [Möbius], which was deployed along the main road toward Villers-Bocage. He briefed them on his impressions of the fighting and the situation and deployed them against the town.

The Mk IVs mentioned in Wittmann's citation did not in fact try to enter Villers-Bocage but took up a screening position 1500m to the north at Villy-Bocage.

Between 1130 hours and noon two companies of the Queen's joined the Battalion anti-tank and carrier platoons in Villers-Bocage, to be followed later by a third company.

The 22 Brigade War Diary says that at 1235 hours there were five Tigers and another unspecified tank trying to encircle A Squadron 4 CLY on Point 213. The History of the Panzer Lehr Division confirms that a few of its Mk IVs which had been undergoing maintenance at Parfouru, 4km north-east of Villers-Bocage, took part in this action.

At 1240 hours Viscount Cranley, somewhere on Point 213 but out of touch with his A Squadron, radioed that he was surrounded; and at about 1300 hours the surviving tanks of A Squadron and some seventeen men of A Company 1 RB surrendered. Cranley was captured separately and turned up in a German prisoner-of-war camp near Argentan on the 15th.

A vivid description of the final moments on Point 213 is provided by Christopher Milner in *Desert Rats at War*:

Suddenly there was a rumble of tanks from the east and as I darted round to the front of the cottage I was astonished to find that the tank shooting seemed to have ended and that some tank officers in black berets were standing about talking to one or two of our officers in the middle of the main road. Since there had been no shooting and everyone seemed very friendly I took them to be members of the RTR [who also wore black berets] and stepped out to join the conversation, only to be frozen in my tracks when I realised they were German tank crews!

The leading Battlegroup of the 22nd Armoured Brigade had ceased to exist. But the losses, although serious—twenty Cromwells, four Firefly Shermans, three Stuarts, three artillery Shermans, sixteen carriers, fourteen halftracks and two 6 pdr anti-tank guns—would pale into insignificance by comparison with those which would result from the failure of Operation PERCH. 4 CLY suffered four killed and five wounded, and 1 RB nine killed on the 13th of June. It would seem that virtually all the rest of the Battlegroup became prisoners—the relevant War Diaries speak of seventy-six and ninety-four men 'missing' respectively. Christopher Milner managed to escape.

Some time after 1300 hours Möbius ordered his 1st Company Tigers to advance into Villers-Bocage. They were accompanied by the Panzer Lehr Mk IVs. A description of how the British saw the next moments is given by Lieutenant Colonel Gordon in a citation for Major 'Tiny' French, who commanded C Company of the Queen's:

A report was received that several Mk VI Tiger tanks were moving down the main street towards the square. Major French immediately ordered his Company to disperse into the houses in the side streets which overlooked the main road and to be prepared to take aggressive action. He then personally took a PIAT and together with a small party armed with sticky bombs, went off further into the town in the direction from which the enemy tanks were approaching. He found four Mk VI tanks and one Mk IV in the main street and approached the leading one from a side street to within twenty yards. He fired two rounds with his PIAT while his party threw their sticky bombs. The results of this attack could not be observed but it caused one tank to move forward where it was driven on to the waiting [Queen's] 6 pdr anti-tank guns and the guns of our waiting tanks [B Squadron 4 CLY] and completely destroyed. During this attack one of the enemy tanks blew down a house near which Major French was standing and he was wounded in the leg, but in spite of this he returned to collect his Company and take them to their allotted positions.

Senior SS Sergeant Werner Wendt, a Tiger commander in the 1st Company reported:

There was fire from all corners. We were battling anti-tank guns and infantry. Even today I can still picture SS Second

Lieutenant Lucasius as he was knocked out by close range weapons. He bailed out. His burns looked frightening.

At least one Tiger and one Type IV were knocked out by PIATs and by sticky bombs dropped from upper storey windows or thrown from ground floors. More were claimed by the Queen's anti-tank platoon and B Squadron. In 1979 Möbius told the former Chief of Staff of 12th SS, Hubert Meyer, that his Company withdrew after losing three tanks 'to close range weapons'. Six Tigers and two Mk IVs were found in the town after the battle and the 1st and 2nd SS Tiger Companies suffered a total of ten killed and twelve wounded during the day.

The 1/7 Queen's War Diary says that, following the withdrawal of the Tigers, the three Queen's companies moved to cover the main approaches to Villers-Bocage, together with the Battalion anti-tank guns and B Squadron tanks.

Some time after 1430 hours Brigadier Ekins, commander 131 Brigade, paid a short visit to Lieutenant Colonel Gordon in the town. By this time it was raining. Gordon, a highly experienced officer, told him that enemy infantry were beginning to infiltrate his positions—these were in fact from a scratch force hastily put together by Panzer Lehr, possibly reinforced by the leading elements of the 2nd Panzer Division. Ekins said he thought the situation was hopeless and left, not to be seen again by anyone until the following morning—quite what he was doing in another Brigade commander's sector at all remains a mystery.

At 1525 hours Gordon drove back to the 22 Brigade Tactical Headquarters near Amayé. Brigadier Hinde had reappeared there during the afternoon but seemed reluctant to discuss the rapidly deteriorating situation with his staff or issue positive orders. Gordon explained that unless his Battalion was reinforced it would soon be overwhelmed. He wrote later, 'I don't think Looney quite appreciated that I was rapidly losing control of my companies because so many tank hunting parties were dispersed in the nearby houses'—a situation not helped by the paucity of radios in an infantry battalion at that time. In the meantime General Erskine had finally recognised the urgent need for more British infantry and at 1500 hours he placed another Queen's battalion under Hinde's command. 1/5 Queen's moved forward from the Livry area at 1515 hours.

At 1600 hours B Squadron reported enemy infantry in the south-east corner of Villers-Bocage and at 1650 hours Hinde told Erskine that the position in the town was 'unsatisfactory'. A withdrawal was sanctioned, with the proviso that the high ground just to the west, around Point 174, should be held at all costs.

At 1700 hours, only fifteen minutes before 1/5 Queen's started to arrive in Villers-Bocage, Hinde gave orders for 1/7 Queen's and B Squadron 4 CLY to commence their withdrawal and join what Major 'Boy' Burton, the second-in-command of 1/5 Queen's, described as, 'most of the Armoured Brigade, less a battalion of tanks, the greater part of two armoured reconnaissance units and a Regiment of Royal Horse Artillery' sitting impotently only two miles west of Villers-Bocage.

By 2000 hours 1/7 Queen's and B squadron 4 CLY, together with the rest of 22 Brigade were in position on the high ground to the west of the town which they were forced to defend the following day and evening. 1/7 Queen's suffered 128 casualties in the two days fighting.

At 1200 hours on 14th June, Bucknall decided to withdraw the whole Division to positions north-east of Briquesard during the forthcoming night. In his personal diary[6] he claimed to have received Dempsey's agreement to this withdrawal at 1400 hours. The move was covered by the noise of 300 RAF aircraft which dropped over 1,700 tons of bombs south and east of Villers-Bocage, and on Evrecy where one Tiger of the 3rd Company of the 10st SS Heavy Panzer Battalion was destroyed and three others put out of action. There were twenty-nine casualties including the Company commander wounded and a Knight's Cross holder, SS Second Lieutenant Günther killed.

And so ended the battle of Villers-Bocage. The Germans were in occupation of the town and would remain so for another two months. Chester Wilmot summed up the battle in his book. *The Struggle for Europe* as follows:

Thus the fruits of the initial success, which might have been turned into a striking victory, were handed back to the enemy. Erskine's troops suffered no defeat after the first costly encounter with the single Tiger.

POST MORTEM

Having chronicled the battle, it would seem appropriate to discuss what went wrong, not least because the failure of PERCH inevitably necessiated a series of extremely costly operations to remove the Germans from the Caen sector.

In retrospect it has to be said that the 7th Armoured Division had been asked to carry out a type of operation for which it was untrained and for which its commanders were not mentally tuned—Blitzkrieg. Lieutenant General Dempsey had said on 12th June:

Provided this [the operation] is carried out with real drive and speed, there is a chance that we will get thro' before the front congeals.[7]

And as we have already heard, Montgomery saw it as a potential 'turning point of the battle'. Above all it needed what Monty had specified to his Army in England before D-Day:

To be able to concentrate our armour and push fairly strong armoured columns rapidly inland to secure important ground. . . . Offensive eagerness is not only necessary in the soldier; it is essential in the officer, and especially in the senior officer and commander. Inaction, and a defensive mentality, are criminal in any officer—however senior.[8]

In the event, many of his commanders at every level—company, battalion, brigade, division and corps—failed him, and more importantly failed their men. They displayed none of the panache, drive, imagination or willingness to take risks which this operation demanded. One can only guess at what might have happened if the roles been reversed and men like Kurt Meyer, Jochen Peiper and Max Wünsche had been in command, with their tanks operating, like those of the British, under conditions of total air superiority.

Many excuses have been offered in mitigation of this disaster. One is that the 'bocage' made it difficult and dangerous for the British tanks and gave an advantage to the Germans. In his official report after the battle, Brigadier Hinde said:

> The country on both sides of the main road Villers-Bocage—Caen is much closer than it appears on the map and it was easy for enemy tanks to remain hidden close to the road.

This is an extrordinary statement, as it is a clear criticism of his own command ability and that of his subordinates. If it was true that enemy tanks could easily hide close to the line of advance, then why did he not insist upon proper air or at least ground reconnaissance?

Another reason given for the failure of Operation PERCH is that the 7th Armoured Division lacked sufficient infantry for its task. This argument ignores the fact that most of 1 RB and two battalions of the Queen's remained uncommitted on the critical day and that one complete infantry brigade (151) was in Corps reserve; in fact two infantry brigades of the 49th Infantry Division were also unemployed—they were released to the 50th Division on the night of 13th June. Any of these three infantry brigades could have been allotted to Erskine before his Division set off on its epic task, and the blame for this failure to concentrate sufficient forces at the right place at the right time must be laid at the door of Bucknall, the commander of XXX Corps.

But the major reason given, both at the time and since the war, for the failure of PERCH, was the unexpected arrival of the 2nd Panzer Division on the southern outskirts of Villers-Bocage during the late morning of 13th June. This is a curious argument; first because, as we shall see, 2nd Panzer's tanks were nowhere near Villers-Bocage at this time, and second because, even if *both* the Division's Panzer-Grenadier Regiments had arrived together, they would still have had only the same number of infantry companies as the 7th Armoured Division—sixteen. (Army Panzer Divisions had only four Panzer-Grenadier battalions, unlike those of the Waffen-SS which had six.)

Montgomery wrote to the British Chief of the General Staff in London on 14th June:

Late last evening 2 Pz Div came into the battle. It counter-attacked 7 Armd Div in the Villers-Bocage area and we took some prisoners. A real good dogfight went on all evening.

The men of 22nd Armoured Brigade and the Queen's would hardly have agreed with the last remark, but the whole business of 2nd Panzer is a myth anyway. Only part of the Reconnaissance Battalion and various advance parties arrived on the 13th; when a company of 1/7 Queen's ran into enemy on the outskirts of Villers-Bocage at around 1100 hours, these turned out to be a 2nd Panzer Division staff car with two motor-cycle escorts—hardly the deployment of a Panzer Division advancing to contact! Dietrich's Chief of Staff, Fritz Kraemer, confirmed in his post-war interrogation that the only combat element of 2nd Panzer to arrive in the Caumont sector on 13th June was part of the Reconnaissance Battalion. The fact that there was only minor sniping and a few patrols against the British positions west of Villers-Bocage during the night 13th–14th June is highly significant, as is the XXX Corps Intelligence Summary for the same night:

It seems surprising that at a moment when the enemy had a chance of dealing our troops around Villers a decisive blow, his attack should have been so halt-hearted and ill-timed.

Even Hinde admits in his official report:

During the evening [13th] enemy infantry, mainly south of the road, confined their activities to patrolling and sniping; enemy shelling was negligible.

The simple fact is that neither 2nd Panzer Division nor Panzer Lehr was capable of launching 'a decisive blow' against 'the Desert Rats' on the night of 13th June or on the day of the 14th. In an interview with Milton Shulman, General Heinrich von Lüttwitz, the commander of 2nd Panzer, said that the trains bringing his tanks were hit so many times by Allied aircraft, that they had to finish the journey from Amiens by road, and 'it was not until *18th June* [author's emphasis] that eighty of the 120 tanks that originally started finally limped into the line around Caumont.' Yet the mere suggestion that 2nd Panzer had arrived in the Caumont—Villers-Bocage area was enough, apparently, to frighten most of the senior British commanders including, as we shall see, Montgomery himself.

Even on 14th June, German offensive capablity was very limited. The first attack on the new British positions to the west of the town did not come until 1100 hours; it was from the east and carried out only by infantry. According to the History of Panzer Lehr it was mounted by their reinforced Divisional Reconnaissance group.[9]A second attack developed at around 1930 hours on the southern front manned by 1/5 Queen's and this was almost certainly launched by personnel of 2nd Panzer. They were supported by four Tigers of Möbius's 1st Company. Exaggerated reports of the strength of the second attack—'a brigade of Panzer-Grenadiers on a one battalion front'—led to urgent requests for additional artillery support leading, according to the British Official History, to 160 guns (eighty-four British and seventy-six American 155s) going into action to support the defenders. Even so, reports of eleven German tanks being destroyed and several hundred Germans killed, mainly by artillery, are certainly much exaggerated. One Tiger was damaged and later recovered. In his official report Hinde wrote, 'It is questionable whether the expenditure of artillery and small arms ammunition was justified *by the scale of the enemy's efforts.*' [author's emphasis]. Unfortunately, the call for support from American guns gave the impression that matters were much more serious than they really were and led to a totally false picture being painted in later years. David Eisenhower, Ike's grandson, in his book *Eisenhower at War 1943–1945,* wrote in 1986, 'US V Corps artillery intervention had prevented a rout, but the British had been forced to retreat.'

No, excuses will not do. This was a serious defeat and the real reason for it is clear—the incompetence of the senior commanders. The whole operation was badly set up and, as already mentioned, some of the officers who led it were unprofessional and mentally incapable of carrying it through when unforeseen complications arose. Hinde's initial decision to halt at Livry on the evening of the 12th, instead of advancing the mere 6km to Villers-Bocage, is incomprehensible. Halting was unlikely to confuse anyone—it was inevitable that British troops would turn east and seek the high ground south of Tilly. Hinde's infantry could have done it on their feet before midnight and Villers-Bocage could have been made a fortress before first light, making it a perfect platform for further advance.

But it was when things started to go wrong that the command system really fell apart. Hinde, Ekins and Cranley all appear virtually to have ceased commanding at the most critical times in the battle; but, because their staffs and subordinates thought, correctly, that they were still somewhere in the battle area, they were naturally reluctant to issue orders with which their commanders might disagree. Erskine's failure to use 131 Brigade which, with a complete tank battalion, two infantry battalions and an artillery regiment, was sitting doing nothing of value except 'holding a firm base' between Livry and Torteval from 1100 hours, must be placed in Montgomery's category of 'criminal.' Had the Divisional commander personally moved forward and taken a firm grip on the situation, the results could have been dramatic. If he had visited Hinde's Headquarters near Amayé he would have seen that only half of 22 Brigade had been committed—there were in fact more than enough troops available within his Division to hold on to Villers-Bocage and Point 174, *and* to occupy the high ground at Maisoncelles Pelvey as required in the original plan. According to the 22 Brigade War Diary, at 2130 hours on 13th June, after the withdrawal from Villers-Bocage, the Armoured Brigade still had 155 tanks operational, well over 100 of which had not fired a shot all day—and of course, this figure does not include the Cromwells of the Divisional Armoured Reconnaissance Regiment, the 8H, or the 17 pdrs of the Divisional Anti-Tank Regiment, the Norfolk Yeomanry, which had taken no part in the battle at all. The number of uncommitted infantrymen has already been mentioned.

At the higher level Bucknall, the commander of XXX Corps, did not seem to comprehend that by withdrawing the 7th Armoured Division on the nights of the 13th and 14th, instead of reinforcing or even sacrificing it, he forfeited all chance of Panzer Lehr weakening its front at Tilly, which was clearly its centre of gravity, and so of opening the way for his reinforced 50th Division and reserve Infantry Brigade—in other words, of stretching I SS Panzer Corps, and Panzer Lehr in particular, to a point where it would break. His policy was a negation of Blitzkrieg. One can only wonder once again at what might have happened if the roles had been reversed and a Panzer division had suddenly appeared at the rear of the British front north of Tilly?

It is not surprising that after 13th June neither Montgomery nor Dempsey had any real faith in Erskine or Bucknall; within two months they and Hinde had been sacked and Ekins was no longer serving. Dempsey made his feelings very clear in a post-war interview with Chester Wilmot:

> This attack by 7th Armoured Division should have suc-
> ceeded. My feeling that Bucknall and Erskine would have to
> go started with that failure. . . . If he [Erskine] had carried
> out my orders he would never have been kicked out of
> Villers-Bocage, but by this time 7th Armoured was living on
> its reputation and the whole handling of that battle was a
> disgrace. Their decision to withdraw was made without
> consulting me; it was done by the Corps commander and
> Erskine.[10]

However, we may notice that, whilst he may not have ap-proved the initial withdrawal on the evening of the 13th, he certainly agreed with the subsequent move back on the night of the 14th. His personal diary has the following entry for that day:

> I agreed to 30 Corps' proposal to withdraw leading elements
> of 7 Armd Div from the Villers-Bocage area to the Caumont
> area.[11]

The failure of Operation PERCH and the steadfast defence of the Tilly area by Panzer Lehr caused Montgomery to revise his plans yet again. On 14th June he wrote to the British Chief of Staff, Field Marshal Sir Alan Brooke:

The arrival of 2 Pz Div. . . . puts a different complexion on the problem. . . . I have not yet sufficient strength to be offensive on both flanks of Second Army. . . . I am going to put all my offensive power, ammunition and so on, into the offensive by XXX Corps on the right of Second Army.

As might be expected, the man who caused all the trouble, Michael Wittmann, was awarded Swords to his Knight's Cross for his amazing performance on 13th June and promoted to SS Captain. His citation ended, 'With the count of 13th June, Wittmann has achieved a total number of victories of 138 enemy tanks and 132 anti-tank guns with his personal Panzer.'

We shall hear more of this remarkable man as our story unfolds.

NOTES

1. Wilmot, *The Struggle for Europe*, p. 306. 2. Meyer, Hubert, *The History of the 12th SS Panzer Division Hitlerjugend*, p. 71. 3. Meyer, Kurt, *Grenadiers*, p. 130. 4. Dempsey Diary, PRO WO 285/9. 5. The following account is based on: A. The War Diaries of XXX Corps, 7 Armd Div, 22 Armd Bde, 131 Inf Bde, B. 4 CLY, 1/5, 1/6, 1/7 Queen's, 1 RB; C. Lt Col Gordon's personal account dated 18 Jun 44; D. Helmut Ritgen's *Die Geschichte der Panzer Lehr Division in Westen 1944–1945*; E. Hubert Meyer's *History of the 12th SS Panzer Division* Hitlerjugend; Sepp Dietrich's citation for Wittmann; F. Kraemer, *I SS Panzer Corps in the West*, MS C-024, IWM, London, AL 2727/1–2. G. Lt Col Gordon's citation for Maj French dated 17 Jun 44. H. Brigadier Hinde's official report on 22 Armd Bde operations 6–15 Jun 44; I. Lindsay and Johnson's unpublished *History of the 7th Armoured Division*, dated Sep 45; J. Carlo D'Este, *Decision in Normandy*; K. Personal discussions and correspondence with Maj Gen Gordon and various officers and soldiers of 1/7 Queen's, Maj Milner of 1 RB, the Brigade Major of 22 Armd Bde Lt Col Joe Lever, Capt Dyas and other members of 4 CLY, and Brig Hinde's personal driver. 6. Bucknall Diary, IWM 80/30/1 (8). 7. Dempsey Diary, PRO WO 285/9. 8. Montgomery, *The Memoirs of Field Marshal Montgomery*, pp. 243–244. 9. Ritgen, *Die Geschichte der Panzer Lehr Division im Westen 1944–1945*, p. 138. 10. D'Este, *Decision in Normandy*, p. 196. 11. Dempsey Diary, PRO WO 285/9

12 | 14th to 24th June—
Lull Before the Storm

The commander of the 12th SS Panzer Division HJ, Fritz Witt, was killed by a shrapnel wound to the face on the morning of 14th June at his Headquarters in Venoix, near Caen. At the age of thirty-six, this holder of the Knight's Cross with Oak Leaves, German Cross in Gold and the Iron Cross 1st and 2nd Class, had fallen victim to naval gunfire. Dietrich immediately appointed the senior remaining commander in 12th SS, Kurt Meyer, to succeed him and SS Lieutenant Colonel Karl-Heinz Milius took over the 25th SS Panzer-Grenadier Regiment. He was replaced in the 3rd Battalion by a Knight's Cross holder, Wehrmacht Captain Fritz Steger. The Divisional Command Post was quickly moved to Verson, 4km to the southwest and only 3km from Dietrich's own Headquarters, which was surprisingly far forward, at Baron. It should be noted that the radio trucks of these Headquarters were always located well away from the Headquarters itself, sometimes as far as 2km away, and then connected by telephone cables. Despite this, as we have already seen, Allied intercept units still managed to locate many German command posts.

With the situation in the Panzer Lehr sector becoming increasingly critical, Witt had already asked for permission to shorten his line and withdraw some of his forward elements, particularly Mohnke's 26th SS Panzer-Grenadier Regiment in the area of Cristot, Brouay and le Mesnil-Patry, and Bremer's 12th SS Reconnaissance Battalion, which was holding a 3km frontage south of les Haut Vents—a task for which it was neither structured nor equipped. The request had initially been refused but, after further urging by Meyer, it was finally agreed that a new, shorter, line could be adopted on the night 15th-16th June in conformity with a small withdrawal by Panzer Lehr. The move back went undetected and the new front connected with the 25th Regiment at Franqueville and then ran from St Mauvieu, along the south side of the Mue stream and then west, about 1000m north of the main road, to Fontenay. The units of Mohnke's Regiment and the HJ were deployed from east to west as follows: 1st Battalion, 12th SS

Pioneer Battalion, 2nd Battalion, 12th SS Reconnaissance Battalion, 3rd Battalion. The Mk IV tanks of the 2nd SS Panzer Battalion were positioned across the whole front in anti-tank ambush positions and all the Panthers withdrawn to the Noyers area as a reserve force. Mines were laid on the exits from le Mesnil-Patry and the whole Divisional front was now well balanced and reasonably strong. Meyer's biggest worries were the total absence of any replacements for the 1,149 casualties the HJ had suffered to date and the fact that he had only fifty-two Mk IVs, thirty-eight Panthers, ten Wespe (105mm SP guns) and five Hummel (150mm SP guns) combat ready on 16th June.[1] The devastating effects of Allied air power and the seemingly limitless numbers of artillery rounds raining down on their positions were finally beginning to drain the morale of his soldiers. Even the LAH veterans said they had never experienced anything like it before—not even in Russia. Meyer described the problem thus, after a briefing at his Command Post:

> I see worried faces during the situation report. Without talking about it openly we know we are approaching a catastrophe. . . . Faced with the enemy's enormous naval and air superiority, we can predict the breakdown of the defensive front. The tactical patchwork of battles has cost us the irreplaceable blood of our best soldiers and is destroying precious material. We are already surviving on subsistance levels. Up to now we have received neither a single replacement for our comrades, wounded or killed in action, nor one tank or gun.[2]

No sooner had the HJ completed its withdrawal on the 16th than two battalions of the British 49th Infantry Division, 1/4 King's Own Yorkshire Light Infantry (1/4 KOYLI) and 11th Royal Scots Fusiliers (11 RSF), supported by a troop of the 24L, launched an attack to seize Brouay and Cristot and the 3rd Canadian Division advanced on le Mesnil-Patry; the whole attack was supported by 250 artillery pieces, naval gunfire and fighter-bombers. Not surprisingly it succeeded, and if the Germans had not already withdrawn they would undoubtedly have suffered heavy casualties.

The following two days saw intense fighting—in and around the dominating Parc de Boislonde, 1000m north of Fontenay—between Mohnke's men, supported by a few Mk IV tanks, and troops of the British 49th Infantry Division, particularly the 6th and 7th Battalions the Duke of Wellington's Regiment (DWR), and a troop of tanks from the 24L, part of the 8th Armoured Brigade. At the end of the period 12th SS had suffered 151 casualties, including forty killed,[3] but the British had lost four tanks and 324 men. 6 DWR was so badly mauled and dispirited, having lost 236 men, that it was returned to England for reorganisation. A full report on its state on 30th June can be read in the Public Record Office—it makes sad and disturbing reading.

On the same day, 18th June, the British 50th Infantry Division finally captured Tilly. Rather than expose the flank of Mohnke's Regiment, Meyer ordered the abandonment of the Parc de Boislonde and so it became a no-man's-land. He had decided to hold the northern half of Fontenay with Mk IVs supported by Panzer-Grenadiers in ambush positions and dispose the bulk of Mohnke's 3rd SS Panzer-Grenadiers in the southern half. Thus it would remain for a further week.

During the whole period from 8th to 24th June the front to the north and north-west of Caen, in the sector of the 25th SS Panzer-Grenadier Regiment and 21st Panzer Division, remained relatively quiet. The non-arrival of German infantry divisions meant that there was still no possibility of relieving any, or even part, of the committed Panzer divisions, and it would be some days yet before the bulk of the reinforcing Panzer divisions arrived. General Paul Hausser's II SS Panzer Corps, comprising the 9th and 10th SS Panzer Divisions, had left Poland on 12th June but could not be expected before the 25th and, as we shall see, the Leibstandarte was having an extremely difficult time moving from Belgium. Only the 2nd SS Panzer Division DR had reached the battle area at St Lô, and that was held in Army Group reserve. As yet therefore there was no possibility of launching a major counter-attack.

It will be remembered that Montgomery had decided, following the Villers-Bocage débâcle, to launch a single sledgehammer blow on the west side of Caen. The offensive, to be known as operation EPSOM, was originally scheduled for 23rd June but, quite unexpectedly, in the early hours of 19th June a violent summer storm developed in the Channel and lasted three days. The interruption to the landing of men and supplies meant that EPSOM had to be postponed. The scale of the interruption can be judged by the following figures: in the period 15th to 18th June, before the storm, the British landed 15,774 soldiers, 2,965 vehicles and 10,666 tons of stores; in the period of the storm, 19th to 22nd, the figures dropped to 3,982 men, 1,375 vehicles and only 4,286 tons of stores.[4] As well as causing a postponement to Montgomery's planned offensive, the storm had another positive effect for the Germans—the poor flying weather allowed them to carry out resupply and troop movements without fear of attack by fighter-bombers.

A combination of all these factors meant that, in the short term, neither side was capable of serious attack in the Caen sector and this led to an uneasy lull in the fighting.

In Belgium on 17th June the 1st SS Panzer Division LAH loaded on to trains at Eeklo, Maldegem, St Kruis and Moerbeke stations.[5] But not all the Division's units were ready to move—the 5th SS Flak Company had no vehicles and remained in air defence along the Albert canal, while the 1st SS Reconnaissance Company, 3rd SS Panzer Artillery Battalion, all except one company of the Werfer Battalion and even some elements of Peiper's 1st SS Panzer Regiment, had to be left behind.[6]

Owing to incessant air attacks the trains were directed further and further east. They eventually arrived in a concentration area around Reims, Château Thierry, Villers Cotteréels, Soissons and Laon, from where the journey had to be continued by road at night to another assembly area at Dreux, Evreux and l'Aigle. It was to be 6th July before the whole Division reached the battlefield.

On 23rd June SS Major General Teddy Wisch's advanced Headquarters set up at la Bagottière, 20km south-east of Caen, and when the first LAH minor units arrived they were positioned between Caen and Falaise in the Fôret-de-Cinglais.[7]

NOTES
1. Meyer, Hubert, *The History of the 12th SS Panzer Division Hitler-jugend*, p. 78. 2. Meyer, Kurt, *Grenadiers*, p. 134. 3. Meyer, Hubert, op. cit., p. 85. 4. Ellis, *Victory in the West, Vol I, The Battle of Normandy*, p. 274. 5. Lehmann & Tiemann, *The Leibstandarte IV/I*, p. 115. 6. Ibid. 7. Ibid., p. 118.

13 25th June to 1st July—Operation EPSOM and the Battle of the Odon

The aim of Operation EPSOM was to cross the Odon and Orne rivers and capture the high ground astride the Caen-Falaise road, north-east of Bretteville-sur-Laize, thus isolating Caen and exposing the German right flank in Normandy. It was to be carried out by three Corps—Phase I, code-named MARTLET, was to begin on 25th June with XXX Corps capturing the commanding ground around Rauray and then, after taking Noyers, exploiting south to Aunay-sur-Odon. With its right flank thus protected, the recently landed VIII Corps was then, in Phase II, to carry out the main thrust on 26th June through the positions of the 3rd Canadian Infantry Division. As the operation progressed I Corps was to eliminate the Germans to the north of Caen and, after capturing Carpiquet airfield, to clear the city itself. There was to be a concurrent thrust out of the airborne bridgehead east of the Orne. The whole plan was therefore highly ambitious. From a tactical point of view it was flawed, in that the main attack by the three divisions of VIII Corps—two infantry and one armoured—would be on a very narrow section of the front (6km) between the Carpiquet airfield and Rauray, in column, using the same centre-line and having to fight in parts through extremely difficult country. Whilst the early stages of the attack would be through hedgeless fields of standing corn, the intermediate stage would be 'bocage', leading to the thickly wooded valley of the Odon. After that the ground rose to a commanding ridge south of the river, before dropping steeply again to the Orne which itself was dominated by high ground to its east. All the important roads, railways and rivers ran across the line of advance. It is surprising that the senior commanders involved in this operation did not realise that full achievement of the mission, even against a weak enemy, was almost certainly beyond the capabilities of their troops and equipment.

General Sir Richard O'Connor's VIII Corps was a very large one, having been reinforced by two tank brigades and a specialist tank battalion—it numbered some 60,000 men and 600 tanks and was to be supported by the fire of over 900 guns, three naval cruisers and the fighter-bombers of the Second Tactical Air Force. It will not have escaped the reader's notice that this awesome force was to be directed, in the main, at the left half of the 12th SS Panzer Division HJ.

Sepp Dietrich knew that the Leibstandarte had been allotted to his I SS Panzer Corps and that the 16th Luftwaffe Field and 276th Infantry Divisions were due to relieve his Panzer Divisions. He was also aware that none of these forces was likely to arrive before a predictable British onslaught on his tired troops.

There is some confusion over the number of casualties sustained by the HJ before the opening of Operation EPSOM and the whole subject of German casualties will be discussed in more detail at the end of this chapter. Suffice it to say at this stage that, in the opinion of this author, this confusion is due mainly to exaggerated figures quoted by German generals and apologists after the war, attempting to excuse their defeats and make their efforts sound even more heroic. Kurt Meyer, as we know, talks in his memoirs of his Division already 'surviving at subsistence levels' and Fritz Kraemer, in his post-war interrogation,[1] gives estimates of only thirty to forty men left in each of the 12th SS Panzer-Grenadier companies and a mere thirty tanks left in the whole Division on 20th June. This gives an entirely false picture, not least because there were in fact more tanks combat ready on the eve of Operation EPSOM than there had been on 16th June—fifty-eight Mk IVs and forty-four Panthers. There were in addition an estimated eighteen Mk IVs and ten Panthers under repair and expected to be operational in a short time. The Division also had 233 SPWs and scout cars and seventeen heavy anti-tank guns combat ready, with forty-four and eleven respectively under short-term repair.[2] Nevertheless, it is true that by 25th June some of

the SS Panzer-Grenadier battalions and the HJ Reconnaissance
and Pioneer Battalions had suffered badly.

25TH JUNE

It is important to understand the deployment of the 12th SS
Panzer Division before the battle. The Fontenay sector was
held by the 3rd SS Panzer-Grenadier Battalion of Mohnke's
26th Regiment, supported by his Regimental Reconnaissance
and Pioneer Companies, and the 8th SS Panzer (Mk IV) Company. In Fontenay itself strongpoints had been set up in many
of the damaged or destroyed houses. To the west, a battalion of
Panzer Lehr was in position south of St Pierre-sur-Seulles. The
St Mauvieu sector was held, from left to right, by the 2nd SS
Panzer-Grenadier Battalion, the Divisional 12th SS Pioneer
Battalion (north of Cheux), and the 1st SS Panzer-Grenadier
Battalion with its Headquarters in the Château la Mare (to as
far east as the Caen-Bayeux railway line), backed by the other
four Mk IV SS Panzer companies in the sequence 6th, 5th, 7th,
and 9th. These had all prepared alternative positions. Three SP
and three towed artillery batteries were also located behind
Mohnke's Regiment. One eminent military historian has suggested that the presence of the Divisional Pioneer Battalion in
a forward defensive position was a sign of having to 'make do
and mend'. Not so—unlike Allied engineers who, as already
stated in Chapter IV, were engineers first and alternative infantrymen second, German pioneers were looked upon as elite
infantrymen and were specially trained in street fighting and
the construction of sophisticated defensive positions. It is also
worth noting that because the Germans, in order to allow
freedom of movement for their armour, did not believe in
extensive minefields, and because they always aimed to capture
bridges intact rather than build them, there was far less engineer work for their pioneers to do than there was for their
Allied counterparts.

Kurt Meyer's previous command, the 25th SS Panzer-Grenadier Regiment, now under SS Lieutenant Colonel Milius, was
still holding the front from Franqueville to Epron in well reinforced positions. The 3rd SS Panzer Artillery Battalion, with its
heavy 150mm guns and 100mm cannons, was in support.

In reserve, to the north of Noyers, Meyer had Bremer's 12th SS Reconnaissance Battalion and Jürgensen's 1st SS Panzer (Panther) Battalion. Significantly the III Flak Corps with three Regiments, comprising some sixty to eighty 88mm guns, had taken up positions between St André-sur-Orne and Aunay-sur-Odon, behind the HJ and Panzer Lehr Divisions. The 4th Flak Regiment of this Corps was in the area of Mouen, Noyers and Evrecy.

The idea that Meyer's Division had prepared a classic German defence position, with Battle Outposts, Advance and Main Positions is wrong. The number of casualties already received and the width of the front, 18km, precluded any chance of creating a position with any real depth. Advance and Main positions were therefore combined, more or less on the line of the Caen-Fontenay road, and there were no HJ troops on the Odon itself or to its south. Only the 88mm guns of the 4th Flak Regiment were to be found there.

At 0415 hours on 25th June the Allied artillery barrage by 250 guns opened up and shortly afterwards Major General 'Bubbles' Barker's 49th (West Riding) Infantry Division, with the 8th Armoured Brigade under command, set out on the MARTLET part of Operation EPSOM, its first full-scale operation of the war. The Division was made up mainly of men from Yorkshire but it also contained two Scottish and two East Anglian battalions. It had been given an additional artillery battalion and anti-tank battery, and had the fire of five more artillery battalions and parts of two anti-aircraft brigades, firing in a ground role, on call. It was also to be supported by fighter-bombers as needed and suppressive fire was to be brought down on suspected strongpoints, such as Juvigny, Tessel and Cheux, on the flanks of its advance. Parts of 146th Infantry Brigade, supported by 24L tanks, moved towards Bas de Fontenay on the right flank and elements of 147th Brigade with the Nottinghamshire Yeomanry (tanks) towards Fontenay itself on the left. The 70th Brigade and the tanks of the 4/7 DG were kept in reserve.

The artillery produced a 'wall of fire' behind which the infantry advanced on foot. With daylight came a thick ground mist which reduced visibility to as little as five metres and led to general confusion—the tanks halted and although the infantry plodded on without them, few knew where they were. Air support was out of the question.

Despite the delays and chaos, the 4th Lincolnshire and Hallamshire Battalions of the 146th Brigade secured Bas de Fontenay and the western part of Fontenay by 0915 hours and around midday the tanks caught up. By early afternoon the 1st/4th Battalion, King's Own Yorkshire Light Infantry (¼ KOYLI) had reached the spur of ground north of Vendes and occupied what were called the Tessel woods. These attacks cost the British 263 men killed and wounded, but their success posed a serious threat to the west flank of Mohnke's 26th SS Panzer-Grenadier Regiment. In order to rectify the situation SS Major Olboeter personally led the small reserve of his 3rd SS Panzer-Grenadier Battalion, supported by Mk IV tanks from the 8th SS Panzer Company, in an unsuccessful counterattack to secure his flank and clear the Tessel woods. A disturbing account of the fighting was given by the commander of C Company ¼ KOYLI in, 'Worm's Eye View. The Recollections of Lewis Keeble.'

It was a hell of a day. . . . The first shock was that this advance was supposed to be protected by smoke, but we were utterly exposed. . . . H-hour was postponed. Two members of the company couldn't stand it and shot themselves in the foot in quick succession. . . . The fire support, similar to or even greater than for Cristot. More of it behind the Start-Line than in front of it. . . . Off we go, the blast from a shell knocks me over, but only one little flesh wound. . . . Where are the boys? Not here. I go back—'come on'. Through the hedge again, still no boys. Back again—'COME ON!' They came. Through more hedges. Up to the edge of the wood. Bloody murder; people dropping dead. . . . Hitlerjugend prisoners. . . . During the attack one of my platoons ran away and was brought back at pistol point by Tug Wilson, my second-in-command. . . . We were being counter-attacked by infantry and two tanks. The same platoon ran away again. . . . Eventually it all died down. The enemy retired, leaving two knocked out tanks and quite a lot of dead. . . . I was sure they'd be back and stood to the whole Company all night. . . . But they didn't come.

The story on the Fontenay-le-Pesnel front was very different. The initial attack was again bedevilled by the mist and despite intense fighting throughout the day, 11 RSF was unable to take the village. Even after a further Battalion, 7 DWR, supported by tanks, anti-tank guns and heavy mortars, was thrown in as late as 2100 hours in the evening, it could not be cleared; fighting continued throughout the night. Olboeter's 3rd SS Panzer-Grenadiers, supported by the Regimental Reconnaissance, Pioneer and Infantry Gun Companies, and stiffened by the Mk IVs of Prinz's 2nd SS Panzer Battalion whenever needed, would not give way and it soon became obvious that there was no chance of capturing the high ground around Rauray, as required by the British plan, before dawn on the 26th. The RSF lost 201 men in the day's fighting, and the Germans claimed five British tanks knocked out. Kurt Meyer gives a graphic, if rather dramatic description of the battle of Fontenay as he witnessed it:

Screaming rounds tear the last buildings to pieces. . . . The smoke of exploding projectiles obscures the view. It is impossible to determine the main defensive line. The artillery drums and drums. The village is like a simmering cauldron. Heavy shells drill deep into the earth and leave smoking craters behind. . . . I jump into a crater and watch the enemy [Nottinghamshire Yeomanry] tanks attack Fontenay. Firing continuously, feeling secure, the steel colossi are moving slowly towards the rubble of Fontenay. Our anti-tank guns are destroyed by the crazy artillery fire. The Grenadiers hold their Panzerfausts tightly. Panzerfaust against tank! What a contrast! And what a heroic spirit this contrast reveals! The first tank is smoking now. . . . The forward enemy tanks are fighting the Grenadiers in the rubble and the tanks further back have not yet noticed our tanks. . . . The tank versus tank action starts. There are casualties on both sides. Thick, black, oily smoke rolls over the battlefield. . . .

Battle weary Grenadiers wave to me yelling out jokes, their eyes shining. It mystifies me where these youngsters are getting the strength to live through such a storm of steel. They assure me again and again that they will defend the rubble to the last round and will hold their positions against all-comers.[3]

Major General Barker, commanding the 49th Division wrote in his diary:

Unfortunately the Boche took a lot of turning out of Fontenay and was in some strongly fortified houses at the east end which the Battalion in that sector couldn't clear. In the evening the Boche had luckily withdrawn after the hammering we gave them.[4]

Dietrich and Meyer were acutely conscious of the gap that had opened up between the HJ and Panzer Lehr Divisions—the way south through Noyers to Villers-Bocage and Aunay looked dangerously vulnerable. Accordingly, at about 1400 hours, Max Wünsche, commander 12th SS Panzer Regiment, was ordered to plug the gap and link up with Panzer Lehr. He was to use three Panther companies of Jürgensen's 1st Battalion, supported by Panzer-Grenadiers from Olboeter's 3rd SS Battalion and Bremer's 12th SS Reconnaissance Battalion. It is concerning this stage that we hear in various regimental histories of encounters with 'Tiger' tanks. Even the Divisional commander wrote in his diary for the day:

We knocked out six Tigers, two Panthers and four other tanks and took quite a few prisoners—all first class troops of 12 SS PZ Div. . . . These Tiger and Panthers are a nuisance.[5]

In reality there were no Tiger Is engaged in opposing the British in the early stages of operations MARTLET or EPSOM—the HJ had none and Panzer Lehr's original eight were not employed on the extreme right of the Division; it has to be realised, however, that the power of German propaganda was such that all Allied soldiers expected to see a Tiger every time they heard the sound of tanks and, although in both cases much smaller, the Mk IV did look similar to a Tiger I and the Panther to a King Tiger.

By 2230 hours KG Wünsche was 500m from the Fontenay-Juvigny road and contact was established with Olboeter's men in Fontenay. Although it had not reached the original line and had lost a few tanks, the KG had managed to restore the situation in the HJ sector but, despite the loan of the 12th SS and I SS Corps Escort Companies to Panzer Lehr, the gap on that Division's right flank remained. Dietrich knew he would have to give some ground and he pulled his line back to south of the Fontenay-Juvigny road, giving up Fontenay itself (as mentioned by General Barker) and the Tessel woods. The 12th SS forward positions in this sector now ran from north of le Haut du Bosq, through Rauray, to le Manoir from where a link was established with Panzer Lehr at Vendes.

At the end of the day the HJ still held the essential ground; it had cost them 188 men[6] but the British VIII Corps would have to advance in the morning with an open flank. It seemed to the Allied commanders that Phase I of EPSOM had failed. In essence this was true, but of course Dietrich and Meyer had no idea that the main attack was yet to come and their eyes were fixed on their vulnerable western flank where they expected further attacks from the area of the Tessel woods on the 26th. Dietrich therefore ordered a counter-attack for the morning of 26th June by both 12th SS and Panzer Lehr, with the aim of restoring the original line from Fontenay to Juvigny. Meyer complained that he had insufficient forces for the task and was initially promised the Tigers of the 101st SS Heavy Panzer Battalion; in the event they could not be assembled in time and Meyer had to fall back on his own resources. According to Hubert Meyer,[7] the 12th SS Chief of Staff, the attack was to be made with all the Division's Panther and Mk IV companies except the 9th, which remained in ambush positions to the west of Carpiquet airfield. Infantry support, particularly for clearing the Tessel woods, was to be provided by the unfortunate Olboeter's 3rd SS Panzer-Grenadiers and Bremer's SS Reconnaissance Battalion. This strong force moved to its forming-up area in heavy rain during the late hours of the night 25th–26th June, exposing the other two Battalions of

Wilhelm Mohnke's 26th SS Panzer-Grenadier Regiment to the
onslaught of one armoured and two infantry divisions. But,
unknown to the Germans, the 49th Infantry Division had also
been ordered to attack again on the morning of the 26th to
cover the flank of the main attack by VIII Corps.

26TH JUNE

The British attack on the left flank of the HJ front was
carried out by the 1st Battalion Tyneside Scottish with tanks of
the 4/7 DG. Their task was to capture Tessel-Bretteville and le
Manoir and then to secure the vital ground at Rauray. The
right flank of this attack was to be supported by the 12th
Battalion, King's Royal Rifle Corps (KRRC) and the 24L from
the Tessel woods. These moves coincided precisely with those
of Wünsche's KG counter-attacking from Rauray toward the
same area—the two forces inevitably met head-on. Kurt Meyer
observed this armoured clash from the village of Rauray where
he and Wünsche had gone to oversee the advance of the German force. He described it thus:

> A bitterly contested tank versus tank action develops. The
> hedgerows, difficult to see through, don't allow our tanks to
> take advantage of their guns' longer range. Lack of infantry
> is an especial disadvantage. Intense artillery fire makes co-
> operation enormously difficult and effective command and
> control virtually impossible. . . . The awful columns of
> oily smoke hang in the sky again. Each column means a
> tank's grave. . . . It starts to rain, thank God. We are now
> protected from the fighter-bombers. . . . A runner from
> the 2nd Battalion (Mk IV) rushes up to me and shouts,
> 'Tanks side by side on the Battalion's right flank!' . . . This
> is the major attack I expected! The corner-stone of the Ger-
> man front in Normandy [Caen] is now at stake![8]

This account was written long after the event and with the
benefit of hindsight. Even so, it is an accurate description in
that the British VIII Corps had indeed started its major thrust
south from Norrey and le Mesnil-Patry. Meyer acted
promptly—he halted Wünsche's counter-attack, made him responsible for the defence of Rauray and ordered the Mk IV

Panzer companies to return as quickly as possible to their ambush positions behind the main body of Mohnke's 26th SS Panzer-Grenadier Regiment centred on Cheux and St Mauvieu—right in the path of VIII Corps. Meanwhile he returned to his Divisional Headquarters at Verson, where he was made fully aware of the strength of the British attack. In his memoirs he made clear his dissatisfaction with the way he was required, by Dietrich, to fight the battle:

> Corps [I SS Panzer] can only give one answer. 'Positions must be defended to the last cartridge! We have to fight for time. II SS Panzer Corps is on the way to the front.'
>
> As so often in the past, command is being conducted according to tactical and not strategic considerations. Important decisions are not taken. The system of elastic defence is rejected. We have no other choice than to sell our lives as dearly as possible.[9]

The opening artillery barrage by 344 field and medium guns to prepare the way for the attack by VIII Corps commenced at 0730 hours. Even the British soldiers, picking their way under heavy combat loads through shattered villages like Bretteville-d'Orgueilleuse and Norrey on their way to the Start-Line, found it awesome:

> Between the rain showers we watched the reflection of the gun fire from the low clouds. The horizon was trembling and a thousand eerie lightnings criss-crossed the night sky. For a long time we watched in silence. Then, someone said what we were all thinking, 'We have to go into that!' Our breathing became a little faster, our hearts were beating a little harder. Those eighteen-year-olds of the Hitlerjugend Division, strong in their youthful trustfulness and youthful fire, were selling their lives at a high price.[10]

The weather in England on 26th June was so bad that almost no aircraft took off to support the ground troops. Only the Spitfires, Typhoons and Mustangs of Air Vice-Marshal Harry Broadhurst's 83 Group, based in Normandy, were able to take part and their 500 or so missions were severely disrupted by low cloud and ground mist. As the day wore on the rain became torrential.

Behind the artillery barrage, which advanced 90m every three minutes, Major General MacMillan's 15th Scottish Division, with the lumbering Churchills of the 31st Tank Brigade under command, set off. The 44th (Lowland) Brigade, with 9 RTR less a squadron, advanced on the left, directed on St Mauvieu and, on the right, Brigadier Barber's 46th (Highland) Brigade with 7 RTR was tasked with capturing Cheux and the high ground to its south and le Haut du Bosq. Specialist tanks and medium machine-gun companies from 1st Middlesex accompanied both Brigades. It was then intended to seize the crossing over the Odon with Brigadier Machintosh-Walker's 227th (Highland) Brigade and a squadron of 9 RTR tanks.

For nearly every Scot it was his first action. The idea of two infantry brigades advancing in line is impressive—but, as John Keegan correctly points out in his book *Six Armies in Normandy,* no commander puts everything 'in the shop window', and in reality not more than twenty-four platoons, each of about thirty-five men, 800 in all, led the attack.

True to their training the young Waffen-SS soldiers, in their cleverly camouflaged and carefully prepared positions, allowed the creeping artillery barrage and first lines of Scottish infantry to pass over them. Then they opened fire, causing havoc among their attackers. Minefields, carefully laid by the 12th SS Pioneers to the south of le Mesnil-Patry, delayed and halted the tanks—7 RTR alone lost nine tanks[11], and the men of the 9th Cameronians soon lost the protection of the artillery barrage as they fell behind to deal with their ferocious enemy. As Chester Wilmot aptly described it, 'The troops of the 12th SS. . . . fought with a tenacity and a ferocity seldom equalled and never excelled during the whole campaign.'[12]

The situation was not helped by the fact that radio communications between the tanks and infantry broke down and every time a rifle shot rang out it was assumed to be a sniper; a dreadful fear of this type of enemy soon developed—the War Diary of the Gordons even talks about 'sniper fever'. Lieutenant General H. G. Martin's *History of the 15th Scottish Division* has this to say on the subject:

Enemy snipers had survived the barrage in plenty in the high corn. . . . Light machine guns, too, and mortars kept coming to life everywhere. The right forward company of the Cameronians ran into particularly stiff opposition and had all its officers hit but one. That day the mopping up of snipers had been made the responsibility of reserve platoons and companies, who were thus diverted from their main job of maintaining the momentum of the attack. Subsequently this arrangement was to be changed.

In most cases the 'culprit' was no more than a Panzer-Grenadier firing his normal weapon from a standard, but carefully prepared, defensive position. Much of the confusion was due to the fact that in the British army snipers were issued with camouflaged smocks. In the Waffen-SS, unlike the rest of the German army, Panzer-Grenadiers normally wore camouflaged jackets. It is significant that when the twenty-nine-year-old Lieutenant Colonel Michael Carver, later to be Field Marshal the Lord Carver, took over the 4th Armoured Brigade on 27th June, he gave orders that all talk of 'snipers' was to cease and they were to be referred to as 'isolated enemy riflemen'.[13]

The whole of the open, undulating and sodden battlefield was swept by fire from Wünsche's Panthers on the high ground at Rauray, and from SS Panzer-Grenadiers in the villages and woods to the north of the Odon. The importance of Rauray cannot be over-emphasized—as usual Meyer and Wünsche had secured the vital ground. German artillery was also very effective, particularly the 88s of the Flak Regiment firing from the Odon valley. Despite this bitter resistance, by 1130 hours Lieutenant Colonel Campbell's 2nd Glasgow Highlanders had reached but not cleared Cheux—pockets of resistance remained. It cost them twelve officers and nearly 200 men to capture and hold on to the village. By midday the Cameronians, even after hand-to-hand fighting and the loss of 131 men, had only managed to clear the northern half of le Haut du Bosq.

Meanwhile on Brigadier Money's 44th Lowland Brigade's front it had taken all day for the 8th Royal Scots to clear la Gaule and for 6 RSF to get into St Mauvieu. The Royal Scots suffered 110 casualties and, according to the 141st Regiment War Diary, three flame-throwing Churchill tanks were lost eliminating the last defenders of St Mauvieu. Mohnke's men counter-attacked twice but the Scots held on to the village. The RSF War Diary recorded twenty-one killed, 113 wounded and nine missing in the day's fighting.

On the left flank, Wünsche's Panthers and a few men of Bremer's SS Reconnaissance Battalion were heavily engaged in halting the tanks of 4/7 DG and 24L and the infantry of the Tyneside Scottish and 12 KRRC in their attempted thrusts from the direction of the Tessel woods. A separate, but supporting, attack by the 1st Nottinghamshire Yeomanry and 7 DWR, followed later by 11 DLI, from Fontenay towards Rauray was also stopped by the 6th SS Panzer Company returning to its original positions.

On the right flank, the 1st SS Panzer-Grenadier Battalion, although it had lost St Mauvieu except for a few strongpoints by midday, was still in position to the east and north-east of the village, with the 9th SS Panzer Company dug in behind it covering Carpiquet airfield. Contact with Müller's 12th SS Pioneers south of Cheux had been lost, that Battalion having been overrun by the 7th Battalion Seaforth Highlanders and tanks of 7 RTR—three Churchills went up in flames in the process.

The 2nd SS Panzer-Grenadier Battalion had also been forced back from its positions between Cheux and Fontenay. But once again Mk IVs of the 5th and 8th SS Panzer Companies, returning from KG Wünsche, had stopped the advance of 7 RTR at and to the west of le Haut du Bosq.

With the 15th Scottish Division now poised on a line from St Mauvieu to Cheux, the main threat as Meyer saw it was to Mouen and Verson and he pleaded with Dietrich to send reinforcements. The 3rd Tiger Company from the 101st SS Heavy Panzer Battalion was forthcoming and moved in the early evening to Grainville, just 2km to the west of Colleville. Kraemer also sent a message saying that Panzer and assault gun companies were being attached from 21st Panzer, which like the HJ's own 25th SS Panzer-Grenadier Regiment had not been involved in the main attack. He then, most sensibly, moved Dietrich's Headquarters to a new location 3km south-east of Baron.

Kurt Meyer's worries about Mouen and Verson turned out to be correct. Shortly after midday, O'Connor ordered 'Pip' Roberts to send his 11th Armoured Division tanks through the 15th Scottish Division to seize the crossings over the Odon. The Shermans of the 2nd Fife and Forfar Yeomanry were to advance via le Haut du Bosq and Grainville to the Gavrus bridges and those of the 23rd Hussars (23H) through Colleville to the one at Tourmauville. A Squadron of the Divisional Armoured Reconnaissance Regiment, the 2nd Northamptonshire Yeomanry, was to lead. However, since the tanks had no way of talking to the 15th Scottish infantry through which they would have to pass, their close support would be limited to a single motor battalion—8 RB. An additional problem lay in Cheux which, with major elements of two Divisions now trying to get through it, was a complete bottleneck, choked with rubble. As General Martin put it in his *History of the 15th Scottish Division*:

> What little space there was left in the lanes of Cheux seemed to be filled by our own tanks, closed down [against German artillery and mortar fire] and deaf to all appeals. No one who was in Cheux that morning is likely to forget the confusion.

It was after 1400 hours by the time the Reconnaissance Squadron of the 11th Armoured Division reached the high ground to the south of the village. Shortly afterwards it lost two Cromwells and the remainder were withdrawn. Similarly, when the Shermans of the 2nd Fife and Forfar Yeomanry tried to move to the west of Cheux they became involved with Mk IVs of Prinz's 2nd SS Panzer Battalion and were halted in le Haut du Bosq with the loss of four tanks. They were to lose another five before the day was out. The tanks of the 23H, having bypassed St Mauvieu, ran into trouble as soon as they tried to cross the crest south of Cheux. Four Shermans went up in flames—the victims of at least one Tiger of the 101st SS Heavy Panzer Battalion sited north of Grainville.

At 1800 hours MacMillan ordered his reserve 227th (Highland) Brigade to try to clear a way for the armour. But the severe congestion in Cheux, coupled with the Panthers at Rauray and the Mk IVs of the 5th and 7th SS Panzer Companies, soon checked the advance of Lieutenant Colonel Young's 10th Highland Light Infantry (HLI) on the right flank, and when tanks of 9 RTR and men of Lieutenant Colonel Colville's 2nd Gordon Highlanders (Gordons) finally reached the high ground south of the village, still in torrential rain, they came under sustained fire from Milius's 15th SS Reconnaissance Company, and from two Panzer companies and some assault guns of the 21st Panzer Division which had arrived, as promised by Kraemer, just in the nick of time. Despite this fire, one company of Gordons managed to reach Colleville, on the Caen—Villers-Bocage railway line by 2200 hours; but it was isolated and when 9 RTR, having lost nine tanks,[14] withdrew the Highlanders were forced to follow suit and pull back to the vicinity of Cheux. A Tiger from the 101st SS Heavy Panzer Battalion, which was now down to eighteen operational tanks, played a significant part in stopping 9 RTR.

The limit of the advance on the 26th was only 6km from the British Start-Line and the Odon had not even been reached, let alone crossed. 12th SS had held and frustrated all attempts to sweep it aside. But the cost had been high—eighty-eight killed, 230 wounded and 412 missing; a total of 730 men.[15] SS Major Siegfried Müller's 12th SS Pioneer Battalion, which was seriously depleted anyway and had been right in the path of the main British attack, suffered 323 casualties and was reduced to about half strength. But amazingly, Müller and nine of his Headquarters staff survived in their bunker and returned to German lines during the night, as did many other battered remnants which had been cut off during the fighting. Surrender was not considered an option. In the mist and rain they reached the new Divisional line without interference from the British and many units were able to reform by the following morning. The new line ran from Marcelet, where it linked in with the 25th SS Panzer-Grenadier Regiment at Carpiquet, to the high ground south of Cheux, to Rauray and on to Vendes. In his report for 26th June,[16] Meyer, as well as claiming over fifty British tanks destroyed, was able to report that he still had forty-seven tanks and fourteen heavy anti-tank guns combat ready; despite this he had little optimism about his prospects for the next day.

27TH JUNE

During the night and early morning of 27th June troops of the 43rd (Wessex) Infantry Division took over some of the ground so dearly won by the 15th Scottish Division on the previous day. Its 129th Infantry Brigade relieved the 44th Low-landers in St Mauvieu and la Gaule and the 214th Brigade was told to take over in the Cheux area, releasing the 227th High-land Brigade for another attempt to seize the bridges over the Odon. Major General 'Pip' Roberts' 11th Armoured Division, with the 4th Armoured Brigade under command, stood ready to exploit any success.

Dietrich had been surprised that VIII Corps had not contin-ued its attack during the night, but he knew that something drastic had to be done, and done quickly, if the British thrust into the heart of his Corps was not to lead to its destruction. Facing the projected strike by the 227th Highland Brigade and 11th Armoured Division between Marcelet and Grainville, were the 1st and 2nd SS Panzer-Grenadier Battalions of Mohnke's 26th Regiment, the remnants of the 12th SS Pio-neers, thirty Mk IVs of Prinz's 2nd SS Panzer Battalion and weak Panzer and Assault Gun companies from 21st Panzer. Bremer's 12th SS Reconnaissance Battalion was filling a gap north of Colleville.

Still facing the British 49th Division on the left flank around Rauray, Max Wünsche had seventeen Panthers of Jürgensen's 1st SS Panzer Battalion and Olboeter's 3rd SS Panzer-Grena-diers. Some other Panthers had been moved 2km to the south-east into the area around Grainville. There were also about twelve Tigers of the 2nd and 3rd Companies of the 101st SS Heavy Panzer Battalion operating in the Verson—Grainville sector on this day. And of course the 88s of the 4th Flak Regiment were still in position to the rear.

Since the leading elements of the Leibstandarte could not be expected before the 28th and Hausser's II SS Panzer Corps would not be able to come to the rescue before the 29th,

Rommel approved a request by Dollmann that a Panzer battalion of the 2nd Panzer Division from the St Lô area and a KG of the 2nd SS Panzer Division DR, which had finally arrived from southern France, be used to relieve the pressure on I SS Panzer Corps. Dietrich was informed accordingly and he directed that they attack the flank of VIII Corps in the Cheux area from the direction of Rauray as soon as possible.

The British plan for the 27th was for 10 HLI, with a squadron of Churchills from 7 RTR, to seize the Odon crossings at Gavrus, and for the 2nd Battalion, The Argyll and Sutherland Highlanders (officially abbreviated to A and SH, but known, even in *The History of the 15th Scottish Division*, as the Argylls), also with a squadron of Churchills, to seize the crossing at Tourmauville. The 29th Armoured Brigade was then to exploit the crossings, while the 159th Infantry Brigade secured the bridgehead. H-Hour for these attacks was either side of 0500 hours. Concurrently, the 70th Infantry Brigade of the 49th Division was to clear Rauray and advance to Noyers.

The attack by 10 HLI and its accompanying Churchills was a total failure. Four Mk IVs of SS Captain Hans Siegel's 8th SS Panzer Company, with Siebken's 2nd SS Panzer-Grenadiers and some 12th SS Pioneers positioned between Grainville and le Haut du Bosq, supported by the 1st and 2nd SS Panzer Artillery Battalions, saw to that. At the end of the day, and after receiving 112 casualties, the Highlanders were back where they started. Exact tank casualties are unknown but, after several losses, the Churchills turned away and, accompanied by the infantry, disappeared behind the hill south of Cheux. Siegel's own Mk IV was knocked out at around midday and he suffered severe burns.

In the meantime the German counter-attack against the flank of VIII Corps at Cheux had met with very limited success. The KG of 2nd SS Panzer Division DR did not materialize, but at 0930 hours seventeen Panthers from 2nd Panzer Division,[17] without support from Panzer-Grenadiers, attacked north-east towards le Haut du Bosq and Cheux. They reached both villages but ran into tanks of 7 RTR and the Fife and Forfars and the infantry-manned anti-tank weapons of the 5th Battalion, The Duke of Cornwall's Light Infantry (DCLI). Af-

ter losing certainly four, and possibly five, Panthers the remainder withdrew. Hubert Meyer complained later that the
commander of the 2nd Panzer Division unit made no contact
with the HJ Headquarters before his attack and would probably have met with greater success if he had. Nevertheless, the
attack had helped to disrupt and delay the advance by the
reinforced 227th Highland Brigade.

Because of the chaotic situation south of Cheux, the orders
given to Lieutenant Colonel Tweedie of the Argylls to move as
quickly as possible on the bridge at Tourmauville could not be
implemented for several hours. But when they did get going
the Argylls, supported by the 23H, soon captured Colleville
from the 12th SS Reconnaissance men and at 1500 hours advanced through Tourville and Mondrainville. At 1700 hours,
against no opposition, since the 88s in the are had moved out,
the Argylls crossed the intact bridge at Tourmauville and
quickly established a small bridgehead south of the Odon. At
1900 hours two squadrons of the 23H with a company of the 8
RB and most of the Argylls were across, and as darkness fell
the tanks took up positions on the lower slopes of the strategically important Hill 112—of which more later. They were followed across the Odon, commencing at 2145 hours, by the rest
of 8 RB and two battalions of the 159th Infantry Brigade (11th
Armoured Division);[18] the other Battalion of the Brigade, the
3rd Monmouths, ended up in Mouen, north of the river.

Further attempts to seize the crossing at Gavrus from the
east, via Tourville and Grainville, by Lieutenant Colonel Vil-
lier's 9th Cameronians, with support from 7 RTR, were unsuccessful due to the Panthers in the area. Three Shermans were
lost and by 2200 hours the Scots were back in the eastern edge
of Grainville.[19]

By late afternoon the 70th British Infantry Brigade, led by
11 DLI and supported by tanks of the 8th Armoured Brigade,
finally captured Rauray on the western flank, but later attempts to move south across the high ground towards Brettevillette met with no success and cost over 100 casualties.[20]
They ran into determined resistance from Olboeter's men,
ably supported by Panthers and a few Mk IVs, and the 26th

Regimental Pioneer, Reconnaissance and Infantry Gun companies.

As darkness fell the troops of the 11th Armoured and 15th Infantry Divisions took up defensive positions, expecting the inevitable German counter-attack. With this mass of troops, and the tanks of two more armoured brigades, the 31st and 4th, in the small area south of a line from Norrey to le Mesnil-Patry (Map 3) and north of the Odon, conditions were chaotic and did not augur well for the following day's operations.

The day's fighting had not been as costly to the HJ as that of the 26th—191, including forty-four killed.[21] But the front had given way and the British were across the Odon; despite their problems, there was little doubt that they would try to expand their bridgehead in the morning. It was true that the HJ still held the vital flanks of this penetration at Mouen and Grainville and that the salient was dangerously narrow, but the British, at least at this stage, were not to repeat the Villers-Bocage mistake and pull back. Meyer had very little left with which to prevent them pushing further south and east. He had no option but to abandon Marcelet during the night 27th–28th June and pull Krause's dangerously exposed 1st SS Panzer-Grenadiers, the original defenders of St Mauvieu, and the 9th SS Panzer Company back to the western edge of Carpiquet airfield. He was also able, for reasons which will be explained later, to withdraw the bulk of Wünsche's armour from his western flank and relocate it in the vulnerable Fontaine-Etoupefour—Hill 112 area. The new HJ line therefore ran from Carpiquet airfield to Haut de Verson, on to Fontaine-Etoupefour, Hill 112, Esquay, Gavrus and Grainville, and finally to Brettevillette. The most vulnerable gap lay between Verson and the Carpiquet airfield. Everything that could be made available had now been thrown into this line, including the 5th SS Battery gunners who had lost their guns, the reinforcing tanks from 21st Panzer Division, Luftwaffe Flak, and a mortar battalion from the 83rd Werfer Regiment. The Divisional Command Post was moved to Louvigny.

It was during this night of 27th–28th June that the final 'player' in I SS Panzer Corps, arrived to take part in the battle of Normandy—1st SS Panzer Division LAH—or at least part of it. SS Lieutenant Colonel Albert Frey, with the staff of his 1st SS Panzer-Grenadier Regimental Headquarters, and the 1st and 2nd SS Panzer-Grenadier Battalions under SS Lieutenant Colonel Schiller and SS Lieutenant Colonel Max Hansen respectively, arrived in an assembly area around Venoix; the 3rd Battalion and the other Regimental units had yet to catch up. The remainder of the LAH would take another week to arrive.

Dietrich allocated Frey's Regiment to the HJ Division and Meyer, delighted to have some additional forces with which to try to cut off the British salient, immediately ordered it to be ready to counter-attack from the area east of Verson, astride the Caen to Villers-Bocage road, at midday on the 28th and to link up with a KG from the 2nd SS Panzer Division DR in the Grainville area. For the first time in their history, units of the two Divisions bearing Hitler's name on their sleeves were to fight side by side.

28TH JUNE

The loss of the bridge over the Odon had caused consternation at Seventh Army Headquarters. General Dollmann, already reeling from the loss of Cherbourg to the Americans on the 26th and fearing the worst from Hitler's ordered investigation into the reasons for its loss, panicked. At 0810 hours he ordered Hausser 'to attack immediately in order to clear out the breach south of Cheux'[22] with his II SS Panzer Corps (9th and 10th SS Panzer Divisions). This order was certainly not in accordance with the plan approved by Hitler during his only visit to the Normandy front on 17th June, which called for the major counter-stroke to be launched at the seam of the British and American armies in the direction of Bayeux. But it did not matter anyway because Hausser replied that his Corps was not ready and could not attack before the 29th.

One of the most extraordinary things about the German command system on 28th June was that, at this most critical time in the campaign, there was no one senior to Dollmann left in Normandy to countermand his order—Hitler had called both von Rundstedt and Rommel back to Berchtesgaden. Having given the order and been told that it could not be carried out, Dollmann committed suicide. This meant that the Head-

quarters of CinC West (von Rundstedt), Army Group 'B'
(Rommel) and Seventh Army (Dollmann) were all without
commanders. The relevant Chiefs of Staff were left with awesome responsibilities; they did not shrink from them.

At 1300 hours General Hausser advised Seventh Army that,
although he preferred to use the 29th to fight a containing
action whilst he organised his Corps for a proper attack on the
British salient, he could, if necessary, launch a counter-attack
on that day.

At 1500 hours Headquarters Army Group 'B' informed Seventh Army that Hitler had, pending the return of von Rundstedt and Rommel, appointed General Hausser to assume
supreme command in the invasion sector. He was thus the
first Waffen-SS office to command an army. Lieutenant General Pemsel, the Seventh Army Chief of Staff, advised Hausser
to stay with his Corps to organise the counter-attack, at least
until the following morning. This extraordinary decision to
remove a Corps commander just before a vital counter-attack
inevitably set off a chain reaction which did nothing to help
the success of the forthcoming operation—for example, the
commander of one of the two Divisions due to carry out the
attack, Willi Bittrich, had to give up the 9th SS Panzer Division
Hohenstaufen in order to take command of II SS Panzer
Corps.

At 1700 hours the Seventh Army area of responsibility was
split—General Geyr von Schweppenburg and his Headquarters Panzer Group West were reactivated and made responsible
for the invasion front from the Seine to a line running roughly
through Caumont to Bayeux. He was to command I and II SS
and XLVII Panzer Corps and the LXXXVI Infantry Corps.

Von Schweppenburg wasted no time in confirming the order for II SS Panzer Corps to attack from a line running from
Noyers to Gavrus, with the mission of capturing Baron,
Mouen and Cheux and destroying all enemy south of the Caen
to Villers-Bocage road. At 1800 hours he asked Hausser to
confirm that he would be ready and Pemsel did so, on behalf
of his new commander.

The chaotic situation on the German side was matched, in a
different way, on the British. Dietrich and Meyer watched the

desultory moves of the British armoured and infantry divisions with amazement. Their lack of aggressiveness was due, in part, to the fact that there was almost total congestion in the middle of the salient around Cheux, caused by minefields, isolated pockets of SS and general destruction. No one seemed capable of solving the problem and so the vast majority of the tanks and other vehicles sat immobile.

But the lack of strong offensive action was also because ULTRA intercepts had detected the planned German counter-attack, and the moves of II SS Panzer Corps had of course been picked up. O'Connor, who was not privy to ULTRA, held discussions at the Headquarters of the 15th Scottish Division at 1000 hours, and with the approval of Dempsey, who was aware of the ULTRA intercept, ordered the 11th Armoured Division not to attempt any crossings of the Orne. He had decided to strengthen his bridgehead against the expected German counter-attack and not to advance further until his infantry divisions had cleared the ground between Cheux and the Odon and captured the bridges at Gavrus. Unbelievably, the British were handing back the initiative! However, the order to launch Hausser's Corps without proper preparation would prevent the Germans from making the best use of it.

Dietrich's decision to allocate the Leibstandarte KG of Albert Frey to 12th SS had provided Kurt Meyer with a valuable and much needed counter-attack force. Recall that he aimed to use it to cut off those British elements which had crossed the Odon, by attacking from the Verson area towards Mouen and Colleville and linking up with a KG Weidinger in the Grainville area. This KG, named after its commander, SS Lieutenant Colonel Otto Weidinger, had been attached to Panzer Lehr from the 2nd SS Panzer Division on Rommel's authority. It comprised the Headquarters and SS Pioneer, Infantry Gun, Reconnaissance and Flak Companies of the Der Führer Regiment, and two SS Panzer-Grenadier Battalions. The exact composition of Frey's force is uncertain but it certainly included the Leibstandarte's 1st and 2nd SS Panzer-Grenadier Battalions, at least part of one of Jürgensen's Panther companies, a composite MK IV group based on the 4th Company of the 21st Panzer Division, and support from a mortar battalion of the 83rd Werfer Regiment. Up to three Tigers of the Corps 101st SS Heavy Panzer Battalion also took part in this action.

During the night 27th–28th, KG Weidinger took over on the right flank of Panzer Lehr on a line to the west of Grainville, Rauray and Tessel, thus releasing Wünsche's tanks for action at the southern end of the British salient.

Frey was not entirely happy with the prospects for his attack and said later:

> I received the attack order from SS Brigadier Kurt Meyer. I immediately made him aware that I could not execute the order without the support of heavy weapons. I therefore requested a delay until the LAH's artillery could arrive. He answered my objection by saying that the artillery of the 12th SS Panzer Division would support my attack. I started the attack at the designated time, but it was with a heavy heart that I gave the order. As I feared, there was no artillery liaison officer with me and the 12th SS artillery did not take any action of its own accord. The enemy offered immediate and heavy resistance. A remarkable feature of the resistance was the machine gun fire. It was very heavy and fell with equal intensity along the entire attack sector. It appeared that they were firing it from their tanks.[23]

This was not an auspicious start for the expected cooperation between the two designated SS Divisions of I SS Panzer Corps, and Frey's allegation that he lacked artillery support is, not surprisingly, denied by the Chief of Staff of 12th SS.

Frey's attack was launched at 0600 hours with Schiller's 1st SS Panzer-Grenadier Battalion LAH on the right and Max Hansen's 2nd on the left. The Regimental Headquarters remained in Bretteville-sur-Odon.

The 1st SS Panzer-Grenadiers were soon involved in heavy fighting on the northern outskirts of Mouen against a company of the 3rd Monmouths, the detached element of the 11th Armoured Division's Infantry Brigade—the rest of the Battalion had moved to the Tourmauville bridge area at first light. One of the five 21st Panzer Division's Mk IVs advancing with the Battalion claimed three tanks knocked out—they turned out to be Stuarts of 3 CLY. On the left, Max Hansen was wounded for the ninth time in the early stages of the advance in Verson and SS Lieutenant Herford took command of the 2nd Battalion. The joint advance continued over a series of wide ridges into Mouen itself and the left flank company reached the area of Tourville. At 1945 hours an attack by 10 HLI, supported by 3 CLY tanks, coming south from the Cheux area, hit the north flank of Frey's force and resulted in heavy and confused fighting which lasted throughout the night and ended the prospect of any further advance. The CLY lost four Shermans before darkness fell.[24] Frey's LAH KG had succeeded in taking its initial objectives but it had been unable to link up with Weidinger's KG—the latter had spent the day resisting the attempts of the 49th Infantry Division to move south from Rauray.

The British efforts on 28th June were, as we have heard, mainly concerned with trying to widen their slender salient and clear the remaining German pockets of resistance within it. A major aim was to capture Hill 112. 'Hill' is a misnomer—it is the most significant feature in the whole area; from it you can see Caen, 9km to the north-east, Carpiquet airfield, Cheux, Point 213 of Villers-Bocage fame, Mont Pinçon, 18km to the south-west and the Bourguébus ridge to the south-east of Caen. Lying between the Odon and the Orne, it is in reality the eastern height at the end of a 2km broad ridge which runs, like a stranded whale, from Evrecy in the west almost to Maltot in the east. In 1944 it was completely open with a small wood near the summit. It was vital to both the Allies and the Germans and was to become the scene of terrible fighting. Hausser called it the 'key to the backdoor of Caen' and without taking it the British had no hope of crossing the Orne. The problem, which the British would discover the hard way, was that the wide summit of Hill 112 was in plain view from the far side of the Orne, particularly from the Bourguébus ridge south of Caen.

By 1200 hours two squadrons of the 23H with their affiliated Motor Company of 8 RB, all part of the 29th Armoured Brigade, having beaten off a counter-attack by at least the ten Mk IVs of the 5th Company of Prinz's 2nd SS Panzer Battalion at about 0930 hours, were struggling to reach the summit of

Hill 112. On the northern slopes they came under sustained fire from more of Wünsche's tanks in the area of Fontaine-Etoupefour and its associated Château. Casualties soon reached an unacceptable level and, after beating off a further counter-attack, the group was ordered to withdraw to the Baron area. At 1530 hours the Hussar Battlegroup, which had by then lost five Shermans and was running out of tank ammunition, was relieved by 3 RTR[25] and the rest of 8 RB. This force had to repel yet another attack at 1700 hours by some of the thirty Panthers and Mk IVs operating in this sector. But this time it was the British who would not be moved. It is unclear which 12th SS infantry units were supporting Wünsche's tanks in the fighting for Hill 112.

At the end of the day 3 RTR, the 2nd Fife and Forfar Yeomanry and the riflemen of 8 RB were still holding the northern slopes of Hill 112 and the depleted Hussars were back in Tourmauville. The salient south of the Odon measured only seven square kilometres—it contained 152 combat ready tanks of the 11th Armoured Division,[26] a tank battalion from the 4th Armoured Brigade, and four battalions of infantry!

It is interesting to note the tenacity displayed by some members of the HJ, and the methods used to ensure that the maximum number of tanks were always in action. During the first counter-attack against the 23H by the 5th SS Panzer Company, now led by an SS Second Lieutenant named Porsch, a Mk IV commanded by SS Second Lieutenant Kunze was knocked out. Yet another Second Lieutenant, Willi Kändler, described what happened later:

At around 1700 hours our total number, through newly arrived Panzers, was back to nine. The 6th Company. . . . was also there. This time we tried to attack the hill by swinging wide to the left around a small wood in front of the square wooded area. . . . We again came under heavy fire from tanks, had a few Panzer losses and had to withdraw again to our starting positions. . . . In the late evening hours. . . . a reconnaissance VW . . . reported. . . . a Panzer IV with its engine running and a dead soldier sitting in front of it. This could only be the Panzer of

Helmut Kunze . . . in front of the Panzer, the loader, Howe, was lying on his back, his blue eyes open . . . Helmut Kunze sat dead in his commander's seat. The shell seemed to have hit him directly in the back. To his left sat his dead gunner. The Panzer engine had been running since noon. . . . I had the two scouts cover toward the enemy and drove the Panzer under its own power almost to our position. Just before I got there, it ran out of fuel and stopped . . . The Panzer, with a new turret, was back in action few days later.[27]

Senior SS Sergeant Willy Kretzschmar described what happened after his tank was hit:

We inspected our damage—a clean hit had gone through between the engine and fighting compartments. . . . except for a small shrapnel stuck in my right thigh, we all escaped with just a scare. The driver took the vehicle to the repair shop. I remained in Esquay with the rest of the crew. . . . In the afternoon, more Panzers of the 5th Company arrived. My crew and I took over a Panzer which had come back from the repair shop.[28]

How different from many Allied crews who would, no doubt, have been delighted to have accompanied their damaged tanks to the rear.

After being relieved of responsibility for the Tourmauville bridge by the 159th Brigade during the morning, 2nd Argylls sent two platoon-sized patrols through the entangled woods on the south side of the Odon towards Gavrus. To their amazement they found the two small stone bridges there intact and undefended. One company was immediately sent to secure the farthest one and, not surprisingly, the rest of the Battalion was soon ordered to follow. After an appalling journey through the steep-sided forest, dragging their 6 pdr anti-tank guns with them, the Argylls secured the bridge area before darkness fell. This was splendid work but sadly the Battalion was isolated because the HJ was still between it and the nearest British troops at le Valtru. A concurrent attack by 46 Brigade, designed to link up with the move by the Argylls, had started at first light. The 9th Cameronians with support from 7 RTR reached and held Grainville by 1300 hours. At the same time the 7th Seaforth Highlanders, with Churchill tanks, moved through Colleville and fought their way into le Valtru, which they held against a counter-attack by KG Weidinger. Seventy-six men were lost in the fighting.[29] Neither Battalion, however, was able to break through to the Argylls at the Gavrus bridges, a mere 2km away.

On the eastern flank of the British salient the 10 HLI supported by 3 CLY moved on Mouen. As we have heard, they ran into KG Frey's counter-attack and fighting continued well into the night in a very confused situation.

The day's losses for the Leibstandarte and KG Weidinger are unknown. 12th SS lost another seventy-eight, including twenty-two killed.[30] The heaviest losses were predictably in Wünsche's 12th SS Panzer Regiment.

29TH JUNE

The major counter-attack by II SS Panzer Corps was due to start at 0600 hours on 29th June but had to be postponed. During the morning Hausser reported, 'The offensive cannot begin until the afternoon. Our concentrations are under continual artillery and air bombardment.' And again at 1340 hours, 'The enemy is causing heavy losses by fighter-bomber attacks. . . . and the Panzer Divisions cannot bring up all their tanks due to lack of fuel.'[31]

The attack itself will not be described in any detail because this book is restricted to the actions of I SS Panzer Corps. Nevertheless, important elements of Dietrich's command were meant to be involved—namely, the 12th SS Panzer and Artillery Regiments, 12th SS Reconnaissance Battalion, 3rd SS Panzer-Grenadier Battalion of Mohnke's Regiment, a company of the Corps Tiger Battalion, Frey's KG from the Leibstandarte and the 83rd Werfer Regiment. Whilst the rest of 12th SS remained on the defensive, these forces were intended to support the main counter-attack from the west by themselves attacking from the south and east. In the event this plan came into conflict with the British decision to use the 15th Scottish and 43rd Wessex Divisions to clear and enlarge their bridgehead astride the Odon and then for the 11th Armoured Division to continue its advance towards the Orne. As a result of these British efforts, none of Kurt Meyer's units would be free to support the main German counter-attack.

On the eastern flank of the British salient the 43rd Wessex Division, with support from 7 RTR, captured Mouen by 1100 hours and went on to take Baron by the early evening, forcing Frey's Leibstandarte KG to pull back to Verson and Fontaine-Etoupefour. Herford's 2nd SS Panzer-Grenadiers claimed twelve British tanks destroyed during this fighting and this is confirmed in the 7 RTR War Diary. Meanwhile the 15th Scottish Division was fighting to clear the Grainville and le Valtru areas and preparing an attempt to break through to the Argylls on the Gavrus bridges. But some of the heaviest fighting of all took place on the ridge topped by Hills 112 and 113. On the western side of this feature 44 RTR with infantry of the KRRC, detached from the 4th to the 29th Armoured Brigade, moved on Evrecy via Hill 113. There they ran into the advancing 10th SS Panzer Division and by the end of the day had been forced to withdraw for the loss of twelve tanks. A concurrent advance by part of 3 RTR from the north-west side of the Hill 112 towards Esquay was stopped by six Tigers of the 1st Company of the 101st SS Heavy Panzer Battalion under the command of SS Captain Rolf Möbius.

Meanwhile at 0800 hours, on Hill 112, 8 RB reoccupied the small wooded area 300m east of the summit which Wünsche's tanks and Olboeter's Panzer-Grenadiers had vacated during the night, only to come under intense fire from both direct and indirect weapons for the rest of the day. Some fifty six-barrelled Nebelwerfers were available. One British officer described the Nebelwerfer fire as follows:

> A howling and wailing grew until it filled the sky, rising in pitch as it approached, and ending in a series of shattering explosions all round us. . . . Then more squeals, the same horrible wail, and another batch of thirty-six bombs exploded astride us, so that the pressure came first from one side, then from the other, then from both at once.[32]

On the north-eastern slopes of the ridge the Fife and
Forfars, attempting to support this move, became engaged in a
duel with Wünsche's Panzers positioned around Eterville and
the nearby Château de Fontaine and had difficulty holding on
to their positions.

The counter-attack by the 9th and 10th SS Panzer Divisions
of Bittrich's II SS Panzer Corps met with little success. The few
tanks which did break through to Cheux were destroyed and a
small incursion between le Valtru and Grainville was soon
pushed back. The village of Gavrus was taken for a short time
but then lost, and the furthest advance was to Hill 113, north
of Evrecy. British tank and anti-tank forces, and in particular
artillery and air forces, were much too strong for a daylight
attack. The Second Tactical Air Force was out in strength all
day and inflicted heavy casualties on the attacking tanks.

But despite their success in defeating this attack, Dempsey
and O'Connor—influenced partly by captured documents and
aerial reconnaissance—became convinced that they had yet to
receive the main counter-attack. At 2030 hours the tanks of
the Royal Scots Greys (Greys), part of 4th Armoured Brigade,
were ordered to withdraw to the north bank of the Odon and
at 2100 hours the whole of the 29th Armoured Brigade was
also told to pull back,[33] leaving the small bridgehead to the
south to be held by the infantry of two brigades. Any thought
of continuing the advance towards the Orne was abandoned—
at least for the present. Once more the British were relinquish-
ing the initiative. At 2100 hours a rainstorm lasting five hours
turned the ground into a quagmire, making life a misery for
the infantry and movement treacherous for the armour.

30TH JUNE TO 1ST JULY

By first light on 30th June the tanks of the 4th and 29th
Armoured Brigades had, as ordered, withdrawn back across
the Odon over the Tourmauville bridge. During the night the
riflemen of 8 RB had pulled back from Hill 112 in driving
rain, but the remaining infantry south of the river, including
the Argylls still at the Gavrus bridges, awaited the predicted
German onslaught. Behind them the 4th Armoured Brigade
was positioned in the area of Cheux to meet any attacks from

the south-west, whilst the bulk of the 29th Armoured Brigade, now safely north-east of Cheux, protected the eastern flank.

As far as the Germans were concerned it was of paramount importance to keep the British off the vital ridge south of the Odon. Accordingly, after preparatory fire by the 12th SS Artillery and 83rd Werfer Regiments, and another Werfer Regiment supporting the 10th SS Panzer Division, Prinz's Mk IVs and Olboeter's weary SS Panzer-Grenadiers, under the overall command of Max Wünsche, advanced from the south-east and east, whilst parts of 10th SS moved in from the south and south-west. By 0730 hours Prinz's Mk IVs had reached the crest of Hill 112 and at midday the whole northern slope was in German hands. SS Second Lieutenant Willi Kändler described the attack as follows:

> Early in the morning rockets from our launchers, trailing veils of smoke, howled into the English positions in the small square wood. [In fact they were unoccupied]. These launchers decided the success of the attack during that morning. This was our fourth attack on Hill 112, and it was crowned by the capture of the square wood and the hill. As we drove up, we saw numerous destroyed vehicles, among them knocked out Sherman tanks.[34]

A member of the 6th SS Panzer Company later wrote:

> The rocket launchers were firing right above us towards the hill. The Grenadiers reported that the 'Tommies' were on the run. . . . When we reached the top, it was all over. Some tank engines were still running, but no one could be seen inside. Grenadiers from Frundsberg [10th SS] were already coming up the other side. Some hours later they came under a heavy artillery barrage and suffered heavy losses.[35]

After severe fighting the Argylls were forced to abandon their bravely held bridgehead at Gavrus to 10th SS. They had suffered 245 casualties, including twenty-nine killed.[36] By the evening of the 30th the British bridgehead south of the Odon had to all intents and purposes ceased to exist—the Germans held a line from 1,500m north-west of Carpiquet, to Verson, to Eterville, to Hill 112, to 200m south-east of Tourmauville, to the southern edge of Les Vilains, to the northern edge of Gavrus, to le Valtru, to some houses south-west of Grainville, to the southern edge of Tessel-Bretteville. Operation EPSOM was at an end. It had cost the 12th SS Panzer Division HJ dear but its performance would go down in history as a classic defensive operation. As Panzermeyer himself put it, 'The 15th Scottish, 43rd, 49th Infantry and 11th Armoured Divisions have lived off the marrow of the 12th SS.' He went on to say[37] that his Division was left with the combat power of a weak battle group. This, as we shall see, was an understatement.

EPSOM had cost the British VIII Corps 4,020 casualties, of which 2,720 were suffered by the 15th Scottish Division alone.[38] Some days later Montgomery wrote to the Divisional commander, Major General MacMillan:

> Please congratulate the Division from me and tell all officers and men that I am delighted with what they have done. I am sending you a present of 180,000 cigarettes. I hope the men will enjoy them. Good luck to you all.[39]

But in fact much had gone wrong on the British side and, despite what may have been said and written later about drawing as much German armour as possible on to the British sector, there can be no doubt that EPSOM had been a major effort to break through the German defences to the west of Caen, and it had failed. Outdated military philosophies and old-fashioned discipline born and nurtured on the parade ground, had been shown to be badly wanting. It is hardly surprising that Michael Carver had found it necessary to sack his Brigade second in command and Chief of Staff[40] within a few days of taking command of the 4th Armoured Brigade, or that he should find that one of his senior commanding officers 'had lost his grip'.[41] And at a higher level the commander of the 159th Infantry Brigade and two of his commanding officers had to be sacked following EPSOM.[42] Dempsey's decision to go on the defensive at a critical stage in his offensive is just as incomprehensible as Bucknall's over Villers-Bocage—perhaps even more so in view of his overwhelming superiority in firepower: witness being able to call, at very short notice, for 100 heavy bombers to obliterate Villers-Bocage on 30th June in order to interrupt 9th SS Panzer's part in the counter-at-tack. It is clear that if the Germans had their problems as a result of EPSOM, the British did too.

But before leaving this operation we must come back to the question of German casualties. Very precise figures are given by the former Chief of Staff of the HJ, Hubert Meyer, in his extremely detailed book *The History of the 12th SS Panzer Division Hitlerjugend*. Up to 16th June he quotes a total casualty figure of 1,149, and for the heavy fighting during EPSOM a further 1,244 men—a total of 2,393 and a daily rate of about 100. On the other hand, analysing the figures given in Meyer's book by Regiment and unit, we come up with the slightly higher figure of 2,662:

12th SS Panzer Regiment	324—13% of unit strength
25th SS Panzer-Grenadier Regiment	383—11%
26th SS Panzer-Grenadier Regiment	1,017—30%
12th SS Panzer Reconnaissance Battalion	250—25%
12th SS Panzer Pioneer Battalion	490—43%
12th SS Panzer Artillery, Divisional	
Escort Coy & others	198
TOTAL	2,662

This is 13% of total strength and 22% of combat strength.

Three things are of note: first, even the highest figure is less than that suffered by the Canadian 3rd Infantry Division and 2nd Armoured Brigade (2831)[43] during the first six days of the Normandy fighting (approximately 470 per day); second, the similarity with the casualty rate of the 15th Scottish Division during EPSOM (2,720); and third, whichever figure is taken it contradicts Kurt Meyer's statement in his memoirs[44] that after EPSOM his Division had only a combat value of a weak battle group. It is also interesting that the 12th SS strength return dated 3rd July shows twenty-two Panthers and thirty-nine Mk IVs operational, with another fifteen of each in short-term repair—a total of ninety-one tanks. The strength return for I SS Panzer Corps troops dated 1st July[45] shows the 101st SS Heavy Panzer Battalion still had eleven Tigers operational and a further nineteen in short-term repair. This implies that only fifteen Tigers, thirteen Panthers and forty-three Mk IVs had been lost during this initial period of heavy fighting. One Panzer company commander, SS Lieutenant Bando of the 5th, had been killed.

For his outstanding performance during June, Max Wünsche was later awarded Oak Leaves to his Knight's Cross. SS Majors Olboeter and Krause, and SS Captain Hans Siegel, the commander of the 8th SS Panzer Company, were to receive the Knight's Cross for their actions.

NOTES

1. Kraemer, *I SS Panzer Corps in the West*, MS C-024, IWM, London, AL 2727/1-2. 2. Meyer, Hubert, *The History of the 12th SS Panzer Division Hitlerjugend*, p. 93. 3. Meyer, Kurt, *Grenadiers*, pp. 134–135. 4. Delaforce, Patrick, *The Polar Bears*, pp. 74–76. 5. Ibid., p. 74. 6. Meyer, Hubert, op. cit., p. 99. 7. Ibid., p. 100. 8. Meyer, Kurt, op. cit., pp. 135–136. 9. Ibid., p. 137. 10. Howe J, 'Baptism of Fire', *Western Mail*, 27 Jun 81. 11. 7 RTR War Diary, 26 Jun 44, 12. Wilmot, *The Struggle for Europe*, p. 343. 13. Carver, *Out of Step*, p. 192. 14. 9 RTR War Diary, 26 Jun 44. 15. Meyer, Hubert, op. cit., p. 112. 16. Ibid. 17. Ibid., p. 116. 18. 11 Armd Div War Diary, 27 Jun 44 19. 9 Cameronians War Diary, 27 Jun 44. 20. 11 DLI War Diary, 27 Jun 44. 21. Meyer, Hubert, op. cit., p. 120. 22. Ibid., p. 126. 23. Lehmann & Tiemann, *The Leibstandarte IV/I*, p. 121. 24. 227 Inf Bde & 3 CLY War Diaries, 28 Jun 44. 25. 23H War Diary, 28 Jun 44. 26. 29 Armd Bde War Diary, 27 Jun 44. 27. Meyer, Hubert, op. cit., p. 122. 28. Ibid., p. 121. 29. Seaforth War Diary, 28 Jun 44. 30. Meyer, Hubert, op. cit., p. 125. 31. Wilmot, op. cit., p. 345. 32. Belfield & Essame, *The Battle for Normandy*, p. 114. 33. VIII Corps War Diary, 29 Jun 44. 34. Meyer, Hubert, op. cit., p. 128. 35. Ibid., p. 129. 36. Martin, *History of the 15th Scottish Division 1939–1945*, p. 347. 37. Meyer, Kurt, op. cit., p. 142. 38. Martin, ibid. 39. MacMillan Papers, IWM. 40. Carver, op. cit., p. 192. 41. Ibid. 42. Hastings, *Overlord, D-Day and the Battle for Normandy 1944*, p. 175. 43. Stacey, *The Official History of the Canadian Army in the Second World War, Vol III, The Victory Campaign*, p. 140. 44. Meyer, Kurt, op. cit., p. 142. 45. I SS Panzer Corps Meldung No 00851/44 dated 1st July 1944.

The funeral of General Dollmann, the former commander of the Seventh Army, took place on the morning of 2nd July.

The previous day Field Marshals von Rundstedt and Rommel had returned from their meeting with Hitler at Berchtesgaden 'angry and disgruntled', but having agreed to continue a policy of aggressive and unyielding defence. It was Rommel's last meeting with his Führer. When he had said, 'Mein Führer, I must speak bluntly. I cannot leave here without speaking on the subject of Germany', Hitler's voice had rung out, 'Field Marshal, be so good as to leave the room. I think it would be better like that.'[1]

Waiting for Rommel on his return was an appreciation of the situation, prepared on 30th June by General Geyr von Schweppenburg, commander Panzer Group West, and supported by General Hausser, commander Seventh Army. It stated that the Panzer divisions were being so seriously worn down that a withdrawal to a new line which included Caen South, the Orne as far as Bully, and then west to Avenay, Villers-Bocage and the area around Caumont, was essential. It further recommended the redeployment of Dietrich's I SS Panzer Corps (then comprising 12th SS, part of 1st SS, Panzer Lehr and 21st Panzer Divisions) as soon as possible for refitting. Rommel forwarded the report to von Rundstedt with his concurrence. At midnight on 30th June, Rundstedt's Chief of Staff informed Hausser's Chief of Staff that the planned withdrawal from Caen North would be approved by his commander. Rundstedt, having told Rommel to go ahead with the limited withdrawal, informed OKW and forwarded von Schweppenburg's report with its various concurrences, to support his decision. The reaction was not long in coming. During the early evening of 1st July von Schweppenburg received instructions from Rommel's Headquarters to halt all preparations for the planned withdrawal. These instructions were based on a Führer Order received by Rundstedt at 1740 hours. Von Schweppenburg's response was transmitted by Rommel to von Rundstedt. It said:

If the requested straightening of the front does not occur within a few days, the 9th, 10th, 12th SS and Panzer Lehr Panzer Divisions will burn out to the extent that they will no longer be usable.

We are here not talking about 'running away', but rather about a sensible and methodical removal from the fire of ships' artillery for which the men are helpless targets at the present time.[2]

That night Rundstedt, in answer to the question, 'What shall we do?' from Keitel, Chief of the OKW, made his famous reply, 'Make peace, you fools!'[3]

The following morning, 2nd July, one of Hitler's adjutants arrived at von Rundstedt's Headquarters with another decoration for the ageing Field Marshal, and more importantly, a letter from the Führer relieving him of his command. Field Marshal Günther Hans von Kluge was already on his way to take over. It was later stated that Rundstedt had asked to be replaced for health reasons. On the same day von Schweppenburg was told by Rommel that he was to be replaced by the forty-eight-year-old General Heinrich Eberbach, Inspector of the Panzerwaffe,—Rommel added the words, "I'm next on the list!"

There was to be no early respite for Dietrich's 'boys'.

NOTES

1. Irving, *Trail of the Fox*, pp. 363–364. 2. Meyer, Hubert, *The History of the 12th SS Panzer Division Hitlerjugend*, p. 133. 3. Wilmot, *The Struggle for Europe*, p. 347.

15   4th to 5th July—Operation WINDSOR —the Battle for Carpiquet

It will be remembered that Operation EPSOM should have included the capture of Carpiquet village and its airfield by the Canadian 3rd Infantry Division and 2nd Armoured Brigade. However, the failure to clear the VIII Corps salient quickly and expand the British bridgehead across the Odon led, on 30th June, to the postponement of this part of the operation.

By 4th July Dietrich's I SS Panzer Corps was constituted as

Hitler had originally intended it—with only the 1st and 12th SS Panzer Divisions under command. 21st Panzer was now part of LXXXVI Corps and Panzer Lehr had joined 2nd Panzer in the XLVII Panzer Corps. Together with II SS Panzer Corps, these three Corps now formed General Eberbach's Panzer Group West which was generally facing Dempsey's Second British Army.

At the tactical level, the morning of 4th July saw the forward positions of the 25th SS Panzer-Grenadier Regiment of Meyer's HJ Division along a line from just south of Cambes in the east, to Buron, to Gruchy, to Authie, to Franqueville. Recall that this Regiment had been uninvolved in the EPSOM fighting and had suffered relatively few casualties—under 400 since 7th June.

To the south-west of Milius's 25th Regiment, Wilhelm Mohnke's depleted 26th SS Panzer-Grenadier Regiment was holding Carpiquet village and airfield, and then a line to the south, through les Jumeaux to Eterville, which was held by Albert Frey's 1st SS Panzer-Grenadier Regiment LAH. Contact had been established with the 10th SS Panzer Division near Eterville.

The western edge of Carpiquet village was occupied by the 3rd Company and a platoon of the 1st Company of SS Lieutenant Colonel Bernhard (Papa) Krause's 1st SS Panzer-Grenadier Battalion. Two light infantry guns were in position at the east end. The rest of the Battalion had set up on the southern edge of the airfield after withdrawing from Marcelet during EPSOM. Krause's men were able to use the old Luftwaffe airfield defences for cover. The eastern part of Carpiquet was covered by the 88mm Flak guns of the 2nd Battery of the 12th SS Flak Regiment, in position in St Germain-la Blanche-Herbe. For armoured support there were five Mk IVs of the 9th SS Panzer Company, under SS Lieutenant Buettner, at the south-east corner of the airfield and parts of the 4th Panther Company in reserve on the reverse slope at Bretteville-sur-Odon. Fire support was available from the HJ's 3rd SS Panzer Artillery Battalion and elements of the 83rd Werfer Regiment under the command of Lieutenant Colonel Böhme.[1]

The Canadian operation to capture Carpiquet and its airfield was code-named WINDSOR. It was considered to be an essential prerequisite to the capture of Caen itself. The attack was to be made by Brigadier K. G. Blackader's 8th Infantry Brigade, reinforced by the Royal Winnipeg Rifles. Tank support was to be provided by the Fort Garry Horse (10th Armoured Regiment) and three squadrons of specialist tanks, including one of flame-throwers, from the British 79th Armoured Division. Massive fire support was available in the form of naval ships, including the battleship HMS *Rodney,* and twenty-one artillery battalions, together with two squadrons of Typhoon "tank-busting" aircraft from 83 Group, on call if needed. The 3rd Canadian Infantry Division War Diary speaks of 760 guns being available for the operation.

The day began at 0500 hours with artillery barrages from both sides—the Germans had anticipated the Canadian attack and caught the leading companies as they crossed their Start-Lines with more than 200 shells and their dreaded Nebelwerfers. Needless to say, the defenders of Carpiquet suffered even more and the village was totally destroyed.

By 0632 hours the men of the North Shore and Chaudière Regiments, each with a squadron of tanks, had reached the village and started to clear through it. It took them until 1400 hours to complete their mission—against a single, under-strength SS Panzer-Grenadier Company. Kurt Meyer described the German tactics in his book *Grenadiers:*

> The Grenadiers know their job. The Company commander is to withdraw, fighting a delaying action, to the eastern edge of Carpiquet. . . . and tempt the attacking Canadians to enter the village. There are 88mm guns positioned in ambush just to the east of Carpiquet. Furthermore, the outskirts of the village lie within the field of fire of waiting tanks. . . . Our artillery and mortars are already zeroed in on the village.

According to the historian of the Chaudière Regiment, Carpiquet became an inferno, and even after the village was captured the 88mm guns of the 2nd SS Flak Company in the western part of St Germain prevented any further movement to the south or east by either tanks or infantry.

The concurrent attack by the Royal Winnipeg Rifles across the completely open ground from Marcelet, apart from suffering badly from Nebelwerfer fire from the moment the advance began, soon ran into strong resistance from the rest of Krause's 1st SS Battalion and the Mk IVs in the southern hangars and on the southern edge of the airfield. It was 0900 hours before the leading companies reached the first hangars and by then they were in real trouble. Their attached tanks had assisted only by firing from static positions, and although they and some flame-throwers did eventually move forward at about 1300 hours,[2] the Canadians were still unable to make any real progress. The Fort Garry War Diary says that at 1540 hours they and the Winnipegs were forced to withdraw back to the area of a small wood 800m west of the hangars. Buettner's Mk IVs, occasionally assisted by the 4th SS Panzer Company's Panthers, had prevented any significant advance by the Canadian tanks. One Panther commander, SS Senior Sergeant Rudolf, was awarded the Knight's Cross for his actions this day—he was credited with knocking out six Shermans.

SS Senior Sergeant Wohlgemuth, the leader of the anti-tank platoon of Krause's 4th Company, again describes what it was like in the battle for the southern hangars:

> I was located in a former ammunition bunker. The explosions were of such violence that bits of concrete inside the bunker burst from its walls. Once the artillery fire had moved to the rear, I leaped ahead some 10m to the front squad of the mortar platoon to repel the expected attack. Sergeant Daniel and Corporal Kordahs of the mortar platoon had been killed. Also, our artillery observer was dead from a 25cm long fragment of a ship's shell sticking in his back. There was no problem repelling the infantry attack. We concentrated our fire at the massed groups of attacking infantrymen until they retreated.[3]

Another attempt to advance by the Winnipegs at about 1600 hours met with failure when the Panthers, from their reserve positions at Bretteville, moved on to the ridge south of the airfield at 1750 hours.[4]

Since there could be no question of the planned exploitation by the Queen's Own Rifles to seize the eastern parts of the airfield, Brigadier Blackader ordered the attack halted at 2100 hours.[5] Five squadrons of rocket-firing Typhoons were called in against the SS tanks and artillery around the airfield—the Germans said later they suffered no equipment casualties from these attacks. By 2130 hours B Squadron of the Fort Garrys and the Winnipeg survivors were back at Marcelet.

The 4th of July cannot be called a successful day for the Canadians. They had captured Carpiquet village and advanced to take the undefended northern hangars of the airfield, but Meyer's men still held the vital southern hangars and control tower. Canadian casualties had been heavy—377 killed, wounded and missing, with the Winnipegs and North Shore Regiment suffering most with 132 each.[6] Some idea of the reinforcement system can be gained by the fact that the Winnipegs received 200 new men the following day![7] Krause's Battalion lost 155 men including SS Captain Eggert, the commander of the 1st SS Panzer-Grenadier Company,[8] but his men had fought an epic battle. A single depleted Battalion, supported by less than a company's worth of tanks and six 88mm guns, had fought off four battalions of infantry and the equivalent of more than two tank battalions, supported by over 700 guns, naval gunfire and ground attack aircraft. It is hardly surprising that Panzermeyer described Krause as:

> The backbone of the defence as so often in the past. Bernhard Krause is the premier Grenadier in his Battalion. He speaks to his Grenadiers like a father in his deep, quiet voice. There are no surprises to fear from [Krause's] section of the battle line.[9]

There are no reports of any German tanks being lost in this action. A strength return for 5th July shows eighteen Panthers and nine Mk IVs ready for action. This figure had increased dramatically by 7th July to twenty-eight Panthers and thirty-two Mk IVs, which gives an indication of the rapid repair capabilities of the German army.

Although the Canadians had failed to capture the airfield, their advance into the flank of 12th SS threatened Caen itself and worried Dietrich and Meyer. Accordingly, a night

1. On the occasion of the 1936 Berlin Olympics, Theodor (Teddy) Wisch heads the Leibstandarte SS Adolf Hitler Guard of Honor. Seven years later he was the commander of the 1st SS Panzer Division LAH.

2. Hitlerjugend recruiting poster 1943.

3. Kurt Meyer, Fritz Witt and Sepp Dietrich with Field Marshal von Rundstedt, early 1944.

4. Sepp Dietrich, commander I SS Panzer Corps, with Field Marshal Erwin Rommel, commander Army Group B.

5. Lieutenant General Omar Bradley, commander First US Army, General Sir Bernard Montgomery (Monty), commander 21st Army Group and Lieutenant General Miles Dempsey, commander Second British Army.

6. Wilhelm Mohnke, Walther Ewert, Kurt Meyer, Dr. Besuden and Teddy Wisch, 28th May 1943.

7. Near Kharkov 28th May 1943—officers of the LAH celebrate Dietrich's birthday—front row: Kurt Meyer, Hugo Kraas, Sepp Dietrich, Albert Frey, Weiser, Rudolf Sandig, Bernhard (Papa) Krause, Schönberger (Hubert Meyer behind Sandig).

8. (left) Teddy Wisch, commander of the 1st SS Panzer Division LAH.

9. (right) Kurt Meyer (Panzermeyer), commander 25th SS Panzer-Grenadier Regiment HJ on D-Day and 12th SS Panzer Division HJ from 16th June until 6th September 1944.

10. Panzermeyer driving Fritz Witt, his Divisional commander, on a reconnaissance in Normandy in early June 1944. The Regimental Medical Officer mounts the pillion. It is difficult to imagine equivalent Allied officers doing the same thing.

11. Max Wünsche, commander 12th SS Panzer Regiment.

12. Wünsche, slightly wounded on 9th June, with injured Rudolf von Ribbentrop, commander 3rd company 1st SS Panzer Battalion HJ. It is again hard to envisage an Allied armored brigade commander in similar circumstances.

13. Jochen Peiper being awarded the Knight's Cross in 1943. In June 1944 he was commanding the 1st SS Panzer Regiment LAH.

14. Kurt Meyer, Jochen Peiper, Max Wünsche and Sepp Dietrich celebrate Peiper's release from prison in December 1956.

15. Erich Olboeter, commanding
officer 3rd Battalion, 26th SS
Panzer-Grenadier Regiment HJ.

16. Michael Wittmann,
22nd June 1944.

17. Hans Waldmüller, seen on right,
commanding officer 1st Battalion, 25th SS
Panzer-Grenadier Regiment HJ.

18. Gerd Bremer,
commanding officer 12th
SS Reconnaissance
Battalion HJ.

19. Despite the disaster of the Falaise Pocket, Sepp Dietrich, Field Marshal Model and General Heinrich Eberbach are still cheerful—late August 1944.

20. Monty with Major General Stanislaw Maczek, commander 1st Polish Armored Division. (Courtesy PISM)

21. Lieutenant General Guy Simonds, commander II Canadian Corps.

22. Retreating German column destroyed on Mont Ormel by troops of the Polish 1st Armored Regiment and 9th Infantry Battalion, 18th August 1944. Panther in the foreground and Sherman top right. This is the first time since 1946 that this picture has been printed the right way around! (Courtesy PISM)

23. St. Lambert-sur-Dives, early afternoon 19th August 1944. Canadian troops are in control of the northern part of the village, but the heaviest fighting is yet to come. Major David Currie VC, second from left.

24. German column destroyed in the "Corridor of Death" near Moissy. (Courtesy PISM)

25. Calvary on Mont Ormel after the Battle. (Courtesy PISM)

26. Private John Wellington of the US 90th Infantry Division meets Corporal Grabowski of the 1st Polish Armored Division in Chambois on 19th August 1944. (Courtesy PISM)

27. Tiger I of the 101st SS Heavy Panzer Battalion knocked out by British infantrymen of 1/7 Queen's in Villers-Bocage, 13th June 1944.

28. Panthers knocked out on the Chambois-Vimoutier road on "Maczuga" by the Shermans of the Polish 1st Armored Regiment, August 1944. (Courtesy PISM)

29. Panther of the 1st SS Panzer Battalion HJ knocked out by Canadian troops during the attack on Bretteville l'Orgueilleuse on the 8th June 1944.

30. German Mark IV tank, knocked out by Polish troops near Chambois, 20th August 1944. (Courtesy PISM)

31. The much feared dual-roled 88mm anti-aircraft/anti-tank gun. Note the high profile and lack of protection for the crew. (Courtesy PISM)

32. SPW 251—standard German half-track armored personnel carrier. This engineer version belonged to the 12th SS Panzer Pioneer Battalion HJ.

33. Sherman of the Royal Scots Greys or Fort Garry Horse knocked out by the LAH on 1st August during the unsuccessful attack on Tilly-la-Campagne.

34. Cromwell of 4 CLY knocked out by Michael Wittmann in Villers-Bocage, 13th June 1944.

35. British Sherman tank mounting a 17 pdr anti-tank gun—
known as "Firefly."

36. Second British Army M-10 with 3-inch anti-tank gun and
50 cal machine gun.

counter-attack by Frey's 1st SS Panzer-Grenadier Regiment
LAH was ordered to recapture the village and relieve Krause's
Battalion. But since the attack was to be launched from the
north, it involved a move of 8km just to get to the jump-off
position.

Frey's 2nd SS Panzer-Grenadier Battalion reached the eastern edge of the airfield and allowed the withdrawal of Krause's
men to be accomplished without difficulty.

Shortly after midnight SS Lieutenant Colonel Wilhelm
Weidenhaupt's 3rd SS Panzer-Grenadier Battalion attacked
south towards Carpiquet from the line of the Route Nationale
13. One of its companies was hit by its own supporting artillery and suffered considerable casualties, but by first light the
Battalion had overrun a company of the Chaudières[10] and
reached the line of the railway. However, further attempts to
get into the village were stopped by Allied artillery fire and the
stubborn resistance of the North Shore and Chaudière Regiments. Meyer ordered the attack halted and told Weidenhaupt
to take up defensive positions on the line of the Route Nationale 13. Frey's Regiment appears to have received 118 casualties
in the fighting.[11]

At the request of Kurt Meyer, Lieutenant Colonel Böhme of
the 83rd Werfer Regiment was awarded the German Cross in
Gold for his personal valour and the performance of his Regiment on 4th and 5th July.

The most important consequence of the HJ's tenacious defence of the Carpiquet airfield was that it led Dempsey to
believe that it would be impossible to take Caen quickly and
without unacceptable casualties unless he was assisted by
Bomber Command. It also led to severe recriminations on the
Allied side. After the failure to take the airfield, commander I
Corps, Lieutenant General Crocker, wrote to Dempsey:

> The Div [3rd Canadian] as a whole carried out its D-Day
> tasks with great enthusiasm and considerable success. Once
> the excitement of the initial phase passed, however, the Div
> relapsed into a very nervy state. . . . Exaggerated reports of
> enemy activity and of their own difficulties were rife; every-
> one was far too quick on the trigger, and a general attitude

of despondency prevailed. Everyone was naturally tired and a bit shaken by the first impact of real war and there was a quite understandable reaction after the pent-up excitement of the assault. It was just here and now that the steadying hand of the Commander was required. It was totally lacking, indeed the state of the Div was a reflection of the state of its commander. He was obviously not standing up to the strain and showed signs of fatigue and nervousness (one might almost say fright) which was patent for all to see.

In this last day or two 3 Cdn Div has started active operations again. . . . The limited success of this operation I am afraid I can only attribute to a lack of control and leadership from the top. When things started to go not quite right all the signs of lack of calm, balanced judgement and firm command became evident again.

Dempsey sent this letter on to Montgomery with a recommendation for Major General Keller's removal. Montgomery passed both letters to Lieutenant General Henry Crerar, commander 1st Canadian Army, with the comment:

I have little to add to these letters. I definitely agree with them. . . . [Keller] has certain qualities which are assets. But taken all round I consider he is not good enough to command a Canadian division; the Canadian soldier is such a magnificent chap that he deserves, and should be given, really good generals.

Any suggestion of an anti-Canadian bias on the part of any of the British officers concerned can be discounted—one of Montgomery's own protégés, the commander of the famous 51st Highland Division, was sacked at this time. In the event, General Keller survived, only to be wounded later in the campaign.

NOTES

1. Meyer, Hubert, *The History of the 12th SS Panzer Division Hitlerjugend*, p. 134. 2. Winnipeg Rifles War Diary, 4 Jul 44. 3. Meyer, Hubert, op. cit., p. 137. 4. 8th Cdn Inf Bde War Diary, 4 Jul 44. 5. Winnipeg Rifles War Diary, 4 Jul 44. 6. Stacey, *The Official History of the Canadian Army in the Second World War, Vol III. The Victory Campaign*, p. 155. 7. Winnipeg

Rifles War Diary, 5 Jul 44. **8.** Meyer, Hubert, op. cit., p. 140. **9.** Meyer, Kurt, *Grenadiers*, p. 144. **10.** 8th Cdn Inf Bde War Diary, 5 Jul 44. **11.** Lehmann & Tiemann, *The Leibstandarte IV/I*, p. 129.

16 | 7th to 11th July— Operation CHARNWOOD and the Battle for Caen

7TH JULY—THE BOMBING

By 7th July I British Corps had been reinforced to a strength of 115,000 and Montgomery and Dempsey had plans to use it, in conjunction with Air Marshal Sir Arthur Harris's Bomber Command, to take Caen by frontal assault—all previous attempts to capture this D-Day objective having failed. The declared mission was to clear Caen as far as the Orne, and then to establish bridgeheads across the river. The British 3rd Infantry Division was to attack on the eastern flank, Major General Lyne's 59th Infantry Division in the centre, and Keller's 3rd Canadian Infantry Division from the west. Tanks of the 27th British and 2nd Canadian Armoured Brigades were to be in support, together with specialist tanks from the British 79th Armoured Division; additional artillery was to be provided by the guns of two Army Groups Royal Artillery and of the Guards Armoured and 51st Infantry Divisions, reinforced by naval gunfire from HMS *Rodney*, a monitor and two cruisers. In conjunction with this massive assault, VIII British Corps was to be at twenty-four hour's notice to launch another attack from the west with its 43rd Infantry Division, designed to reach the Orne in the region of St André.[1] This would involve the capture of Hill 112.

Sir Arthur Harris agreed with the ground commanders that, for safety reasons, bombs would be dropped no nearer than 6000 yards to the attacking Allied troops. This meant that the bombs would fall over 5km behind the German forward defences and virtually guaranteed that the vast majority of the defenders of Caen would survive unscathed. Since the attacking troops would be unable to follow the bombing closely, it was further decided to mount the air attack the evening before the ground attack and to set most of the fuses to detonate the

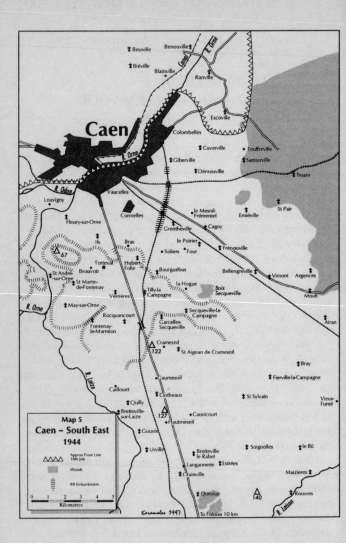

Map 5
Caen – South East
1944

	Approx Front Line 18th July
	Woods
	RR Embankment

0 1 2 3 4 5
Kilometres

Kavamales 1997

To Falaise 10 km

bombs six hours later. It was hoped that the destruction caused would prevent the Germans from bringing reinforcements through the city. Suggestions that the bombing was carried out the evening before the attack because of a forecast of bad weather for 8th July are incorrect.[2]

It will not have escaped the reader's notice that the planned onslaught was destined to fall on Dietrich's I SS Panzer Corps in general and Meyer's 12th SS Panzer Division HJ, with its reinforcing Regiment from the Leibstandarte, in particular. On the HJ's right, to the east of la Bijude, the newly arrived 16th Luftwaffe Field Division, with a Panzer battalion left behind by 21st Panzer Division when it moved away, held the front to the Caen canal. On the left of 12th SS, to the south and west of Verson, the II SS Panzer Corps had taken over.

On 5th July Hitler had ordered that 12th SS should be relieved as soon as possible. But since its planned relief, the 271st Infantry, had not yet arrived, Meyer's Division was still deployed as follows: the 25th SS Panzer-Grenadier Regiment from la Bijude through Buron to Franqueville; the 2nd SS Panzer-Grenadier Battalion of the 26th Regiment in St Germain-la-Blanche-Herbe; the 3rd Battalion of the same Regiment and the Divisional Escort Company in reserve in the north-west part of Caen and Krause's exhausted 1st Battalion resting to the south of the city, along with Bremer's 12th SS Reconnaissance Battalion and one of the Divisional artillery battalions.[3]

Albert Frey's 1st SS Panzer-Grenadier Regiment LAH, now complete, was holding a line from Franqueville through les Jumeaux to the western part of Eterville[4] and the Leibstandarte's 1st SS Artillery Battalion had caught up.

The four batteries of the 12th SS (88mm) Flak Battalion were deployed throughout the 12th SS area of responsibility, with many guns sited to fight tanks as well as aircraft, and the Werfers of the HJ and the 3rd Battalion of the 83rd Regiment were sited north and west of Caen.[5]

Bear in mind that the HJ had thirty-two Mk IVs and twenty-eight Panthers combat ready on 7th July. Nine Mk IVs of the 5th Company were in ambush positions in Buron and Gruchy, five of the 9th Company on the eastern edge of Carpiquet airfield and eleven Panthers from the 1st, 2nd and 4th Companies between Bretteville and Eterville. This left eighteen Mk IVs and seventeen Panthers of the 3rd Company which had just been re-equipped, in reserve near Ardenne and in the western outskirts of Caen.[6] Meyer's Headquarters was located in part of the ancient Abbaye aux Dames.

Following an artillery and naval bombardment of Caen which started at 2000 hours on 7th July, the aerial onslaught began at 2150 hours and lasted until 2230. It was carried out by 467 Lancaster and Halifax heavy bombers and followed by ground attack aircraft which attacked specific point targets. Some 6,000 actual bombs (2,500 tons) were dropped which destroyed the city, blocked all routes and killed several hundred French civilians. Miraculously the Cathedral, Abbaye-aux-Hommes and Hôpital du Bon Sauveur, where many civilians had sheltered, were not hit. German casualties were minimal. The HJ lost two Mk IVs and under twenty men,[7] and the LAH even less.[8]

Although Allied artillery continued to pound the southern approaches to Caen and German forward positions throughout the night, the morale of the young SS men apparently remained high, sustained to some extent by, as they saw it, the rather pathetic results of this huge effort. Kurt Meyer's comments on this aspect of the attack are interesting:

> The air raid seems to be the prelude to the main assault. Every last Grenadier is at the ready. The gunners stand by for orders to lay down a curtain of fire in front of our own lines. We wait. The phones are silent. We stare tensely out into the night awaiting the enemy ground force's attack. Minutes pass without the silence being broken. It is inconceivable but true. The Allies are making no attempt to exploit the tremendous bombing operation.[9]

8TH JULY—THE ATTACK

H-Hour for Operation CHARNWOOD was 0420 hours on 8th July. It began as usual with a shattering artillery barrage by 656 guns, behind which the two British Divisions advanced towards their objectives. H-Hour for the Canadians was de-

pendent on how well the initial British attacks proceeded and
was finally ordered for 0730 hours.

As far as Meyer's 12th SS Panzer Division and the attached
Leibstandarte Regimental group were concerned, the relevant
Allied objectives were: la Bijude and Epron for the 176th British Infantry Brigade, reinforced with a tank battalion and anti-
tank, machine-gun and specialist tank units; Galmanche for
the 197th British Infantry Brigade, similarly reinforced and
with an extra infantry battalion; and Buron, Gruchy, Authie
and Franqueville for the 9th Canadian Infantry Brigade and
Sherbrooke Fusilier tanks. The 8th Canadian Infantry Brigade
and Fort Garry Horse tanks were to take Carpiquet airfield
once the outskirts of Caen had been reached by the rest of the
3rd Canadian Division. (Kurt Meyer believed this attack
should have been launched at the same time with the aim of
cutting off the retreat of his Division).

Despite further air attacks lasting two hours by 250 medium
bombers of the Ninth US Air Force against strong points, gun
areas and suspected Headquarters, Meyer's men fought with
their usual tenacity. The British 59th Division committed
seven infantry and two tank battalions, and the Canadians
nine infantry and two tank battalions during the day.

Meyer, after visiting Milius in the Command Post of the
25th SS Panzer-Grenadier Regiment in the Ardenne Abbey and
Karl Ritzel's SS (88mm) Flak Battery at Cussy, where he found
the Battery commander himself laying a gun, eventually returned to his own Headquarters in the early evening. He reported to Dietrich by telephone that since the 16th Luftwaffe
Field Division had collapsed, his right flank was dangerously
exposed and the British (9th Infantry and 33rd Tank Brigades)
had penetrated into the outskirts of Caen.

Milius's 1st SS Battalion had had to give up la Bijude, and
Epron was therefore threatened; the remnants of the 2nd SS
Battalion were cut off in Glamanche and the British (1/7 Royal
Warwicks) had reached St Contest at 1550 hours; the 3rd SS
Panzer-Grenadier Battalion was surrounded by the Canadians
in Buron. A counter-attack at 1730 hours by two Panther pla-
toons of von Ribbentrop's 3rd SS Panzer Company had failed
to relieve the crisis and seven tanks had been lost in the pro-

cess. Gruchy, Authie, Franqueville and Carpiquet airfield had all fallen to the Canadians although at terrible cost (the North Shore Regiment alone lost 262 men, including sixty-two killed).[10]

At 1830 hours Major General Keller committed the Canadian 7th Infantry Brigade and by 2130 hours Cussy had fallen to the Canadian Scottish with help from two Winnipeg companies; SS Captain Ritzel and the last survivors of his 1st SS 88mm Flak Battery had died over their guns but had made their enemies pay dearly—the Canadian Scottish lost thirty-four killed, sixty-eight wounded and two missing.[11] The Regina Rifles had only been prevented from taking the Ardenne Abbey by artillery and Werfer fire and a counter-attack by Panthers and Frey's 3rd SS (LAH) Panzer-Grenadiers. Another counter-attack by the 3rd SS Panther Company failed to recapture Cussy.

Allied hopes of reaching the Orne bridges in Caen with light reconnaissance elements of the British Inns of Court and Royal Canadian Hussar Reconnaissance Regiments were dashed when they came under fire and ran into mines in St Germain-la-Blanche-Herbe. But by now Meyer knew that his tired Division was being overwhelmed and he begged for permission to withdraw what was left of his command. Dietrich refused, saying a Führer Order demanded that Caen be held at all costs. Meyer was furious, but his Chief of Staff pleaded with his opposite number at I SS Panzer Corps and finally Fritz Kraemer said the magic words:

> If you are thrown back to the southern banks of the Orne while fighting a superior enemy, it could never be considered to be a withdrawal contrary to orders.[12]

This was enough for Meyer and he gave the necessary orders. When one considers the casualties suffered by Dietrich's 'boys', even Hitler could never have accused them of givin up prematurely. Hubert Meyer gives firm figures of 423 killed, wounded and missing.[13] This does not include those for Milius's 3rd SS Panzer-Grenadier Battalion, which are not recorded; nor yet those for the 3rd Leibstandarte Panzer-Grenadier Battalion at Franqueville. The latter's commanding officer, Weidenhaupt, was certainly wounded and a conservative estimate would add a further 200 to the overall total. A strength return dated 9th July shows only eighteen Panthers and ten Mk IVs operational, indicating a probable loss, for one reason or another, of ten Panthers and twenty-two Mk IVs on 8th July.

At 1915 hours Rommel approved the withdrawal of all heavy weapons from the Caen bridgehead and a regrouping south of the Orne.[14] Eberbach, commander Panzer Group West, had undoubtedly encouraged him to do so—he had paid a valuable and dangerous visit to Meyer's Command Post during the morning and was fully in the picture.

But it was one thing to order a withdrawal and quite another to execute it when locked in battle with a determined enemy. In the case of 12th SS the operation was carried out with typical Waffen-SS aggression. Wünsche's 12th SS Panzer Regiment—or rather the thirty or so tanks available—was ordered to free the encircled parts of Milius's 25th SS Panzer-Grenadier Regiment, and the Divisional Escort Company and Olboeter's exhausted and depleted SS Grenadiers were told to cover the Division's withdrawal. Bremer's severely weakened 12th SS Reconnaissance Battalion was given the task of right flank protection and what was left of Müller's 12th SS Pioneers told to provide a close-bridge garrison on the Orne bridge in Caen and be prepared to blow it on order. A new line was designated along the southern bank of the Orne, with the 25th Regiment from the eastern edge of Vaucelles to the bend in the river, and Frey's 1st LAH Regiment from there to the north of Louvigny and on to the west of Eterville. Meyer's Command Post was to move first to Faubourg de Vaucelles and later to Garcelles.

9TH JULY—THE WITHDRAWAL

Meyer wrote later that if the Allies had continued their attacks during the night his Division would almost certainly have been destroyed. They did not; but even so the withdrawal during the night of 8th–9th July was a nightmare. SS Major Waldmüllers' 1st SS Panzer-Grenadier Battalion was described as "like a breakwater against a tidal wave" in its defence of the

Epron area against the 6th North Staffords and the tanks of
the 13th/18th Hussars. The Battalion was only able to withdraw due to the efforts of its 1st Company, and in particular a
platoon under SS Senior Sergeant Schümann. He and most of
his men were killed but some of them were still holding on
two days later. The forty or so survivors of the 7th Company
of the 2nd SS Battalion who had held Galmanche, escaped in
the darkness by silently by-passing their enemies.

The Ardenne Abbey, which had seen so much fighting, was
finally abandoned by Milius at midnight although survivors
were still resisting there up to 0135 hours on the 9th.[15]

Spasmodic resistance continued north of the Orne during
the following day. Mâlon was finally reported clear at 1245
hours, Bitot at 1350 and la Folie at 1640 hours. British patrols
reached the centre of Caen around midday but progress
through the rubble-filled streets was painstakingly slow. The
bombing, first on 6th-7th of June and then again on 8th July,
had devastated the city. It seems the lessons of Monte Cassino
had been forgotten.

The Canadians took till 1430 hours[16] to clear St Germain-la-
Blanche-Herbe and they needed the assistance of tanks to push
the Divisional Escort Company and the remnants of
Olboeter's 3rd SS Battalion back into, and through, Caen.
Olboeter himself was one of the last to cross the Orne bridge
and once the stragglers were across the SS Pioneers blew it.
They then all formed part of the defence on the south bank.
The HJ lost another sixty-three men in the day's fighting.[17]

Montgomery's men had finally reached their D-Day objective—they were over a month late and even now they had
taken only the northern part of Caen. The cost had been appalling—3,817 casualties. The 3rd and 59th British Divisions
took well over 1,000 each on 8th July alone and the 3rd Canadian Division received 1,194 in the two days fighting—more
than it suffered on D-Day.[18] At least eighty Allied tanks had
been knocked out.[19] The ratio of Allied casualties to German
was more than six to one, but this is hardly surprising in view
of Allied tactics which in the case of infantry divisions usually
meant using tanks to support attacks rather than to lead them.
And it will probably not have escaped the reader's notice that

by this stage of the campaign the casualties suffered by the Canadian 3rd Infantry Division and 2nd Armoured Brigade (4,138), were higher than those received by the 12th SS Panzer Division which had done considerably more fighting.

And the bombing? Had it achieved anything of military value, other than to lift the morale of the Allied soldiers as they watched wave after wave of aircraft streaming over them the evening before the attack? Professor Solly Zucherman, scientific adviser to Air Chief Marshal Sir Arthur Tedder, Eisenhower's Deputy, and a supposed expert on Allied bombing policy, visited the target area immediately afterwards and reported that there were almost no signs of German equipment or dead in the target area. Later remarks[20] by Montgomery's chief operations officer, Major General David Belchem, that the area was known to contain enemy defensive and headquarters locations and that the bombing caused extensive damage to those headquarters and eliminated many enemy gun emplacements, are quite simply not true. Tedder refused to give Zucherman's report a wide circulation on the grounds that, "He had never read a more demoralising document."[21] The destruction of Caen had been for nothing.

It would be wrong to leave the battle of Caen without some personal reminiscences. SS Second Lieutenant Willi Kändler, commanding five Mk IVs of the 5th SS Panzer Company, recalled his part in the battle:

> We were able to watch our hits easily. With our Panzer alone we knocked out five Sherman tanks. . . . With our machine guns we forced enemy infantry into the ground and inflicted heavy losses on them. During these hours we fired 10,000 aimed rounds of machine-gun ammunition. . . . Each of our Panzers landed hit after hit while we suffered no losses. The hedges provided us with good cover. We frequently moved the Panzers small distances to new positions so as to reduce the enemy's chances of accurately targeting our muzzle flashes.[22]

But not everyone was as fortunate—SS Sergeant Heinz Freiberg was one of von Ribbentrop's Panther commanders in a tank battle, almost certainly with the Canadian Sherbrooke Fusiliers:

As we passed an opening in a wall there were two sudden explosions. The Panzer of Sepp Trattning and another stood in flames. We immediately fired both MGs at the wall opening. I spotted some movement there and then a further flash. Already we were hit in the turret mantlet and the armour-piercing shell dropped into the fighting compartment . . . the gunner was wounded in the face and I had a small shrapnel wound in my left arm. The turret crew bailed out immediately and because of heavy MG fire took cover behind the Panzer. The driver and radio operator had not noticed this activity and sat placidly in the Panzer, its engine running quietly. I jumped back on the 'crate', yelled the order 'backward march!' . . . and we set out for Ardenne. After a few metres drive, the pedestal of our antenna, which I had used as a foothold, was shot off. Thus, I lost a heel. After some 500m we reached our infantry where our gunner and loader had already arrived.[23]

And now one from the infantry—SS Sergeant Siegfried Bleich of the 1st Company of Waldmüller's 1st SS Panzer-Grenadier Battalion, after being ordered to fight its way back to Caen from the Epron area:

Together with a corporal I searched the terrain for wounded men, but also in the hope of finding Panzerfausts in the abandoned positions.

In the field we found a boy who had dragged himself back this far, despite a wounded foot, but could go no further. I carried him on my back through the haze caused by the phosphorous grenades. I seldom felt so worn out as I did after this ordeal. Someone had found a wheelbarrow and was pushing it ahead of him. Only when I got closer in the falling darkness did I notice that our Chief was riding in it. . . . Suddenly, armour noises were coming closer. Of course the boys were very excited, until someone hailed us. Waldmüller had sent our Panzers forward to bring us back. At that time we were down to barely thirty men.[24]

Perhaps the last word should go to Meyer himself. After the withdrawal, he found some of Waldmüller's men in a bunker on the edge of Caen:

> The soldiers, totally exhausted by the fighting, have fallen into a deep sleep. The officers have taken over guard duty. Late-comers stumble into the bunker and collapse. . . . The soldiers of the 12th SS Panzer Division are at the end of their physical endurance. . . . They went to war weeks ago with fresh, blooming faces. Today, camouflaged muddy steel helmets shade emaciated faces whose eyes have, all too often, looked into another world. The men present a picture of deep human misery; but it is no use, they can't rest any longer. . . . Each Grenadier has to be woken individually. They stagger drowsily out of the bunker and hang their ammunition round their necks once again; the heavy machine-gun belts drag the half-awake Grenadiers forward. Swearing, they hitch themselves to two heavy infantry guns and turn back towards the burning town.[25]

During the evening and night of 9th July the rest of SS Major General Teddy Wisch's 1s SS Panzer Division Leibstandarte began to arrive in the Caen sector. The 1st SS Panzer-Grenadier Battalion and part of the 2nd, from Rudolph Sandig's 2nd SS Regiment, were attached to Frey's Regiment and took up positions in depth on the right flank; they ran from the southern edge of Caen to le Mesnil. Of course Frey's 1st Regiment was already committed—SS Lieutenant Colonel Schiller's 1st SS Panzer-Grenadier Battalion around Louvigny, Herford's 2nd from le Mesnil to Eterville and SS Captain Graetz's 3rd SS Panzer-Grenadier Battalion on the hills west and south-west of Maltot (Weidenhaupt had been wounded on the 8th). The first LAH Sturmgeschütz (StuG) Company to arrive was sited in depth at Louvigny. The rest of Sandig's Grenadiers took up another position in depth running from the Caen to Falaise main road to the junction of the Odon and Orne rivers.

Kurt Meyer decided to move most of what was left of Wünsche's 12th SS Panzer Regiment, less than thirty tanks, to new positions to the south-east of Maltot during the last hours of the 9th and the 2nd SS Panzer (Mk IV) Battalion of Jochen Peiper's 1s SS Panzer Regiment was held in reserve in the area of Bully—this was in fact in the sector of II SS Panzer Corps. A strength return shows this Battalion had sixty Mk IVs combat ready on 9th July. Peiper's 1st Panther Battalion had thirty tanks operational and Heimann's Sturmgeschütz Battalion forty-one StuGs. Although not all these units had arrived by first light 10th July, the south-west sector of the Caen front was, nevertheless, strongly held, and the remainder of the LAH would arrive in the next few hours.

A member of Sandig's 2nd SS Panzer-Grenadier Regiment, Werner Josupeit, remembered his journey to the front on 9th July:

> We moved under the cover of darkness and with large distances between the elements. We took the Route Nationale towards Caen. To our left (on Hill 112) there was the constant flash of artillery fire. Its thunder grew louder and louder. Then we heard the strange chatter of British machine-guns. A few comrades with experience at the front were sitting opposite me in the truck. In the flickering light I could see fear on their faces. The rest of us did not have a clue what lay before us. We were wound up for action. Some of us sang. (I thought it over later. I realized that the comrades who had done the most singing that night were not with us on the next transport. They were killed, wounded or missing. Was that just a coincidence?) Last year I drove that road once more and called those pictures back to memory. After forty years they still gave me a chill down my spine.[26]

NOTES

1. Ellis, *Victory in the West, Vol I, The Battle of Normandy*, p. 310. 2. Ibid., p. 312. 3. Meyer, Hubert, *The History of the 12th SS Panzer Division Hitlerjugend*, p. 141. 4. Lehmann & Tiemann, *The Leibstandarte IV/I*, p. 132. 5. Meyer, Hubert, op. cit., p. 141. 6. Ibid. 7. Ibid., p. 143. 8. Lehmann & Tiemann, op. cit., p. 132. 9. Meyer, Kurt, *Grenadiers*, p. 145. 10. Stacey, *The Official History of the Canadian Army in the Second World War, Vol III, The Victory Campaign*, p. 161. 11. Cdn Scots War Diary, 8 Jul 44. 12. Meyer, Hubert, op. cit., p. 147. 13. Ibid., p. 150. 14. Panzer Group West War Diary. 15. 7 Cdn Inf Bde War Diary, 8 Jul 44. 16. 9 Cdn Inf Bde War Diary, 9 Jul 44. 17. Meyer, Hubert, op. cit., p. 151. 18. Stacey, op. cit., p. 163. 19. Ellis, op. cit., p. 316. 20. Belchem, *Victory in Normandy*, p. 150.

21. D'Este, *Decision in Normandy*, p. 317. 22. Meyer, Hubert, op. cit., pp. 144–145. 23. Ibid., p. 146. 24. Ibid., p. 148. 25. Meyer, Kurt, op. cit., p. 150. 26. Lehmann & Tiemann, op. cit., p. 134.

17 | 10th to 11th July—Operation JUPITER and the Battle for Hill 112

In conjuction with Operation CHARNWOOD the British VIII Corps was ordered to advance to the Orne in the region of St André-sur-Orne. The operation was code-named JUPITER and involved seizing the high ground between the Odon and Orne in the general area of Hill 112 and Maltot. Major General G. I. (Butcher) Thomas's 43rd (Wessex) Infantry Division was given the task and reinforced by two regiments of the 31st Tank Brigade, the 4th Armoured Brigade and the 46th Highland Brigade. Thomas's plan was for his own infantry brigades with tank support to take Hill 112 and Maltot and then for the 4th Armoured Brigade to exploit to the Orne. Additional artillery support was to be provided by guns of two Army Groups Royal Artillery and the 11th Armoured and 15th Scottish Divisions; ground attack aircraft were to be available all day. H-Hour was set for 0500 hours on 10th July.

Covering the attack area in the sector running from Bretteville-sur-Odon to south-east of Maltot were some thirty tanks of Wünsche's 12th SS Panzer Regiment and four LAH units— the 1st SS StuG Battalion (forty-one StuGs) and the three battalions of Frey's 1st SS Panzer-Grenadier Regiment. Responsibility for the main ridge running from Hill 112 to Hill 113 lay with SS Brigadier Harmel's 10th SS Panzer Division Frundsberg. There is some confusion over which formation was responsible for Eterville since both 1st and 10th SS Divisions claim to have fought there. It seems probable that a battalion of the 22nd SS Panzer-Grenadier Regiment (10th SS) was in position in and to the north-west of the village and the 2nd SS Panzer-Grenadier Battalion LAH was on the reverse slope to its east.

At 0615 hours the 5th Battalion The Dorsetshire Regiment (5 Dorset), part of the 130th Infantry Brigade, reported it had captured the Château de Fontaine; in reality fierce fighting

continued there for the rest of the morning. Nevertheless, this
was the signal for its sister Battalion, 4 Dorset, with Churchills
in support, to advance and by 0800 hours it had reached
Eterville. Both the 22nd SS Panzer-Grenadiers and Herford's
2nd SS Panzer-Grenadier Battalion had been forced to withdraw—the latter to Athis.

The 7th Battalion The Hampshire Regiment reported it had
taken Maltot at 0915 hours but that its attempt to dig in 400
yards south of the village had been prevented by tank fire.[1] At
1035 hours the Battalion said nine of its supporting tanks had
been knocked out and German infantry and Tiger tanks were
infiltrating back into the village. At least one of the Tigers was
from Möbius's 1st Company and the others were a platoon of
SS Lieutenant Colonel Hans Weiss's 102nd SS Heavy Panzer
Battalion which had moved in from St Martin. The infantry
were those of SS Lieutenant Hasse's 11th Company of the 3rd
SS Panzer-Grenadier Battalion; Hasse was to be awarded the
Knight's Cross for his actions on this day. 5 Dorset, after its
struggle to clear the Château de Fontaine, attempted to move
on and make contact with the Hampshires at Maltot but failed
in the face of Tiger tanks and the 22nd SS Panzer-Grenadiers.
By 1400 hours the Hampshires had been deprived of their
prize.

Meanwhile the 129th Brigade had advanced on Hill 112, but
the infantrymen of the 4th Somerset Light Infantry (SLI) and
tanks of 7 RTR could not get beyond the crest[2]—again, almost
all the Churchills were lost. An officer of the Greys described
the scene on Hill 112:

> The skyline was dominated by Churchill tanks 'brewing-up',
> not a pretty sight. They had all gone just too far over the
> ridge and were being knocked out like ninepins by the en-
> emy who were in extremely good positions. . . . there
> were dead and wounded men lying all over the ground in
> the long grass, rifles stuck in the ground marking the posi-
> tions of their owners—a gruesome sight. . . . Tank crews
> who had managed to escape from their flaming vehicles
> were crawling back, their clothing and all exposed parts of

their bodies burnt, black all over from smoke, oil and cordite fumes.[3]

Back on the British left flank 4 Dorset and a squadron of 9 RTR renewed the attack on Maltot at 1620 hours. They reached the village after terrible losses, only to suffer more from an attack by a squadron of RAF Typhoons. At about 1830 hours the Germans launched a strong counter-attack with SS Panzer-Grenadiers and some of Wünsche's tanks. The Dorset defence lost cohesion and after all the Battalion's anti-tank guns were destroyed, the Brigade commander ordered the remnants to withdraw.[4]

At 1930 hours the 5th Battalion Duke of Cornwall's Light Infantry (5 DCLI), from Thomas's reserve 214th Infantry Brigade, supported by fourteen Churchills of 7 RTR, was ordered to attack to relieve the pressure on 4 SLI and to make a final attempt to take Hill 112. The rifle companies advanced through the carnage of the previous fighting and the rusting hulks of British and German tanks knocked out two weeks before. Despite heavy casualties, part of the Battalion managed to dig in near the small wood on the summit but at last light the surviving Churchills withdrew and the British were left holding a line from Eterville through Fontaine-Etoupefour and its Château to the northern slopes of the elusive Hill 112.[5] It had been a costly day—7 and 9 RTR had lost thirty-nine tanks between them,[6] the Greys three Shermans and a Stuart,[7] 5 Dorset had incurred 208 casualties[8] and 4 SLI 189.[9]

Field Marshal The Lord Carver, then commanding the 4th Armoured Brigade, gives an alarming version of events on 10th July in his book, *Out of Step*:

Thomas's plan was for two brigades of his division to capture the ridge. . . . 4th Armoured Brigade was then to thrust through six miles to the Orne and try to capture a bridge over it. It looked like Balaclava all over again. . . . The only stipulation I insisted on was that, before launching my leading regiment over the crest of Hill 112, the square wood on its reverse slope must be firmly in our hands. If it were not, my tanks would be shot up from the rear as they went forward. After further heated argument and objections from the infantry, it was agreed. . . .

The infantry attack was launched [with]. . . . the Churchills of the squadron of 9 RTR supporting the final phase of the attack being almost all knocked out by anti-tank fire from this wood, which the infantry had not cleared. Having confirmed this myself . . . I [said] I would not order my leading regiment over the crest towards the river Orne until the wood had been cleared of enemy, as had been agreed. . . . Thomas came on the set [radio] himself and said that his information from his infantry brigades was that all the objectives had been secured, and that I must start my forward thrust. I said I was on the spot, as his infantry brigadiers were not, and that if he did not believe me, he could come and see for himself. This, not surprisingly, did not please him. He insisted that I should order my tanks to advance over the crest. I said that if I did, I expected that the leading regiment would suffer at least 75% casualties. . . . He asked me which regiment I proposed to send. I told him it was The Greys. [Scotland's only professional cavalry Regiment!] 'Couldn't you send a less well-known regiment?' he replied, at which I blew up. Finally he accepted my arguments.

Around midnight a major counter-attack by Frey's 1st and 2nd SS Panzer-Grenadier Battalions LAH was launched against the hills to the north of Maltot and Eterville respectively. The latter changed hands a number of times during the night and at dawn was held by the 9th Cameronians, who had relieved 4 Dorset, whilst Maltot remained in German hands. The ferocity of the fighting can be judged by the fact that one company of Graetz's 3rd SS Panzer-Grenadier Battalion lost forty-four men during the night.[10]

At 0615 hours on the 11th the 2nd SS Panzer-Grenadier Battalion LAH, supported by Leibstandarte StuGs and elements of the 22nd SS Panzer-Grenadier Regiment (10th SS Panzer Division), recaptured most of Eterville. They lost it again by 1415 hours but with help from the 1st SS Panzer-Grenadier Battalion LAH the eastern edge had been retaken by nightfall. The Glasgow Highlanders, who had relieved the Cameronians during the afternoon, lost eighty-five men during their short time in the village,[11] but the British claimed three StuGs[12] and over 100 Germans killed in this fighting. By last light the LAH line had been re-established from Maltot to Louvigny.

Also during the early hours of 11th July the 10th SS Panzer Division, with Tigers from II SS Panzer Corps, attacked the depleted 5 DCLI on Hill 112, but they could not fully secure it and the summit became a no-man's-land. In less than twelve hours the DCLI had lost their second commanding officer and 254 men, including twenty-six shell shocked and nine suffering from complete exhaustion.[13]

Michael Carver described the events of the 11th as he saw them.

> A fresh attack was made in the early hours of the next day, the infantry [5 DCLI] being joined in the wood by a squadron of the Greys at first light; enemy artillery fire was so heavy that the infantry were withdrawn, and, as it was no place to leave tanks on their own, the Greys came with them. The Germans also counter-attacked elsewhere and the 31st Tank Brigade lost many of the Churchill tanks. . . . Thomas was now resigned to the failure of his operation.[14]

The Greys lost five Shermans on the 11th although the 4th Armoured Brigade claimed nine German tanks knocked out.[15]

Late on the first day of JUPITER the 8th Canadian Brigade, which by then had been attached to Thomas's 43rd Division, started to cross the Odon on the eastern flank and this brought the number of Allied brigades between the two rivers to five infantry and two armoured—a superiority of some ten to one in infantry and much more in tanks. But at the end of one of the bloodiest battles of the Normandy campaign, the Allies had failed to eject the men of the I and II SS Panzer Corps from the vital ground between the Odon and Orne. Graphic descriptions of the misery and horror suffered by those who fought on Hill 112 and around Maltot can be read in Major J. J. How's excellent book, *Hill 112 Cornerstone of the Normandy Campaign.*

But some German reserve units, such as the LAH's 2nd SS Panzer Battalion at Bully, had not even been committed to battle. Most of the men of this Battalion spent the two days trying to dig in their tanks. Gerhard Stiller of the 7th SS Panzer Company gave an indication of a professionalism so often lacking on the Allied side:

> As dawn approached [10th July], we finished camouflaging the vehicles. . . . Dig in—but how? There was perhaps a 30cm layer of top soil with solid rock below. . . . In desperation the crews grabbed pick-axes. But we had only two per Panzer. . . . We hacked away the whole day. . . . If we got tired the bomber attacks kept reminding us of the need to keep working. . . . We tried blasting out holes with hand grenades and blasting cartridges. Finally, the Company commander issued a strict order: 'No blasting with our own ammunition supplies'. . . . It took us more than two days to get anywhere near dug in. We worked practically round the clock. Meanwhile, the order could have come at any time: 'Prepare to march!'. . . . Hacking, digging and blasting makes a man thirsty. We found barrels of cider in the cellars of Bully. The rabbits from the farmer's hutches, left to fend for themselves after the flight of their owners, soon found their way into the Panzer crews' cook pots. Water was scarce, however, because many of Bully's wells had caved in.[16]

The Official British History admits to two thousand casualties in Operation JUPITER and says that little ground was gained. However, since it was the British and not the Germans who were doing the attacking, it is difficult to understand its claim that the 10th SS Panzer Division, 102nd SS Heavy Tank Battalion and part of 1st SS Panzer Division had been *held* (author's emphasis) in the fight and even more incomprehensible that the writer completely fails to mention the Hitlerjugend Division.[17]

Early in the morning of 11th July, Meyer's battle-weary Division was finally pulled out of the line and the Leibstandarte took over the sector known as 'Caen South'. Even then it was required to leave behind the 12th SS Panzer Artillery Regiment in support of the LAH and Siebken's 2nd SS Panzer-Grenadier Battalion on the Orne at St André. The rest of the 12th SS concentrated in the area Sassy, Condé, Garcelles, Potigny, Bons for refitting.

Two other things happened during JUPITER. On 10th July Michael Wittmann, having returned from the Berghof where Hitler had awarded him Swords to his Knight's Cross for his action at Villers-Bocage, assumed command of what was left of the 101st SS Heavy Panzer Battalion—von Westernhagen was suffering badly from a previous head wound and could no longer carry on. And the following day Möbius's 1st Tiger Company handed over its last three tanks to the 2nd and 3rd Companies and left Normandy forever. The remainder of the Battalion would shortly be withdrawn to the Forêt de Cinglais for refitting.

NOTES

1. 7 Hamps War Diary, 10 Jul 44. 2. 7 RTR & 4 SLI War Diaries, 10 Jul 44. 3. Carver, Second to None, p. 115. 4. 9 RTR & 4 Dorset War Diaries, 10 Jul 44. 5. 129 & 130 Inf Bde War Diaries, 10 Jul 44. 6. 31 Tk Bde War Diary, 10 Jul 44. 7. Carver, op. cit., p. 117. 8. 5 Dorset War diary, 10 Jul 44. 9. 4 SLI War Diary, 10 Jul 44. 10. Lehmann & Tiemann, The Leibstandarte IV/I, p. 139. 11. Martin, History of the 15th Scottish Division 1939–1945, p. 64. 12. Carver, op. cit., p. 119. 13. 5 DCLI War Diary, 11 Jul 44. 14. Carver, Out of Step, p. 194. 15. 4 Armd Bde War Diary, 11 Jul 44. 16. Lehmann & Tiemann, op. cit., pp. 139–140. 17. Ellis, Victory in the West, Vol 1, The Battle of Normandy, p. 318.

18 | 12th to 17th July—R & R

The Caen South sector which 1st SS Panzer Division LAH took over on 11th July ran from Maltot on the west flank to the Caen-Falaise road on the east. SS Lieutenant Colonel Frey's 1st SS Panzer-Grenadier REgiment still held the forward line with its 1st Battalion and the 1st SS StuG Company at Louvigny, 2nd Battalion at Eterville and 3rd Battalion, together with the 2nd SS StuG Company, at Maltot. The 3rd (SPW) SS Panzer-Grenadier Battalion of SS Lieutenant Colonel Rudolf Sandig's 2nd Regiment was positioned in Divisional reserve at St André, whilst his 2nd Battalion held the south-western section of Caen itself. The 2nd SS Panzer (Mk IV) Battalion LAH, less a company in Corps reserve, was still in depth at Bully. The rest of the Leibstandarte was concentrated 10km to the south in the Forêt de Cinglais.

On 12th July intense fighting continued around Eterville and Maltot and attempts by the 8th Canadian Infantry Brigade to take the vital area of Louvigny were defeated. Powerful support for the defenders was provided by both the LAH and HJ SS Artillery Regiments—it will be recalled that the latter had been left behind when 12th SS was pulled out.

German plans to relieve their Panzer Divisions with infantry were at last taking shape. By 11th July most of Panzer Lehr had already been extracted and moved across to engage the Americans and now, after two relatively quiet days on the 13th and 14th, the newly arrived 272nd Infantry Division joined I SS Panzer Corps and began to take over the Caen South sector from the Leibstandarte. During the nights of the 14th and 15th, the bulk of 1st SS moved to a new concentration area astride the Caen-Falaise road (Route Nationale 158) between Ifs and Cintheaux. SS Lieutenant Colonel Fritz Schröder's over-worked 12th SS Artillery Regiment and SS Major Fend's 12th SS Flak Battalion, both from the HJ, were left behind to support the new infantry Division, and the 2nd SS (Mk IV) Panzer, 1st SS StuG, 3rd SS (SPW) Panzer-Grenadier and 1st SS (SP) Artillery Battalions LAH were all left west of the Orne in a Corps reserve role.

Meanwhile, the Hitlerjugend Division was licking its wounds. The recorded casualties for 12th SS during Operations CHARNWOOD and JUPITER are 595.[1] Taking into account the figures given in Chapter 13 and again analysing Hubert Meyer's figures, we have a maximum of 3,304 and a minimum of 2,988 casualties for the period 6th June to 11th July—far less than those quoted in most books, or those indicated in Kurt Meyer's book, *Grenadiers*, where he says, 'More than 20% of the soldiers had been killed in action and more than 40% reported as wounded or missing.' Presumably he was talking about combat, rather than total, strength; but even in this case his figures would amount to an unrealistic total of

7,200. It is surprising that both the British and Canadian Official Histories say that Meyer's Division had been reduced to a fighting strength of only one battalion by the end of JUPITER. It is plain that it had not. Nevertheless, 3,304 is 28% of the fighting strength of 12th SS and there is no doubt that its fighting capability had been severly reduced. An analysis of Hubert Meyer's figures reveals that, as absolute minimums, the personnel strengths of the major fighting elements of the HJ had been reduced as follows: the Panzer Regiment by 16%, the 25th Regiment by 25%, 26th Regiment by 30%, Reconnaissance Battalion by 25% and Pioneer Battalion by 43%.

Tank casualties during this period are difficult to establish with any precision. According to Hubert Meyer,[2] seventeen replacement Panthers arrived during the first week in July and were used to re-equip von Ribbentrop's 3rd SS Panzer Company (this contradicts his commander's statement that no replacement tanks were received during the fighting in June and the first half of July); we have therefore a starting figure of ninety-six Panthers and ninety-six Mk IVs. Furthermore, if Hubert Meyer's figures of forty-eight Panthers and forty-six Mk IVs operational or in short-term repair on 11th July are correct, it means the Division had lost forty-eight Panthers and fifty Mk IVs in the fighting up to that date—almost exactly half its strength.

Clearly a major restructuring and reinforcement of 12th SS Panzer Division was required. It is known that thirty-six new Mk IVs were on their way by 17th July.[3] In the meantime a reorganisation within Wünsche's 12th SS Panzer Regiment, based near St Sylvain, produced eighteen Panthers and twenty-one Mk IVs ready for action by 16th July. Similar reorganisations and amalgamations of the SS Panzer-Grenadier battalions ensured that Milius's 25th and Mohnke's 26th SS Panzer-Grenadier Regiments, in the Sassy and Ouilly areas respectively, had some combat effective units by 17th July. The 1st and 3rd SS Panzer-Grenadier Battalions of the 25th Regiment amalgamated under Waldmüller, and Siebken's 2nd Battalion of the 26th Regiment provided men for Krause's 1st and Olboeter's 3rd Battalions. Siebken and his staff, together with Milius and the other command elements of the 25th Regiment were withdrawn back to base areas near Vimoutiers in order to receive reinforcements from the Divisional Replacement Battalion and men combed out of rear support units.

On 16th July, to the amazement and dismay of Dietrich and Kurt Meyer, von Kluge ordered the HJ to move at once to the Lisieux-Pont l'Evêque area. This order had originated with Hitler who was concerned that there might be another landing to the east of the Orne. In a directive dated 8th July, the day EPSOM was launched, he had predicted:

A thrust forward on both sides of the Seine to Paris. Therefore, a second enemy landing in the sector of Fifteenth Army, despite all the risks this entails, is probable; all the more so, as public opinion will press for elimination of the positions for long-range [V1 and V2] fire on London.

Allied deception efforts were still paying dividends.

Accordingly, on the evening of 16th July, a strong KG under the command of Max Wünsche set out for the designated area. It comprised a mixed Panzer Battalion under SS Major Jürgensen, consisting of thirteen Panthers and eighteen Mk IVs, Krause's 1st SS Panzer-Grenadier Battalion and Olboeter's 3rd (SPW) SS Panzer-Grenadier Battalion, both of Mohnke's 26th Regiment, and a Wespe battery of 105mm howitzers. The rest of 12th SS, less the 3rd Artillery Battalion, was due to follow during the night 17th-18th July. It had only eight tanks ready for action but was expecting the further thirty-six already on their way.

The rest period had been depressingly short—as it would be for the remainder of Dietrich's I SS Panzer Corps, including the 101st SS Heavy Panzer Battalion, which was resting near Granville-Langannerie with seventeen operational Tigers and eight more in short-term repair, and the 7th Werfer Brigade which had been attached.

During the afternoon of 17th July, Field Marshal Erwin Rommel visited Sepp Dietrich's I SS Panzer Corps Headquarters at Urville. Teddy Wisch and Kurt Meyer had been ordered to attend and were congratulated on the recent performances of their Divisions. All three Waffen-SS commanders stressed the desperate need for air cover from the Luftwaffe—something the Field Marshal hardly needed telling. Shortly after leaving he was severely wounded during an air attack; the place where it happened was called, ironically, St Foy-de-Montgomery! Rommel was not replaced—von Kluge personally took command of Army Group 'B'.

NOTES

1. Meyer, Hubert, *The History of the 12th SS Panzer Division Hitlerjugend*, p. 153. 2. Meyer, Hubert, op. cit., p. 153. 3. Ibid, op. cit., p. 154.

19 | 18th to 21st July—Operation GOODWOOD and the Battle for the Bourguébus Ridge

The political and military reasons for launching operation GOODWOOD have been discussed in virtually every book written about the Normandy campaign. In essence, by 10th July the Allies were facing a crisis. The vital port of Cherbourg was not yet operational, the Americans had failed to achieve their planned break-out, German occupation of Caen South was blocking the way to the Falaise Plain and insufficient ground had been captured in the Allied bridgehead for the necessary airfields to be constructed. Significantly, four German infantry divisions had reached Normandy in early July, with the aim of releasing Panzer divisions for their classic counter-attack role and operations against the Americans. Montgomery was thus facing criticisms from all quarters. If his declared strategy of breaking out from the west was to succeed, it was essential that he create a sufficient threat on the Caen flank to hold and attract the German armour which might otherwise be used against the Americans.

Consequently, and having already failed to achieve a breakthrough to the west of Caen, Montgomery decided to launch a strong armoured thrust on the east side—from the Orne bridgehead on 18th July. As he put it in a letter to Field Marshal Sir Alan Brooke on the 14th:

The Second Army is now very strong. . . . and can get no stronger. . . . So I have decided that the time has come for a real 'showdown' on the eastern flank, and to loose a corps

of three armoured divisions into the open country about
the Caen-Falaise road.[1]

This was to be followed by a breakout by the US First Army
around St Lô (Operation COBRA) on the 20th. Both attacks
were to be preceded by massive aerial bombardments.

In the case of the Second Army sector, subsidiary attacks
between Caen and Tilly-sur-Seulles (Map 3) by the newly arrived XII Corps and the veteran XXX Corps, were planned to
last from the night of 15th July until the 17th. These were
designed to divert German attention and gain what ground
they could.

The Germans were certainly not distracted from the main
threat; indeed, they predicted it precisely. On 16th July an
ULTRA intercept revealed that the commander of Luftflotte
(Air Fleet) 3, Field Marshal Sperrle, had signalled his units that
a major British attack was 'to take place south-eastwards from
Caen about the night 17th–18th.' In the event the diversionary
attacks gained little ground and the cost was appalling—another 3,500 casualties,[2] of which 964 were suffered by the injured 15th Scottish Division.[3] The details need not concern us
here.

The plan for Operation GOODWOOD was for three British
armoured divisions, under General O'Connor's VIII Corps, to
carry out the main attack towards the enormously important
and almost featureless Bourguébus ridge to the south-east of
Caen, and the village of Vimont in the low, flat ground to its
east. At the same time Lieutenant General Guy Simonds's
newly arrived Canadian II Corps, with its 2nd and 3rd Canadian Infantry Divisions and 2nd Armoured Brigade, was to
capture the southern part of Caen from Colombelles to
Vaucelles, bridge the Orne and be prepared to exploit south to
a line from St André-sur-Orne to Verrières, where it would
hopefully link up with a British armoured division. This part
of the plan was code-named ATLANTIC; in addition, Lieutenant General Crocker's I British Corps was to secure the left
flank of the main assault by clearing the east side of the
planned salient to a line from Emiéville, through St Pair to
Troarn.

On 15th July Montgomery issued a personal memorandum to O'Connor in which he made clear his intentions for VIII Corps:

> To engage the German armour in battle and write it down to such an extent that it is of no further value to the Germans as a basis of the battle. To gain a good bridgehead over the Orne through Caen and thus improve our positions on the eastern flank. Generally to destroy German equipment and personnel, as a preliminary to a possible wide exploitation of success. . . . The three armoured divisions will be required to dominate the area Bourguébus-Vimont-Bretteville [sur Laize], and to fight and destroy the enemy.[4]

However, on 17th July, just before the attack, Dempsey restricted the VIII Corps objectives by specifying them as Vimont for the Guards Armoured Division, Garcelles-Secqueville and St Aignan-de-Cramesnil for the 7th Armoured and Verrières and Rocquancourt for the 11th.

The German defences facing Dempsey's Second Army attack were considerable and, unknown to Allied intelligence, laid to a depth of some 12km. The two relevant Corps of General Eberbach's Panzer Group West in this sector were Dietrich's I SS Panzer Corps and General Obstfelder's LXXXVI Corps. The latter, to the east of the Caen-Falaise road, had its 346th Infantry Division in position from the coast near Cabourg to just north of Touffreville and the remnants of the badly mauled 16th Luftwaffe Field Division from there to Colombelles. The bulk of Feuchtinger's 21st Panzer Division formed the third Division in LXXXVI Corps and its 192nd Panzer-Grenadier Regiment with a Luftwaffe Panzerjäger battalion was positioned from Colombelles to the Orne bridge in Caen South. Behind these screen forces was KG von Luck, named after the commander of the 125th Panzer-Grenadier Regiment of 21st Panzer Division, Major Hans von Luck. He had just been recommended for the Knight's Cross and had only returned from three days leave in Paris on the morning of the attack. His KG consisted of his own 1st and 2nd Panzer-Grenadier Battalions and the 200th Sturmgeschütz Battalion. This latter unit, commanded by a Major Alfred Becker, was to play a critical part in the forthcoming battle; it had five batteries for a total of thirty SP armoured 75mm assault guns and twenty SP armoured 105mm howitzers, all of which could be used in an anti-tank role. The batteries were sited in or near the villages of Giberville, Démouville, Grentheville, le Mesnil-Frémentel and le Poirier[5] which dominated the proposed British axis. On the eastern flank of Feuchtinger's Division, his 1st Panzer Battalion with twenty-two Mk IVs and the 503rd Heavy Panzer Battalion of Captain Fromme with thirty-six Tigers, including one company with Tiger IIs, were in position to support KG von Luck and to act as a Divisional reserve. They were assembled under the cover of orchards, copses and barns in the area from Sannerville to Emiéville.[6] In addition, the 9th Werfer Brigade had been attached to LXXXVI Corps and one of its battalions was sited near Grentheville, whilst a four gun battery of a Luftwaffe 88mm Flak battalion was near Cagny where Major Becker also had his Headquarters. It is noteworthy that, once again, there were no German anti-tank minefields, thus allowing freedom of movement for their armour.

Further south, on the ridge behind Bourguébus, the Reconnaissance and Pioneer Battalions of the 21st Panzer Division were protecting the artillery of the three Divisions of the LXXXVI Corps and, very significantly, an 88mm anti-tank battalion and two 88mm Flak battalions with a total of seventy-eight 88mm guns in the area of the Bois Secqueville. According to Rommel's records, there were 194 artillery pieces and 272 Werfers (1,826 barrels) in the sector;[7] unfortunately for the Allies there were insufficient bombers available for these to be targeted during the morning of the 18th. Offers to attack them later were rejected by Dempsey who believed that if he was to succeed at all, his armour must by then have reached the Bourguébus ridge.

Dietrich's I SS Panzer Corps was on the left of the Caen-Falaise road. The 272nd Infantry Division, which had relieved the LAH, was in a forward position from the Orne bridge in Caen to near Eterville (Map 3). The twenty-five Tigers of the Corps 101st SS Panzer Battalion (only seventeen operational) were around Grainville-Langannerie and Wisch's 1st SS Panzer

Division LAH was, unknown to British intelligence, in reserve in the area between Ifs and Cintheaux. It will be remembered, however, that its 2nd SS Panzer, 1st SS StuG, 3rd SS (SPW) Panzer-Grenadier and 1st SS (SP) Artillery Battalions were acting as a separate Corps reserve on the west side of the Orne.

The other Division of Dietrich's I SS Panzer Corps, 12th SS, was still reorganising and recovering. KG Wünsche had, by 17th July, moved to an area to the north-west of Lisieux; there it was joined by the newly activated 1st SS Panzerjäger Company HJ of SS Lieutenant Georg Hurdelbrink, with its ten new Jagdpanzer IVs. The rest of 12th SS was some 8km north of Falaise preparing to follow on. Suggestions that this move to the Lisieux area was part of a strategic plan by von Kluge to meet any breakout to the east of Caen are wrong. As pointed out in Chapter 18, 12th SS was directed there in response to Hitler's fear of a second Allied landing between the Seine and Orne rivers.

It has also been suggested that Rommel was personally responsible for the layout of the German defences. This is not true, although his views would undoubtedly have been taken into account by the man who had the overall responsibility— the much respected and combat-experienced holder of the Knight's Cross—General Heinrich Eberbach. He decided the basic structure of the Caen sector defences, and the details were worked out by the two Corps and six divisional commanders.

A strength return dated 17th July shows Jochen Peiper's 1st SS Panzer Regiment LAH with fifty-nine Mk IVs and forty-six Panthers combat ready, and Heinrich Heimann's 1st SS Sturmgeschütz Battalion with thirty-five StuGs. The total number of operational armoured vehicles available to I SS Panzer and LXXXVI Corps on the morning of 18th July was therefore 219 tanks and ninety-five StuGs and SP armoured assault guns; but it has to be remembered that forty-nine of these were with KG Wünsche, temporarily attached to another Corps in the Lisieux area. In addition there were eight Tigers, thirty Panthers and twenty-five Mk IVs in short-term repair, giving a grand total of 377 German tanks, StuGs and SP armoured assault guns—many more than Allied intelligence

estimated at the time and most historians and commentators
have recorded since.

There were a great many drawbacks to the GOODWOOD
plan drawn up by Dempsey, approved by Montgomery and
due to be implemented by O'Connor, with support from Simonds and Crocker. In the first place the bridgehead to the
east of the Orne, from which the attack was to be launched,
was far too small to accommodate three armoured divisions—
the Guards, 7th and 11th. They would therefore have to follow
one behind the other, not only across the three double bridges
over the Orne and its canal between Ranville and the sea (a
distance of only 4km), but also through the protective British
minefields which could not be gapped until the last moment
as they were under German observation. In fact the Germans
had a commanding view over the three double bridges and the
whole Orne bridgehead from the Colombelles factories. And
then, after negotiating the minefields, the problems were by no
means over. The initial, very flat 'corridor' along which the
tanks were required to move was less than 2km wide for the
first 5km owing to the factory area of Caen on the west side
and a forested ridge to the east. This meant that, even after his
armour emerged from the minefields, O'Connor would still be
able to manoeuvre with only one of his three armoured brigades. Another significant problem was that, after the first
8km, the leading tanks would be beyond the range of most of
the artillery support since the guns would be to the west of the
Orne until all the tanks and infantry had cleared the bridges
and assembly area. Only the few 25 pdr SP close support batteries moving with the forward tank regiments would be in
range.

It is hard to imagine a worse or more complicated plan—
three divisions, with 877 tanks and a total of over 8000 vehicles, were required to cross a canal and a river, and then to
advance in column (six brigades one behind the other),
through a minefield and along a narrow corridor, to objectives
15km away.

In order to understand the GOODWOOD battle it is important to begin by describing the ground over which it was
fought. Recall that the main objective of the whole operation

was the Bourguébus ridge which overlooked the southern exits
of Caen. The villages of Bras, Hubert-Folie, Bourguébus and la
Hogue at the northern and north-eastern end of this ridge
dominated the whole very flat area to their north and east—an
area which had little or no cover for attacking troops. They,
like most Norman villages, have houses built of brick and
stone and strong walls surrounding gardens, farmyards and
orchards, making them ideal for defence.

The railway lines from Caen to Troarn (now a motorway)
and Caen to Vimont were not obstacles, though of course they
inevitably took a little time to cross; and they had no real
importance other than as report lines. Much more significant,
and usually not even shown on maps in most books, was the
railway line coming out of the north-east part of Caen and
then running south past the west side of Giberville and
Grentheville, between Hubert-Folie and Bourguébus and then
on past the west side of Tilly to the quarries and mines south
of Grainville. It was highly significant for two reasons—one, it
ran along a high embankment (which still exists) for 4km
from south of Giberville until it reached Bourguébus, and was
therefore a serious obstacle requiring even tanks to use its
underpasses; and two, because it was, and still is, impossible to
see to the west of it from the villages of le Mesnil-Frémentel
and Grentheville. In effect it divided the battlefield into two
quite separate parts—the eastern part dominated by
Bourguébus and la Hogue and the western by Hubert-Folie
and Bras.

Despite stating that his men were 'raring to go', the commander of the leading Armoured Division (11th), Major General 'Pip' Roberts, had severe misgivings about the plan and he
'remonstrated' about it with O'Connor, both verbally and on
paper.[8] He was concerned that, although his mission was to
reach the high ground at Verriéres and Rocquancourt on the
western flank, he was first required to capture the villages of
Cuverville, Démouville and Cagny. This would necessitate the
use of his 159th Infantry Brigade, an armoured regiment and
an artillery battalion (half his Division) and, as he put it,
'make me fight with one arm tied behind my back.' O'Connor
agreed that he need only 'mask' Cagny until the following

(Guards) Division cleared the village, but said the rest of the plan must stand and if Roberts did not like it he would find another division to lead the attack. Roberts gave in.

The final plan therefore was for the 11th Armoured Division to take the high ground to the west, as already described, then for Major General Adair's Guards Armoured Division to follow and after Cagny, swing to the east and reach Vimont, following which Erskine's 'Desert Rats' would exploit south to Garcelles. 200 guns were to provide a creeping barrage behind which the tanks would advance, and a further 350 guns, mainly mediums and heavies, were available to engage point targets as required. An Air Support Signal Unit was provided to enable each armoured brigade and division to call in ground attack aircraft, and the leading Brigade, Brigadier 'Roscoe' Harvey's 29th, had with it an airman in a tank who could talk direct to the fighter-bombers. Significantly, his tank was knocked out early on in the battle—German tank and anti-tank gunners were trained to engage command and 'special' tanks as a top priority.

18TH JULY—THE ARMOURED CORRIDOR

Operation GOODWOOD began at 0525 hours with an artillery barrage against known and suspected anti-aircraft batteries. Ten minutes later 1,100 British heavy bombers dropped a carpet of high explosive bombs on the eastern parts of Caen, the area from Touffreville to Emiéville and in the vicinity of Cagny. They were followed at 0700 hours by 482 Allied medium bombers which used fragmentation bombs on the axes of the armoured divisions, whilst 300 fighters and fighter-bombers went for known strong points and gun positions. Dust and smoke from the initial attacks made it difficult for aircraft in the later waves to find their targets and many had to abort their missions. Then, for half an hour starting at 0800 hours, 495 American heavy bombers dropped further fragmentation bombs designed to do maximum damage to the defenders but not to impede the advance of the British tanks. Some of these also had trouble with smoke and dust, as did fighter-bombers later in the day—they had great difficulty finding targets on what became a very confused battlefield. A total of 7,700 US tons of bombs was dropped. Major Bill Close, a leading squadron commander in 3 RTR, recalled later, 'It really did seem that nothing could live under the bombardment, but how wrong we were!'[9]

The results of these attacks have been described many times before and there is no need to repeat them in detail. Most of the forward German positions were destroyed and the Panzer reserves in the Sannerville-Emiéville area were badly affected; but amazingly, all the armoured assault gun batteries except the one in Démouville survived, as did most of the rest of KG von Luck—even the Panzer-Grenadier Battalion in Colombelles was able to withdraw later under the cover of darkness with remarkably few casualties. It is also worth mentioning that the commander of the 3rd Company of the 503rd Tiger Battalion, Lieutenant (later Bundeswehr Major General) Freiherr von Rosen, personally described to the author in 1981 how one of his 57-ton tanks was literally turned upside down by the force of the explosions, and how one of his men was driven insane and two more committed suicide during the attack. Four of his Tigers were destroyed and the rest had to be dug out of the earth and debris which covered them. That his Company recovered to fight at all on that first morning is an indication of its high morale and professionalism.

The Leibstandarte and Hitlerjugend Panzer Divisions were virtually unaffected by the bombing, as was the Corps 101st SS Heavy Panzer Battalion.

In order not to arouse German suspicions (in fact they were fully aware that a major attack was coming that morning due to the noise made by so many tanks) only Brigadier Harvey's 29th Armoured Brigade crossed into the bridgehead east of the Orne before H-Hour. When the artillery barrage opened up at 0745 hours some of the shells fell short, killing and injuring a number of the forward tank crews who were out of their vehicles awaiting the order to advance. According to Bill Close, 'This happening a few seconds before we were to start, added considerably to the confusion, and we set off after the barrage in some disorder.' Dust, smoke and cratering in the path of the two leading squadrons of 3 RTR, trying to advance with thirty-two Shermans in line abreast, soon added to the chaos.

Fortunately for them they met no opposition before the Caen-Troarn railway line, which they reached at 0830 hours, but even though the artillery barrage was advancing at a rate of only 8kph, the leading tanks were soon left behind. At the railway there was a planned fifteen minute pause to allow the tanks to cross and sort themselves out, but even then not all could catch up—in fact they averaged only a walking pace of 4kph in the first hour and a half. Not surprisingly the 2nd Fife and Forfar Yeomanry, who were following and were meant to come into line with 3 RTR after emerging from the minefield, soon caught up with the rear tanks and added to the confusion, whilst the third Regiment of the Brigade, 23H, dropped right back due to the traffic congestion and poor visibility. Shortly after 0900 hours the main barrage ended and the tanks were on their own except for their own close support SP batteries.

The two leading Regiments pushed on towards the Caen-Vimont railway line and at last, between the Troarn and Vimont roads, they managed to change from column to line, with 3 RTR passing to the west of le Mesnil-Frémentel and the Fife and Forfars to the east; but, as the latter crossed the Caen-Vimont road at about 0930 hours, the rear squadron together with the supporting motorized infantry company of 8 RB and SP artillery battery were suddenly engaged by Becker's assault guns from positions in le Mesnil-Frémentel and le Poirier—twelve Shermans went up in flames.[10] The German gunners had deliberately let the two leading squadrons pass unhindered, for they were to be dealt with by other assault guns in Grentheville. Major Becker was skilfully withdrawing his batteries in accordance with the British advance, and three of them would shortly take up new positions to the south-east of Four, and in Soliers and Hubert-Folie. Brigadier Churcher's 159th Infantry Brigade, which would have been invaluable for dealing with these assault guns, was fully engaged clearing the villages of Cuverville and Démouville to the north.

The leading squadron of 3 RTR also lost five or six of its Shermans to fire from le Mesnil-Frémentel and was now faced with the problem of the north-south railway line running along the steep embankment. Its commander, Bill Close, led the rest of his Squadron under an embankment bridge at about 1000 hours and deployed without further loss 1km short of the Cormelles factory area. The remainder of Lieutenant Colonel Silvertop's 3 RTR and accompanying 8 RB infantry company soon followed, but at noon ran into effective anti-tank fire from Bras and Hubert-Folie and even some 88mm fire from Bourguébus. This could have come from Tigers of Wittmann's 101st SS Heavy Panzer Battalion. Sherman after Sherman went up in flames.

During the morning General Eberbach had become aware of the size of the Allied attack and particularly of the threat along the line of the Caen-Vimont railway. He therefore ordered Dietrich, who although focusing on the Canadian attack out of the centre of Caen was also aware of the threat to the right flank of his Corps, to move the Leibstandarte to the area of the Bourguébus ridge and launch a counter-attack as soon as possible. Dietrich agreed to release back to the LAH that important and large part of the Division which was still west of the Orne. No doubt with the help of SS Lieutenant Colonel Jochen Peiper, the renowned commander of the 1st SS Panzer Regiment, Wisch made his plan as follows: SS Major Kuhlmann's 1st SS Panzer Battalion (forty-six Panthers) was to advance from the area east of Rocquancourt, through Cagny, and push the enemy back across the Caen-Troarn railway line; it was to be assisted in this operation by SS Major Kling's 2nd SS Panzer (Mk IV) Battalion and SS Captain Heimann's 1st SS StuG Battalion as soon as they arrived from west of the Orne (both officers were holders of the Knight's Cross); Panzer-Grenadiers from both Frey's and Sandig's Regiments were to advance to and hold the Four-Soliers area, and to secure Bras for Heimann's StuGs. With admirable speed the first reconnaissance elements of the LAH arrived in the Bourguébus area around noon.

The movement of 1st SS Panzer Regiment to the battle area went undetected by Allied aircraft and its arrival on the Bourguébus ridge at about 1245 hours coincided with that of the already depleted Fife and Forfar Yeomanry, whose two remaining squadrons were advancing past Four towards Soliers and the ridge running from Bourguébus to la Hogue.

Within minutes they lost twenty-nine tanks including their commanding officer's.[11] The situation was so bad that at 1258 hours the 23H, in reserve in the Grentheville area, were ordered not to advance south of Soliers.[12]

Allied fighter-bombers were very active during the day but seem to have had difficulty in finding and effectively engaging the German armour in the dust and smoke and general confusion of the battlefield. The main problem was that after the tank with the RAF liaison officer was hit during the morning, no one on the ground was really capable of talking directly to the pilots or of indicating to them the required targets.

Behind Brigadier Harvey's 29th Armoured Brigade there had been increasing chaos as units became delayed and mixed up. Worse still, as the leading tanks of the 5th Guards Armoured Brigade approached Cagny at 1015 hours[13] they themselves were engaged by the four Luftwaffe 88s which von Luck had ordered, at pistol point, to take up anti-tank positions in the north-west part of the village. These guns had to be dealt with before any further advance could be made and, while the 2nd Armoured Grenadier Guards tried to do this, 1st Armoured Coldstream and 2nd Armoured Irish Guards bypassed Cagny at about 1230 hours[14] and took a detour through le Mesnil-Frémentel in order to advance along the line of the railway to Vimont. Unfortunately this put them right across the path of the 7th Armoured Division and only added to the confusion. Major-General Roberts had asked VIII Corps for assistance from the 7th Armoured Division at 1145 hours[15] but, as the 7th Divisional War Diary put it, '[7th Armoured was] badly congested by the Guards Armoured Division who came too far west and blocked our exit against the 11th Armoured Division'.

In the meantime the 2nd Armoured Grenadiers advancing on Cagny were hit by a counter-attack from the remains of the 21st Panzer armoured reserve consisting of up to ten Tigers and nine Mk IVs. This failed when two of the Tigers were mistakenly engaged and knocked out by the Luftwaffe 88s in Cagny.[16] The remaining tanks withdrew and were then ordered to Frénouville, where von Luck's Headquarters was located, and the le Poirier area, with a view to blocking the open German flank to the south-east of Caen.

At 1430 hours the 23H were ordered to advance past the sad remains of the Fife and Forfars towards Soliers and Four.[17] They were soon halted by Becker's assault guns in Soliers, the tanks of the LAH on the ridge and the German armour in the area of le Poirier and Frénouville. As they tried to withdraw, just before 1500 hours,[18] every tank in C Squadron was destroyed. *The Story of the 23rd Hussars* relates that:

> With no time for retaliation, no time to do anything but take one quick glance at the situation, almost in one minute, all its tanks were hit, blazing and exploding. Everywhere wounded or burning figures ran or struggled painfully for cover, while a remorseless rain of armour-piercing shot riddled the already helpless Shermans.

In post-war interview with Milton Shulman, Teddy Wisch claimed that he was personally in command at this action.

By 1506 hours[19] the remnants of the Fife and Forfars had pulled back to the north of the Caen-Vimont railway line and twenty-two minutes later 3 RTR's position on the west flank was reported to have 'deteriorated'.[20] The Regiment had already pulled back to the north-south railway line at 1400 hours after reporting the ground to its front 'covered by tanks and anti-tank guns.'[21]

At 1600 hours when Roberts met his Corps commander and Erskine of the 7th Armoured Division just behind le Mesnil-Frémentel, his Armoured Brigade was in complete disarray and his Infantry Brigade was still tied up at the north end of the corridor. Grentheville had been cleared but Frénouville, le Poirier, Four, Soliers, la Hogue, Bourguébus, Hubert-Folie and Bras were all in German hands—in other words, all the vital ground. Roberts had already called forward his only armoured reserve, the 2nd Northamptonshire Yeomanry, and he demanded, not unreasonably, that the 7th Armoured Division move forward to fill the gap between himself and Adair's Guards. However, the 7th Armoured had been seriously delayed getting through the minefields and, as we have heard, further disrupted in its advance in the narrow corridor north of le Mesnil-Frémentel. It has been suggested that Erskine, who certainly thought the whole operation was a waste of armour, displayed undue caution on this day and perhaps deliberately delayed his leading armoured Regiment, saying there was no way through between the 11th Armoured Division and the Guards. This is difficult to believe because it would have required the collusion of both the Brigade commander, Brigadier Hinde, and the commanding officer of 5 RTR, not to mention the various staffs. Whatever the truth, 5 RTR did not arrive at the Caen-Vimont railway line until 1800 hours[22] and by then it was too late to help—it had taken two hours to move the 3km from the Caen-Troarn road to Grentheville.

In the meantime the 32nd Guards Brigade had reached Cagny at 1600 hours—the 88mm gun crews blew up their guns before withdrawing—but it took until 2000 hours before the village was finally cleared; le Poirier fell to the 1st Coldstream Guards at 1630 hours.[23] Attempts by 2nd Armoured Irish Guards to advance on Vimont at 1900 hours again failed in the face of German tanks and assault guns around Frénouville. The War Diary of the Guards Division says sixty Shermans were damaged during the day, of which fifteen were 'knocked out'.

At 2000 hours Herford's 2nd SS Panzer-Grenadier Battalion of the 1st Regiment arrived to join the LAH's StuGs in Bras. The latter claimed to have surprised some fifteen to twenty tanks on the northern edge of the village earlier in the evening. According to the LAH semi-official history:

> Rettlinger [a Knight's Cross holder] organized the attack. . . . 2nd Company moved around Bras from the east [Hubert-Folie]; the 1st Company moved around from the north. The pincers caught the enemy tanks. . . . two of their tanks burst into flames immediately and some took direct hits. Panic overtook the enemy. . . . We lost not a Panzer. By then it was 1900 hours.[24]

These were the Cromwells of the 11th Armoured Divisional Reconnaissance Regiment, the 2nd Northamptonshire Yeomanry, which Roberts had committed in a final attempt to achieve his mission. Sixteen tanks were lost in this forlorn attempt to take the ridge from the north.

By the time darkness fell the remnants of 11th Armoured's four tank Regiments had withdrawn to the north of Soliers and the Caen-Vimont railway line. The 29th Armoured Brigade had lost at least 125 Shermans during the day's fighting—thirty-three from the 23H, forty-five from 3 RTR (the unit War Diary says forty-nine) and forty-seven from the 2nd Fife and Forfars.[25] The 159th Infantry Brigade had finally caught up and was dug in around le Mesnil-Frémentel. With the 32nd Guards Brigade in defence around Cagny and the 5th Guards Armoured Brigade to the west of a line from Emiéville to Frénouville, the situation at the southern end of the 'armoured corridor' was, as in EPSOM, both crowded and confused.

One of the reasons given for the VIII Corps débâcle on 18th July was a lack of infantry. Hans von Luck, in his book *Panzer Commander,* certainly criticized British tactics. He pointed out that the tank attacks were almost always carried out without infantry support and there was therefore no one immediately available to eliminate troublesome anti-tank nests. This is an over-statement in that a motorized infantry battalion was an integral part of each of the two armoured brigades involved, but it is certainly true that the potential of the three infantry brigades in VIII Corps was largely wasted. A plan which deprived the leading 11th Armoured Division of its Infantry Brigade, a lack of armoured personnel carriers and poor cooperation between infantry and armour ensured that the British tanks in GOODWOOD operated virtually unsupported. There were twelve infantry battalions available in VIII Corps (three of them mechanized) to support nine tank regiments and three armoured reconnaissance regiments, and yet five of them saw no action on 18th July. As Belfield and Essame point out in their book, *The Battle for Normandy:*

> None of the senior officers on the spot appeared unduly perturbed by these hold-ups [at the bridges] and the urgently needed infantry were allowed to sit phlegmatically in their trucks which edged forward at a snail's pace. The 7th

Armoured Division, at the tail of the tank column, took little or no part in the first day of GOODWOOD.

Panzermeyer's comments on the poor performance of British armour on that day are also very apt:

> Where is the spirit of the Light Brigade at Balaclava in the Crimean War? The enemy tanks drag themselves across the ground like turtles, their power is not concentrated.[26]

But despite the terrible tank casualties in O'Connor's VIII Corps the cost in human terms was surprisingly light—521[27] in all, and only eighty-one killed in the four tank Regiments of the 11th Armoured Division; even more surprising, the four infantry Battalions of the same Division suffered a total of only twenty casualties.

The Canadians had in the meantime cleared the Colombelles factory area, penetrated into Vaucelles and, early on the 19th, bridged the Orne—all at a cost of less than 200 men. The Germans withdrew from the Caen suburbs during the night and took up new positions on the western end of the Bourguébus ridge where the bulk of the LAH was now located.

On the eastern flank, the 3rd British Infantry Division and other troops of I British Corps cleared Touffreville and Sannerville during the day and reached the outskirts of Troarn, but attempts to advance further south were firmly blocked by the German defenders in the Emiéville and St Pair sector. The cost had been relatively heavy—651[28] and eighteen tanks,[29] but this time the bombing had undoubtedly helped the attackers.

In summary, at midnight on the 18th the Germans had lost Caen but were still holding all the villages to the south of the Caen-Vimont railway except Grentheville, and were defending a firm line running north from Frénouville, through Emiéville, to Troarn.

During the night the LAH reorganised slightly, giving Frey's 1st SS Panzer-Grenadier Regiment responsibility for the Bras, Hubert-Folie and Bourguébus sector and Sandig's 2nd Regiment the area of le Poirier, Four, Soliers and la Hogue.

But what had happened to the 12th SS Panzer Division? The 12th SS Artillery Regiment and 12th SS Flak Battalion were still in position and in action to the west of Bourguébus in support of the 272nd Infantry Division, and KG Wünsche was in an assembly area to the north of Lisieux. There is a general belief that the rest of 12th SS, comprising two strong KGs with tanks, was sitting in reserve north of Falaise on 17th July and that on the 18th it was used to thicken up the German defences to the south-east of Caen and repel the British Guards and 11th Armoured Divisions. Not so. 'The rest' of 12th SS, in terms of combat ready troops, consisted of little more than one KG under the command of SS Major Hans Waldmüller. On 17th July, General Eberbach, suspecting that the British were about to attack, cancelled the plan for this group to join KG Wünsche and at about midday on the 18th, worried by the strength of the VIII Corps attack, he asked von Kluge if he could use the Hitlerjugend Division. However, permission could not be given without OKW agreement since, on 16th July, Hitler had expressed himself intent on preserving the HJ.[30]

12th SS Panzer Division was released to I SS Panzer Corps at 1500 hours on the 18th and ordered to take over the sector from Emiéville church to Frénouville from 21st Panzer as soon as possible.[31]

Interestingly, the Germans had appreciated that the ground due east of Vimont, along the Route Nationale 13, was quite unsuitable for armoured forces, being only just above the water table. KG Wünsche was therefore wasted near Lisieux. The more likely British axis was through Airan and then on to cross the Dives river near St-Pierre-sur-Dives. It was therefore decided to concentrate the HJ with its centre of gravity in the Vimont area. While it would not be too difficult to move KG Waldmüller forward during the night, the destroyed bridges over the Dives would present serious problems for Wünsche. All concerned, von Kluge, Eberbach, Dietrich and Meyer, knew that the HJ could not be fully in position before midday 19th July at the earliest—fortunately for the Germans, the British were to allow it the necessary time.

19TH JULY—SIDE BY SIDE

During the night 18th-19th July the Luftwaffe made one of its few effective raids against the British bridgehead east of the Orne. It caused heavy personnel casualties amongst some of the administrative echelons and replacement tank crews for the Guards and 11th Armoured Divisions. The vital bridges were not hit.

Although both the forward British armoured divisions had full strength infantry brigades available and in the right place, neither attempted the one operation which the Germans were dreading—a night attack by infantry; instead they 'consolidated their gains'. Moreover, VIII Corps took no offensive action during the morning of 19th July either—it was 'reorganising for further action.'[32] Not so with the Germans: at 0700 hours a counter-attack from Four by a company of Sandig's 2nd SS Panzer-Grenadier Regiment recaptured le Poirier.[33]

O'Connor met his three Divisional commanders at midday and told them to resume their attacks. The 11th Armoured Division was to capture Bras and Hubert-Folie beginning at 1600 hours, and then at 1700 hours the 7th Armoured was to capture Bourguébus—now known to the soldiers as 'Buggersbus'—and then exploit to Tilly-la-Campagne and Verrières, whilst the Guards were directed to retake le Poirier and then advance to Vimont.[34]

Besides carrying out the counter-attack against le Poirier already mentioned, the men of the Leibstandarte spent the morning improving their defences and preparing further ones in depth. The 7th SS Panzer Company of Knight's Cross holder SS Lieutenant Werner Wolff joined the 3rd SS Panzer Company in the Tilly area and the rest of Kuhlmann's 1st SS Panzer (Panther) Battalion moved up behind the ridge to the east of Bourguébus. As a result of observed British movements only two StuGs were left in Bras with Graetz's 3rd SS Panzer-Grenadiers and the remainder of Heimann's Battalion moved to better positions between the village and Hubert-Folie which, along with Soliers, was held by the 1st Battalion of the 1st SS Panzer-Grenadier Regiment. The 2nd SS Battalion was

defending the ridge from Bourguébus to Tilly and SS Lieutenant Colonel Rudolf Sandig's 2nd SS Panzer-Grenadier Regiment continued to defend the right flank of the LAH sector in
le Poirier, Four and la Hogue.

The leading elements of Meyer's 12th SS Division HJ arrived in the forward area at 0530 hours on the 19th. By midday KG Waldmüller had taken over the 21st Panzer Division
positions on both sides of the Cagny-Vimont road at Frénouville, with the emphasis on the west side, and the Divisional Escort Company was behind it at Bellengreville. The
ground here is flat but supports several woods. KG Wünsche
arrived on the high ridge running north-south in the
Argences-Moult-Airan area around noon. The tanks took up
positions there as an armoured reserve, whilst Krause's SS
Panzer-Grenadiers moved in on Waldmüller's right flank and
Olboeter's SPW Battalion occupied Emiéville. The 8th SS Panzer Company (Mk IVs) of SS Lieutenant Höfler took up ambush positions astride the Vimont road between Krause's and
Olboeter's Battalions, and Hurdelbrink's 1st SS Panzerjäger
Company gave depth behind Frénouville. Bremer's under-
strength 12th SS Reconnaissance Battalion was located near
Meyer's Headquarters at Ruel, close to Airan and Müller's
12th SS Pioneer Battalion was used throughout the sector laying mines and constructing obstacles. The thirty-six replacement Mk IVs destined for Prinz's 2nd SS Panzer Battalion
were still on their way and did not arrive in time for the
fighting on the 19th. Nevertheless, for the first time since its
formation, the two designated Divisions of Hitler's I SS Panzer
Corps Leibstandarte were to fight side by side.

Despite the severity of the fighting on the second day of
GOODWOOD when all three British armoured divisions attacked, little coverage is given to it in the history books—
eighteen lines in Ellis's Official History and only ten between
four of the best known British and American writers on the
Normandy campaign.

In the afternoon of 19th July elements of the 32nd Guards
(Infantry) Brigade attacked Emiéville but were beaten off by
Olboeter's Grenadiers who suffered a loss of only two killed
and six wounded. A larger attack at 1900 hours by the same

Brigade easily retook le Poirier,[35] when the company of the Leibstandarte's 2nd SS Panzer-Grenadier Battalion there withdrew under orders to Four. However, further attempts by the Guards to advance on Frénouville failed against Waldmüller's and Krause's men backed by the Jagdpanzers. The 5th Guards Armoured Brigade inexplicably remained idle. Its War Diary records, 'It was reported that a screen of 88s barred any further progress in the direction of Vimont and it became more important that we should hold Cagny so that the 7th and 11th Armoured divisions on our right flank should be able to advance.'

The attack by the 11th Armoured Division began at 1600 hours when the 2nd Northamptonshire Yeomanry advanced on Bras.

It was to be followed by 3 RTR which, once Bras was secured, had the task of capturing Hubert-Folie. According to the Yeomanry War Diary they attacked with two squadrons from the north-north-west, but the 29th Armoured Brigade says the Regiment mistakenly advanced from the west.[36] It does not matter—by 1620 hours the attack had failed. Lieutenant Colonel Silvertop, commanding 3 RTR, therefore decided to join in the action and advance on Bras from the north-east. One StuG was destroyed in this attack and the other withdrew leaving the Grenadiers without intimate armoured support. A member of Graetz's 9th Company reported:

> The tanks rolled up. Two, five, eight, ten, we stopped counting. They approached our foxholes carefully. Dread and fear paralysed us. We knew they would pulverize us. Those of us who survived were taken prisoner.[37]

At 1710 hours 3 RTR emerged on the south-west side of the village and by 1730 hours 8 RB was mopping up.[38]

Following the fall of Bras, the 2nd Northamptonshire Yeomanry was ordered to advance on Hubert-Folie at 1810 hours. The village was defended by parts of Schiller's 1st SS Grenadiers and the 2nd SS StuG Company. The advance broke down in confusion after twenty minutes when the Yeomanry was reduced to only a squadron's worth of tanks[39] by fire from the

StuGs and Peiper's Panzers, hull down on the ridge to the south.

At 2000 hours the 2nd Fife and Forfar Yeomanry, with only twenty-five tanks organised into two squadrons, was ordered to take Hubert-Folie. Fortunately for them they found no enemy[40]—the LAH defenders had withdrawn to the dominating line 2km to the south, near Verrières, where Peiper's tanks were already in position. At the end of the day Heimann's 1st SS StuG Battalion had only three operational StuGs left—two had been destroyed and the other fifteen damaged.[41]

The concurrent attack by the 7th Armoured Division's 22nd Armoured Brigade against the Leibstandarte forward defences in Four and Soliers was initially delayed by Sandig's SS Panzer-Grenadiers before they withdrew as planned to the Bourguébus-la Hogue ridge. This withdrawal had enabled 3 RTR to advance on Bras without danger. But then, as the 5 RTR tanks surged forward just before 1900 hours on either side of Bourguébus, they ran headlong into Jochen Peiper's 1st SS Panzer Regiment and lost eight Shermans.[42] There was nothing to be done but pull back into Four and Soliers.

Hitler's Leibstandarte SS Panzer Divisions had, to all intents and purposes, held firm. The HJ had given no ground and, as darkness fell, the LAH was still holding the vital ground from la Hogue through Bourguébus to Beauvoir.

During the 19th, on the left flank of Dietrich's I SS Panzer Corps, the Canadian 2nd Infantry Division had cleared Cormelles, Fleury-sur-Orne and Hill 67, just to the north of St André, and by midnight Ifs, to the northwest of Bras, had been secured; however, at 1550 hours on the 19th, Dempsey had ordered Simonds's II Canadian Corps to take over Bras and Hubert-Folie from the British 11th Armoured Division as a matter of urgency—and this would bring the Canadians face to face with the Leibstandarte on the 20th.

20TH TO 21ST JULY—A BAD DEAL

At 1000 hours on 20th July, Lieutenant General Miles Dempsey gave orders that the 7th Armoured Division was to complete the capture of Bourguébus and then VIII Corps was to hold its current positions with infantry whilst its battered

armour was to be withdrawn. GOODWOOD was, to all intents and purposes, over.

General Simonds told Keller's 3rd Canadian Infantry Division to relieve the badly mauled 11th Armoured Division.
When it did so the soldiers were shocked by what they saw—
one of them later described how the sight of so many
smouldering Shermans made them feel sick.[43] At the same
time, the 2nd Canadian Infantry Division was told to advance
and establish itself on the Verrières feature astride the Caen-
Falaise road.

Before Dempsey's order to halt was received, the Guards
Armoured Division took Frénouville and Emiéville—both villages had been abandoned by Waldmüller's and Olboeter's SS
Grenadiers. These withdrawals were carried out in order to
shorten the HJ line, but further attempts by the Guards to
advance towards Vimont were strongly resisted and failed.
Low, threatening clouds precluded any Allied air support.

The new 12th SS line ran from the Château St Pierre Our-
sin, east of Emiéville, to a point half way between Frénouville
and Bellengreville. But Kurt Meyer had already decided that
his depleted Division could no longer man a continuously
defended line and so during this day he reconnoitred a series
of potential strongpoints running from Vimont to St Sylvain,
8km to its southwest, which he ordered should be prepared.

When the 7th Armoured Division began its advance it
found Bourguébus similarly abandoned by the Leibstandarte's
1st SS Panzer-Grenadiers; but when the tanks of 4 CLY and a
company of 1 RB tried to continue across the gently rising
ground towards Verrières they came under heavy fire and were
stopped in their tracks.[44] The LAH, supported by tanks of
Wittmann's 3rd Tiger Company was, as usual, on the vital
ground and had decided this far was enough. But Brigadier
Hinde's 22nd Armoured Brigade was not the only formation
attacking Verrières on the morning of the 20th, for it will be
remembered that the Canadians had also been ordered to take
the ridge, and their 6th Infantry Brigade had crossed the Orne
that morning preparatory to doing so. After hurried consulta-
tions between II Canadian and VIII British Corps, it was
agreed at midday that the British would withdraw to the east

of the Caen-Falaise road and provide fire support for the Canadian attack. The British got the best deal.

The attack began at 1500 hours supported by both Canadian and British artillery and ground attack Typhoon aircraft. Despite the fact that this was a full scale attack, the Canadian infantry advanced on their own, unaccompanied by tanks which for some strange reason were held back in a counter-attack role.[45]

A foothold was secured by the Camerons of Canada in the relatively unimportant village of St André-sur-Orne, defended by the 272nd Infantry Division, and Lieutenant Colonel Clift's South Saskatchewan Regiment reported it had two companies on its objective by 1730 hours. This objective, around Verrières and the farms at Beauvoir and Torteval, was held by some of Max Junge's 2nd SS Grenadiers (SS Captain Karck, another Knight's Cross holder, had been killed in an accident on 3rd July) and two companies of the LAH's SS Reconnaissance Battalion. But at about 1700 hours a violent rain-storm turned everywhere into a sea of mud and, just as the Canadians were denied air support, a violent counter-attack from the direction of Verrières by the 5th and 6th Companies of Kling's 2nd SS Panzer Battalion, supported by a StuG company and elements of the 1st SS Panzer-Grenadier Regiment, hit the Saskatchewans. They were overrun, suffering 208 casualties including their commanding officer and sixty-five men killed.[46] The same force then turned on the Essex Scottish Regiment, which had moved up to occupy the area between Beauvoir and St André, causing it heavy casualties. By 2100 hours two companies had been broken. It was during this period that Albert Frey, commander of the LAH's 1st SS Panzer-Grenadier Regiment, was severely wounded by artillery fire near Garcelles; SS Lieutenant Colonel Joachim Schiller, commanding officer of the 1st Battalion took over and SS Captain Lotter replaced him.

Heavy fighting continued throughout the night of 20th-21st July, as did the torrential rain which turned the whole battlefield into a quagmire, terminating any hopes which Montgomery, Dempsey, O'Connor or anyone else might have had of continuing GOODWOOD.

On the morning of the 21st the LAH launched another
heavy counter-attack against the Canadian centre and the Essex Scottish once more suffered heavy casualties, bringing their
total in the two days to 301.[47] Despite a counter-attack that
evening by the Canadian Black Watch, supported by tanks of
the 1st Hussars and Sherbrooke Fusiliers, which reached the
road between Torteval and St André and enabled the survivors
of the Essex Scottish to withdraw, Wisch's men re-took the
vital Torteval and Beauvoir farms. The strategic Verrières ridge
remained firmly in the hands of the Leibstandarte. There is a
very sad comment in the War Diary of the Essex Scottish Regiment concerning its part in the battle:

> It is not a pleasant picture to realise that so many of the
> battalion have been lost, especially as the action was unsuc-
> cessful and so many of the casualties could have been
> avoided by better planning and the observance of the proce-
> dures that our training had led us to believe would be fol-
> lowed before going into battle. All the rules of man
> management were either violated or ignored, by the sudden
> move ordered after midnight, the loss of sleep by all ranks, a
> poor breakfast and little or no noon meal before battle and
> the general or detailed picture or plan, if known, was not
> given to the junior officers or troops.

Not surprisingly, the commanding officer, Lieutenant Colonel Bruce Macdonald, was sacked.[48] He became the Canadian
representative on the SHAEF Court of Inquiry investigating
war crimes, then headed the No 1 Canadian War Crimes Investigation Unit and by a strange twist of fate, ended up as the
Chief Prosecutor at Kurt Meyer's trial!

GOODWOOD was over. The strategic results, failures, successes and implications of this operation have been discussed
many times. This author will confine himself to four basic
statements. First, of the four objectives specified by Dempsey—Vimont, Garcelles, Hubert-Folie and Verrières, only Hubert-Folie had been captured, and one assigned by
Montgomery, Bretteville-sur-Laize, was still over 8km away.
Second, Montgomery's aim of 'writing down' the German armour had not been achieved (this point will be discussed

later). Third, the cost for what was achieved was enormous—
British losses (VIII and I Corps only) were 3,474,[49] and Canadian casualties amounted to 1,965, including 441 dead.[50] Reports that the British lost over 400 tanks are certainly much
exaggerated—a careful study of the relevant documents indi-
cates a maximum of 253 for the period of GOODWOOD and
many of these were reparable. Fourth, Montgomery's vital aim
of holding the bulk of the German armour on the eastern
flank, to prevent it being used against the intended American
breakout in the west, was achieved.

With regard to 'writing down' the German armour, the
claim in the British Official History that the LAH and 21st
Panzer Divisions lost 109 tanks on 18th July[51] is another exag-
geration. One can however, account for forty-one tanks and
six assault guns knocked out in the initial bombing, and
Wisch, the commander of the LAH, mentions a figure of
twelve Panthers and one Mk IV lost on the same day. We also
know that the LAH Sturmgeschütz Battalion had seventeen
StuGs knocked out or badly damaged on the 18th and 19th,
although only two of these were total write-offs. It is confirmed that the HJ suffered no tank or Jagdpanzer casualties
during the fighting[52] and that on 20th July the LAH still had
seventeen Panthers and forty-six Mk IVs operational. Therefore, the figure given by Major General 'Pip' Roberts, commander of the 11th Armoured Division, in an interview at the
British Staff College in 1979 and used in the British Army
training film on GOODWOOD—75 German tanks and assault
guns destroyed—can be accepted as accurate. This is only 20%
of the total German armoured strength in the I SS Panzer
Corps sector and cannot possibly be described as the 'writing
down' of armour as required by Montgomery.

Needless to say, the failure to break through in GOOD-
WOOD caused a major row in the highest echelons of the
Allied command. Eisenhower was furious and made his famous remark that the Allis could hardly expect to advance
through France at a rate of a thousand tons of bombs per
mile! Tedder, Leigh-Mallory and all the senior air commanders
were equally angry. Many officers at SHAEF wanted Montgomery sacked and Eisenhower himself to take command of

all land forces—even Churchill, who was never particularly fond of Monty, began to have doubts about his ability. There is little doubt that whilst Montgomery would remain, even to this day, a hero to most of the British fighting soldiers who served under him, his reputation with many senior officers and military historians would be forever tarnished. Sadly for him, his chance of remaining as overall land force commander ended with GOODWOOD.

German personnel casualties were relatively light. In the case of the HJ most were caused after GOODWOOD by Allied artillery fire; the total loss for the period 19th July to 4th August was 134, including eighteen killed.[53] Figures for the LAH over the period 16th July to 1st August are 1,092 lost including 243 killed.[54] Nevertheless, the personnel losses in Dietrich's SS Panzer Divisions, and those in Bittrich's II SS Panzer corps, had reached a level which was causing great concern. At 180 hours on 19th July an entry in the Panzer Group West War Diary[55] shows that General Eberbach had expressed the view that:

> We need many men and much material. Dietrich and Bittrich, in particular, are shocked by how little help they are getting from the SS main command office in the way of replacement forces,

and that he had requested replacement forces for both Corps. Eberbach had also asked that the Chief or Deputy Chief of Staff of the OKW visit Normandy to get a first-hand impression of the desperate situation.

POSTSCRIPT

Two things happened during this period which are pertinent to our story—one minor and the other momentous. Wilhelm Mohnke, commander of the 26th SS Panzer-Grenadier Regiment HJ and the only senior commander in I SS Panzer Corps without a Knight's Cross, was awarded this honour by the Führer in recognition of his performance, and that of his men, during the fighting to date. And on 20th July there was an attempt to assassinate Adolf Hitler. A few men in Dietrich's Corps heard about it on the radio and the news spread like wild-fire. Hubert Meyer's reaction, typical of the Waffen-SS, is interesting:

> It was incomprehensible that soldiers would attempt a coup against the supreme military leadership while they were themselves involved in bitter defensive fighting against the enemy who demanded 'Unconditional Surrender', not willing to negotiate a cease-fire or even peace.[56]

This view is agreed by Kurt Meyer who records[57] that he met few German officers during his captivity who supported the assassination attempt.

The Adjutant of the LAH's 1st SS Reconnaissance Battalion had this to say:

> The aspect of the attempted assassination which disturbed us the most was its timing. On the one hand, each day was making us see that our weeks of fighting were serving an increasingly hopeless cause. On the other hand, only a few days before the attempt, the Division had destroyed more than a hundred British tanks.
>
> At that point there were still hours and even days when we did not feel by any means beaten. Those were the times when circumstances were at least even on the two sides; to speak clearly, the times when the Allies had not just turned their commanding air power on us and strafed or bombed us into the dirt. . . . Even without the attempted murder, it was bad enough that we were being commanded from the Rastenburg or from the Obersalzberg! Our thoughts at the time had nothing to do with Adolf Hitler as a person or with his position as Commander-in-Chief.
>
> The years of war and our daily confrontation with all its harshness had turned us into 'front pigs'. Our lack of understanding and inner rejection of everything we heard from 'up there' or 'back home', led us to accept only one last 'Heimat', one final homeland. That was our unit, our 'little heap' of men. . . . We, the men of the Leibstandarte were no Praetorian Guard. We were simple front soldiers and that was a deeply felt self-identification.[58]

NOTES

1. Directive No. M 511. 2. Ellis, *Victory in the West, Vol I, The Battle of Normandy*, p. 334. 3. Martin, *History of the 15th Scottish Division 1939–1945*, p. 347. 4. Stacey, *The Official History of the Canadian Army in the Second World War, Vol III, The Victory Campaign*, p. 168. 5. Von Luck to author, Heidelberg, 18 Nov 81. 6. Von Rosen to author, Heidelberg, 18 Nov 81. 7. Meyer, Hubert, *The History of the 12th SS Panzer Division Hitlerjugend*, p. 155. 8. Major General Roberts interviewed at the British Staff College, Camberley, 1979. 9. Major Close interviewed at the British Staff College, Camberley, 1979. 10. 29 Armd Bde & 2 F&F War Diaries, 18 Jul 44. 11. 29 Armd Bde War Diary, 18 Jul 44. 12. Ibid. 13. Gds Armd Div War Diary, 18 Jul 44. Ian Hogg in *The Guns of World War II* confirms that all German artillery weapons were issued with anti-tank ammunition—even 128mm Luftwaffe AA guns on Flak towers in major cities! 14. Ibid. 15. 11 Armd Div War Diary, 18 Jul 44. 16. Meyer, Hubert, op. cit., p. 158. 17. 23H War Diary, 18 Jul 44. 18. 29 Armd Bde War Diary, 18 Jul 44. 19. Ibid. 20. Ibid. 21. 3 RTR War Diary, 18 Jul 44. 22. 29 Armd Bde War Diary, 18 Jul 44. 23. Gds Armd Div, War Diary, 18 Jul 44. 24. Lehmann & Tiemann, *The Leibstandarte IV/I*, p. 153. 25. 29 Armd Bde War Diary, 18 Jul 44. 26. Meyer, Kurt, *Grenadiers*, p. 154. 27. Wilmot, *The Struggle for Europe*, p. 362. 28. Ibid. 29. Ellis, op. cit., p. 343. 30. Meyer, Hubert, op. cit., p. 156. 31. Panzer Group West War Diary. 32. Ellis, op. cit., p. 346. 33. 11 Armd Div War Diary, 19 Jul 44. 34. 22 Armd Bde War Diary, 19 Jul 44. 35. 32 Gds Bde War Diary, 19 Jul 44. 36. 29 Armd Bde & 2 Northamptonshire Yeomanry War Diaries, 19 Jul 44. 37. Lehmann & Tiemann, op. cit., p. 159. 38. 29 Armd Bde, 3 RTR & 8RB War Diaries, 19 Jul 44. 39. British Army War Study of Operation GOODWOOD dated 1979. 40. 2 Fife & Forfar War Diary, 19 Jul 44. 41. Lehmann & Tiemann, op. cit., p. 160. 42. 22 Armd Bde War Diary, 19 Jul 44. 43. Hastings, *Overlord D-Day and the Battle for Normandy 1944*, p. 278. 44. 4 CLY War Diary, 20 Jul 44. 45. Stacey, op. cit., p. 175. 46. Ibid., p. 176. 47. Essex Scottish War Diary, 22 Jul 44. 48. Stacey, op. cit., p. 176. 49. 21st Army Group 'A' Branch War Diary. 50. Stacey, op. cit., p. 176. 51. Ellis, op. cit., p. 346. 52. Meyer, Hubert, op. cit., p. 163. 53. Ibid. 54. LAH Meldung No. 00980/44 dated 1 Aug 44. 55. Lehmann & Tiemann, op. cit., pp. 160–161. 56. Meyer, Hubert, op. cit., p. 160. 57. Meyer, Kurt, op. cit., p. 194. 58. Lehmann & Tiemann, op. cit., p. 286.

20 *25th July—Operation SPRING and the Battle of the Plain*

Operation SPRING was launched by the II Canadian Corps at 0330 hours on 25th July to coincide with a major US First Army offensive on the western flank codenamed COBRA. At this time Dietrich still had the 272nd Infantry Division, sup-

ported by elements of 2nd Panzer and 9th and 10th SS Panzer
Divisions, defending the left-hand section of his Corps area to
the east of the Orne, the 12th SS Panzer Division HJ in defence
in the Vimont sector and 1st SS Panzer astride the Route Nationale 158, the main Caen to Falaise highway. As an important reserve he had the balance of 9th SS in position to the
north-west of Bretteville-sur-Laize. Dietrich had been told by
von Kluge on 23rd July that both the LAH and HJ would
shortly be relieved by infantry divisions; but before this was to
happen the LAH, and indeed the 272nd Infantry Divisional
Group, would have to withstand the onslaught of operation
SPRING.

The aim of the operation, as defined by Montgomery, was
to capture the area Fontenay-le-Marmion, Point 122 (also
known as Cramesnil spur) and Garcelles—the exact area held
by the Leibstandarte. To help in this task II Canadian Corps
had been allocated the British Guards and 7th Armoured Divisions, giving it a total of four divisions, two of them
armoured, and an additional armoured brigade. The successful conclusion of this operation was to be followed by a XII
Corps attack west of the Orne on the 28th to capture Evrecy
and Amayé, and finally VIII Corps was to attack through II
Canadian Corps, down the Falaise road, to cover the capture
by the British Guards of the large wooded area to the east of
Garcelles. When all this had been achieved, Monty intended to
launch several armoured divisions towards Falaise in a re-run
of GOODWOOD. The role of the LAH in frustrating Montgomery's plans would therefore be crucial.

How was 1st SS deployed to meet Operation SPRING?
Starting on the east side of the Caen-Falaise highway, the area
from inclusive la Hogue to just north-east of Tilly-la-
Campagne (Tilly) was defended by Max Junge's 2nd SS Panzer-Grenadier Battalion of Sandig's 2nd Regiment, together
with the 3rd SS (88mm) Flak Company. Tilly itself had been
made into a strongpoint, with Dinse's 3rd SS (SPW) Panzer-
Grenadier Battalion, Wolff's 7th SS Panzer (Mk IV) Company
and a company of Scheler's 1st SS Pioneer Battalion. To the
west of Tilly, near the Caen-Falaise highway, Herford's 2nd SS

Grenadiers of the 1st Regiment were in position with the re-vamped 2nd SS StuG Company.

There were strong forces in depth—the 1st SS Panzer-Gren-adier Battalion of Sandig's Regiment was to the north of Sec-queville, the 2nd SS Werfer Company just south of Tilly, the rest of Scheler's SS Pioneers in Garcelles and, most impor-tantly, Kling's 2nd SS Panzer Battalion, less the 5th and 7th Companies, was in reserve just to the east of Garcelles.

The vital area from the Caen-Falaise road to and inclusive of Verrières, was held by Fritz Lotter's 1st SS Panzer-Grenadier Battalion less its 3rd Company, the 12th SS Heavy Panzer-Grenadier Company of Graetz's Battalion and the 15th SS (Pi-oneer) Company, all from Schiller's 1st Regiment, together with SS Lieutenant Werner Sternebeck's 5th SS Panzer Com-pany and the reorganised 1st SS StuG Company. Forward of these main positions in Torteval there was a screen force pro-vided by the 1st SS Reconnaissance Battalion and, in depth behind them at Rocquancourt, there was a strong reserve com-prising four SS Grenadier Companies from the 1st Regiment and the 3rd SS Sturmgeschütz Company. The other two SS 88mm Flak companies were at Caillouet and St Aignan where the rest of Knittel's 1st SS Reconnaissance Battalion provided yet another reserve.

On 25th July the 2nd SS Panzer Battalion had forty-one operational Mk IVs and the 1st SS Sturmgeschütz Battalion had been re-equipped with thirty-two StuGs. It is unclear whether Kuhlmann's 1st SS Panzer (Panther) Battalion was still with the LAH at this time or had been pulled out to reinforce the Hitlerjugend. Hubert Meyer says that by 31st July it was part of a reinforced KG Wünsche reserve force but he does not say when it moved across. *The Leibstandarte IV/I* by Lehmann and Tiemann records it as part of the LAH armoured reserve to the east of Garcelles on 24th July and goes on to mention it taking part in a counter-attack on the eve-ning of the 25th. However, this must be questioned since it says the Battalion had only 'about ten Panzers' when we know that in reality it had thirty-one operational Panthers on that day. Certainly Jochen Peiper's 1st SS Panzer Regimental Headquarters was located in the Château at Garcelles-Secqueville at this time.

With or without the 1st SS Panzer Battalion LAH, the whole defensive layout facing II Canadian Corps was typical of German military thinking and destined to cause major problems for the attacker.

Lieutenant General Guy Simonds's plan called for Major General Foulkes's 2nd Canadian Infantry Division to take May-sur-Orne and Verrières, and Keller's 3rd Division to capture Tilly. Erskine's British 7th Armoured Division was due to advance down the centre-line to seize the Cramesnil spur, whilst the 2nd Division pressed on to Fontenay-le-Marmion and Rocquancourt and the 3rd Division to Garcelles. The British Guards Armoured Division was to clear the woods to the east of Garcelles once the 3rd Infantry had secured the village. It was an ambitious plan involving an advance of over 10km.

Although the Canadian plan for SPRING looked on the face of it reasonably simple and logical, in reality it left a lot to be desired. For example, it sounds perfectly reasonable for an Infantry Division to be given the task of capturing Tilly; the attack was however to be carried out, not by the Division, not even by one of its Brigades, but by just one Battalion—the poor North Nova Scotia Highlanders. Only after Tilly had fallen and the 'Desert Rats' had secured Point 122, was the Highland Light Infantry of Canada due to advance on Garcelles. The rest of Brigadier Cunningham's 9th Infantry Brigade and the whole of Foster's 7th were being held for the exploitation phase and the entire 8th Brigade of Brigadier Blackader was, inexplicably, to be in reserve. The only thing which can be said for this plan is that it was simple.

The 2nd Canadian Infantry Division's plan was quite the opposite, over complicated and seriously flawed. In the first place the selected Start-Line for the attack, the St André to Hubert-Folie road, was not even in Canadian hands; and then, almost as if to ensure that there would be chaos, the three Brigades of the Division were muddled up. The 6th Brigade lost two of its battalions to the other Brigades so that they could secure the Start-Line, but then each of those two Brigades lost one battalion to Brigadier Young's 6th Brigade in order to provide a reserve. The main attack was to be delivered against Verrières by the Royal Hamilton Light Infantry (RHLI) and against May-sur-Orne by the Calgary Highlanders. A second phase, due to begin at 0530 hours, was to involve Lieutenant Colonel Cantlie's Black Watch of Canada and a tank squadron of the 1st Hussars taking Fontenay-le-Marmion, with the Royal Regiment of Canada (Royals) and another Hussar squadron passing through Verrières to capture Rocquancourt.

Perhaps to add even more flavour to this 'cocktail', 'Looney' Hinde's 22nd British Armoured Brigade was to move forward from Ifs in a counter counter-attack role and to be ready to exploit to Point 122 and, just for good measure, the British 27th Armoured Brigade, from a different Corps, was to secure the left flank. If the reader is now thoroughly confused, he will know what it was like for those who attended General Simonds's 'O' Group on 23rd July.

Although the Allied heavy bomber force was now required to support the American breakout attempt in the west, medium bombers were available to help the Canadians in SPRING, as was a powerful force of Canadian and British artillery.

On the evening of 24th July sixty medium bombers took part in a preliminary air attack on the German positions, but due to very effective German Flak only fifteen aircraft succeeded in attacking their targets.

The main night attack by the Canadians which began at 0330 hours was meant to be helped by what was termed 'artificial moonlight'—light created by reflecting searchlight beams off clouds. According to the commanding officer of the North Nova Scotias, all it achieved when it did come on, was to silhouette his men as they advanced from Bourguébus towards Tilly. Despite heavy artillery support, his three attacking companies had little hope anyway against Dinse's Battalion of SS Panzer-Grenadiers, supported by Pioneers and Wolff's Mk IV Panzer Company. During the attack seventy-four medium bombers bombed the woods to the east of Tilly, around la Hogue, for two hours beginning just after 0600 hours, but it did nothing to help the Canadian attack, and even when the rest of the Nova Scotias were thrown in, together with their carriers and SP anti-tank guns, they could not prevail. The unit War Diary noted that A and C companies were pinned down when 'the enemy opened the door, let them in and trapped them' and the 9th Infantry Brigade Diary described the Battalion as being 'decimated'. The squadron of Fort Garry Shermans allocated to support the attack complained that it was unable to help effectively 'as Panther tanks remained between our tanks and the advancing infantry'. It withdrew at 1715 hours having lost eleven of its sixteen tanks.[2] Eventually permission was given for the surviving Canadians to withdraw back to Bourguébus. About 100 made it under cover of darkness. The Battalion had suffered 139 casualties, including sixty-one killed.[3] According to the Official Canadian History[4] the LAH, 'had fought with genuinely fanatical determination and skill.' Considering many of its soldiers were much younger than their Canadian counterparts and had received less than three months training, this was praise indeed.

Manfred Thorn, the nineteen-year-old driver of one of Wolff's Mk IVs in the 7th SS Panzer Company, described his part in the day's events:

> Our Panzer was well camouflaged, huddled up against the wall of a house. . . . the three [Canadian]tanks had not seen us yet. One shot from our gun would have brought us certain death. . . . I turned the motor on and put it in reverse . . . We wanted to fire at the three tanks, which were still standing in the same spot, from behind. . . . We moved along the road to the east, out of Tilly. . . . turned south again, back toward Tilly. . . . When we were about 20m from the tanks we opened fire. The first one burst into flames and the other two took some hits. The crews bailed out.[5]

A platoon commander in Wolff's Panzer Company, SS Second Lieutenant Stiller, gave a wider picture.

> The [SS] infantry crouched in their foxholes. The Panzer crews lay under their Panzers. Mortar and artillery shells rained down on us. . . . The sun was still low when Tom-

mys' tanks approached from the north-west. That was good for us; they had to aim right into the sun. Our orders were, 'Let them get closer!'. . . . Finally the white flare went up! Fire at will! The tracer trajectories shot out of our ambush positions. Shell after shell flew out of the barrels, and more Panzers raced up to join our line. Five minutes of that and the Tommys [sic] stopped in their tracks. . . . Behind us, however, there was a thundering sound. Heavy Nebelwerfers pulled up, and for 500m in front of us the terrain turned into a hell. The Tommys fled from the field like rabbits. One of the tanks must have taken a direct hit, for it simply disappeared. Others stopped where they were and became smoking witnesses to the destruction. . . . We hunted down some more Canadians who had left their vehicles and hidden in the houses.[6]

The attack by the 3rd Canadian Infantry Division was over. It will not surprise the reader to learn that the commander of the 9th Infantry Brigade and two of his commanding officers were sacked.[7] Major General Keller survived again.

Meanwhile, Wisch's men to the west of the Caen-Falaise highway had adjusted their deployment to meet the attack of Foulkes's 2nd Canadian Infantry Division. The 1st, 2nd and 15th SS Panzer-Grenadier Companies of the 1st Regiment had moved forward into prepared positions in the tree and hedge line on the northern edge of Verrières, where they were well supported by the 4th and 12th SS Heavy Companies and the 5th SS Panzer and 1st SS StuG Companies, whilst parts of the 3rd, 9th and 11th SS Panzer-Grenadier Companies from the reserve force in the Rocquancourt area had moved forward to a perfect reverse slope blocking position 400m south of Verrières. There were therefore two SS Panzer-Grenadier Battalions, well supported by armour and with further reserves available, in the sector into which initially one Canadian infantry Battalion, the RHLI, and later the Royals and part of a British tank battalion, 1 RTR, were to be committed. The ratio of attackers to defenders was too low even though the former had strong artillery and air support.

Because of difficulties in securing the Start-Line, Lieutenant

Colonel Rockingham's RHLI could not advance until 0410 hours and consequently lost the benefit of the artillery barrage.[8] The dug-in Panzers and StuGs initially gave the Canadians a lot of trouble, but when 17 pdrs of the 18th Battery, 2nd Anti-tank Regiment, firing from the Torteval Farm area, knocked out four of the tanks, and field and medium artillery came to the rescue, Sternebeck's tanks with the StuGs and SS Grenadiers were forced to make a fighting withdrawal. By 0750 hours the RHLI had, against the odds, captured Verrières. It was a magnificent achievement. Werner Sternebeck described part of this action:

> The Canadian infantry stood even with, even between, our Panzers. . . . The enemy penetration meant we had to abandon the Company's position along the hedgerows. . . . In just a few minutes the Company lost four or five Panzers and men from each crew. My own Panzer was crippled. The rest of the Company, three or four Panzers, were unable to keep a firm grip on Verrières. The Grenadiers and our Company were forced to abandon the town. . . . During this attack, the Canadians enabled us to take our wounded with us. They did not fire on us as we collected our comrades, even though they were in a position to do so.[9]

Between 0900 and 1000 hours the Royals and two troops of 1 RTR moved through the RHLI with the aim of taking Rocquancourt. When they reached a line about 400m south of Verrières they ran into exceptionally heavy artillery concentrations as well as anti-tank and machine gun fire. 1 RTR reported thirty German tanks hull-down on the ridge between Rocquancourt and Fontenay.[10] Certainly all the armoured assault guns of the 1st SS StuG Battalion were in that area and it is possible that some Mk IVs of the 6th and 8th SS Panzer Companies from the reserve near Garcelles could have been deployed to meet this threat. C Company of the Royals was almost annihilated when it tried to continue the advance, and the attack completely bogged down. This was hardly surprising in the face of the two SS Panzer-Grenadier Battalions and the German armour.

Further to the west, on the left flank of the LAH, the Black Watch of Canada had already lost its commanding officer and taken many casualties in clearing remnants of the 272nd Infantry Division from their intended assembly area in St Martin-de-Fontenay. After an inevitable reorganisation they eventually moved forward again at 0930 hours, six hours late, in an attempt to reach their objective of Fontenay-le-Marmion. This move was meant to be aided by a squadron of the 1st Hussars giving fire support from the village of May, but as soon as the men of the Black Watch crossed their new Start-Line they came under fire from that village, from the Verrières ridge and even from across the Orne. Part of the problem was that on entering May, Lieutenant Colonel MacLauchlin's Calgary Highlanders with a squadron of 1st Hussars had run into tanks of either the 2nd Panzer or 9th SS Panzer Division fighting with the 272nd Infantry and, after losing four Shermans and some 177 men,[11] had been forced to withdraw. May, abutting the Orne, was the westerly bastion of Dietrich's defence.

When a mere sixty surviving men of the Black Watch finally reached the crest of the Fontenay-Verrières ridge, they found dug-in Grenadiers and were pinned down by machine gun and tank fire. Afterwards, the officers of the Black Watch said that of about 300 men who attacked Fontenay, not more than fifteen returned to Canadian lines.[12] When the area was taken later in the campaign, the acting commanding officer, twenty-six-year-old Major Griffin, was found lying amongst his men. Although precise casualty figures for this day are unclear, the Official History believes the Black Watch lost 307 men,[13] making it the highest number in a single day for any Canadian unit in WWII except for the Dieppe operation.

At 1730 hours General Simonds issued further orders. An hour later the 2nd Division, supported by the whole II Corps artillery, was to capture Rocquancourt and at first light the following morning, Fontenay-le-Marmion was to be attacked. All the 3rd Division was asked to do was to 'make Tilly firm' during the night. It shows just how out of touch Simonds's Headquarters was—Tilly had never been captured.

At exactly the time Simonds's new directive was being issued, the LAH reserve of about ten Mk IVs and an SS Panzer-

Grenadier Battalion (which one is unclear, but possibly Graetz's) counter-attacked the Canadians in Verrières from a start point in a wooded area between Rocquancourt and Fontenay-le-Marmion. Eight Panzers reached the RHLI positions and the situation was only saved by twelve rocket-firing Typhoons of 181 and 182 Squadrons RAF. According to the Germans, three Panzers were knocked out by the Typhoons.[14] At the end of the day the RHLI were still in possession of the village—it was the only unit to have taken and held its objective in operation SPRING but it cost forty-six dead, 154 wounded and five anti-tank guns.[15]

Later that evening Simonds went to Dempsey and recommended that the whole operation be called off—the Army commander agreed. The Official History estimate of casualties incurred is 1,500 with 450 dead.[16] It goes on to say:

> The 2nd Canadian Corps attack had struck a stone wall. The result is not surprising, in view of the strength of the Germans' positions and the powerful force of high-category troops which was holding them.[17]

At the end of the day the LAH was holding the line la Hogue to Tilly, to a point just to the south of Verrières, and the 9th SS was still in May. The question of casualties will be discussed in the next chapter. Suffice it to say here that the Leibstandarte Corps had again played an essential part in thwarting Allied, and particularly Montgomery's, intentions.

NOTES

1. AEAF Daily Summary No 188. 2. Fort Garry Horse War Diary, 25 Jul 44. 3. Stacey, *The Official History of the Canadian Army in the Second World War, Vol III, The Victory Campaign*, p. 190. 4. Ibid. 5. Thorn to author, Feb 94. 6. Lehmann & Tiemann, *The Leibstandarte IV/I*, p. 166. 7. Stacey, op. cit., p. 190. 8. RHLI War Diary, 25 Jul 44. 9. Lehmann & Tiemann, op. cit., pp. 168–169. 10. 1 RTR War Diary, 25 Jul 44. 11. Calgary Hldrs War Diary, 25 Jul 44. 12. Stacey, op. cit., p. 192. 13. Ibid., p. 194. 14. Lehmann & Tiemann, op. cit., p. 172. 15. RHLI War Diary, 25 Jul 44. 16. Stacey, op. cit., p. 194. 17. Ibid.

Apart from the almost constant Allied shelling, the period between Operation SPRING and the 1st of August was a relatively quiet time for both the LAH and the HJ and, since we have strength returns for this date, it is a convenient time to address the subject of casualties and reorganisation.

The Leibstandarte return dated 1st August[1] shows a total strength of 20,395 all ranks and a figure of 1,092 killed, wounded and missing for the period 16th July to 1st August. The fact that there is a difference of only 867 between the 1st July and 1st August strength returns is probably accounted for by the fact that many of the lightly wounded, in this case 225, remained with the Division and were not evacuated; this was standard practice in the German army. One of those who was evacuated was SS Lieutenant Colonel Grensing, the LAH Chief of Staff, who was seriously wounded by artillery fire on 25th July. Even so, when one considers that the period 16th July to 1st August covered both GOODWOOD and SPRING, the LAH losses were not unduly high—particularly when compared with those suffered by Allied divisions during the same period.

With regard to armour, the LAH had thirty one Panthers, forty-one Mk IVs and thirty-two StuGs operational on 25th July, the day of SPRING, and thirty-three Panthers, thirty Mk IVs and twenty-two StuGs on 28th July. It would appear therefore that it probably lost eleven Mk IVs and ten StuGs during the fighting around Tilly and Verrières. The fact that there is an increase in the Panther force may indicate that the 1st SS Panzer Battalion had indeed been withdrawn to reinforce KG Wünsche before SPRING, as already suggested. It is of note that by 31st July Kling's 2nd SS Panzer Battalion was back up to a strength of sixty Mk IVs and Rettlinger had twenty-nine StuGs.

What of the Hitlerjugend? Manpower was still a major problem for Kurt Meyer. His Chief of Staff, Hubert Meyer, in his History of the Division, details 134 more casualties for the period 19th July to 4th August,[2] which brings our maximum and minimum totals in Chapter XVIII to 3,438 and 3,122 respectively. However, it has to be said that in the difficult and often chaotic conditions in which the HJ found itself by this time, the chances of accurate casualty reporting were minimal. All that can be said in summary is that by 4th August 12th SS had certainly suffered somewhere in the region of 3,500 casualties. The figure of 6,164 quoted by Hubert Meyer[3] from the Panzer Group West War Diary can be dismissed as a crude attempt by Eberbach's Headquarters to emphasise the undoubted crisis and obtain reinforcements.

Nevertheless it is hardly surprising that on 1st August Dietrich asked for 2,000 replacements for the HJ from the Waffen-SS Training and Replacement Battalion. According to Hubert Meyer only 261 recruits arrived, but he goes on to point out that other reinforcements may have been sent from Panzer, Pioneer or other specialist training units.[4] Kurt Meyer maintained that he had to make do with just a company's worth of anti-tank gunners and received no Grenadiers at all.[5]

Dietrich probably had a new-found confidence on the day he demanded the reinforcements, for it was on 1st August that he was promoted to the rank of SS Oberstgruppenführer (full general), with seniority back-dated to 20th April 1942! Hitler had wanted to promote him on the original date but had been advised against it because it would have made Dietrich senior to Hausser.

Both von Kluge and Dietrich were anxious to relieve 12th SS with an infantry division and set it up as a Corps reserve force. This happened gradually over the period 23rd July to the night of 3rd–4th August, when the 272nd Infantry Division, itself relieved by the 9th SS Panzer Division, finally took over the HJ sector.

The first stage in this reorganisation happened when KG Wünsche was strengthened by the addition of Kuhlmann's 1st SS Panzer (Panther) Battalion LAH and the Corps 101st SS Heavy Panzer Battalion. These were added to Jürgensen's 1st SS Panzer (Panther) Battalion and Olboeter's 3rd SS (SPW) Panzer-Grenadier Battalion, to give Wünsche a total of sixty-one Panthers, four Mk IVs (one source says seventeen) and nineteen Tigers,[6] plus the strong SPW Panzer-Grenadier Battalion. This force was ready as a Corps reserve by 31st July with its Command Post in Fierville-la-Campagne.

The second part of the reorganisation began when Krause's 1st SS Panzer-Grenadier Battalion was relieved on 2nd August. The rest of Kurt Meyer's 12th SS Panzer Division, including the whole of the 12th SS Panzer Artillery Regiment and the Werfer and Flak Battalions (but less KG Wünsche), then became known as KG Meyer. It was thus another strong reserve within Dietrich's I SS Panzer Corps and was deployed in the St Sylvain, Bray, Vieux-Fumé and Maizières area. It had twenty-two (some say thirty-nine) Mk IVs and twenty-seven Jagdpanzer IVs.[7]

It did not take long for part of these newly created reserves to be called up for action. On 2nd August, in response to the crisis which had developed in the II SS Panzer Corps area, KG Wünsche and Wisch's Leibstandarte, which was already deployed, were ordered to provide a 'Fast Group'. This was needed to help counter a thrust by the British 11th Armoured Division which had captured le Bény-Bocage and was threatening Vire (Map 1) in the rear of the German forces which were attempting to seal off the eastern flank of the by now successful American breakout (Operation COBRA). The British Operation was code-named BLUECOAT and although it made painfully slow progress in its early stages, it threatened to drive a wedge between Eberbach's Panzer Group West and Hausser's Seventh Army. It was the slowness of this advance, particularly by XXX Corps, that led Dempsey on 2nd August, with Montgomery's approval, to sack the Corps commander, Lieutenant General Bucknall. The following day Major General Erskine, Brigadier 'Looney' Hinde and the Artillery commander and Chief of Staff of the 7th Armoured Division were also fired. Although the 'Desert Rats' strongly resented this action, and even today some still think it was wrong, many outside the Division thought they should all have gone after Villers-Bocage.

A number of historians have suggested that 7th Armoured and some of the British infantry divisions were over-tired by this stage of the campaign. One who took part in BLUECOAT wrote:

For two months they had pinned down most of the enemy's divisions. When the offensive [BLUECOAT] began they were already weary with the endless routine of marching and fighting; they were already punch-drunk with battle.[8]

But when one compares the amount of time actually spent in combat between these divisions and the Hitlerjugend, one can only suppose that leadership, motivation and tactical handling accounted for the difference in performance and morale.

The 'Fast Group' sent to help II SS Panzer Corps was titled Reconnaissance Group Olboeter after the name of its commander, SS Major Erich Olboeter, of whom we have already heard much. It comprised the 2nd SS Panzer Company under SS Lieutenant Gaede, with thirteen Panthers, the 9th SS (SPW) Panzer-Grenadier Company, six Wespes of the 1st SS Battery, 12th SS Panzer Artillery Regiment and six armoured cars from the LAH's 1st SS Reconnaissance Battalion. The group was attached to II SS Panzer Corps late on 2nd August and ordered to move to the Vire area. It arrived on the evening of 3rd August but, apart from a claim of knocking out six British tanks on 7th August, we know little of its actions in the period up to 8th August when it was urgently recalled to its parent formation to help stem a huge attack by the Canadian II Corps. Nevertheless, it undoubtedly played a part in plugging the potentially disastrous gap between Hausser's and Eberbach's forces.

While most of Panzermeyer's Division had a relatively quiet time during this period, the Leibstandarte was still having trouble with the Canadians. The left-hand Divisional boundary changed during the night 28th–29th July when the 9th SS Panzer Division took over from the 272nd Infantry Division. The new line ran from east of Torteval, to east of Verrières, to inclusive Rocquancourt.

During the night 29th–30th July the Essex Scottish captured a group of farm buildings to the north-west of Tilly from SS Panzer-Grenadiers of Schiller's 1st Regiment at a cost of thirteen killed and nineteen wounded.[9] Herford's 2nd SS Panzer-Grenadier Battalion from the same Regiment, together with Dinse's 3rd from the 2nd Regiment, Wolff's 7th SS Panzer

Company and the 2nd SS StuG Company, were all holding the strongpoint of Tilly. They correctly interpreted the action by the Essex Scottish as the precursor of a major attack. For reasons unknown, Georg Preuss's 10th SS Panzer-Grenadier Company of Schiller's 1st Regiment was also part of the Tilly defences, bringing the total number of Grenadier companies in the area to nine—although most of them were of course seriously depleted.

The First Canadian Army of Lieutenant General Crerar had been activated on 23rd July and with Second British Army it formed 21st Army Group. Crerar immediately ordered Simonds to keep up the pressure south of Caen in order to stop the Germans redirecting their forces against the American breakout. He was also anxious to capture Tilly in order to prevent German observation into the Orne bridgehead. It is one of the most dominating villages in the whole area. Accordingly, an attack by Foulkes's 2nd Infantry Division was organised for the night 31st July–1st August.

The Canadian attack was to be carried out by the Calgary Highlanders, part of Brigadier Megill's 5th Infantry Brigade, aided by a squadron of tanks from the Scots Greys, and with heavy support from the artillery of two divisions and an Army Group. A diversionary attack at 0100 hours on 1st August from Bourguébus towards la Hogue by D Company of Lieutenant Colonel McQueen's Lincoln and Welland Regiment of the newly arrived 4th Canadian Infantry Division, was soon brought to a halt by Panzer-Grenadiers of the 2nd Regiment, ably supported by Werfer and artillery fire.

At 0230 hours Lieutenant Colonel MacLauchlan's Calgary Highlanders advanced behind a massive artillery barrage astride the track leading into Tilly from the previously captured farm buildings to the north-west. Once again the odds were stacked heavily against them; German artillery and mortar fire and fog prevented the Canadians keeping up with their own barrage[10] and although one company got into the village, it was soon ejected by local counter-attacks. It withdrew to the area of the railway track to the west of the village. A second attack at 0730 hours[11] supported by a troop of the Greys did no better and, when two of the tanks were lost at about 0930 hours,[12] the Calgary Highlanders withdrew to their Start-Line. A graphic description of some of this fighting is given by the previously quoted platoon commander in the 7th SS Panzer Company, SS Second Lieutenant Stiller:

> A wall of fire rolled slowly across the railway tracks and transformed the western side of Tilly into an inferno. . . . The punishment lasted over two hours. Shell after shell hit every square metre of the terrain. The men in their holes and under the Panzers nearly suffocated in the fumes from exploding light and medium calibre shells. . . . The Canadians moved past the town hall at a funeral march tempo. They seemed afraid of mines. . . . The first enemy tank approached from the right. It was only 30m away when Pager sent a tank shell right through the side of its turret. It pulled back and we scored a second hit on the upper part of its hull. The crew bailed out and we chased them away with a burst of machine gun fire. We had barely finished the job when a second tank rumbled up. 'Enemy tank at 11 o'clock! Fire at will!' The shell went straight into the turret and this tank pulled back too. More machine gun fire cleared the area of enemy soldiers and chased the infantrymen back across the railway tracks.[13]

At 1430 hours Brigadier Megill ordered a third attack by the exhausted Highlanders; this time it was supported by a squadron of the Fort Garry Horse. It did no better—the Leibstandarte would not give ground and the Highlanders lost 178 men.[14]

The penultimate attack against the LAH in Tilly was launched at 2345 hours by Lieutenant Colonel McQueen's Lincoln and Welland Battalion, without a preceding artillery barrage in the hope of gaining surprise. Even though by this time the defenders had been much reduced in numbers, due to Dinse's 3rd SS (SPW) Panzer-Grenadier Battalion being redeployed to the LAH's left flank between Rocquancourt and May-sur-Orne, the attack was easily defeated and by 0700 hours the Canadians were back in Bourguébus; the cost was fifty-eight men, including twelve dead.[15]

The diarist of the Calgary Highlanders described a further bombardment of Tilly on 2nd August:

> At 1800 hours the Typhoons arrived and Tilly went up and then down in a mess of smoking rubble. . . . Shortly afterwards our artillery played terrifically heavy fire into the rubble and many air bursts were fired directly over Tilly as well. . . . the seemingly impossible has happened because we are once again receiving MG fire from the slits at Tilly. The Hun is like a rat and comes up for more no matter how hard we pound him.[16]

One of the 'Huns' and a member of the 7th SS Panzer Company, Rolf Ehrhardt, wrote:

> Tilly was a tiny and, in the context of the entire war, insignificant town. But none of the men who spent even a few days in that inferno will ever forget its name.[17]

The final attacks against the LAH in the Tilly sector came on 5th August—the very day it was relieved by the 89th Infantry Division. The Canadians were suspicious that a relief operation might be under way and during the afternoon sent patrols against Tilly and la Hogue. The same evening they launched the Argylls of Canada, with the 29th Armoured Regiment (The South Albertas), against Herford's 2nd SS Panzer-Grenadiers in the rubble of Tilly. At the same time a weak company of the Lake Superior (Motor) Regiment and a squadron of the 22nd Armoured Regiment (Canadian Grenadier Guards) moved against Junge's 2nd SS Panzer-Grenadiers in la Hogue. Both attacks were costly failures. It was in this latter battle that the only Knight's Cross to be earned by a Waffen-SS Panzer-Grenadier in the entire war was won by Grenadier Erich Göstl. Despite being the only man not killed or wounded in his squad and being blinded in both eyes, he continued firing in the direction of any enemy he could hear. When he was eventually found, his rescuers discovered that he had collapsed with exhaustion only after being wounded again in the hand and having his machine gun put out of action. He typified the tenacity of the Leibstandarte's performance during this 'relatively quiet time.'

At 1935 hours, whilst the fighting around la Hogue and Tilly was still going on, Wisch received an order to dispatch two Panzer and two Panzer-Grenadier battalions, plus an SP artillery battalion, to the area Tinchebray, St Corniers, Beauchêne, le Châtellier and Flers, to the south-east of Vire, that night! This extraordinary order stemmed from Hitler's directive to von Kluge to use his Panzer Divisions to counter-attack the Americans at Avranches in a desperate attempt to stem the tide which was engulfing western Normandy and Brittany. In fact Hitler himself saw this situation as an oppor-tunity to cut off and destroy large numbers of Americans rather than a crisis measure. Von Kluge, Hausser, Eberbach and Dietrich, who knew the real situation, saw things very differently and when Eberbach told Dietrich to release both the Leibstandarte and Hitlerjugend Divisions for this counter-attack the latter was shocked—he would be left with no ar-mour with which to face the extremely strong First Canadian Army and he would be losing his 'boys'. He was given the 89th Infantry Division to replace the LAH and as events turned out the HJ could not be extracted and remained under his com-mand. But Wünsche had to give up Kuhlmann's 1st SS (LAH) Panzer Battalion and, after only eighteen days fighting along-side its sister Division, the Leibstandarte began its 100km move to the west on the night of 5th August. As far as the Waffen-SS were concerned the battles of 'Unforgettable Tilly' were over at last. The last elements of the LAH were relieved by the 89th Infantry around midnight.

Two other things happened on 5th August—Eberbach's Panzer Group West was redesignated Fifth Panzer Army and Dietrich was awarded Diamonds to his Knight's Cross. He was immediately summoned to the Führer's western Headquarters to receive the decoration.

NOTES

1. LAH Meldung No 00940/44 dated 1 Aug 44. 2. Meyer, Hubert, *History of the 12th SS Panzer Division Hitlerjugend*, p. 163. 3. Ibid. 4. Ibid. 5. Meyer, Kurt, *Grenadiers*, p. 155. 6. Meyer, Hubert, op. cit., p. 163. It is of interest that the 101st lost eleven Tigers between 7th and 31st July. 7. Ibid. 8. Belfield & Essame, *The Battle for Normandy*, p. 185. 9. Essex Scottish War Diary, 29 Jul 44. 10. 5th Cdn Inf Bde War Diary, 1 Aug 44. 11. Ibid. 12. Greys War Diary, 1 Aug 44. 13. Lehmann & Tiemann, *The*

Leibstandarte IV/I, p. 176. **14.** Stacey, *The Official History of the Canadian Army in the Second World War, Vol III, The Victory Campaign*, p. 206. **15.** Ibid. **16.** Calgary Hldrs War Diary, 1 Aug 44. **17.** Lehmann & Tiemann, op. cit., p. 179.

22 | 6th to 9th August — Another Orne Bridgehead

During the period 4th and 5th August, General Eberbach shortened his frontage by withdrawing from the ruins of Villers-Bocage, Aunay and Evrecy and setting up a new line from Vire to Mont Pinçon, on to Thury-Harcourt and then across the Orne to the Bourguébus ridge. This withdrawal became necessary because of the requirement to provide a strong Panzer group for Hitler's great counter-offensive against the Americans. Coincidental with this German redeployment, on 4th August Montgomery issued a new Directive which was designed to break the 'hinge' of the German defences south of Caen and trap the bulk of von Kluge's forces west of the Orne. The Directive, addressed to Crerar's First Canadian Army, gave as its objective:

> Break through the enemy positions south and south-east of Caen in order to capture as much terrain as is necessary to cut off the enemy forces which are now facing the Second Army and to impede their withdrawal to the east, if not making it impossible altogether.[1]

Vire fell to the Americans on 6th August, and on the same day the British took Mont Pinçon and their XII Corps moved towards the Orne in the Thury-Harcourt sector.

Responsibility for the German front from Thury-Harcourt to la Hogue lay with the 89th and 271st Infantry Divisions of Dietrich's, now inappropriately named I SS Panzer Corps. The 89th Infantry was deployed from inclusive la Hogue to a point to the north-west of St Martin-de-Fontenay—the old positions of the Leibstandarte. On the 89th's left, the 271st Infantry Division, after pulling back to the steep east bank of the Orne on the 6th of August, was manning a series of outposts along the river to a point just to the north of Thury-Harcourt. The only reserve available to Dietrich was Meyer's 12th SS which, it will be recalled, had been split into three groups—KG Meyer, KG Wünsche and Fast Group Olboeter; but also recall that the latter was already deployed in the area just to the east of Vire in support of II SS Panzer Corps and would not return until the 8th.

Artillery fire began to fall in the Grimbosq and Thury-Harcourt sectors at 1840 hours on the 6th of August and during the night the infantry battalions of Brigadier Fryer's 176th Infantry Brigade of the 59th (Staffordshire) Division, with support from two squadrons of the 107th Regiment RAC, established a bridgehead 1000m deep on the steep east bank of the Orne to the south of Grimbosq.[2] By 0800 hours on the 7th a bridge had been constructed at le Bas (today called Grimbosq Halte), just to the west of Brieux.[3] Two counter-attacks by the 271st Infantry Division failed to dislodge the British and during the day the 6th North and 7th South Staffordshire and 7th Royal Norfolk Battalions enlarged their bridgehead to a width of about 3km and depth of 1500m, running from Lasseray in the north to Brieux in the south. It was clearly time for Dietrich to deploy part of his armoured reserve and he ordered Wünsche to restore the situation.[4]

Wünsche deployed the 3rd SS Panzer (Panthers) and 8th SS Panzer (Mk IV) Companies, each with about seventeen tanks, a minimum of five and maximum of ten Tigers from SS Lieutenant Wendorff's 2nd Company of the 101st SS Heavy Panzer Battalion with the unit Flak Platoon, the 1st and 3rd SS Panzer-Grenadier Battalions of Mohnke's 26th Regiment, less the 9th Company with Olboeter, and SS Major Karl Bartling's 3rd SS Panzer Artillery Battalion HJ.

During the move towards the British bridgehead the KG came under attack by a force of fifty-four Mitchell medium bombers but the German Flak was so effective that thirty-six were hit and some were too badly damaged to return to England.[5] German casualties were minimal.

After the 3rd SS Grenadiers had swept through the Forêt de Grimbosq, a combined Panzer and Panzer-Grenadier attack was launched at 1830 hours, supported by artillery. Tanks soon reached the narrow streets of Grimbosq and at 2021 hours Tigers were reported near the Orne and within 400m of

the bridge at le Bas[6] which they engaged with high explosive
rounds. According to the 34th Tank Brigade War Diary, the
107th Regiment lost twenty-eight tanks during the fighting on
the 7th. Most of the 7th South Staffords were forced back
across the river but artillery forward observers had a grand-
stand view of the whole area from the hills to the west of the
Orne and, with seven regiments of artillery firing at a rate of
1000 rounds per gun per day,[7] the slender bridgehead survived. The ground troops were aided by two sorties of nine
RAF Typhoons each from 438 and 439 Squadrons which attacked Wünsche's force between 2115 and 2140 hours with
500lb bombs.[8]

During the night another infantry battalion, 1/7 Royal
Warwicks, reinforced the depleted British force and Wünsche's
tanks were forced to pull back from the river.[9] Later on the 8th
the 147th Regiment RAC relieved the badly mauled 107th.[10]
Wünsche had prevented the expansion of the bridgehead but
despite further attacks he could not destroy it. In view of the
major crisis developing to the south-east of Caen, he was ordered to break off his action and move to the Potigny (Map 7)
area with all speed. By the time he withdrew he had lost nine
Panthers and 122 men.[11] Several of the Tigers were damaged
but none was a total loss.

The British had stubbornly and successfully defended their
bridgehead—it cost the 6th North Staffordshire Battalion seventy-six casualties[12] and Lieutenant Colonel Ian Freeland's 7th
Norfolks forty-two killed, 111 wounded and seventy-three
missing.[13] Captain David Jamieson of the 7th Norfolks was
awarded the Victoria Cross for his part in this fighting.

NOTES

1. Directive No M 516 dated 4 Aug 44. 2. 34 Tk Bde War Diary, 7 Aug
44. 3. 176 Inf Bde War Diary, 7 Aug 44. 4. Kurt Meyer incorrectly identifies this Battlegroup as KG Krause in his book, *Grenadiers*, p. 155. 5. Ellis,
Victory in the West, Vol I, The Battle of Normandy, p. 411. 6. 176 Inf Bde &
6 N Staffs War Diaries, 7 Aug 44. 7. 7 R Norfolk War Diary, 7 Aug 44. 8.
Squadron Operations Record Books, PRO, London. 9. 176 Inf Bde and 6
N Staffs War Diaries, 7 & 8 Aug 44. 10. 34 Tk Bde & 147 Regt War Diaries,
8 Aug 44. 11. Meyer, Hubert, *The History of the 12th SS Panzer Division
Hitlerjugend*, p. 169. 12. 6 N Staffs War Diary, 8 Aug 44. 13. 7 R Norfolk
War Diary, 8 Aug 44.

6th to 10th August—The Mortain Counter-Attack

BACKGROUND AND OPERATION COBRA

In order to understand the place of the Leibstandarte in the American sector of the battle of Normandy it is necessary to go back in time. The Allies had always dreaded a repetition of the war of attrition suffered by their armies in France in World War I and yet by early July it seemed that events might be leading that way. If the British and Canadians were bogged down and agonizing in front of Caen and the Odon, then the Americans were suffering as much or more in what they called 'The Battle of the Hedgerows'. Their problems were basically those of geography and space. Cherbourg had been captured but its facilities were far from operational and supplies still had to enter Normandy over the Omaha and Utah beaches; and there was insufficient space from which to mount the breakout operation required in the Allied master plan. Only one major lateral road east of Carentan was in American hands and even that was under enemy fire. Everything seemed to favour the defence—the sluggish streams which flowed north through marshy flood plains to converge on Carentan, a belt of 'bocage' 10 to 15km deep to the east of the Vire river, the hills beyond the extensive marshes of the upper Seves and the large Fôret Mont Castre. The scale of the 'bocage' problem can be judged by the fact that in a single aerial photograph of the US sector one can see 3,900 hedged enclosures in an area of less than 20 square km.

So as to provide the space needed for the breakout, a major First US Army offensive was ordered in early July to gain the line Coutances-Marigny-St Lô. It did not go well—by the middle of the month when the attack was halted, it had taken VIII Corps twelve days to gain 11km and VII Corps had lost 4,800 men in taking 15 square km of ground.[1] General Bradley then declared the primary goal to be St Lô and the road leading west from it towards Periers. It cost the three infantry divisions of XIX Corps 10,077 casualties to achieve it.[2] Whilst many British and Canadian people are aware of the heavy American casualties on Omaha beach on D Day, few know of

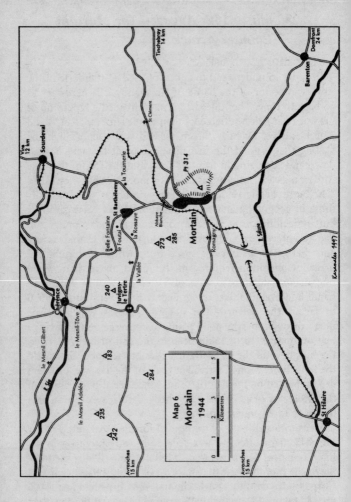

Map 6
Mortain
1944

Kilometres
0 1 2 3 4 5

Avranches
15 km

Avranches
15 km

le Mesnil Gilbert

Cherence

le Mesnil-Tôve

le Mesnil Adelée

△ 235

△ 242

△ 183

△ 284

Juvigny
le Tertre
△ 240

la Vallée

le Foutal
Belle Fontaine

St Barthelemy

la Toumerie

la Rossaye

△ 273
△ 285
Abbaye
Blanche

Mortain

Romagny

R. Sélune

Pt 314

St Clément

Sourdeval

Vire
12 km

Tinchebray
14 km

Barenton

Domfront
24 km

St Hilaire

Kimmodes 1997

the suffering endured by the men of the First US Army before the breakout.

By 18th July the Battle of the Hedgerows had earned the space needed for the breakout—Operation COBRA. The Americans had fought through the areas of marsh, river and 'bocage' and were poised on the higher, more favourable ground south of the St Lô-Periers highway. With St Lô and the high ground around it secure, the war of attrition seemed to be coming to an end at last.

It will be remembered that COBRA should have been launched on 20th July, two days after the beginning of GOOD-WOOD. In the event it had to be postponed until the 25th because bad weather prevented the heavy aerial bombardment which was considered an essential prerequisite of both operations.

Facing Bradley's First US Army was General Paul Hausser's exhausted Seventh Army. It had been depleted by Hitler's insistence on 'standing fast' and withdrawals 'from hedgerow to hedgerow only'. On 15th July the commander of the LXXXIV Corps, von Choltitz, reported to Hausser,[3] 'The whole battle is one tremendous bloodbath, such as I have never seen in eleven years of war.' Montgomery's strategy of pulling the German Panzer divisions and reserves on to Dempsey's Second Army on the eastern flank had worked—by 25th July Dempsey was facing fourteen divisions, of which seven were armoured with 600 tanks, whilst Bradley was opposed by nine hotchpotch divisions, of which only two were armoured with a total of just over 100 tanks.

We do not need to discuss COBRA in any detail other than to say that despite its difficulties and tragedies, such as a major 'Blue on Blue' bombing of American troops, it was highly successful. Unlike the majority of British and Canadian tank units, American armoured battalions were prepared to operate at night and so by the morning of the 27th the high ground at le Mesnil-Herman had been occupied and the way to the south was open. On the afternoon of the 28th Coutances was captured. By then half a dozen German infantry divisions had been cut to pieces and LXXXIV Corps had disintegrated. As

US columns poured down the roads between Coutances and
the Vire even the Americans were astonished by their success.

By 30th July General George Patton's Third US Army was
fully operational and his 4th Armoured Division, after advancing 40km in thirty-six hours, reached Avranches. When darkness fell on 1st August the Americans were across the river at
Pontaubault and had entered Brittany. On the same day Bradley assumed command of the 12th US Army Group, General
Courtney Hodges took over First Army and von Kluge warned
OKW, 'The left flank has collapsed.'

Bradley now ordered Hodges to seize the area Vire-Mortain
whilst Patton was to secure the line St Hilaire-Fougères-
Rennes and then turn west into Brittany. In a characteristic
feat of organisation and personal leadership, George Patton
funnelled seven divisions down one road and across the one
bridge at Avranches in seventy-two hours.

It is not this author's intention to discuss the higher strategy
of the Normandy campaign with all the arguments about
wasted efforts in Brittany and large and small envelopments.
For the purposes of this book it is sufficient to say that
Mortain was captured by 2nd August and the following day
Bradley ordered Patton to leave minimum forces in Brittany
and use his main strength to drive eastwards. On the 4th
Rennes was secured and Montgomery issued a directive which
ended, 'The broad strategy of the Allied Armies is to swing the
right flank towards Paris and to force the enemy back to the
Seine.'

Montgomery was not the only person to issue a new directive on 4th August. Hitler did the same. With the Seventh
Army front still intact from Mont Pinçon to Vire and then
south to Barenton, he ordered von Kluge to launch a counter-
offensive from the Vire-Mortain area, aimed first at Avranches,
with the aim of cutting off all American forces to the south of
that line, and then north-east to the Channel coast to drive the
Allies back into the sea. It was a highly imaginative plan but
although it involved the use of eight of the nine Panzer divisions in Normandy and the entire reserves of the Luftwaffe,
both von Kluge and Hausser knew it would be impossible to
assemble these forces before the collapse of the entire front to

the west of the Orne—they also knew that there was no point in arguing!

Hitler was also insisting that the attack should not be made until, 'every tank, gun and plane was assembled.' Every detail was specified including the exact roads and villages through which the assaulting troops were to advance. General Blumentritt, Chief of Staff CinC West, complained after the war to Milton Shulman, 'All this planning had been done in Berlin with large-scale maps and the advice of the generals in France was not asked for, nor was it encouraged.' The operation was code-named LÜTTICH. The Americans called it the Mortain counter-attack. Suggestions that the Allies were forewarned of Hitler's intentions through ULTRA intercepts have been effectively dismissed in Ralph Bennett's authoritative book *Ultra in the West*.

6TH AUGUST

When Patton's tanks approached Le Mans (Map 1) on 6th August, von Kluge began to panic. It was clear that the German southern flank was wide open, but he was reassured by Jodl from OKW that afternoon that he 'should not worry about the extension of the American penetration, for the delay [in launching the counter-offensive] would mean cutting off so much more.'

Von Kluge and Hausser knew that the Führer Order was sounding the death knell of the Seventh Army and that any delay in launching the counter-attack would only exacerbate matters. They therefore resolved to attack during the night 6th–7th, long before all the necessary forces could be assembled. They were encouraged in this decision by a visit to Seventh Army on the afternoon of the 6th by Luftwaffe General Bülowius, Fighter West commander, who said 300 fighters could be committed over the attack area on the 7th.[4] Although this new plan fell far short of Hitler's vision of a campaign-winning counter-stroke, he surprisingly acquiesced.

The Germans had detected only one US infantry division and part of an armoured division in the path of their attack. Against this relatively small force von Kluge and Hausser planned to use General Hans von Funck's XLVII Panzer Corps with the 116th and 2nd Panzer Divisions, 2nd SS Panzer Division DR with a KG from the 17th SS Panzer-Grenadier Division[5] and hopefully, part of the Leibstandarte. However, a large part of 1st SS had remained west of the Orne in Army Group 'B' reserve[6] and so, as Hausser described in his postwar interrogation,[7] 'the main body of the 1st SS Panzer Division. . . . was to serve as a second wave in the attack on Juvigny.'

Von Funck's counter-attack was to be launched between the Sée river in the north and the Sélune in the south. Although not significant barriers, these small rivers would at least give the flanks of the offensive some protection. The main German thrust was to be in the centre, through St Barthélemy (spelled St Barthélmy on 1944 maps) and Juvigny, initially by von Lüttwitz's 2nd Panzer Division. Since his Division had suffered some 40% casualties to its combat strength, von Lüttwitz was to be strongly reinforced—by SS Major Kuhlmann's 1st SS Panzer Battalion from the LAH and by another Panzer battalion and anti-tank company from the 116th; this was expected to give von Lüttwitz a strength of about 100 tanks.[8] As we have heard, it was envisaged that by the time the breakthrough by 2nd Panzer had been achieved, the rest of the Leibstandarte would have arrived and be able to lead the final advance to Avranches.

The remainder of the relatively fresh but now seriously weakened 116th Panzer Division, with only about twenty-five tanks, was to protect the northern flank by advancing from the area west of Sourdeval to engage enemy forces north of the Sée. Its initial objective was le Mesnil-Gilbert.

SS Brigadier Baum's reinforced 2nd SS Panzer Division was only about 60% combat effective and had less than thirty tanks. Its task was to capture Mortain by encirclement and then advance west and south-west to St Hilaire, whilst the Panzer Lehr reconnaissance elements looked after the southern flank.

Although well under 200 tanks would be available for the assault on 7th August, it was hoped that a sufficient number of tank reinforcements and replacements would be furnished during the advance with the arrival of the 9th and 10th SS

Panzer Divisions and the Panther Battalion of 9th Panzer Division.[9]

At 1630 hours on 6th August SS Major General Wisch, commanding the 1st SS Panzer Division LAH, reported that his tanks, having driven 70km, would need refuelling before commitment and anyway they could not arrive before 2200 hours.[10]

At 2200 hours von Funck reported to Hausser that the leading elements of the Leibstandarte were still at Tinchebray, some 20km from their required positions and with some very difficult country still to cover. The route through Yvrandes, Ger and St Clement was narrow and winding, with high banks skirting the poor roads and the deep valley of the Egrenne to be crossed. 2nd Panzer Division had therefore no chance of receiving its extra LAH Panther tanks in time for the planned H—Hour. Nor it seems had Lieutenant General Graf von Schwerin's 116th Panzer Division produced its share of extra forces for 2nd Panzer, with the result that von Funck went as far as to ask for von Schwerin to be sacked.[11] There is no doubt that von Funck, Hausser and particularly von Lüttwitz were unhappy with the way things were going—the latter was missing not only his extra tanks but also an assault gun brigade and additional artillery which had been promised from the II Parachute Corps. Hausser is recorded as saying, 'I must say this is a poor start. Let's hope that tonight's loss of time will be compensated for by morning fogs tomorrow.'[12] Such sentiments contrast oddly with a statement in his April 1946 interrogation about 'our own well-prepared attack.'

Facing the XLVII Panzer Corps attack General Hodges had basically just one Division—the 30th Infantry, nicknamed 'Old Hickory'. It had already suffered badly in the Normandy fighting—between the 7th and 13th July during the attack on the Vire, it incurred 3,200 casualties and on the 25th another 662 fell to attacks by American aircraft.[13] Its attached tank Battalion, the 743rd, lost thirty-eight tanks and 133 crewmen during July[14] but had since received thirty-three replacement tanks and crews.

Robert L. Hewitt's *Work Horse of The Western Front* gives a vivid picture of the Division's move to the Mortain sector:

By morning of August 6, the entire Division was on the road. Most of the trip was more like a celebration than a move into battle. August 6 was a warm bright Sunday and the local citizenry thronged the roads to wave, throw flowers and offer drinks to the passing soldiers. At Mortain itself hotels and cafés were open and crowded with customers.

And when the men of the 1st Infantry Division, whom they were relieving, told the GIs there was not a German within a hundred miles who wanted to continue the fight, they began to relax and look forward to a few days' rest before continuing what promised to be an easy advance east to the Seine and Paris. The only thing to mar their pleasure was when some of the later convoys were strafed by several flights of German fighter-bombers.[15] Old Hickory had no way of knowing that within six hours of its commander becoming responsible for the Mortain sector, it would be engulfed by Hitler's latest offensive.

Major General Leland Hobbs deployed the 30th Infantry Division as follows: the 120th Infantry Regiment, less a battalion required for a separate task, took over in the town of Mortain and on Hill 314 immediately to its east; the 117th Infantry Regiment occupied St Barthélemy and the area to its west, and the 119th Infantry, less a battalion detached to the 2nd Armored Division, was in reserve about 5km to the west of Juvigny. Each Regiment had a TD company of the 823rd TD Battalion in support. On Hobb's right flank the VII Corps cavalry was reported in position as far south as le Teilleul, 14 km south of Mortain, and he was told that the 39th Infantry Regiment of the 9th Division was around Grand-Dove—le Mont-Turgon 4 km to his north, and the 8th Regiment of the 4th Infantry Division was to the west of that. He had no direct contact with any of them. In fact the 30th Infantry Division was dangerously exposed on both flanks.

7TH AUGUST—OPERATION LÜTTICH

We left a major part of the Leibstandarte moving hurriedly west during the night of 5th–6th August and, as we have heard, its leading elements had only reached Tinchebray by

2200 hours on the 6th—H-Hour for the attack was 2400 hours! By 0200 hours on the 7th, only Gustav Knittels' 1st SS Reconnaissance Battalion, Kuhlmann's 1st SS Panzer Battalion (not more than forty-three Panthers) with about seven Mk IVs of the 5th Mk IV Company, and the SPW Battalion of Sandig's 2nd SS Panzer-Grenadier Regiment had arrived.[16] Knittel's Battalion joined the right wing of 2nd Panzer's thrust towards le Mesnil-Tôve and the rest of the force, under SS Major Kuhlmann, formed a major part of the left-hand assault group aimed at Juvigny. Amazingly, other Mk IVs spent the 6th and 7th August 'resting in woods by Bretteville-sur-Laize';[17] whether they were without orders or deliberately left behind is unclear.

It is interesting that Hausser's Chief of Staff, von Gersdorff, used the late arrival of the LAH Panzer Battalion as an excuse for events on 7th August:

> Immediately before the beginning of the attack, friction oc-
> curred at XLVII Panzer Corps. Due to mistakes by the
> Lower Command the Panzer Battalion of the Leibstandarte,
> which was to be brought up to the 2nd Panzer Division, was
> greatly delayed and was not yet ready for action at 2400
> hours. . . . Therefore, the left attack group of 2nd Panzer
> Division was only able to launch the attack on Barthélemy
> at dawn of 7th August.[18]

Needless to say, the Leibstandarte did not accept that it was to blame for its late arrival. The Divisional History relates:

> The Division's elements had only a short summer night to
> travel 70 to 80km [in fact over 100km] right across the
> supply routes of two armies engaged in full-scale combat. In
> addition, the 2nd SS Panzer Division, 2nd Panzer Division,
> the 116th Panzer Division and the entire II SS Panzer Corps
> were moving along the same march route just ahead of the
> LAH. . . . Just the supply and repair elements of these five
> armoured divisions were enough to fill the roads to capac-
> ity. . . . Responsibility for all these difficult manoeuvres
> fell on the shoulders of the commander [Wisch] and his

tiny staff. There was no support from a trained General Staff officer.[19]

The XLVII Panzer Corps attack ran into difficulties from the start. In the northern sector von Schwerin's 116th Panzer Division got nowhere. It had been unable to disengage properly before the planned H-Hour and did not attempt to advance until 1630 hours. At 2050 hours its highly decorated commander was sacked. In the south Baum's 2nd SS Panzer Division encircled Mortain, mainly from the south, and advanced as far as Romagny, 2km to the south-west, and St Jean-du-Corail to the south. But when the morning fog lifted US artillery and Allied air power threatened any further advance and a halt was called. A major factor in this situation was the valiant and undefeated stand by the surrounded 2nd Battalion of the 120th Infantry Regiment of Old Hickory on Hill 314 which was to go down as an epic in American military history. The Battalion lost more than 300 men killed and wounded during the siege. No less critical were the actions of a platoon of A Company, 823rd TD Battalion and men of the 120th Infantry at the l'Abbaye Blanche roadblock to the north of the town—they inflicted astonishing casualties on the northern thrust of 2nd SS Panzer and remained undefeated when the Germans finally withdrew four days later.

But how did the Leibstandarte fare? There are many misconceptions regarding its status and possible employment. Most books, and indeed some German reports, talk about 'The 1st SS Panzer Division' as though it was a complete entity, and many American writers describe it as one of the strongest and best equipped divisions in the German army. Nothing could be further from the truth—on 7th August it did not even exist as a coherent Panzer Division. On 5th August, when it was relieved by the 89th Infantry Division south of Caen and before it began its move west, the Leibstandarte had forty-three Panthers, fifty-five Mk IVs and twenty-nine StuGs combat ready. But as we have seen, only the Reconnaissance, Panther and SPW Battalions reached the concentration area before first light on the 7th and they had already been allocated to the 2nd Panzer Division. Another part of the

LAH, KG Schiller, had been subordinated by Hausser to the 84th Infantry Division to help stem the enemy attack south of Vire. It consisted of the Headquarters of Schiller's own 1st SS Panzer-Grenadier Regiment, a composite battalion of SS Panzer-Grenadiers from the same Regiment, an artillery battalion, a Werfer battery and four or five StuGs. It fought with the 84th Division from the 7th until the night of 10th August. The balance of Wisch's Division—which therefore comprised Sandig's 1st and 2nd SS Panzer-Grenadier Battalions, about twenty StuGs of Heimann's 1st SS Sturmgeschütz Battalion and Scheler's 1st SS Pioneer Battalion—was still on the move towards the Mortain area when the attack began and had not even reached St Clément when darkness fell that night. And some elements, such as the Mk IVs of the 7th SS Panzer Company, did not even start to move west from the Bretteville-sur Laize area until the night of the 7th and took until the 10th just to get to Domfront.[20] Hitler's criticism of von Kluge for not committing the LAH as an exploitation force through 2nd SS Panzer in the southern sector on the morning of the 7th, with which some historians have agreed, ignored reality.

The right hand group of von Lüttwitz's 2nd Panzer Division, including the Leibstandarte's Reconnaissance Battalion, made reasonable progress during the early hours of the 7th. Its attack route lay down a narrow, wooded valley as far as Bellefontaine but then the country opened up and the way to the west was relatively unrestricted. At 0315 hours the Americans reported an enemy penetration between the 117th and 39th Infantry Regiments in the vicinity of le Mesnil-Tôve.[21] Further reports said that at least twenty tanks, supported by infantry (members of Knittel's SS Reconnaissance Battalion), forced the Cannon Company of the US 39th Infantry to abandon its vehicles and guns in that village. Before 0800 hours this force reached the outskirts of le Mesnil-Adelée, where a company of the reserve 119th Infantry Regiment had established a road block. The Germans were 10km from their start point but still 25km from Avranches. By then, as with Baum's advance south-west of Mortain, they were vulnerable to Allied artillery and air power and out on a limb. The column halted.

At 0730 hours Combat Command B of the 3rd Armored

Division was attached to the 30th Infantry[22] and one combat
team was given orders to restore the situation in conjunction
with the 3rd Battalion of the 119th and a company of the
743rd Tank Battalion. The combined force was to strike north
from Juvigny to retake le Mesnil-Tôve and if possible cut off
the Germans. With the failure of the 116th Division to advance on its right, von Lüttwitz's column was indeed vulnerable on both flanks. The 3rd Armored Division tank and
infantry combat teams advanced shortly after 1310 hours,[23]
forcing the Germans to fight hard to hold le Mesnil-Tôve. The
Americans, however, lacked the strength to break through; by
last light Knittel's companies were successfully defending the
western and southern approaches to the village[24].

Despite the delays already mentioned, the Panthers of
Kuhlmann's 1st SS Panzer Battalion and attached Mk IVs of
the 5th Company arrived in their assembly area to the east of
St Barthélemy before first light on the 7th and were ready to
move forward by 0430 hours. They were joined by Dinse's
SPW mounted 3rd SS Panzer-Grenadier Battalion which had
been placed under Kuhlmann's command for the attack[25]. The
assembly area proved to be cramped and unsuitable and the
prospect of advancing in thick fog over unseen ground so soon
after an exhausting approach march could not have been attractive. In fact had Kuhlmann and his men been able to see
what lay ahead of them they would have been appalled. The
initial part of their route was through 'bocage' with high banks
along the narrow roads, there was no chance of deploying
cross-country and visibility was restricted, even without the
fog, to less than 100m. They would therefore have no chance
to use their splendid tank guns effectively. But worse was to
come—although the country opened out beyond St
Barthélemy, they were destined to advance along a high, narrow, whale-like ridge towards Juvigny with no cover whatso-
ever from the dreaded Allied fighter-bombers!

At 0550 hours, following a forty-five minute artillery barrage on the American positions in and around St Barthélemy
which did little damage, the Leibstandarte tanks moved in
from the east and south-east and the 2nd Panzer Mk IVs and
assault guns from the north and north-east. The village was

held by A and C Companies and three 57mm anti-tank guns of Lieutenant Colonel (later Major General) Robert Frankland's 1st Battalion of the 117th Infantry. They were supported initially by four 3″ TDs of 3rd Platoon, B Company, 823rd TD Battalion, and later by two guns of the 1st Platoon of the same Company. B Company of the 117th was in reserve further along the ridge to the west of the village in an area called le Foutai (known to the Americans as le Fantay).

Frankland had been expecting to move into a simple assembly area and was surprised to find he was required to defend the village. His Battalion strength was 828 but 190 of these men had only joined the unit within the previous three days;[26] everyone was tired having been on the move all day, there were no detailed maps of the area and some of the fox-holes and outposts vacated by the 1st Infantry Division had to be occupied under conditions of darkness. This was particularly serious for the TD crews who found many of the former positions of the SP armoured M-10s of the 1st Infantry totally unsuitable for their low-slung, towed guns.

Kuhlmann was also in for a surprise. He had been expecting to drive straight through St Barthélemy but soon found he had to clear the southern part of the village in order to get on to the Juvigny road—the thirty or so Mk IVs, and the assault guns and Grenadiers of the 2nd Panzer Division had been ordered to attack the northern sector of the village only. The fog, which rose and fell like a stage curtain, made it difficult for attacker and defender alike and in chaotic fighting most engagements took place at less than 50m and in some cases hand to hand. The tanks were unable to deploy and conditions generally could not have been more unsuitable for an armoured attack. Even so by 0808 hours the Panthers had broken into the C Company positions—in fact at 0810 hours Frankland gave orders that the Panzers were to be allowed to pass through.[27] This tactic, reminiscent of the Hitlerjugend's in the Caen fighting, caused many casualties to Dinse's SS Grenadiers as they tried to follow up behind the tanks.

According to the 30th Infantry Division log, the 117th Regiment reported at 0922 hours, 'Everything under control'; but it went on to say, 'we have no reserve and have to shuttle troops back and forth.' Within the hour the picture changed dramatically—the Regimental log shows the following entry timed at 1035 hours: 'tanks have broken through A and C Companies and heard [sic] advancing toward B Company.' The log also shows that at 1046 hours the 1st Battalion Command Post (CP) at la Rossaye, 1100m west of the village church, was under attack. The 117th Infantry Regimental CP was only 400m to its south.

At 1130 hours the Army Group 'B' War Diary placed KG Kuhlmann 1km west of St Barthélemy and this is confirmed by the log of the 117th Infantry which states that at 1125 hours enemy 'tanks and infantry are on the road advancing toward the Regimental CP from St Barthélemy.' At this time Frankland's Battalion was desperately trying to establish a defence line at la Rossaye but things were getting so bad that A Company of the 105th Engineer Combat Battalion, supporting the 117th, had to be called in to provide protection for the Regimental CP. It claimed a Mk IV tank knocked out at 1200 hours[28] and this has to be added to the main claim, by B Company of the 823rd TD Battalion, of eight enemy tanks destroyed in the St Barthélemy sector during the morning, with two more probables.[29] All six TDs were lost in the process as were the three infantry 57mm anti-tank guns.

At 1218 hours a temporary defensive line had been 'built up on the high ground east of the CP'[30] but there were no reserves. The 2nd Battalion of the 117th Infantry had been placed under the command of the 120th Regiment at 0315 hours to help meet the crisis at Mortain, the 3rd Battalion was holding the north flank between Juvigny and St Barthélemy and the two remaining battalions of the reserve 119th Regiment were busy trying to hold le Mesnil-Adelée and to recapture le Mesnil-Tôve. No tanks were available to help out since the 743rd Tank Battalion, permanently attached to the 30th Infantry, was operating in support of the 119th and 120th Infantry Regiments.[31] The only heavy weapons left were the other five TDs of B Company, 823rd TD Battalion,[32] which had been sited to cover the St Barthélemy-Juvigny road. Frankland's command had by now lost seven officers and 327 men,[33] many of them prisoners, and the TD Company forty-three men.[34] The following description was provided by the temporary Regimental Commander, Lieutenant Colonel Johnson, and Lieutenant Colonel Frankland in After Action interviews made shortly after these events:

About twenty-five men of A Company worked their way back to the line finally established that afternoon. About fifty-five men of C Company, plus the battered platoon of B Company reached the new position. And after reaching that line the Battalion got the heaviest concentration of artillery they had ever experienced.[35]

The 30th Infantry History also points out that the 1st Battalion was:

Crippled even more [than the casualties indicate] by disorganisation and isolation of its small units. Some men of the Battalion fought and hid in isolated bands for two days before they succeeded in rejoining their companies.[36]

But in spite of everything the Americans had delayed the Germans for six critical hours and there is no doubt that the resistance at St Barthélemy against both KG Kuhlmann and the elements of von Lüttwitz's 2nd Panzer Division, during a period when bad weather prevented ground attack aircraft from intervening in the battle, was crucial to the success of the American defence on 7th August. The leading elements of KG Kuhlmann were still some 3km short of Juvigny when the first Typhoons appeared overhead shortly after 1230 hours.[37]

The 300 aircraft promised by the Luftwaffe had never materialized. On the Allied side:

It was agreed. . . . that the Typhoons, armed with rocket projectiles, of the Second Tactical Air Force, under the control of the AOC 83 Group [Air Vice-Marshal Harry Broadhurst], should deal exclusively with the enemy armoured columns, while the American fighters and fighter-bombers [of US Major General 'Pete' Quesada's IXth Tactical Air Command] should operate further afield to prevent enemy aircraft from interfering with our air effort and, in

addition, to destroy the transport and communications
leading up to the battle area.[38]

The result of this agreement was that once the morning fog
lifted the German armoured columns were at the mercy of
dedicated ground attack aircraft—the 7th of August has not
been called 'The Day of the Typhoon' without good reason.

At 1215 hours Wing Commander Charles Green, commander of 121 Wing RAF, led a flight of six aircraft from an
airfield at le Fresne-Camilly, to the east of Bayeux, on an
armed reconnaissance of the Vire-Flers-Domfront area and
spotted a 'large concentration of enemy tanks and motor
transport . . . at St Barthélemy, north of Mortain'. From
then on, until 2040 hours, the XLVII Panzer Corps armoured
columns were exposed to a furious and non-stop attack. There
were never less than twenty-two aircraft over the Mortain sector during this period and at the height of the attacks, between
1500 and 1600 hours, there were no less than eighty-eight
Typhoons in the air. A total of 458 individual Typhoon sorties
were flown on 7th August, of which 271 struck the German
forces in the Mortain sector—247 were armed with anti-ar-
mour rockets and twenty-four with 500 or 1000lb bombs.

Broadhurst's 83 Group, flying from le Fresne-Camilly and
the Canadian strip at nearby Lantheuil, furnished 224 of these
missions with the balance coming from Air Vice-Marshal
Brown's 84 Group. A further 131 sorties attacked targets
around and to the east of Vire and for various reasons another
fifty-six failed to find targets. Only four aircraft were lost.[39]

The Luftwaffe had been rendered completely impotent by
the Americans, who flew some 200 sorties. At 1740 hours Luftwaffe Colonel von Scholz reported to Seventh Army,[40] 'our
fighters were hard pressed by enemy fighters from the moment
they took to the air. They could not reach the target area.' He
did not need to tell XLVII Panzer Corps—at 1500 hours the
Chief of Staff told Seventh Army they had 'not seen a single
German plane all day.'

The G-3 Daily Report of Hausser's Advance Command Post
recorded the following statement for 7th August,[41] 'Continuation of the attack during the midday hours was made impossi-

ble because of enemy air superiority', and at 1940 hours von Gersdorff told the Army Group 'B' Chief of Staff, 'The attack has bogged down since 1300 hours because of heavy enemy fighter-bomber operations and the failure of our own Air Force.'[42] Hausser himself told von Kluge at 2150 hours on the 7th, 'Terrific fighter-bomber attacks. Considerable tank losses. The Corps have orders to continue their attacks as soon as the air activity decreases.[43]'

Exact German losses on this day will never be known. RAF pilots claimed a total of eighty-four tanks destroyed, thirty-five probably destroyed and twenty-one damaged, plus a further 112 other vehicles destroyed or damaged. The IXth US Tactical Air Command, which flew 441 sorties over the period 7th to 10th August, made claims of sixty-nine tanks destroyed, eight probably destroyed and thirty-five damaged and 116 other vehicles destroyed or damaged. Confirmed results on the ground were somewhat different. Between 12th and 20th August 1944 operational research teams from both the 21st Army Group and Second Tactical Air Force conducted separate investigations in the battle area and then compared and collated their results.[44] They found thirty-four Panthers, ten Mk IVs, three SP guns, twenty-three armoured personnel carriers, eight armoured cars and forty-six other vehicles. Of the forty-four tanks they concluded that twenty had been destroyed by ground fire, seven by air force rockets, two by bombs, four from multiple causes and eleven either abandoned or destroyed by their crews. It is impossible to say how many damaged vehicles the Germans managed to recover. Seventeen Panthers were found in the area over which the LAH had operated (thirteen in the vicinity of St Barthélemy, with the most westerly pair being found 1700m west of the church) and of these, six had been knocked out by army weapons, four by air force rockets and the rest blown up or abandoned by their crews.

Arguments about who stopped the German advance are futile. Without the stubborn resistance of the 30th Infantry Division and 823rd TD Battalion, elements of von Funck's forces might well have reached the vicinity of Avranches before the arrival of the Typhoons. The consequences could have been dramatic. Equally, had the Typhoons not intervened when

they did there is a distinct possibility, some would say proba-
bility, that the Germans would have broken through to the
west. But these are the 'ifs' of history. As with most successful
operations in modern warfare, it was cooperation between all
arms and between ground and air forces that was the essential
ingredient.

Werner Josupeit, a machine-gunner in the Leibstandarte,
described his experience that day:

> The fighter-bombers circled our tanks several times. Then
> one broke out of the circle, sought its target and fired. As
> the first pulled back into the circle of about twenty planes, a
> second pulled out and fired. And so they continued until
> they had all fired. Then they left the terrible scene. A new
> swarm appeared in their place and fired all their rockets
> . . . Black clouds of smoke from burning oil climbed into
> the sky everywhere we looked. They marked the dead
> Panzers. . . . Finally the Typhoons couldn't find any more
> Panzers so they bore down on us and chased us mercilessly.
> Their shells fell with a terrible howl. One fell right next to a
> comrade of mine, but he did not get hurt. These rockets
> burst into just a few big pieces of shrapnel, and a man had a
> chance of not being hit.[45]

It was inevitable that, in the confused fighting of the day,
there would be many cases of attacks on one's own troops.
The 117th Infantry Regimental log records three instances
when its troops were attacked by Allied aircraft, the first timed
at 1505 hours, and of requests for 'any more missions to be
called off.'

But 'Blue on Blue' incidents were not restricted to the RAF;
in the fog some troops were hit by friendly artillery and even
small-arms fire. As one TD man put it, 'We didn't have a
friend in the world that day.'[46]

The *History of Old Hickory* says:

> The events of August 7 brought the 30th Infantry Division
> to the brink of disintegration. . . . The attack had inflicted
> severe damage on the defenders, but it won no decisive
> advantage.[47]

This was true. At 1930 hours Hausser presented von Kluge with three alternatives:[48] hold on until annihilated; withdraw towards the east and allow an Allied breakthrough to the north-east; or fall back towards the north-east and allow the Allies a free run towards Paris. Since Hitler would not even consider withdrawal, the inevitable order came back to renew the attack as soon as further troops could be made available. In the meantime the current situation was to be improved as far as possible and maintained at all costs.

We need not concern ourselves with Hitler's plan for renewing operation LÜTTICH or the forces he proposed to use. Although scheduled initially for 9th August, major events elsewhere in Normandy precluded any chance of it ever being launched. We will confine ourselves to the activities of the Leibstandarte and in this respect there is an interesting entry in the Seventh Army Telephone Log timed at 2200 hours 7th August:

> Hausser to von Funck: 'The remaining parts of the Leibstandarte are still at your disposal to continue the attack. Where do you want them to go?' Funck: 'To St Clement.' Hausser: 'They still have twenty-five assault guns.' Funck: 'I shall have the ordnance officer order the Regiment on the march immediately.'

8TH AUGUST—STALEMATE

During the night 7th–8th the remainder of the Leibstandarte less KG Schiller arrived in the St Barthélemy sector, as did the 3rd Battalion of the US 12th Infantry Regiment (4th Infantry Division), with six tanks and four TDs in support. This new American group reinforced Frankland's depleted Battalion, which now had a total strength of 465[49] but an offensive combat strength of only just over 200.

Some time after first light the 1st and 2nd SS Panzer-Grenadiers of Sandig's 2nd Regiment advanced towards Juvigny and Bellefontaine, with support from tanks and artillery limited due to early morning fog. The Germans say they captured both locations but could not hold them. There is no evidence to support this claim.

The Americans say their attack in the same area by the 3rd

Battalion, 12th Regiment and Frankland's B Company, with tank and TD support, began at 0800 hours. By 1140 hours B Company said it had advanced two hedgerows[50] and after fighting all day the American force pulled back. It had gained only a few hundred metres; two German tanks were claimed. Junge's 2nd SS Panzer-Grenadiers in St Barthélemy and Becker's 1st to their south were not to be moved easily, although von Gersdorff said of the day's events:[51] 'The Division [LAH] again experienced heavy losses, especially in tanks, through enemy air activity and the increased activity of enemy artillery.' The 2nd Panzer Division's northern group, including Knittel's SS Reconnaissance Battalion, had a much more difficult time in the Mesnil-Adelée and Mesnil-Tôve sector. It was attacked by Task Force 1 of Combat Command 'B' of the US 3rd Armored Division and the 3rd Battalion of the 119th Infantry Regiment. Task Force 1 comprised the 1st Battalions of the 33rd Armored and 36th Armored Infantry Battalions and the combined force managed, after heavy fighting, to advance to and capture le Mesnil-Tôve by 1945 hours. This still left the Germans holding the high ground to the east of the village. Von Gersdorff made the following statement about this action:

> When le Mesnil-Tôve was captured by the enemy, the KG was cut off in the area of le Mesnil-Adelée. Its main body was annihilated. The Division [2nd Panzer] was thereby forced into defence on the line east of le Mesnil-Tôve and Hill 280 west of St Barthélemy.[52]

At 1845 hours von Kluge told Hausser:

> Everything must be risked. Besides, at Caen we are dealing with a penetration of unprecedented proportions. I draw the following conclusion: first of all, we have to make preparations to reorganise the attack. Therefore, tomorrow the attack will not be continued, but an attack on the following day will be prepared.[53]

Although von Kluge did not yet know it the Canadian operation TOTALIZE to the south of Caen was in deep trouble—

thanks to the Leibstandarte's partner in I SS Panzer Corps, the Hitlerjugend.

But another event on 8th August was heralding the end of the current 1st SS Panzer Division—at 1700 hours, 100km to the south-east of Mortain, tanks of Major General Haislip's XV US Corps crossed the Gambetta bridge and rolled into the centre of Le Mans.

9TH AUGUST—'THE ATTACK IS TO BE CONTINUED'

Lehmann and Tiemann's *The Leibstandarte IV/I* has concise comment about events on 9th August—'The units spent the day improving their positions, moving in reinforcements and closing all gaps in the line.' On the ground this involved Knittel's 2nd SS Reconnaissance Company occupying Bellefontaine in order to complete the line to Sandig's SS Panzer-Grenadiers, Scheler's SS Pioneers strengthening the northern part of St Barthélemy,[54] and elements of the 1st SS Panzer-Grenadier Regiment also coming into the line. Consequently, when the Americans launched their attack in the St Barthélemy sector with the same force as on the 8th, they got nowhere.

In the east of the le Mesnil-Tôve sector a penetration by the 3rd Battalion of the 119th Infantry was stopped by an immediate counter-attack from elements of 2nd Panzer. Whether or not Knittel's men took part is unknown. German artillery fire completely crippled attempts by tanks of Task Force 1 of the 3rd Armored Division to support this attack. The Divisional History speaks of the Force 'sustaining very heavy casualties'.

During the afternoon Hitler replaced von Funck with General Eberbach and gave tentative orders for the Avranches counter-offensive to be re-launched on 11th August. The new command, which was still to be subordinate to Hausser, was to be called Panzer Group Eberbach and comprised, in name only, two Panzer Corps—XLVII and LVIII. As we shall see, Kurt Meyer's Hitlerjugend Division had saved the day against the Canadians in TOTALIZE and at 1520 hours von Kluge told Hausser's Chief of Staff:

I have just had a decisive conversation with the Supreme Command. Inasmuch as the situation south of Caen has been stabilized again and apparently has not brought about

the bad results which were expected, I have suggested that
we stick to the idea of attack. [It was of course Hitler's
order, not von Kluge's suggestion]. The attack must be prepared and carried out, however, according to plan and
should not be done too hastily. . . . General Eberbach will
arrive at your CP tonight with an improvised staff.[55]

Needless to say most of the officers on Hausser's staff realised that if this last attempt to break through to Avranches
failed, the Seventh Army would be encircled and doomed.
From our point of view it is interesting to note that the main
thrust was still to be through Juvigny—in the LAH sector.

10TH AUGUST—STATUS QUO

During 10th August the Leibstandarte continued to hold its
positions in the St Barthélemy sector. The fighting was bitter
and bloody but the Germans were husbanding their armour
for the next phase of LÜTTICH. Although the Americans
made some minor dents in the German defences, they were
not strong enough to evict their enemy from his well based
positions. In fact, for obvious reasons, a continuation of the
status quo suited Montgomery and Bradley.

To the north-east of Mortain KG Schiller helped to hold and
then push back an American incursion to the south of Vire.
No details are available. Schiller received orders to rejoin the
main body of the LAH during the night 10th–11th when the
Division was due to be pulled out of the line for use in Hitler's
great counter-attack.

But by now the American push towards Alençon was causing von Kluge grave concern. In an attempt to placate Hitler
he asked for Panzer Group Eberbach to be:

Temporarily transferred from the Mortain area [so that it
could be used to] destroy the enemy spearheads thrusting
northwards [and thus] render possible the prosecution of
the decisive offensive [LÜTTICH].[56]

There was no response from the Führer but despite this
Hausser's future intentions are revealed in the Seventh Army
War Diary for this day:

In the night 11–12 August, the 116th Panzer Division and parts of 'The LAH' will be transferred to the LXXXI Corps in the area Carrouges-Alençon-Sées.

POSTSCRIPT

There are two further minor but interesting stories concerning the Mortain counter-offensive. The first is connected with the delayed arrival of the Leibstandarte's 1st SS Panzer Battalion in the attack ara on 7th August and stems from two basic sources. First, von Gersdorff's post-war statement which included the passage:

> The Battalion was in close formation in defile when an enemy fighter-bomber, which had been shot down, fell on the first tank and thus blocked the entire Battalion. Backing out and turning the vehicles took up valuable hours.[57]

This story has been repeated by a local French historian, who locates the incident at or near the le Tournerie crossroads 1500m east of St Barthélemy, and by at least three eminent American, Canadian and British historians. In *The Leibstandarte IV/I* it merely says:

> [The Chief of the 10th Panzer-Grenadier Company, SS Lieutenant] Preuss offered the following report on a *much-discussed incident* (author's emphasis): 'It is true that one fighter bomber we shot down landed on a Panzer and destroyed it. Most other Panzers and Schützenpanzers, however, fell victim to this intensive air bombardment, which lasted hours.'[58]

The story may well be true but this author offers the following comments. First, the 1st SS Panzer Battalion moved from Tinchebray to St Barthélemy during the hours of darkness and, after first light on the 7th, in very foggy conditions— Allied fighter-bombers did not fly under such conditions. Second, although there are many potential bottlenecks between the places mentioned, the area of the le Tournerie crossroads is not one of them. This is not to say however that an aircraft did not crash on to a German vehicle in this area some time after the battle started.

The second story concerns the commander of the 1st SS
Panzer Regiment LAH, Jochen Peiper. There has been much
discussion as to whether or not he was present at St
Barthélemy on 7th August. In 1976 Peiper told the French
police[59] that he had been wounded whilst fighting the Canadians in the Caen sector on 2nd August and had been evacuated
via Paris to a hospital in Tegernsee in Bavaria. Those who do
not accept this usually quote the following statement by former SS Major Ralf Tiemann in his book *The Leibstandarte
IV/I*:

> The armoured force under Obersturmbannführer Peiper
> succeeded in moving past St Barthélemy [on 7th August].
> . . . Peiper suffered a heart attack and had to turn his Regi-
> ment over to the commander of the 1st Battalion,
> Sturmbannführer Kuhlmann.[60]

This statement is backed up to some extent by SS Lieutenant
Georg Preuss, the commander of the 10th SS Panzer-Grenadier Company, who wrote later, 'I heard that Peiper had suffered a heart attack [on 7th August]'. Nevertheless this author
knows of no one who claims to have seen Peiper at Mortain
and the supposition is contradicted by Fritz Kraemer, Chief of
Staff I SS Panzer Corps, in his post-war interrogation[61]—when
referring to the delayed arrival of the 1st SS Panzer Battalion
on 7th August he said, 'If Peiper had been there, this would
not have happened.'

It also has to be said that if Peiper had been present with the
LAH during the 6th and 7th it is most unlikely that a man
with his experience and dynamic personality would have allowed elements of his Regiment's 2nd Panzer Battalion to remain 'resting in woods near Bretteville-sur-Liaze'.

A medical document[62] dated 30th January 1945, signed by
SS Major Kurt Sickel, the medical officer of Peiper's Panzer
Regiment, and witnessed by his Adjutant, SS Captain Hans
Gruhle, shows that Peiper was wounded twice in 1944—once
by shrapnel in the left thigh and secondly with a bullet graze
on the left hand. Exact dates are not given. It also shows that
he had jaundice that year, with connected damage to his gall
bladder. There is separate evidence to show that Peiper was

indeed evacuated to a field hospital on 2nd August 1944 and sent to the Tegernsee Reserve Hospital in Bavaria on 6th August—close to where his wife and children were living at Rottach am Tegernsee!

There are two more fascinating twists to this puzzle. First, the US 30th Division G-2 Intelligence Report for the 'period ending 072200 Aug 1944' details the organisation of the 1st SS Panzer Division LAH but shows Kuhlmann, not Peiper, as the commander of the 1st SS Panzer Regiment. This author is of the opinion that there is no way American intelligence staffs could have obtained this information in time to publish it on the 7th if Peiper had been taken ill on the same day. And second, a gas mask with Peiper's name on it is today on display in the Musée Mémorial de la Bataille de Normandie at Bayeux—it was allegedly found in the Mortain area.

One thing is certain—a man like Jochen Peiper would not wish anyone to think he had suffered a heart attack during a critical battle or that he had been forced to leave a battlefield with jaundice—it is much more heroic to have been wounded.

NOTES

1. CMH Pub 100–13, *St Lô*, p. 91. 2. Ibid., p. 126. 3. 7th Army Telephone Log, 152350 Jul. 4. Gersdorff, US National Archives, MS B-725, p. 35. 5. Ibid., p. 37. 6. Lehmann & Tiemann, *The Leibstandarte, IV/I*, p. 182. 7. Hausser, US National Archives, MS B-179. 8. Gersdorff, op. cit., p. 38. 9. Ibid. 10. 7th Army Daily Reports Vol IV. 11. Ibid. 12. Ibid. 13. Hewitt, *Workhorse of the Western Front*, p. 32 and 37. 14. Ibid., p. 32. 15. Ibid., p. 51. 16. Lehmann & Tiemann, op. cit., pp. 184–185. 17. Manfred Thorn, a 7th SS Pz Coy driver, to author Feb 94. 18. Gersdorff, op. cit., p. 40. 19. Lehmann & Tiemann, op. cit., p. 182. 20. As note 17. 21. 30th Inf Div G-3 Log, 7 Aug 44. 22. Hewitt, op. cit., pp. 60–61. 23. As note 21. 24. Lehmann & Tiemann, op cit., p. 186. 25. Wisch, US National Archives, MS B-358, p. 2. 26. Statistics provided by Capt Freeman, HQ Coy, 1/117 Inf Regt, 16 Aug 44. 27. Unit Journal 117th Inf and Combat interview with Lt Col Frankland. 28. 105th Engr Combat Bn After Action Report No. 54. 29. 823rd TD BN After Action Report for Aug 44. 30. As note 21. 31. 30th Inf Div Report dated 070030 Aug 44. 32. As note 29. 33. As note 26. 34. As note 29. 35. US National Archives. 36. Hewitt, op. cit., p. 60. 37. 7th Army G-3 Daily Report 7 Aug 44. 38. Coningham, Arthur, *Operations Carried Out by 2 TAF between 6 Jun 44 and 9 May 45*, PRO AIR 37/876. 39. Details have been taken from the Operations Records Books of all RAF squadrons involved. These are available in the PRO, London in the series AIR 27. 40. 7th Army Telephone Log, 7 Aug 44. 41. As note 37. 42. As note 40. 43. Ibid. 44. Report No. 4 *Air attacks on Enemy Tanks and Motor Transport in*

the Mortain Area, August 1944 by No. 2 Operational Research Section
(PRO WO 106/4348). **45.** Lehmann & Tiemann, op. cit., p. 185. **46.** Hewitt, op. cit., p. 59. **47.** Ibid., p. 63. **48.** Gersdorff, op. cit., p. 45. **49.** 117th
Inf Unit Journal. **50.** Ibid. **51.** Gersdorff, op. cit., p. 48. **52.** Ibid., p. 47. **53.**
7th Army Telephone Log, 8 Aug 44. **54.** Lehmann & Tiemann, op. cit., p.
188. **55.** 7th Army Telephone Log, 9 Aug 44. **56.** Wilmot, *The Struggle for
Europe*, p. 416. **57.** Gersdorff, op. cit., p. 35. **58.** Lehmann & Tiemann, op.
cit., p. 186. **59.** Brigade Recherches Vesoul Procès Verbal No. 336, 22 Jun
76. **60.** Lehmann & Tiemann, op. cit., p. 186. **61.** Kraemer, *I SS Panzer
Corps in the West*, MS C-024, IWM, London, AL 2727/1–2. **62.** Peiper,
Bestätigung der Verwundungen, 30 Jan 45.

24 | 8th to 11th August—Operation TOTALIZE and the First Battle of Falaise

8TH AUGUST—'AN EVEN BLACKER DAY FOR THE GERMAN ARMY'

The 8th of August 1918 was the start of the great British
offensive east of Amiens, which Ludendorff described later as,
'The black day of the German Army in the history of the war.'
On the eve of the first major offensive by the First Canadian
Army General Crerar told his senior officers that he intended
to make 8th August 1944 an even blacker day for the Germans.
Recall that when this speech was made von Kluge already
knew that Phase I of Operation LÜTTICH had failed.

Guy Simonds was an experienced Corps commander. He
had commanded an infantry division in Sicily and an
armoured division in Italy before taking over the II Canadian
Corps, and it fell to him to carry out Montgomery's directive
of breaking out towards Falaise in the operation code-named
TOTALIZE. In fact Crerar had told him to plan such an operation several days before Monty issued his Directive. For this
task Simonds already had his own 2nd and 3rd Canadian Infantry Divisions and the inexperienced 4th Armoured Division. He was now given the British 51st (Highland) Infantry
Division and 33rd Tank Brigade, and the unblooded 1st Polish
Armoured Division, which was to play a short but dramatic
part in the battle of Normandy. Many of the Poles had been
waiting four years for this moment.

Simonds brought new ideas to the forthcoming battle: first,
he decided to attack at night, without a preliminary bombard-

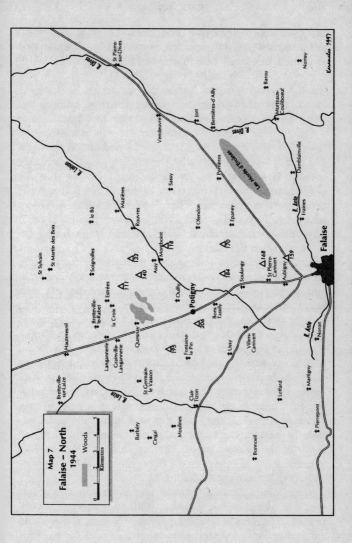

Map 7
Falaise – North
1944

Woods

Kilometres

Kerslake 1997

St Pierre-sur-Dives

R. Dives

St Pierre-sur-Dives

Norey

Barou

Berniéres-d'Ailly

Morteaux-Couliboeuf

Iort

Vendeuvre

R. Dives

Damb)lainville

Les Monts d'Eraines

R. Ante

Perriéres

St Martin des Bois

le 80

Maziéres

Sassy

Olendon

Eraines

Rouvres

Epaney

St Sylvain

Soignolles

△ 132

Montboint

△ 118

△ 170

Hautmesnil

Estrées

la Croix

△ 111

Assy

△ 140

Ouilly

△ 168

△ 159

Falaise

Bretteville-le-Rabet

Quesnay

Potigny

△ 184

Aubigny

St Pierre-Canivet

Langannerie

Grainville-Langannerie

△ 195

Fontaine-le-Pin

△ 206

Bons Tassilly

Soulangy

Bretteville-sur-Laize

St Germain-le-Vasson

Ussy

Villers-Canivet

R. Ante

Noron

Clair Tizon

Lefard

Marigny

Moulines

Pierrepont

Barbery

Cingal

Bonnoeil

R. Laize

R. Laison

ment; second, by removing the 105mm gun from the 'Priest' self-propelled artillery vehicle, he created an open-topped armoured personnel carrier, code-named 'Kangaroo', which gave some of his infantry both mobility and protection; and third, he decided to use RAF night bombers to saturate the flanks of his proposed penetration and American medium and heavy bombers in the breakout phase after first light.

Such a plan demanded extremely accurate navigation by both airmen and soldiers. A trial was carried out on the night of the 6th which proved that the artillery could adequately indicate targets with marker shells and, following this, Air Chief Marshal Sir Arthur Harris agreed to his RAF aircraft taking part as requested. Various other technical aids were adopted to help the ground forces including the use of radio directional beams, artificial moonlight and tracer fired from AA guns down the flanks.

Simonds's plan, in outline, was to obliterate the flanking areas of May-sur-Orne—Fontenay-le-Marmion on the right and la Hogue—Secqueville-la-Campagne on the left with heavy bombers starting at 2300 hours on 7th August; and then to seize Garcelles, the Cramesnil spur, St Aignan, Gaumesnil, and Caillouet features with tanks and the seventy-six Kangaroos of the 2nd and 51st Infantry Divisions. Then, with the aid of a heavy daylight air bombardment—and whilst the same Divisions went on to secure the flanks at Bretteville-sur-Laize on the right and the woods north of Cauvicourt on the left—the 4th Canadian Armoured Division was to secure the area Fontaine-le-Pin—Potigny and the 1st Polish Armoured Division the vital ground to the east of the Caen-Falaise road and south of the Laison stream. The 3rd Infantry Division was, when ordered, to take over the Bretteville-le-Rabet and Point 140 area, dominating the Laison valley.

Some idea of the administrative preparations for this operation are given in the Canadian Official History:[1] 205,000 rounds of artillery ammunition for the 720 guns available and 152,000 gallons of petrol were dumped behind the II Corps positions before H-Hour and an additional 1,069 tons of ammunition and 672 tons of petrol were carried 'on wheels' with the attacking divisions.

Facing this onslaught was the 89th Infantry Division which had been formed only four months previously in Norway. It had moved first to Rouen and then to the south-east of Dieppe in late July, before taking over the Leibstandarte sector only four days before the attack. It comprised two Regiments, each of three infantry battalions and a Fusilier battalion on bicycles, an artillery Regiment of four battalions (one of which had 88mm guns), a Pioneer battalion, and an anti-tank battalion with only one company of 75mm guns available; the other two companies had still to arrive. Most of the officers and NCOs had combat experience.

On the right flank of the 89th Division, the 272nd Infantry Division had some elements near Secqueville; KG Meyer was of course in reserve behind the 89th. Recall that Fast Group Olboeter had not yet returned from the II SS Panzer Corps area and KG Wünsche was still tied up resisting the British bridgehead at Grimbosq. Although Allied intelligence staffs knew that 1st SS Panzer Division had been relieved by an infantry division, they did not know it had moved west and were under the impression that it had gone into a reserve position in depth. This idea may have been helped by sixty-five dummy tanks set up by KG Wünsche during the night 2nd August to the east of St Aignan.

On the 7th, the day before the Allied attack, Meyer moved his force into the area south-east of Bretteville-sur-Laize so that it would be more centrally positioned in the I SS Panzer Corps sector and nearer to the new British bridgehead over the Orne. He had available Prinz's 2nd SS Panzer Battalion with thirty-nine Mk IVs (Fritz Kraemer said twelve of these had been 'borrowed' from the 9th SS Panzer Division)[2], eight combat ready Tigers of Wittmann's 101st SS Heavy Panzer Battalion, twenty-seven Jagdpanzer IVs, Waldmüller's 1st SS Panzer-Grenadier Battalion, the Corps and Divisional Escort Companies, the 12th SS Panzer Artillery Regiment (now commanded by SS Major Oskar Drexler) of three Battalions, less the Wespe battery with Olboeter, and the 12th SS Flak Battalion. In addition, parts of the III Luftwaffe Flak Corps and the 83rd Werfer Regiment were operational in the Corps area. Chester Wilmot estimated that there were some one hundred 88mm and

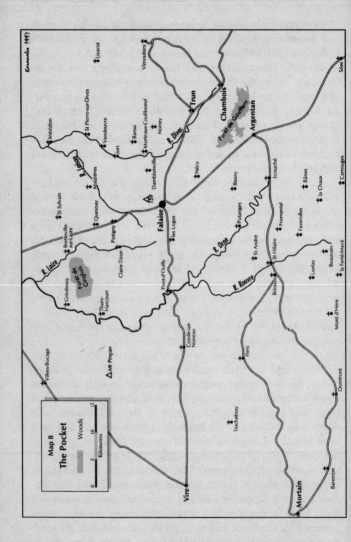

75mm anti-tank capable weapons facing Simonds's Corps,[3] and Kraemer confirmed that there were two 75mm anti-tank battalions and 100 howitzers in the Corps sector.[4]

At 2140 hours on the day Meyer moved his KG to the Bretteville area, von Kluge ordered Dietrich to send the bulk of the Hitlerjugend Division as soon as possible to the area north-west of Condé-sur-Noireau (Map 8), where it was urgently needed to help prevent a British breakthrough between Vire and Thury-Harcourt. Dietrich argued unsuccessfully against this decision and Kraemer, his Chief of Staff, duly confirmed that most of the HJ would indeed move that night, and that KG Wünsche would follow at about 1000 hours the following day, after it had 'dealt with' the Grimbosq bridgehead. As we shall see these proposed moves proved impossible to implement.

Less than two hours after Meyer had been told to move his Division, at 2300 hours on 7th August, 1,020 RAF night bombers began dropping 3,462 tons of bombs on their targets. According to the Canadian Official History not one bomb fell amongst the Canadian or British troops and ten aircraft were shot down during the raid.[5]

At 2330 hours seven Allied armoured groups were ready on their Start-Line running from just north of Tilly to St André— four from the 2nd Canadian Infantry Division and 2nd Canadian Armoured Brigade to the west of the Caen-Falaise highway, and three from the British 51st Highland Division and 33rd Tank Brigade to the east; specialist tanks from the British 79th Armoured Division supported all the columns. It was an incredible sight—each column, which numbered nearly 2,000 men and 200 armoured or semi-armoured vehicles, was four vehicles abreast, less than a metre apart, and each rank was separated by only a few metres. They were led by navigating, mine-clearing and assault engineer tanks; behind them came the assault force of combat tanks and infantry mounted in Kangaroos, followed by infantry support weapons in carriers, armoured recovery vehicles, bulldozers and halftrack ambulances. More tanks brought up the rear. Whilst foot infantry were tasked with capturing May, Fontenay, Rocquancourt, Tilly and Secqueville, these armoured columns had the task of

driving hard for the Phase I objectives as far south as Caillouet, Gaumesnil, the Cramesnil spur and St Aignan. The artillery barrage by 360 guns, which would not commence until
the columns had been moving for fifteen minutes, would cover
a width of 4000 yards astride the Caen-Falaise highway and
would move at 100 yards a minute, lifting in jumps of 200
yards. It should be made clear, though, that relatively few of
Simonds's infantry were carried in the armoured Kangaroos—
the total lift was only about 600 men. The balance rode in
scout cars, halftracks, on the rear tanks, hitched lifts on other
armoured vehicles or walked.

Things began to go wrong right from the start. No one
could see—the dust created by so many tracked vehicles and
the exploding shells formed a blinding curtain, into which the
German artillery fired smoke rounds. This inevitably affected
the bombing programme and the Master Bombers had to order the last waves of aircraft to abort their missions—only
two-thirds of the programme was completed.[6]

On the ground vehicles ran into each other, some strayed
from their correct axes and others got completely lost, some
even ending up in bomb craters well off their intended routes.
Confused drivers and commanders were forced to follow the
tail lights of the vehicle in front and inevitably there were a
number of 'Blue on Blue' incidents, as well as groups running
into strongpoints they were meant to avoid. An excellent description of what it was like appears in Belfield and Essame's
book, *The Battle for Normandy*:

> All went well until the barrage started. The column was
> then immediately enveloped in a dense cloud of dust in
> which it was impossible at more than a few feet to see the
> tail light of the tank in front. . . . When the barrage started
> the needle immediately swung wildly in all directions, and
> the compass became useless. . . . Great shapes of tanks
> loomed up out of the fog and asked who you were. Flails
> seemed to be everywhere and their enormous jibs barging
> about in the dark seemed to add to the confusion. . . . In
> fact, some of the Canadians became mixed up with part of

our column and one Canadian tank spent the rest of the night with us.

In fairness though, it has to be said that orientation in Normandy was never easy; the maps issued to the Allied troops were difficult enough to read in daylight let alone the dark and many of the smaller hamlets like Verrières were not even shown. Villages often had the same or similar names and most of them looked puzzlingly similar.

Despite all the confusion, the new tactics were a success; by first light the British columns were 5km inside the German defences and had secured Garcelles with its Château, park and woods, Cramesnil and St Aignan (now one village). The Canadians had considerably more difficulty finding their way and encountered greater opposition, but by midday they had taken Caillouet and the tiny hamlet of Gaumesnil. Casualties were surprisingly light. The three Canadian infantry battalions lost a total of only sixty-three men.[7] Such was sadly not the case for the foot infantry—two battalions of Seaforth Highlanders lost sixty killed in the final twelve hour battle to take 'the blood-stained stones of Tilly',[8] and the Canadians had suffered 260 casualties, including sixty-eight dead,[9] before all their objectives were cleared.

As soon as Kurt Meyer heard the RAF bombing and then the roar of the Allied artillery he knew a major attack had begun. He immediately moved forward to Urville, where he met Wilhelm Mohnke,[10] who had been seriously deafened by the bombing. Early reports indicated that the 89th Division's forward positions had been overrun and that organised defence had, to all intents and purposes, collapsed. In reality many of the forward 89th Division troops in places like Tilly and Fontenay-le-Marmion fought on stubbornly well into the afternoon.

From Meyer's detailed knowledge of the ground, learned when he had been stationed there as a Reconnaissance Battalion commander in both 1942 and 1943, he knew that the next defendable line was the high ground around Potigny (Map 7) and the natural obstacle of the Laison. This stream, lying in a shallow wooded valley was less than 2m wide and 1m deep;

nevertheless it was to prove a considerable tank obstacle. Meyer knew this and he also knew that if he could delay the Allied attack and give time for the reinforcing 85th Infantry Division to take up a position to the south-east, all might not be lost; its leading elements had already reached Trun (Map 8).

Meyer then drove on to the tactically vital village of Cintheaux which lay only 1000m from the Canadians in Gaumesnil. There he found a single anti-tank platoon from SS Major Hans Waldmüller's KG covering the Caen-Falaise highway. He also found soldiers of the 89th Division fleeing to the rear in disorder. In his inimitable way he described the scene:

> I am seeing German soldiers running away for the first time during these long, gruesome, murderous years. They are unresponsive. They have been through hell-fire and stumble past us with fear filled eyes. I look at the leaderless groups in fascination. My uniform sticks to my body, the fear of responsibility making me break out in a sweat. . . . I jump out of the car and stand alone in the middle of the road, talking to my fleeing comrades. They are startled and stop. They look at me incredulously, wondering how I can stand on the road armed only with just a carbine. . . . They recognise me, turn round, and wave to their comrades to come and organise the defence on the line of Cintheaux.[11]

Panzermeyer then returned to Urville where General Eberbach, the commander of the Fifth Panzer Army, had arrived to assess the situation personally. Thus we have the equivalent of Dempsey or Hodges less than 5km from the nearest enemy troops on a front which has already collapsed. No wonder German soldiers had respect for such officers!

Eberbach approved Meyer's plan to stabilize the situation and orders were immediately given for KG Waldmüller, reinforced by the thirty-nine Mk IVs of Prinz's 2nd SS Panzer Battalion and Wittmann's eight Tigers, to counter-attack and seize the vital ground at St Aignan, currently held by 1st Black Watch and the 1st Northamptonshire Yeomanry tank battalion, and then the woods south-east of Garcelles. The I SS Panzer Corps Escort Company was attached to Waldmüller for this operation, as were the HJ Escort Company and 1st SS

Panzerjäger Company. They had orders to advance in parallel via Estrées, and capture the important ridge line running to the west of St Sylvain. Artillery support for the counter-attack was to be provided by the HJ Artillery Regiment and Werfer Battalion, as well as two or three other Werfer batteries from the 83rd Regiment. SS Major Fend's 12th SS Flak Battalion was to establish an anti-tank barrier astride the Caen-Falaise road at Bretteville-le-Rabet, and KG Wünsche, which had already been ordered to break off its attempt to eradicate the Grimbosq bridgehead, was to take up a blocking position on the hills west and northwest of Potigny. Divisional Headquarters was established in Potigny, although Meyer positioned himself with Waldmüller. The assembly area for Waldmüller's attack was Bretteville-le-Rabet and H-Hour was ordered for 1230 hours.

Owing to poor weather forecasts, which indicated that the daylight bombers might have difficulty in identifying their targets later in the day, H-Hour for Phase II of operation TOTALIZE was ordered for 1355 hours. By this time, the bombers would have prepared the way for the 4th Canadian and 1st Polish Armoured Divisions to thrust forward to their final objectives of Fontaine-le-Pin and the hills to the north of Falaise. Their essential intermediate objectives were Gouvix, Hautmesnil and Cauvicourt, all of which dominated the ground to their north for over 2km.

Kurt Meyer arrived in Cintheaux with SS Major Hans Waldmüller shortly before the American Fortresses appeared overhead at 1255 hours. He was determined to direct the counter-attack himself—as he put it, 'You just cannot lead a tank battle from behind an office desk!' But he was horrified when he saw the massed armour of the two Allied Divisions on either side of the Caen-Falaise highway, and when he spotted a single American bomber flying across his front Meyer correctly surmised that it was a marker aircraft. He ordered the counter-attack to begin at once. By closing with his enemy he hoped to get as many of his men as possible out of the target areas.

Despite some serious delays and not a little confusion (the Polish Division had moved all the way from the Bayeux area

during the night), the Allied Armoured Divisions were ready
to advance as the first of the 678 American B-17 'Flying Fortresses' approached their targets of Bretteville-sur-Laize,
Gouvix, Hautmesnil, Cauvicourt and St Sylvain.[12] According
to Kurt Meyer, one of his Grenadiers shouted to him, 'What
an honour, Churchill is sending one bomber for each of us!'[13]

Intense Flak shot down nine B-17s and for various reasons
181 did not carry out their attacks.[14] The remainder dropped
1,487 tons on the three main targets although only one aircraft
managed to find Gouvix. Unfortunately tragic mistakes by two
twelve-plane groups caused an estimated 315 casualties, including forty-four Poles, and the loss of some fifty-five vehicles
and four artillery pieces to friendly forces. In one case a damaged Fortress bombed short and the rest of the group followed
suite, and in the second, faulty target identification caused
another group to drop near Caen just as a convoy of the 3rd
Canadian Infantry Division was moving through Faubourg de
Vaucelles. The North Shore Regiment lost twenty-three killed
and seventy-five wounded near Cormelles[15] and Major General Keller's Tactical Headquarters was hit and he himself
wounded.

Kurt Meyer claimed to have shaken Michael Wittmann's
hand before wishing him luck on what was to be the Tiger
ace's last mission. His description of the following moments is
characteristic:

> The enemy artillery laid concentrated fire on the attacking
> Panzers. Michael Wittmann's Panzer raced right into the
> enemy fire. I knew his tactic during such situations: Get
> through! Don't stop! Into the dirt and reach a free field of
> fire. All the Panzers hurled themselves into the steel inferno.
> They had to prevent the enemy from attacking, they had to
> disrupt his timetable. Waldmüller pursued with his infantry,
> the brave Grenadiers following their officers. . . . Lost for
> words in the face of the terrific Allied power, I watched an
> endless chain of large four-engined bombers approaching.
> . . . The last waves flew over the strongly attacking KG
> Waldmüller without dropping a single bomb on the

Panzers. The bombers attacked their targets as ordered without concern for the, by this time, changed situation.[16]

The Poles crossed their Start-Line a little precipitately at 1335 hours with their 2nd Armoured Regiment on the left and 24th Lancers on the right, each with a company of 10th Dragoons (Motor Battalion) in support. The 1st Polish Armoured Division Operational Report records that the 2nd Regiment came under heavy fire from the area 2km south-east of St Aignan at 1425 hours and that the Lancers were 'under artillery fire'—no casualty figures are mentioned. At 1520 hours the Polish Report says its 2nd Regiment was in a difficult position with enemy tanks on its left flank, and at 1610 hours II Canadian Corps logged a message from General Maczek's Headquarters to the effect that twenty Tigers (almost certainly Prinz's Mk IVs) were 'covering with fire all country immediately over' the lateral road through St Aignan.[17] The Poles had of course clashed head-on with the Mk IVs and Jagdpanzer IVs of KG Waldmüller. Hubert Meyer says the Polish 2nd Armoured Regiment lost twenty-six Shermans from its two leading squadrons[18] but he gives no justification for this figure. However, it is known that the Regiment received twenty-four replacement tanks and crews the following day and his figure therefore seems very reasonable. With regard to the Lancers, their advance was barred by a shallow valley with a steep southern bank just to the south-east of St Aignan. This tank obstacle was clearly marked on the 1944 'going' map issued to Allied troops (the original still exists) but had obviously been overlooked by those planning the operation. This enforced halt not only exposed the Lancers to the artillery fire already mentioned, but almost certainly to flanking fire from Wittmann's Tigers advancing north from Cintheaux. If this happened, Meyer's statement that the Lancers lost fourteen tanks would not be unreasonable.

Kurt Meyer describes another part of this action in *Grenadiers*:

The Divisional Escort Company reports from the west of St Sylvain that it is in action against the head of the 1st Polish Armoured Division and has destroyed several tanks. The

Poles no longer dare leave the forest of Cramesnil. It is only
later that we hear that this is the Polish Division's first action.

By early evening the Poles had withdrawn to the north-west
of St Aignan.

Waldmüller's counter-attack went on to hit the British in
the St Aignan area—the War Diary of the 1st Northamptonshire Yeomanry admits losing twenty tanks and sixty-three
men, including their commanding officer wounded.

The Canadians did little better. Major General Kitching's
4th Armoured Division was held up right from the start by
resistance near Gaumesnil (including fire from Wittmann's Tigers) and it was 1530 hours before the Royal Regiment of
Canada, a 2nd Infantry Division unit, cleared the way. Even
then the Canadian Grenadier Guards lost their lead tanks to
fire from Cintheaux and it was another two and a half hours
before the Argylls of Canada and South Alberta Armoured
Reconnaissance Regiment evicted the Hitlerjugend from the
tiny hamlet. They claimed forty prisoners and an 88mm. But
the Canadians could advance no further. The deep quarries in
the area presented serious obstacles and SS Second Lieutenant
Willi Klein's small group of SS Panzer-Grenadiers of the 25th
Regiment in the southern part of Hautmesnil, backed by the
88mm guns of Fend's 12th SS Flak Battalion covering the main
Falaise road, were not to be moved.[19]

Simonds's great armoured push had been a dismal failure
against Meyer's few but very determined men. As Meyer put it,
'We have unbelievable luck as the enemy fails to execute a
single co-ordinated assault!', or perhaps even more succinctly,
'A tank attack which is divided into phases is like a cavalry
charge with meal breaks!'[20] His timely counter-attack had ensured that it had no chance of success. The Germans lost 178
men in the day's fighting and a number of tanks including five
Tigers and up to six Mk IVs. The loss of the Tigers was almost
inevitable, for their axis of advance was parallel to the main
Caen-Falaise road, over completely open ground and with
open flanks. It seems that on this fatal occasion the Tiger's
reputation as a virtually invulnerable tank caused even Witt-

mann to throw caution to the wind. It is hardly surprising that he and his crew were amongst those listed as 'missing'!

The lack of progress made by the armoured divisions greatly disappointed General Simonds and he gave orders that the advance was to continue throughout the night, aided by searchlights. Kitching's tanks were to push on down the Falaise road and the Poles were told to seize Cauvicourt at first light. These orders were not executed. As the official Canadian History puts it:

> The tanks withdrew to harbours in the manner to which armoured units had become accustomed in training. Thus, for instance, in the case of the Canadian Grenadier Guards one squadron harboured on the north edge of Cintheaux, while the other two retired to Gaumesnil.[21]

During the night of the 8th–9th KG Wünsche arrived in the Potigny area and at 0300 hours moved into the Quesnay forest. It still had thirty-nine Panthers and was due to be reinforced by thirteen Tigers of the 102nd SS Heavy Panzer Battalion from the II SS Panzer Corps reserve which Eberbach had persuaded von Kluge to release to him.

Although the Canadians had failed to achieve their objectives on 8th August they had made it impossible for Meyer to leave Waldmüller's KG exposed to the north of a line running from Hautmesnil to St Sylvain. He therefore ordered it to withdraw to new positions around Point 140 and on the vital ridge running north of Maizières, Rouvres and Assy (Map 7), where it was to be joined by the 1st SS Panzerjäger Company. Another KG of the 25th SS Panzer-Grenadier Regiment under Bernhard Krause, was to defend from Ouilly to the Falaise highway; and Olboeter's Fast Group, now on its way back from II SS Panzer Corps, was to set up on Point 195, 3km north-west of Potigny, and absorb any stragglers it came across from the 89th Division. As it happened most of the remains of this Division had already taken up defensive positions facing north-east, running from Grainville-Langannerie along the Laize stream to Bretteville, where they linked up with the 271st Infantry Division in the Fôret de Cinglais. After relief by guns of the III Luftwaffe Flak Corps, the two HJ

88mm Flak batteries were ordered to cover the main road
north of Potigny from positions near the road and to the east
of Divisional Headquarters at Tombeau de Marie Joly. All the
remaining 12th SS artillery and Werfers were to withdraw to
the south of the Laison, as was the Divisional Escort Company
which was to form another reserve at Montboint. The majority of these moves were carried out by 2200 hours without
interference, although Fast Group Olboeter would not arrive
from the Vire area until after dark and, as we shall hear, KG
Waldmüller and the Divisional Escort Company were nowhere
near their designated positions when first light came.

Behind this exhausted but well organised defence force the
first elements of Lieutenant General Chill's 85th Infantry Division were due to arrive on the morning of 9th August.

9TH AUGUST—'HIGH GROUND WAS SIGHTED' (Map 7)

It will be remembered that, despite the failure of Hitler's
counter-offensive against the Americans on 7th August, at
1800 hours on the 9th he ordered the attack continued and
personally appointed General Eberbach to command it with a
new and separate Headquarters. Sepp Dietrich was therefore
temporarily appointed to take over the Fifth Panzer Army.

The Allied plan for 9th August envisaged a group known as
'Halpenny Force' (after the name of its Canadian lieutenant
colonel commander) consisting of the 22nd Armoured Regiment (Canadian Grenadier Guards) and Lake Superior (Motor) Battalion, attacking Bretteville-le-Rabet, whilst the 28th
Armoured Regiment (British Colombia) with most of the Algonquin Infantry Battalion was to advance to Point 195,
north-west of Potigny. Bretteville was still held by part of the
89th Infantry and Olboeter's KG had now arrived on Point
195. In concert with the Canadian move, the 10th Polish
Armoured Brigade was to seize the area of la Croix and then
Point 140 above the Laison stream—a feature which it will be
recalled was due to be defended by KG Waldmüller.

The day did not begin well for Meyer's men but would
prove a disaster for Kitching's Division. Willi Klein and his
small group of SS Grenadiers withdrew from Hautmesnil just
before dawn and moved to the Soignolles area where, despite

Meyer's orders for it to move to the area of Point 140 north of the Laison stream, he found most of Waldmüller's 1st SS Panzer-Grenadier Battalion, the 1st Panzerjäger Company and the Corps and Divisional SS Escort Companies. According to Hubert Meyer this KG had 'been pushed to the east and awaited darkness in broken terrain in order to reach German lines during the night'.[22] As a result of this failure to reach his new position Waldmüller sent his Adjutant to Kurt Meyer for further orders. He was told that Prinz's tanks would be sent to help the force so that it could reach its designated defensive positions as a matter of urgency.

Meanwhile a liaison officer from KG Wünsche had tried to make contact with KG Waldmüller on the Point 140 feature; instead, and to his horror, he had found two squadrons of Shermans of the British Columbia Regiment and two companies of the Algonquin Battalion. This may surprise the reader since it will be recalled that this group's objective was over 6km to the south-west—Point 195. However, after advancing at 0200 hours and passing to the east of the Halpenny force preparing to attack Bretteville-le-Rabet, the Canadians had become hopelessly lost. The bulk of Lieutenant Colonel Worthington's force had followed the line of an ancient track called the 'Chemin Heusse'. This route had taken it across KG Waldmüller's path and the resulting skirmish presumably caused the latter to be 'pushed to the east'. With regard to the 90° error in navigation by Worthington's force, it can hardly be explained by 'the light was very poor this early in the morning.'[23] It seems that, as the unit War Diary puts it, 'High ground was sighted and we headed for it.' It further states that Worthington's Battlegroup, including two companies of Lieutenant Colonel Hay's Algonquin Battalion, took up positions at the north-east end of the feature, i.e. approximately 1500m from Point 140 and exactly where the Chemin Heusse ends. It is also clear from the War Diary that the rear elements of the Canadian Battlegroup realised they were heading for the wrong hill but were ordered to 'advance to the high ground in front' and join the commanding officer.

At 0655 hours Worthington reported that he had taken his objective; he went on to say that he was holding there until other troops could come forward to consolidate. As the official Historian puts it, 'In the light of the reports [the force] had made of its whereabouts—[the other troops] could never come.'[24]

As it happened, Worthington's mistake gave Meyer a major headache. He had Canadian instead of German forces in the middle of his main defensive line. Not surprisingly he resolved to deal with the problem ruthlessly and gave Max Wünsche the task. This was not too difficult since his KG, in its concentration area in the Quesnay forest, was less than 3km away. Kurt Meyer, in his memoirs,[25] says that five Tigers and fifteen Panthers were used, with the Tigers taking up positions on the western flank to shoot in the Panthers attacking from KG Krause's firm base on the ridge north of Assy.

During the morning the Canadian group on Point 140 asked for artillery support, but since it had reported that it was on its objective (Point 195), the shells inevitably fell kilometres away from where they were needed. The last radio message from the isolated group came at 0849 hours.[26]

The silence which followed caused great concern at Brigadier Booth's 4th Armoured Brigade Headquarters as well as that of Major General Kitching, and at 0914 hours Lieutenant Colonel Scott's 21st Armoured Regiment (The Governor General's Foot Guards) with the remaining company of Algonquins was ordered to move to support the Worthington group, still believed to be on Point 195. They took an extraordinary seven hours to reach the area of Bretteville-le-Rabet[27] and when they tried to advance south-west towards Point 195 they were shot up from the Quesnay woods[28] and lost between fourteen and twenty-six tanks.[29] At the end of the day they were still in the vicinity of Grainville-Langannerie.

The Algonquin War Diary says that by 1200 hours their commanding officer had been wounded (he lost a leg) and that there were only eight tanks left on Point 140. Infantry casualties at this stage were comparatively light—eight dead and twenty-five wounded.[30]

The KG Wünsche liaison officer sent to contact Waldmüller much earlier in the day, SS Lieutenant Meitzel, had been captured by Worthington's men during the German attack and described what it was like on Point 140:

> I had barely reached the Canadian hedgehog position on Point 140 when our 88mm guns started to fire on the Canadian tanks and infantry. Tigers [the remains of the Wittmann force] and Panthers advanced in order to encircle the positions on the hill. One Canadian tank after another was knocked out and ended up in smoke and flames. Some crews. . . . tried to reach a small wood close by. . . . They took me along. Soon after, the wood came under sustained attacks from fighter bombers to relieve the hard pressed Canadians. My suggestion. . . . to break through to our command post was refused, with thanks! . . . . Only after further fighter bomber attacks did they change their minds. I arrived at our command post again in the late afternoon with twenty-three Canadians and a broken arm.[31]

Panzermeyer reported that none of Wünsche's tanks were attacked by the fighter bombers, which concentrated instead on the poor Canadians.

At 1500 hours the eight remaining Canadian tanks received the order 'all tanks that can still run will make a dash for it; return to original Forming Up Position.'[32]

Although Meyer says that two bicycle companies of the 85th Infantry Division arrived during the day and were used to support Wünsche's tanks by mopping-up on Point 140, it seems quite possible that it was Krause's 1st SS Panzer-Grenadiers who operated in support of the tanks. Infantry were certainly needed, since some parts of the feature were wooded and others covered in gorse. In either case the British Columbia War Diary confirms that the final counter-attack was carried out by two companies of infantry, Panthers and Tigers.

At 2230 hours the Algonquin survivors decided to break out and at 0300 hours the following morning four officers with forty-four infantrymen and five tank men reached Polish lines.[33]

The day had cost the British Columbians 125 men, including Lieutenant Colonel Worthington killed, and forty-seven tanks;[34] the Algonquin War Diary records a total of 127 casual-

ties,[35] although later reports say only thirty-eight men were
lost on 9th August. (For reasons of accessibility the Canadian
memorial commemorating this event lies on the road to
Maizières rather than on Point 140). The final poignant comment in the British Columbia War Diary reads, 'Hill 143 [they
still had the wrong hill] was left to the enemy at 2100 hours,
after having been held for fourteen hours. This, our first day in
action, had been an extremely costly one.' Conversely Kurt
Meyer claimed he suffered no tank losses in this entire action.[36]

During the day the Halpenny force secured Bretteville-le-
Rabet and the Argylls of Canada and the Lincoln and Welland
Battalion occupied Langannerie and Grainville-Langannerie
respectively.

Meanwhile it will be recalled that Waldmüller's KG, including SS Lieutenant Hurdelbrink's 1st SS Panzerjäger Company,
having been 'pushed to the east' during the night 8th–9th, had
set up in the Soignolles area with the Divisional and Corps SS
Escort Companies about 1 to 2km to the south-west of the
village. At 1100 hours the Poles began their advance towards
Soignolles and la Croix. The Cromwells of the 10th Mounted
Rifles Armoured Reconnaissance Regiment found enemy
troops occupying St Sylvain and the 1st and 8th Infantry Battalions were tasked with clearing the village. By 1250 hours the
1st Armoured Regiment was in the western outskirts of
Cauvicourt and the 24th Lancers astride a wood 1000m to its
south-east; each had a company of M-10 anti-tank guns in
support. Soon after this they ran into fire from Waldmüller's
KG including the Panzerjägers, but by 1600 hours the Lancers
had reached the outskirts of la Croix and Point 111 (west) and
Major Stefanowicz's 1st Armoured Regiment, after passing behind them, was in the area of Point 111 (east), 2km north-west
of Rouvres. From this position it, perhaps not unreasonably,
fired on Worthington's Shermans[37]—the Poles could hardly
have expected to find Canadian tanks on their main objective.
But by now both sides had suffered heavily—the I SS Panzer
Corps Escort Company had been virtually wiped out and the
HJ Escort Company almost overwhelmed and forced to find
sanctuary in woods 2km to the north-east of Soignolles. The

anti-tank guns of the combined German force had taken a heavy toll of the Polish tanks[38]—one report mentions twenty-two Shermans being knocked out. The Poles withdrew to the Cauvicourt area.

Warpath, The Story of the Algonquin Regiment describes how the Canadians saw this part of the battle:

Off to the north-east there appeared a dust-cloud which rapidly approached, disclosing a squadron of Sherman tanks. . . . When they reached a point about a mile from the hill, the Germans began to concentrate their fire upon them. This relieved the survivors for the moment and they were able to crawl out of their slits to wave and cheer on the Poles. Morale soared, but the happiness was shortlived, for in practically no time the Polish tanks and artillery began firing at our men. They again dived for cover and burned more yellow recognition smoke. The firing stopped, and the Poles began to concentrate on the body of enemy on the extreme left flank. . . . Their fire seemed effective, and there is no doubt that another counter-attack had been broken up. But the Poles had suffered more severe tank losses in the process, and, heartbreakingly, they began to withdraw to the north. Their withdrawal was even more costly, as tank after tank blew up and brewed before the disappointed gaze of the doomed garrison.

At 1930 hours, following a heavy air and artillery bombardment, the 1st Polish (Highland) Infantry Battalion began its final assault on St Sylvain;[39] by 2200 hours the village had fallen and St Martin des Bois was captured before midnight. The remainder of Waldmüller's force withdrew to its pre-planned positions around Points 132 and 140 sometime after dark, covered by a rearguard provided by the badly battered HJ Escort Company.

By midnight on 9th August the II Canadian Corps front line ran from St Sylvain through Soignolles and Estrées to Langannerie and St Germain-le Vasson. Simonds's intention for the following day was for Kitching's 4th Canadian Armoured Division to seize the high ground at Point 206, just to the west of Potigny and then exploit towards Falaise, whilst the 1st Polish

Armoured Division was to capture the infamous Point 140 and then push on across the Laison to the hills directly north of Falaise on the east of the main highway.

And to counter these plans? The armour available to I SS Panzer Corps was now minimal—twenty Mk IVs, fifteen Panthers,[40] fifteen Tigers, of which seven were from the 102nd SS Heavy Panzer Battalion of the II SS Panzer Corps,[41] and an unknown number of Jagdpanzer IVs—probably about fifteen.

10TH TO 11TH AUGUST—'A FEW CAN HOLD AGAINST MANY HERE'

The first phase of Major General Kitching's plan for his advance south was a night attack by infantry to secure Point 195, just to the north of Fontaine-le-Pin. He then hoped to launch his tanks after first light to take the main objective of Point 206, followed by an exploitation to the south.

Lieutenant Colonel Stewart's Argylls of Canada, by dint of a silent approach, reached Point 195 during the night and had consolidated by first light, together with one troop of 17 pdrs and another of 6 pdrs. The unit War Diary says 'a circuitous route to the east and north-east was chosen as the west was known to be defended heavily. In the morning the enemy awakened to the situation and began to react violently.' This is not surprising since it will be recalled that Olboeter's 3rd SS Panzer-Grenadier Battalion was meant to be defending the two-square-kilometre hill; Kurt Meyer, who says he moved quickly to Point 195 once he knew the Canadians were there, describes events as follows:

> When I reach the hill Olboeter is in the middle of his Grenadiers, leading them in a counter-attack. The enemy has broken into the positions and is just about to capture the entire hill. The Grenadiers attack the enemy spearheads in shock-troop fashion and throw them back in the darkness. The ridge can be held with the help of the tank group. The enemy is made to suffer heavy casualties. By dawn he lies exposed to flanking fire of the Panzers from Quesnay woods. . . . A few can hold against many here.[42]

The Argylls of Canada, helped as we shall hear by a tank battalion, managed to hold on and a stalemate resulted with both sides occupying part of the large hill.

In a similar Canadian operation on the same night, the Lincoln and Welland Battalion had occupied the hill spur near St Germain-le-Vasson, on the Argyll's right flank.[43] Since one company of the Algonquin Battalion and the South Alberta Armoured Reconnaissance Regiment were already south of Langannerie, this meant that the 10th Infantry Brigade was reasonably well established as a firm base for further operations.

By 0906 hours on the 10th, Lieutenant Colonel Halpenny's Regimental Headquarters and two squadrons of tanks of the Canadian Grenadier Guards had moved up on to the northern slopes of Point 195 to support the Argylls; but at 1155 hours, just as they prepared to advance towards Point 206, another SS counter-attack came in, this time supported by 'Goliath' robot tanks.[44] The attack was again beaten off but not before the Grenadiers had lost eight tanks.[45] Just after this the Shermans of the Governor General's Foot Guards were also brought up to reinforce the group on Point 195 but, almost unbelievably, and with Olboeter's men at their mercy, the Canadians made no further attempts to advance. An artillery observer reported twenty-four 88mm guns just to the west of Potigny[46] and they were frightened off—the 88s and Wünsche's tanks to their flank were too much for them. Once again the German armoured reserve had been placed in a strategic position where it could engage attackers on both the left and right flanks (Points 195 and 140) without moving any great distance.

Hubert Meyer comments validly and perhaps a little too politely that, with overwhelming air power and artillery available to them, the Canadian inactivity was 'difficult to understand'! This is uncomfortably true when one considers how few SS Panzers were facing over 200 tanks and how vulnerable were the crews of the 88mm guns—they had no armoured protection and the guns had a high profile.

At 1000 hours Guy Simonds held a conference with his four Divisional commanders—Kitching, Foulkes, Brigadier Black-

ader who had temporarily taken over the 3rd Infantry Division
from Keller, and Maczek of the 1st Polish Armoured. He was
intent on restoring the momentum of the attack. (The British
51st Highland Division had been returned to I British Corps).
Despite Simonds's good intentions, time did not seem to be of
the essence (or was it a matter of slow and hidebound proce-
dures?) because the next attack, by the 3rd Infantry Division
and 2nd Armoured Brigade, was not timed until 1600 hours.
The aim was for this force to seize crossings over the Laison
and then for the Poles, having followed up and secured Point
140, to advance on Sassy.

Before there could be any thought of crossing the Laison it
was essential to clear the Quesnay woods. Unfortunately for
the Canadians, Meyer had made these woods the centre of his
whole defence—bear in mind it was the location of all Wünsche's tanks and Krause's small KG had also taken up positions
in the area. The 88mm guns of the 12th SS Flak Battalion were
to its rear, covering the approaches to Potigny.

Much later than planned, two battalions of the Canadian
8th Infantry Brigade, the Queen's Own Rifles and North
Shores, began their advance at 2000 hours, behind an enormous artillery barrage. The woods had already been hit twice
during the day, at 1105 and 1825 hours, by twenty-four Typhoons[47] but these attacks seem to have had little effect. In
their usual way the SS Panzers and Panzer-Grenadiers allowed
the attacking infantry to get well into the woods before they
retaliated. Supporting artillery fire could not easily be brought
to bear once the Canadians were in the woods and there was at
least one serious case of the guns firing on friendly troops.
Darkness soon added to the confusion and by the time the
Canadians withdrew they had suffered 165 casualties, including forty-four killed.[48]

Meanwhile, the 3rd Infantry Brigade of the 1st Polish
Armoured Division under Colonel Wieronski had been due to
advance from the Estrées area, but the failure of the Canadians
to clear the Quesnay woods combined with intense German
artillery and mortar fire caused the attack to be delayed. Eventually two infantry battalions and the 10th Mounted Rifles
Armoured Reconnaissance Regiment moved towards Point

111 which was defended by a battalion of the 85th Infantry Division with Hurdelbrink's 1st SS Panzerjäger Company in support. By last light the Poles were established on the hill but only after severe losses. SS Second Lieutenant Zeiner of the 1st SS Panzerjäger Company claimed in his diary that his commander, Georg Hurdelbrink, knocked out eleven Cromwells and SS Senior Sergeant Roy seven more during this fighting. They and Hurdelbrink's gunner, SS Corporal Eckstein, were all awarded the Knight's Cross for their actions in the fighting over the period 8th to 11th August.

The take-over of the HJ sector by the 85th Infantry Division began in earnest during the night 10th–11th and was completed during the night 11th–12th. Even then mobile elements of the HJ, including tanks, remained with the 85th Division for another day to give the tired Grenadiers time to settle in. The final handover was at 2100 hours on the 12th and the exhausted remnants of the 12th SS Panzer Division Hitlerjugend, together with its attached Tiger and Werfer units, withdrew to an area to the north-east of Falaise in I SS Panzer Corps reserve.[49]

On the morning of 11th August, the day Wünsche's award of Oak Leaves to his Knight's Cross was announced, Guy Simonds called off all further attacks and ordered his Canadian infantry divisions to relieve the armoured divisions. This order was later amended and the Canadian 7th Infantry Brigade relieved the Poles on Point 111 during the night of 11th August and the 9th Infantry Brigade took over from the 4th Armoured Division. This second operation was not without its difficulties since Wünsche's tanks knocked out a further five Canadian Grenadier Guards' tanks as they withdrew from Point 195 during the afternoon of the 11th.[50] The relief was finally accomplished by 0200 hours on the 12th. Operation TOTALIZE was at an end. It had cost the Canadians over eighty tanks and in his book *Avec Mes Blindés*, General Maczek admits to the loss of sixty-six Polish tanks and 656 men—this to advance only 15km and create a corridor 8km wide. They still had 11km to go to reach their objective of Falaise.

The Hitlerjugend and its attached units had thwarted all attempts by the Allies to break 'the hinge' of the German defence in Normandy—it had cost the HJ another 414 casualties[51] of which a quarter were dead. And yet, as we have heard, in an ironic twist of fate the very success of Kurt Meyer's men allowed Hitler to insist on a second attack at Mortain. Instead of using the precious time bought by the young soldiers of the HJ to extricate his forces, the Führer threw more men and more armour into the noose which would eventually be drawn tight in a small town called Chambois.

On the 12th of August the staff of Wilhelm Mohnke's 26th SS Panzer-Grenadier Regiment and other officers like SS Major Waldmüller of the 25th Regiment were withdrawn to their original locations of 6th June near the Seine; Mohnke was given responsibility for all elements of the HJ withdrawn for refitting. What was left in the forward area? Wünsche's 12th SS Panzer Regiment with between seven and fifteen Panthers and seventeen Mk IVs; seventeen Tigers of the 101st and 102nd SS Heavy Panzer Battalions; two companies of Jagdpanzer IVs of Hanreich's 12th SS Panzerjäger Battalion; the 1st SS Panzer-Grenadier Battalion of the 25th Regiment and the 1st and 3rd Battalions of the 26th Regiment, all seriously understrength; the 12th SS Panzer Artillery Regiment, less two batteries; the 12th SS Werfer Battalion with three batteries; the 12th SS Flak Battalion with one battery of 88s, one of 37mm guns and one battery of 20mm SP Flak which really belonged to Mohnke's 26th Regiment; a 12th SS Reconnaissance group under SS Second Lieutenant Wienecke (all that was left of the Battalion); and a platoon of the Divisional Escort Company.

THE END OF AN ACE

It is hardly surprising that Michael Wittmann, the greatest German tank ace in WWII with 138 tanks to his credit, has been 'claimed' by British, Canadian and Polish units, as well as by the Royal Air Force. Numerous accounts have been written about the action north of Cintheaux (Map 5) on 8th August, most of them relying heavily on supposition and uncorroborated statements.

For some time after the war it was thought that Wittmann had died when his tank was surrounded by a number of Canadian Shermans and shot to pieces. Later, in the 1980s, the credit was given to A Squadron of the British 1st Northampton-tonshire Yeomanry which, it will be remembered, was in a defensive position just south of St Aignan-de-Cramesnil during the period in question, and most commentators were content with this version. However, Hubert Meyer, the former Chief of Staff of 12th SS, recently added to the controversy by writing in the (Old Comrades) magazine *Der Freiwillige*, that tank number 007 (Wittmann's) was hit in the engine compartment by a rocket fired from a Typhoon which blew off the turret. The only thing therefore which can be said with any certainty is that Wittmann did not survive the 8th August fighting against the British, Canadians and Poles.

The final macabre twist to this story came nearly forty years after the event, in March 1983, when exhumations carried out under the supervision of the German War Graves Commission revealed human remains and other artefacts near the Caen-Falaise road at Gaumesnil. A set of false incisor teeth were matched with Wittmann's dental records and an identity disc gave positive identification of the driver of Wittmann's Tiger, Heinrich Reimers. The intermingled remains were buried in a common grave in the German cemetery at la Cambe and are generally accepted as those of Michael Wittmann and his crew.

NOTES.

1. Stacey, *The Official History of the Canadian Army in the Second World War, Vol III, The Victory Campaign*, p. 215. **2.** Kraemer, *I SS Panzer Corps in the West*, MS C—024, IWM London. **3.** Wilmot, *The Struggle for Europe*, p. 410. **4.** Kraemer, op. cit. **5.** AEAF Ops Summary No 202 dated 9 Aug 44. **6.** Ellis, *Victory in the West, Vol I, The Battle of Normandy*, p. 421. **7.** Stacey, op. cit., p. 220. **8.** 2 & 5 Seaforth War Diaries and Wilmot, op. cit., p. 413. First Cdn Army Int Summary No 40 says two Mk IVs were captured intact. **9.** Stacey, op. cit., p. 220. **10.** Meyer, Kurt, *Grenadiers*, p. 157. **11.** Ibid. **12.** Stacey, op. cit., p. 223. **13.** Meyer, Kurt, op. cit., p. 159. **14.** AEAF Ops Summary 8 Aug 44. **15.** North Shore Regt War Diary, 8 Aug 44. **16.** Meyer, Kurt, op. cit., p. 159. **17.** Stacey, op. cit., p. 224. **18.** Meyer, Hubert, op. cit., p. 174. **19.** Ibid., p. 176. **20.** Meyer, Kurt, op. cit., p. 159. **21.** Stacey, op. cit., p. 225. **22.** Meyer, Hubert, op. cit., p. 177. **23.** 28th Armd Regt War Diary, 9 Aug 44. **24.** Stacey, op. cit., p. 226. **25.** Meyer, Hubert, op. cit., p. 177. **26.** Stacey, op. cit., p. 227. **27.** Ibid. **28.** 21st Armd Regt War Diary, 9 Aug 44. **29.** 21st Armd Regt History says 26, 4th Cdn Armd Bde War Diary says 14. **30.** Algonquin Regt War Diary, 9 Aug 44. **31.** Meyer, Hubert, op. cit., p. 177. **32.** British Columbia Regt War Diary, 9 Aug 44. **33.** Algonquin Regt War Diary, 9 Aug 44. **34.** Stacey, op. cit., p.

228. **35.** Algonquin Regt War Diary, 9 Aug 44. **36.** Meyer, Kurt, op. cit., p. 163. **37.** Meyer, Hubert, op. cit., p. 178 and *Warpath, The Story of the Algonquin Regt.* **38.** 1st Polish Armd Div Op Report. **39.** Ibid. **40.** Author's estimate on basis that Garde's 2nd SS Panzer Company with thirteen Panthers returned without loss from the Vire area on 9 Aug and Kurt Meyer mentions fifteen Panthers attacking the Worthington group on 9 Aug without loss. **41.** Meyer, Hubert, op. cit., p. 179. **42.** Meyer, Kurt, op. cit., p. 164. **43.** Lincoln & Welland Regt War Diary, 9 Aug 44. **44.** 22nd Armd Regt War Diary, 9 Aug 44. **45.** Ibid. **46.** 4th Cdn Armd Bde War Diary, 10 Aug 44. **47.** 7th Cdn Inf Bde War Diary, 11 Aug 44. **48.** Stacey, op. cit., p. 231. **49.** Meyer, Hubert, op. cit., p. 181. **50.** GGFG War Diary, 11 Aug 44. **51.** Meyer, Hubert, op. cit., p. 182.

25 | *11th to 18th August — The Second Battle of Falaise*

On 11th August Montgomery issued a new directive which emphasized the predicament of the Germans at Mortain and the urgent necessity to close the narrowing gap between Falaise and Alençon (Map 1) in order to cut them off. Second British Army was to 'advance its left to Falaise' as soon as possible. Crerar's First Canadian Army was in turn ordered to:

> Capture Falaise. This is a first priority and it is vital it should be done quickly. The Army will then operate with strong armoured and mobile forces to secure Argentan.[1]

11TH TO 13TH AUGUST—'RECONNAISSANCE IN FORCE'
(Map 7)

It took an astonishing three days to complete the planning for this 'new', 'vital' and 'urgent' operation and whilst this went on General Guy Simonds ordered the 2nd Infantry Division to make a 'reconnaissance in force' south from Bretteville-sur-Laise, with the aim of threatening the I SS Panzer Corps positions covering Falaise. On 12th August Major General Foulkes was told that his operation was to be upgraded to a major effort and that he was to be given the support of two Army Groups Royal Artillery and the 2nd Canadian Armoured Brigade less one battalion.[2]

The advance of the 2nd Infantry Division via Barbery, 8km to the south of Bretteville-sur-Laize, went reasonably well until it ran into four Tigers of the 2nd Company of the 102nd SS

Heavy Panzer Battalion at Cingal, 2km further south. One Tiger was knocked out for the loss of five Shermans. By last light the Royal Regiment of Canada had captured Moulines, 6km north-west of Potigny. Further progress was made on the 13th and the Calgary Highlanders managed to establish a small bridgehead across the Laize at Clair Tizon, 6km west of Potigny; but when Le Régiment de Maisonneuve tried to expand it that evening they were repulsed with heavy loss by troops of the 271st Infantry Division on the commanding heights east of the river, supported by several Tigers of the 2nd Company of the 102nd SS Heavy Panzer Battalion.[3]

On this same day, 13th August, General Crerar was told by Montgomery that he was giving Dempsey's Second British Army the task of capturing the town of Falaise but that the First Canadian Army was to dominate the Falaise area 'in order that no enemy may escape by the roads which pass through, or near it.' It was further intended that once II Corps had established itself on the high ground north and east of Falaise and when Dempsey's plans to capture Falaise were well advanced, Simonds should exploit south-east and capture Trun (Map 8) as a matter of urgency.[4]

Simonds issued his orders the same day and afterwards made an address to all armoured commanders in which he stressed the necessity of pushing armour to the limits of its endurance and of dismissing any notions that tanks could not move at night or needed infantry protection when they harboured.[5] His plan for Operation TRACTABLE was more or less the same as for TOTALIZE, including heavy bombing; but there was one major difference—it was to be launched in daylight with cover provided by smoke screens. The blow was to fall on the sector east of the Caen-Falaise highway and was to be struck by two vast armoured columns, each comprising one complete armoured brigade; these were each to be followed by two infantry brigades. The War Diary of the Canadian Grenadier Guards says they advanced at 12 mph, in a phalanx 800 yards across and 120 yards deep, with three squadrons in line. The other tank battalions did the same. By now all Shermans had tank tracks welded to their front and sides 'as extra protection against 88s'. Objectives were as follows: on the 4th

Armoured Division front, the 4th Armoured Brigade was to take the strategically important Hill 159 (Map 7), 3km to the north-east of Falaise, whilst the 10th and 8th Infantry Brigades secured Epaney-Perrières and Maizières-Rouvres respectively; in the case of the 3rd Infantry Division front, the 2nd Armoured Brigade was to capture Points 170 and 184, south-west of Olendon, whilst the 9th Infantry Brigade took Montboint and Point 118 and the 7th Infantry Brigade followed up. RAF heavy bombers were to obliterate six targets in the area Quesnay, Fontaine-le-Pen and Bons-Tassilly. The Canadian 2nd Infantry Division was to push south-east from Clair Tizon to protect the right flank and the 1st Polish Armoured Division was tasked with mopping up the RAF target areas. Simultaneously with the main attack the British 51st Highland Division (I British Corps) was to assault on the left to capture le Bû and protect that flank.

Unfortunately for the Canadians an officer in a scout car of the Canadian Hussar Reconnaissance Regiment lost his way on the evening of the 13th and was shot up. On his body the Germans found notes describing all the essentials of the planned operation.

14TH AUGUST—OPERATION TRACTABLE AND THE BATTLE OF THE LAISON (Map 7)

The only reserve available to I SS Panzer Corps on 14th August was the battered remnant of the Hitlerjugend Division and when Panzermeyer, with Max Wünsche, Krause and Olboeter, carried out a reconnaissance to the north of Falaise during the early hours of the morning they were aware that the American XV Corps had already captured Alençon; they knew full well that if the Seventh Army was to have any hope of escape it was imperative to hold for as long as possible against the impending Allied attack in the Falaise sector. Meyer therefore made plans to deploy his slender assets in support of the 85th and 89th Infantry Divisions; Fiebig's 85th, with its Headquarters at Jort, was to the east of the Caen-Falaise highway and the 89th to the west. The 271st Infantry Division was to the left of the 89th.

As a Panzer Division the HJ was now very weak, but Kurt

Meyer's statement[6] that he was down to only 300 Grenadiers is a gross understatement (he speaks later of 500) and is contradicted by his Chief of Staff who mentions a strength of approximately six Panzer-Grenadier companies,[7] i.e., about 1000 Grenadiers.

KG Krause, consisting of the 1st SS Panzer-Grenadier Battalion of the 26th Regiment and a strong platoon of the Divisional Escort Company, was immediately moved across from Olendon to Villers-Canivet on the left flank. At the same time it was decided to send Olboeter's 3rd (SPW) Battalion of the same Regiment to contain the Canadian bridgehead at Clair Tizon, which it did that same morning, after which the weak Escort Company took up positions to the west of Ussy.

Prinz's seventeen Mk IVs were positioned just to the west of Soulangy in order to provide a reserve on the left flank. Between seven and fifteen Panthers, at least eleven Tigers (including six from the 101st) and the two weak companies of Hanreich's 12th Panzerjäger Battalion with about ten Jagdpanzer IVs, supported by Grenadiers of the 1st Battalion of the 25th Regiment, were directed to set up a series of strong points on Hill 159 and at several positions south of the road Falaise—St Pierre-sur-Dives. Hill 159 was the really vital ground in that it dominated Falaise and the Ante (also spelled Aute) stream running to its east. The chances of holding the impending attack were remote—less than fifty tanks and Jagdpanzers against 700 Canadian and Polish tanks. As Kurt Meyer put it, 'His vastly superior number of tanks only have to drive over us at full speed to finish us.' But the commanders and crews of the Shermans lacked the aggressive spirit so evident in the Panzer crews—a spirit personified in a verse of the Panzerwaffe march:

When before us an enemy army appears, we go at full speed to meet it. What is our life worth then for the Army of the Reich? To die for Germany is the greatest honour for us.

At 1135 hours on 14th August the Canadian guns fired marker shells for the seventy-three Boston and Mitchell medium bombers which hit the 85th Infantry positions at Montboint, Rouvres and Maizières in the Laison valley. Five

minutes later the Canadian armoured columns began to roll
across the Start-Line which ran through Soignolles and to the
north of Estrées, and twelve minutes after that the guns began
to lay the thick smoke screen designed to protect the attacking
troops.

Kurt Meyer was scathing in his judgement of the Canadian
tactics:

> Tanks line up in parade ground formation. . . . intending
> to break a way through the defence zone. . . . with steam
> roller tactics. It is a mystery why the Canadians chose such
> an inflexible battle formation. Instead of. . . . [a] loose
> formation, affording the opportunity to use the effect of
> their guns and manoeuvrability to smash the positions and
> make a swift and deep advance into the battlefield, these
> steel monsters roll clumsily and sluggishly over the terrain.
> Precious time is lost as the tanks cross the Laison area since
> they cannot negotiate the swampy ground in their clumsy
> battle formation.[8]

There was indeed chaos as the Shermans tried to negotiate
the stream—one squadron of the 1st Hussars lost eleven of its
nineteen tanks trying to find its way across.

The heavy bombing by 417 Lancasters and 352 Halifaxes
commenced at 1400 hours. They dropped 3,723 tons[9] on the
right flank of the advance, mainly on the 89th Division. Although most of the designated targets were hit, seventy-seven
aircraft bombed 'short', causing 397 casualties to the Canadians as far back as Hautmesnil and ninety-three to the Poles
who also lost three Cromwells. Ironically, forty-four of the
aircraft which hit the Allied troops were Canadian.[10]

Shortly after this bombing and when it was clear that the
attack was not being held, I SS Panzer Corps asked for permis-
sion to pull back to a new line running from Sassy through
Aubigny to Noron, but this was refused and at 1530 hours
Fifth Panzer Army confirmed that the line Mazières-Soulagny-
Bonnoeil (the latter 10km south-west of Potigny), was to be
defended at all costs, otherwise the road running west from
Falaise might be cut.[11]

Events on this western flank of I SS Panzer Corps in the

271st Infantry Division's area were now reaching crisis point. The enemy had already advanced as far as Bonnoeil and during the afternoon Allied tanks reached Leffard, 8km to the north-west of Falaise. After the war Fritz Kraemer, Chief of Staff of I SS Panzer Corps, recalled receiving a last message to the effect that thirty enemy tanks were over-running the Divisional Command Post. In response to this threat a small KG of Wünsche's 12th SS Panzer Regiment, strength unknown, was moved during the evening to an assembly area around Martigny-Pierrepont, 6km west of Falaise. It was in support of the 271st Division but remained under Meyer's command.

By nightfall the Canadians had smashed the Laison defence line. Many infantrymen of the 85th Division had surrendered, unable to resist both the bombing and the overwhelming number of Allied tanks—the 4th Armoured Division, after taking 560 prisoners, had reached Sassy, Perrières and Olendon, and the 3rd Infantry had taken Points 170 and 184, despite a desperate resistance by a few members of the 85th Infantry and some of Wünsche's tanks. But regardless of General Simonds's instructions to his armoured commanders to keep moving at night, they did nothing of the sort and the Germans continued to hold the vital ground north of the St Pierre-sur-Dives road at Perrières, Epaney, Soulangy, Villers-Canivet and the strategic Hill 159. The battle of Falaise was far from over.

The author has been unable to discover any reliable casualty figures for the Hitlerjugend on 14th August but it was on this day that SS Major Karl-Heinz Prinz, the commander of the 2nd SS Panzer (Mk IV) Battalion, was killed. He had been awarded the Knight's Cross on 11th July. Another holder of this coveted medal who died when his tank was knocked out on 14th August was SS Lieutenant Helmut Wendorff, the commander of the 2nd SS Tiger Company.

According to the First Canadian Army Operational Log dated 14th August, some time during that day Montgomery modified his instructions to Crerar and ordered him, not Dempsey, to take the city of Falaise without delay. The only proviso was that this operation was not to interfere with the more important task of capturing Trun and linking up with the Americans.

15TH AUGUST—THE BATTLE FOR HILL 159

During the night 14th–15th I SS Panzer Corps adjusted its positions. On the right flank the 272nd Division linked up with the much weakened 85th Division near Vendeuvre. The latter's line now ran to Bernières-d'Ailly and along the north-west edge of the woods on les Monts d'Eraines. To the great consternation of Fritz Kraemer, and indeed of Sepp Dietrich, the Fifth Panzer Army commander, the Luftwaffe Flak battalion in this area was pulled out during the night without their agreement. In fact all Luftwaffe anti-aircraft artillery was ordered to withdraw that night from what was now called the 'Falaise Pocket' leaving the skies virtually free for Allied aircraft and depriving the Corps of these splendid dual purpose weapons.

On the left of the Corps the 271st Division pulled back to establish quite a strong defence line running, via Noron, to a point 10km south-west of Falaise. Behind this line an anti-tank screen was set up, backed by the few remaining Tigers of the 102nd SS Heavy Panzer Battalion—probably about six.

The Hitlerjugend also redeployed to previously prepared positions—the two Panzerjäger companies moved in small groups to the slopes of les Monts d'Eraines and the woods south-east of Epaney where they could support the Grenadiers of the 85th Infantry, and Wünsche's Panthers and Mk IVs took up ambush positions, again with 85th Grenadiers, on Hill 159. KG Krause, supported by two Tigers, adopted positions in the northern edge of Soulagny with the Escort Company on its right; and to the right of that Olboeter's SS Grenadiers filled the gap across to Hill 159 and Hanreich's Jagdpanzer IVs. The 3rd SS Panzer Artillery Battalion was sited behind the Ante stream and the remaining 88mm SS Flak Battery, under SS Second Lieutenant Hartwig, was also in depth at Morteaux-Couliboeuf. Additional fire support was available from the 83rd Werfer Brigade. An ammunition depot had been discovered in the area so, for once, there was no shortage of artillery ammunition.

The Canadians began their advance again on the morning of the 15th but, despite the extraordinarily weak forces in front of them, they made little progress. It took two infantry battalions and a tank squadron to capture Epaney from the 85th Grenadiers but when two tank battalions, the Canadian Grenadier Guards and the British Columbia Regiment, tried to move to Hill 159 they were bloodily repulsed. As the 4th Canadian Armoured Division diarist put it:

> It appeared that the enemy had once again established an anti-tank screen on the southern [reverse] slopes of the high ground which the Armoured Brigade was unable to penetrate.[12]

Kurt Meyer described it differently:

> Hill 159 is a boiling mountain. Shell after shell explodes around our tanks standing in ambush. . . . The first enemy tanks are burning. Enemy infantry is nailed to the ground by well-aimed bursts of machine-gun fire. . . . Are a mass of tanks suddenly to appear out of the wall of fire? . . . . Will we be lying under the screaming tank tracks any minute? Nothing of the kind happens. The enemy tanks keep their distance and don't overrun us. They stop in front of Hill 159. . . . The 3rd [SS] Artillery Battalion plays an essential part in the success of the defence.[13]

The Canadian Grenadier Guards had only thirty-three Shermans and six Stuarts left at the end of the day.[14]

On the 3rd Infantry Division's front things went little better; it cost the Canadian Scottish 160 casualties to reach and then hold Point 168 to the south-east of Soulangy. Shermans were prevented from joining them on the hill by the two Tigers with KG Krause and the unit War Diary records sadly, 'Thus the Canadian Scottish paved the way with blood for the liberation of Falaise by other Canadian troops.'

At 1815 hours the Winnipegs reached Soulagny but a strong counter-attack at 2100 hours by Krause's men pushed them out and at the end of the day they were back where they started.[15] The 2nd Armoured Brigade, in support of the 3rd Division, lost a total of ten tanks[16] to two 102nd Battalion

Tigers, which came forward from St Pierre-Canivet to help the
beleaguered SS Grenadiers. KG Krause and the SS Escort Company lost a total of forty-two men during the day.[17]

The 1st Polish Armoured Division finished clearing the
Quesnay woods during the morning and then moved across to
the eastern flank via Rouvres and Maizières. Pioneers of the
85th Infantry Division managed to blow the bridges over the
Dives at Vendeuvre and Jort but by early evening elements of
the 10th Mounted Rifles Armoured Reconnaissance Regiment,
reinforced with a company of M-10s and a motorized infantry
company, had forded the river at Jort and moved on to the
high ground just to the east of the village. However, when the
1st Armoured Regiment reached the high ground to the west
of Jort it mistook the 10th Regiment's Cromwells for German
Mk IVs and opened fire causing some casualties. The Germans
claimed three Polish tanks knocked out and five damaged but
none of these are verified. A twelve-man HJ SS Reconnaissance
detachment under SS Second Lieutenant Albert Wienecke
positioned near Jort observed the Polish crossing but could do
nothing about it other than to report its happening. The detachment was soon attacked and destroyed—Wienecke himself
was taken prisoner but managed to escape and reach German
lines.

Similar attempts to ford the Dives south of Jort and at
Vendeuvre failed, but the 9th Polish Infantry Battalion waded
the river during the night and helped to establish a substantial
bridgehead. Engineers began work at once on the demolished
bridges in the two villages.

On the western flank Foulkes's 2nd Infantry Division, after
suffering sixty-five casualties from 'friendly' bombing, eventually discovered that it had no enemy in front of it, the 271st
Division having pulled back as previously described. Even so,
by last light its leading elements were still 2–3km short of
Falaise.

At 2100 hours Fifth Panzer Army issued orders for the
LXXXVI Corps to withdraw behind the Dives river to a line
running from Houlgate on the Channel coast (Map 1) down
to Morteaux-Couliboeuf, and for I SS Panzer Corps to hold a
line from there, along the Ante stream to inclusive Falaise, and

then west through Pierrepont to Pont d'Ouilly, 30km west of Falaise (Map 8). This order was given by Dietrich without reference to von Kluge who was trying to visit Hausser and Eberbach but, as a result of Allied air attacks and traffic jams, lost touch with his Headquarters from 0530 until 2200 hours when he finally turned up at Eberbach's Command Post. The order was impossible to implement because the pathetic remnants of the 85th Infantry Division could not be stretched to link up with Meyer's Division, the most easterly element of which was Hartwig's 88mm Flak Battery on the east bank of the Dives at Morteaux-Couliboeuf. The two weak HJ Panzerjäger companies with some 85th Division stragglers took up positions on the hills north of the picturesque village of Damblainville and Olboeter's SS Panzer-Grenadiers guarded the crossing over the Ante at Eraines. The majority of the remaining tanks, about ten, still held Hill 159, while KG Krause withdrew into Falaise to set up defences in the northern and western edges of the city. The two Tigers attached to the KG remained just to the north covering the approaches.

16TH TO 18TH AUGUST—THE FALL OF FALAISE
(Maps 7, 8 & 9)

On 16th August General Simonds issued orders for the 2nd Infantry Division to clear the city of Falaise and for the 4th Canadian and 1st Polish Armoured Divisions to cross the Dives and advance south-east from Damblainville and Jort respectively. Montgomery had telephoned Crerar during the afternoon and warned him that the German divisions west of Argentan would try to break out between Trun and Falaise and that it was therefore vital to seize Trun and close the gap between the First Canadian and Third US Armies as quickly as possible. By now the retreat was in full swing with Germans streaming back into the surviving salient to the west of the Falaise-Argentan road. Unbelievable targets were beginning to present themselves to the Allied fighter-bombers and it would not be long before artillery and even tanks would be able to participate in the slaughter. But despite Montgomery's direction the advance of the First Canadian Army was to be painfully slow.

During the night of the 15th and morning of the 16th the 1st Polish Armoured Division extended the bridgehead at Vendeuvre and Jort to as far south as Barou and the eastern edges of Morteaux-Couliboeuf but then, instead of exploiting south-east as the situation demanded (Trun was less than 20km away), it was surprisingly told to remain where it was until relieved by elements of the 3rd Canadian Infantry Division.

The concurrent moves by the Canadians soon ran into trouble. Their 4th Armoured Division was held by the few Jagdpanzers and Grenadiers north of Damblainville and the 3rd Infantry Division could not remove Wünsche's tanks from the southern slopes of Hill 159. The unbelievable had happened again—despite their overwhelming strength the Canadians could not prevail. Kurt Meyer was himself wounded in the head by a shell splinter during the fighting on Hill 159. He described in his book *Grenadiers* how he was able 'to continue the battle with a half-shaved head and a couple of stitches.'

For various reasons—such as lack of reconnaissance, traffic chaos and general muddle—the attack by Brigadier Young's 6th Canadian Infantry Brigade against Falaise, originally scheduled for 1300 hours, was delayed until 1525 hours. It was carried out by two battalions of infantry, the South Saskatchewans with 625 men, supported by a squadron of Sherbrooke Fusilier tanks, and the Cameron Highlanders with 667 men and another squadron of tanks—a total of twenty-four Shermans and three artillery battalions were in support. SS Major Bernhard Krause had about 150 SS Grenadiers from his own 1st Battalion and the Divisional Escort Company, two 75mm anti-tank guns and the two Tigers of the 102nd SS Heavy Panzer Battalion with which to defend a city which was in ruins, having been constantly shelled and then devastated by 144 bombers during the night of 12th August.[18]

Street fighting is one of the most difficult and bloody types of operation and the capture of Falaise proved no exception. It took till 1900 hours for the Saskatchewan group to cross the river and it was midnight before the northern section of the city was in Canadian hands—it cost two Shermans and numerous infantrymen. The Camerons failed to penetrate into the western sector. The Shermans supporting them were blocked by the many deep bomb craters and Krause's men fought with their renowned tenacity.

After repeated requests from his generals, Hitler finally agreed during the afternoon of the 16th to a withdrawal across the Orne and Dives.[19] I SS Panzer Corps, aware that its role in holding open an escape route for Panzer Group Eberbach and the Seventh Army was critical, ordered a limited withdrawal during the night 16th–17th to a line from just east of St Pierre-sur-Dives, through the northern edges of Morteaux-Couliboeuf and Falaise, to les Loges, 8km south-west of Falaise. For the Hitlerjugend this meant an even more limited withdrawal—to behind the Ante. Fighting continued throughout the night in Falaise but the bulk of KG Krause with the two Tigers withdrew to the dominating ridges at Villy and Fresné-la-Mère (Map 9). The rest of the HJ, including ten tanks, covered the Ante crossings at Damblainville and Eraines.

In the early morning of 17th August the Argylls of Canada occupied the northern part of Damblainville without difficulty; but when the Algonquin Battalion tried to force the narrow stone bridge they failed and their supporting tanks were unable or unwilling to deploy in the face of the HJ Jagdpanzer IVs and the two Tigers on the high ground south of the Ante. It only took a few shots from the latter to force thirty-five Shermans of the 4th Canadian Armoured Brigade to turn away. Further west the ground at Eraines favours the defence and the Canadians made no attempt to attack.

The Poles did rather better. At 0930 hours their 10th Mounted Rifles Armoured Reconnaissance Regiment reported a large German column moving east on the Crocy-Trun road and a generally chaotic situation with other German columns, comprising everything from tanks to horse-drawn carts, attempting to escape to the north-east. One of the Polish reconnaissance squadrons moving in the direction of Trun lost four Cromwells in under a minute, to anti-tank fire in the vicinity of Point 107, 2km north of the town.[20] It seems likely that this fire came from Hartwig's 88mm Flak guns (Hartwig himself

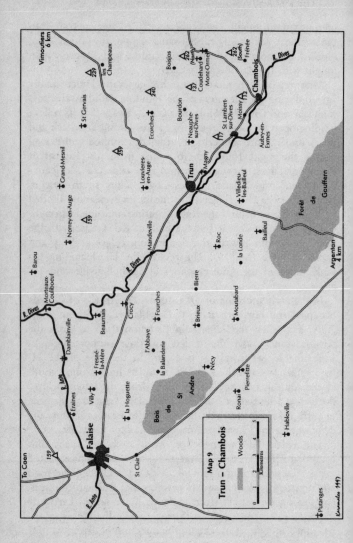

Map 9
Trun – Chambois

Woods

Kilometres
0 1 2 3 4 5

Vimoutiers 6 km

To Caen

R. Ante

159

Falaise

Putanges

St Clair

la Hoguette

Villy

Eraines

Fresné-la-Mère

Dambainville

R. Ante

Barou

Morteaux-Coulibœuf

R. Dives

Beaumais

Crocy

l'Abbaye

la Balanderie

Nécy

Ronai

Pierrefitte

Bois de St Andre

Hablóville

Moutabard

Brieux

Fourches

Bierre

Norrey-en-Auge

159

Mandeville

Roc

la Londe

Bailleul

Argentan 2 km

Forêt de Gouffern

Grand-Mesnil

St Gervais

259

Louvieres-en-Auge

Ecorches

Trun

Magny

Bourdon

Naupahé-sur-Dives

240

259

les Champeaux

239

Boisjos

Coudehard

Mont-Ormel

262 (North)

262 (South)

137

Fréhée

St Lambert-sur-Dives

Moissy

Aubry-en-Exmes

Villedieu-les-Bailleul

Chambois

R. Dives

Knowles 1997

was killed in the fighting) or maybe from a KG of the 21st Panzer Division commanded by Hans von Luck. Whoever it was, it resulted in the 10th Mounted Rifles laagering for the night to the north-west of Louvières.

In the meantime a Battlegroup commanded by Lieutenant Colonel Koszutski and made up of the 2nd Armoured Regiment, the 8th Infantry Battalion and a company of anti-tank guns, had been ordered to seize Point 259, whilst another Battlegroup consisting of the 24th Lancers, 10th Dragoons (Motor Battalion) and an M-10 company, to take the adjacent hills 2km south of Grand-Mesnil. This latter Battlegroup was commanded by Major Zgorzelski, the commanding officer of the Dragoons.

Point 259 was a very large, steep and thickly wooded feature; it was attacked at 1745 hours and by 2245 hours the Koszutski Battlegroup had completed its task—as had Zgorzelski's to its north.[21] The rest of the Polish Armoured Division closed up during the night.

During the same night the Reconnaissance Battalion of the 21st Panzer Division, which had now been allocated to I SS Panzer Corps, took up positions in the Bois de St André with the HJ Divisional Escort Company just to its north at la Hoguette. However, to the south of Falaise there was a large gap which the British filled during the night following the collapse of the 89th Division.

In Falaise itself on the 17th the Saskatchewans were ordered to hold their hard won positions of the previous day; the Camerons were to advance to St Claire, 2km south of the city, whilst Les Fusiliers Mont-Royal were given the awesome job of finishing off those elements of KG Krause which had not received the order to withdraw to Fresné.

The Camerons completed their mission by about 1230 hours. The sixty or so young SS Grenadiers of KG Krause made their final stand in the Ecole Supérieure de Jeunes Filles. They were eventually overcome by two companies of Fusiliers with support from two tanks and some 6 pdr anti-tank guns, during the early hours of the 18th. Lots had been drawn to see which two young Grenadiers should break out to bring a last message to Kurt Meyer. Until 1983 it was believed that apart

from four Germans captured in the Saskatchewan sector, the
rest had died in the school; but in that year a former member
of the KG, then living in England, reported to Hubert Meyer
that he and seventeen others who had been trapped in a separate building in the garden of the school, had managed to
escape and take cover in a local farm where they were later
discovered and captured.

A critical situation was now developing on the eastern flank
of the Hitlerjugend and Meyer was given a KG from the 21st
Panzer Division under the command of a Colonel Rauch, to
help to meet it; this was in addition to the Reconnaissance
Battalion already mentioned. The KG comprised a severely
depleted Panzer-Grenadier Regiment, about eight Mk IVs of
the 22nd Panzer Regiment and an artillery battalion. Meyer
ordered Rauch to counter-attack the Poles who were seriously
threatening Trun. He was told also to keep open a passage
through the town and, at all costs, to prevent an encirclement
of Meyer's Division—not to mention all the other German
forces to the west.

The situation further deteriorated when General Simonds,
having failed at Damblainville, decided to relieve his 4th
Armoured Division on the Ante with the 3rd Infantry and
redirect the 4th to attack further east at Morteaux-Couliboeuf.
Montgomery had telephoned Crerar's Chief of Staff early in
the afternoon to demand resolute action. Brigadier Churchill
Mann recorded the message as follows:

> It is absolutely essential that both Armoured Divisions of II
> Canadian Corps . . . close the gap between First Canadian
> Army and Third US Army. 1st Polish Armoured Division
> must thrust on past Trun to Chambois at all costs and as
> quickly as is possible.[22]

Fortunately for the Germans, and despite their desperate
plight, it was to take another forty-eight hours for this to
happen and the 10km gap to be closed!

Even though KG Rauch was in no position to launch a
serious counter-attack against either the Poles or the Canadians, the Allied advance showed no sign of urgency. When the
Canadian Grenadier Guards reached Louvières-en-Auge that

evening they inexplicably harboured for the night and made plans to attack Trun the following day in cooperation with the Lake Superior Infantry Battalion. The excuse given in the 4th Canadian Brigade War Diary is that the Guards encountered enemy on their way to Trun and consequently had to halt their advance.

Further to the east the situation on the right flank of I SS Panzer Corps was also becoming critical. British forces had pushed east of St Pierre-sur-Dives and it therefore became necessary to pull in the Corps right wing to Montviette, 5km west of Lavarot (Map 8). Promises of two Panzer divisions to help cut off the penetrations by the Poles and Canadians were greeted with scepticism at I SS Panzer Corps.

By now the Germans were presenting targets in the pocket, to quote 35 Wing RAF, 'as had hitherto only been dreamed of.' On this day its aircraft reported, 'a minimum of 2,200 vehicles of all types, including several concentrations so dense as to be uncountable.' Allied Air Forces flew 2029 attack sorties on the 17th.[23]

The threat of complete encirclement was now very real and during the night 17th–18th Meyer pulled back from the Ante. KG Krause stayed firm at Fresné, while Wünsche's few tanks moved to join the Escort Company on the important ground at la Hoguette, north of the Bois de St André. Olboeter redeployed to defend the Dives crossing near Crocy facing north, and most of the Jagdpanzers moved to l'Abbaye, near la Balanderie.

During the evening Field Marshal Model arrived at the Headquarters of Army Group 'B' and, after presenting a letter from Hitler, relieved von Kluge of command. He was the third Commander-in-Chief in less than six weeks. Apart from the unsatisfactory military situation, Hitler had suspected von Kluge of trying to negotiate with the Allies during the time he had been out of touch with his Headquarters on the 15th and he was ordered to report in person to the Führer. The following morning during the flight home, this holder of the Knight's Cross with Oak Leaves and Swords committed suicide by taking cyanide.

NOTES
    1. Stacey, *The Official History of the Canadian Army in the Second World War, Vol III, The Victory Campaign*, p. 234. **2.** Ibid., p. 236. **3.** Meyer, Hubert, *History of the 12th SS Panzer Division Hitlerjugend*, p. 184. **4.** Stacey, op. cit., p. 237. **5.** Ibid., p. 236. **6.** Meyer, Kurt, *Grenadiers*, p. 165. **7.** Meyer, Hubert, op. cit., p. 182. **8.** Meyer, Kurt, op. cit., pp. 166–167. **9.** Stacey, op. cit., p. 243. **10.** Ibid. **11.** Meyer, Hubert, op. cit., p. 185. **12.** Stacey, op. cit., p. 249. **13.** Meyer, Kurt, op. cit., p. 167. **14.** Cdn Gren Gds War Diary, 15 Aug 44. **15.** Winnipeg Rifles War Diary, 11 Aug 44. **16.** Stacey, op. cit., p. 249. **17.** Meyer, Hubert, op. cit., p. 186. **18.** Stacey, op. cit., p. 250. **19.** Army Group 'B' War Diary 16 Aug 44. **20.** 10th Mounted Rifles War Diary. **21.** 1st Polish Armd Div Op Report and Wielogorski, Major T, *Przeglad Kawalerii i Broni Pancernej*, Historical Quarterly, No 147, May–Aug 94. **22.** First Cdn Army War Diary, Aug 44. **23.** AEAF Ops Summary No. 211 dated 18 Aug 44.

26 11th to 18th August— The Leibstandarte Withdraws

On 11th August, the day Montgomery issued orders for the closing of the gap between Falaise and Alençon, the German defence in northern France began to collapse. At noon von Kluge told OKW that he, Hausser and Eberbach, all believed:

> The offensive in the direction of Avranches is no longer practicable, since the enemy has brought up fresh forces. The thrust towards the sea will be a long, tough battle, to which the Panzer troops are no longer equal.[1]

That afternoon Hitler gave his approval for the 'Alençon plan'—the temporary transfer of Panzer Group Eberbach from the Mortain area so that it could be used to destroy the enemy spearheads thrusting northwards into the underbelly of the Seventh Army.

By early evening Wisch had issued orders for the Leibstandarte to move to the Domfront—la Ferté-Macé area (Map 8). The move began at 2300 hours over several different routes.[2]

At 0300 hours on 12th August a Seventh Army liaison officer caught up with Wisch and told him to subordinate his Division directly to Panzer Group Eberbach and await further orders on reaching the area west of la Ferté-Macé.

On its way through Domfront the Leibstandarte column came under artillery fire, but despite the roads being choked with traffic the move continued and at 2100 hours orders were received from Eberbach's Headquarters to defend a line running from la Ferté-Macé to Carrouges. Behind it von Lüttwitz's 2nd Panzer Division would defend the west bank of the Orne to as far south as Ecouché, where the 116th Panzer Division would take up position.[3]

On the morning of the 13th the bulk of the LAH was in position as follows:[4] parts of the 1st SS Panzer Regiment and Dinse's 3rd SS Panzer-Grenadier (SPW) Battalion were in Carrouges and St Sauveur-de-Carrouges, 3km to the north-east; other parts of the 1st SS Panzer Regiment were at Rânes and a hotchpotch of SS Panzer-Grenadier sub-units were in and around la Ferté-Macé. Wisch's Headquarters was at St Martin-l'Aiguillon, near Rânes, but it had been unable to get orders to two companies of Knittel's SS Reconnaissance Battalion and the 2nd SS Panzer-Grenadier Battalion of the 1st Regiment to the south of Argentan.

On the 14th, the day the second Canadian major operation to take Falaise was launched (Operation TRACTABLE), more Leibstandarte sub-units caught up with the mass of the Division and a form of defence was established in the approximate square Lonlay-le-Tesson—la Ferté-Macé—Carrouges—Rânes. At least parts of the following LAH companies are known to have been present:[5] 1st, 5th, 7th and 8th Panzer; 2nd, 3rd, 4th, and 5th Reconnaissance; 6th, 7th, 8th, and 11th of the 1st SS Panzer-Grenadier Regiment and the 2nd, 3rd, 4th, 5th, 6th, 7th, 8th, 14th and 15th of the 2nd; the Headquarters and 1st Company of the 1st SS Pioneer Battalion; parts of the 1st SS Sturmgeschütz Battalion; all the Flak Batteries and the 8th Artillery Battery.

La Ferté-Macé fell to the Americans at 1600 hours on the 14th and by midnight the LAH was holding a line running roughly from the Mont d'Hère in the west, through Beauvain to la Chaux[6] and la Champ-de-la-Pierre 4km further-east. It was opposing parts of the American 90th Infantry and French 2nd Armoured Divisions and, by a strange quirk of fate, its old adversary from Operation LÜTTICH, the US 3rd Armored

Division which was advancing north on the axis Carrouges-
Rânes. Two Task Forces of this Division reported meeting
strong resistance which they were unable to break at Joue de
Bois and Rânes on the 14th.

That night, as during the previous one, elements of 2nd SS
Panzer Division DR passed through the LAH on their way to
an area east of the Dives where they were to form a counter-
attack force.

In confused fighting on the 15th, Wisch's men tried to hold
a sort of 'S'-shaped defensive line from St Hilaire-de-Briouze
to Faverolles and thence to Rânes. At the end of the day the
entire US 3rd Armored Division was 'in a tight position
around Rânes'; its Combat Command A had tried to reach
Fromental but according to the Divisional History 'it could
not get much beyond Rânes.'

The next morning the 3rd Armored launched a coordinated
attack towards Fromental and by the afternoon was fighting in
the outskirts of the town. The Americans claimed fifteen German tanks destroyed and 400 prisoners taken.

By now the Allies were threatening Ecouché and Argentan
and the only way out for the LAH was across the Orne at
Putanges, where the Allied air forces had failed to destroy a
bridge capable of taking the heaviest vehicles.

The final retreat to the north began in the early evening of
the 16th. Although Wisch had little or no idea about the overall situation, his units held intermediate positions during that
night and on the 17th on the prominent ridges at St André, St
Hilaire-de-Briouze and Fromental and at Faverolles. The 3rd
Armored Divisional History records:

> Combat Command A fought its way into Fromental from
> the east [on the 17th]. Task Force 1 of Combat Command B
> attempted to launch an attack on Fromental from the
> south-west. . . . but such heavy resistance was met that
> the town itself was not reached. At about 1700 when all but
> the western part of the town had been cleared of the enemy,
> flights of P-38s heavily bombed Fromental. Combat Com-
> mand A was forced to withdraw because of the bombing,
> and small forces of Germans reoccupied the center and

western parts of the town. . . . Task Force 2 of Combat Command B fought stubborn resistance all day. At 1600 they got across the railroad east of Fromental, seized Hill 216 south of Putanges and remained for the night just south of their objective.

Although US aircraft bombed Fromental in the afternoon, foggy weather during the early part of the day interfered with flying and this allowed sizeable elements of the 1st SS Panzer Division to cross the Orne bridge at Putanges without interference.[7]

After maintaining most of their positions in St Hilaire and Fromental throughout the day of the 17th, the remaining elements of the Leibstandarte in those villages and at St André-de-Briouze received permission to pull out at midnight. Wisch had managed to make contact with Hausser's Command Post at Nécy during the afternoon and had been told that after crossing the Orne the LAH was to assemble in the close and wooded area south of Bissey with a view to continuing the march eastwards via Trun or Chambois depending on the circumstances. The British 11th Armoured Division, which had reached Flers on the night of the 16th, might well have presented Wisch with a major problem at Putanges had it not halted each night[8] instead of pushing on hard for the Orne crossing.

SS Second Lieutenant Stiller, a platoon commander in the 7th SS Panzer Company, described the midnight withdrawal:

I warned my Panzer commanders and driver: 'Run the motors on the lowest r.p.m. possible. We don't want the Americans to notice a thing.' They started their motors on the dot of 0000 hours and we moved to the edge of the forest on cat paws. Who would have thought that Panzer motors could run so quietly? . . . . The Grenadiers stuck to the Panzers like burrs. . . . We finally spotted some vehicles on the road in front of us. It was a horse-drawn unit. . . . The order was given out: 'The Panzers have to go in front! Let the Panzers through! They'll get us out of here!'. . . . It was already getting light as we began our move across the bridge. . . . The Feldgendarmerie directed us to a second-

ary road—that route got us away from the bridge faster.
The bridge could become a living hell at any moment.[9]

Tanks of the British 23rd Hussars and riflemen of 8 RB,
both of the 11th Armoured Division, reached Putanges in time
to have the bridge blown in their faces at 1150 hours on the
18th. At 1237 hours advance elements of the American 33rd
Armored Regiment, part of the 3rd Armored, reached the outskirts of the town and it appeared that the German escape
route had been closed. The British estimated that at least a
battalion of Germans was defending the eastern bank but
when the 3rd Monmouths attacked at midnight there was no
opposition[10]—the LAH had gone!

NOTES

1. Wilmot, *The Struggle for Europe*, p. 416. **2.** Lehmann & Tiemann,
The Leibstandarte, IV/I, p. 191. **3.** Ibid., p. 193. **4.** Ibid., p. 193. **5.** Ibid., pp.
193–195. **6.** Ibid., p. 195. **7.** Ibid., p. 202. **8.** 11 Armd Div War Diary, 16
Aug 44. **9.** Lehmann & Tiemann, op. cit., pp. 208–209. **10.** 11 Armd Div
War Diary, 19 Aug 44.

27 *18th to 25th August— The Last Battle of Normandy*

18TH TO 19TH AUGUST—THE FALAISE POCKET

By first light on 18th August the bulk of the Seventh Army
had managed to cross the Orne and many support and supply
units were already east of the Dives. But with the remnants of
thirteen divisions still inside the Pocket, the German retreat
towards Vimoutiers had yet to reach full flood.

Field Marshal Model arrived at Headquarters, Fifth Panzer
Army at 0900 hours and after a conference with Dietrich,
Eberbach and Hausser's representative, Colonel von Gersdorff,
gave orders that a new front was to be established west of the
Seine. Hausser's Seventh Army, with Panzer Group Eberbach
attached, was to make an initial stand in the Trun area and
then around Vimoutiers—it was to be behind the Dives by
20th August and the Touques, just to the east of Vimoutiers,
by the 22nd. II SS Panzer Corps was to use the severely weakened 2nd and 9th SS Panzer Divisions, which were already
across the Dives and re-organising to the south-west of

Vimoutiers, to launch a counter-attack towards Trun and Chambois with the aim of securing the escape routes. Meanwhile, what was left of the HJ and 21st Panzer Divisions would protect the northern flank of the Pocket while XLVII Panzer Corps, with the 2nd and 116th Panzer Divisions, would continue to hold the south side. The Leibstandarte and 10th SS Panzer Divisions were not to be involved in this operation and were to move initially to l'Aigle and then to Mantes near Septeuil; neither were 17th Panzer or Panzer Lehr, whose remnants were to start moving at once to a refitting area east of Paris. Headquarters I SS Panzer Corps was to be withdrawn at once.

These grandiose orders bore little relation to reality on the ground or what was practicable. Most of the so-called 'divisions' were little more than KGs. In the case of the Hitlerjugend, even 'KG' was becoming an over-statement. When the British 53rd Infantry Division began its advance from south of Falaise towards Nécy on the 18th, the Divisional Escort Company KG under SS Second Lieutenant Stier comprised just two SPWs with fifteen men and two Jagdpanzer IVs. In view of the British move, Wünsche ordered it back to la Balanderie.

The combined Canadian and Polish thrust on the 18th, such as it was, came on the east side of the Dives. Despite the order to link up with the Americans at Chambois as a matter of urgency, the maximum advance on this day was less than 10km. One can only guess at what might have happened had the roles been reversed and men like Wisch, Meyer and Wünsche been in command.

Although General Simonds issued orders on the afternoon of the 18th for his 3rd Infantry Division to take care of the east bank of the Dives down to Trun, and for the Armoured Divisions to push on rapidly to Chambois, there seems to have been little real effort to coordinate the actions of the Canadians and Poles—indeed, it would appear that at unit level neither had much idea what the other was doing, or even trying to do, during the critical period 18th–20th August. Fortunately for the Germans many of the Allied intermediate commanders thought the battle was almost over and all they had to do was mop-up. Such was not the case and as a result of this misunderstanding thousands of Germans escaped to fight another day.

The furthest penetration on the 18th was by a squadron of the Polish Armoured Reconnaissance Regiment which moved through Bourdon and reached the area immediately to the north of Chambois. However, after finding the town well defended and no sign of any other Allied troops, it was ordered back to the area of Point 259.[1] General Maczek claimed later that it was pulled back due to a planned Allied air strike on the town.

Similarly a squadron of the Canadian South Alberta Reconnaissance Regiment reached the northern outskirts of St Lambert-sur-Dives at about 1900 hours. But by 2000 hours two of its tanks had been knocked out—one by anti-tank fire and the other after an attack by two Spitfires—and it was decided, again fortunately for the Germans, to wait until first light on the 19th in order to mount a coordinated attack with an accompanying company of Argylls of Canada.[2] This allowed the Germans to use the bridges in the village during the night without direct interference. Meanwhile, a second squadron of the South Albertas reached Point 117, 2km north of St Lambert, at around midnight.

According to the 4th Canadian Armoured Division's morning situation report for the 18th, there was 'Only slight resistance to forward movement [of] our armour'. This was certainly true since KG Rauch had already withdrawn to the south and another 21st Panzer KG north of Grand-Mesnil, commanded by Hans von Luck, had been outflanked to its south by the Poles. There was therefore no coherent German defence in the area.

By midnight the 4th Canadian Armoured Brigade had moved to the Trun-Vimoutiers road north of Neauphe-sur-Dives, where it was held in a counter-attack role. Following up, the 10th Infantry Brigade occupied Trun and the area immediately to its north-east by last light, whilst the 3rd Infantry Division filled in behind them on the east side of the Dives.

What of the main Polish force? The 1st Polish Armoured Division Operational Report states that General Maczek, from his Headquarters near Norrey, ordered his Koszutski Battlegroup (the 2nd Armoured Regiment, with the 8th Infantry Battalion and an anti-tank company attached), to make 'an immediate stroke at Chambois' at 1930 hours on the 17th.

Lieutenant Colonel Koszutski confirmed later that he received this order during his attack on Point 259 on the evening of the 17th, but said that he decided to wait for a fuel and ammunition resupply before setting off. When he finally gave the order to move, at 0200 hours on the 18th, that resupply had still not arrived.

The Auge countryside through which the Battlegroup was to advance, in fog and at night, was broken and hilly, with narrow twisting roads and tracks, few villages and many scattered farms. Even today, in daylight with a modern map, it is difficult to find one's way. It is hardly surprising therefore that, according to General Maczek, Koszutski employed a local Frenchman to guide his vanguard. Nevertheless, the Battlegroup still lost its way and by 0600 hours it was in the area of les Champeaux—10km north of Chambois and nowhere near its objective. It has been suggested, not unreasonably, that in view of the similarity of the names—Champeaux and Chambois—the guide misunderstood the requirement and led the force to the wrong place. However, suggestions of a misunderstanding about the final objective by the relevant commanders can be discounted. The War Diary of a British unit attached to Maczek's Headquarters throughout the campaign and known as 'Headquarters No 4 Liaison, 21st Army Group', confirms the objective as 'Chambois and the high ground to the north-east.' This unit was headed by a Colonel J.H. Anstice and comprised thirty-five officers and 150 men.

Koszutski's 2nd Armoured Regiment certainly moved off from Point 259 on the correct road, heading east, with the men of the 8th Infantry Battalion mounted on its Shermans. On reaching the main Trun-Vimoutiers road the leading tanks ran into a German column of motorized and horse-drawn transport and there was a short, sharp engagement in which the Germans suffered badly. The Shermans then continued their move to the south-east in the general direction of Chambois, but shortly after crossing the main road and nego-

tiating a steep hill which caused severe problems for some of
the vehicles, they mistakenly turned, (author: probably in the
tiny hamlet of les Lignerits) or were misdirected, to the north-
east and ended up in the area of les Champeaux—another tiny
hamlet lying on the side of a steep hill and consisting of little
more than a church and half a dozen houses. Unfortunately
for the Poles, the Germans were occupying the larger village of
Hostellerie Faroult, which is to be found a few hundred metres
above and to the north-west of les Champeaux, on the main
Trun-Vimoutier road. This, as we have heard, was being used
as a major escape route. Not surprisingly there was a sharp
clash, with casualties to both sides. In his book, *Avec Mes
Blindés*, Maczek claims that this fighting was against the Headquarters and elements of the 2nd Panzer Division, but his
author believes it to be most unlikely that troops of that Division were involved, since it was fighting on the south side of
the Pocket, around Argentan, at the time. However, they may
well have been part of the 2nd SS Panzer Division DR, which
was south-west of Vimoutiers on the 18th preparing to
counter-attack back into the Pockeet—or even, as we shall
hear shortly, from a 12th SS Replacement Battalion under the
command of SS Major Hans Waldmüller! Whatever the truth,
the Poles were apparently delighted to discover from Record of
Service books found on a number of their prisoners that, in an
amazing twist of fate, they were engaging at least some of
those who had invaded their country in 1939!

Fuel was by now an urgent necessity and during its enforced
wait at les Champeaux Koszutski's force suffered further casualties when it was mistakenly struck by American Thunder-
bolts attacking German columns on the main road just above
them. Isolated behind German lines, harbouring casualties and
unable to move, it is hardly surprising that the 1st Polish
Armoured Division Operational Report describes the Battlegroup's situation at this time as 'grave'. It goes on to say that
the 1st (Highland) Infantry Battalion was sent to help.
Maczek's Headquarters later reported, 'half the petrol being
sent to 2nd Armoured Regiment was destroyed through
bombing just after 1700 hours'.

During this same day the highly experienced General

Maczek, whose eye for important ground was legendary, decided to block the exits from Chambois by seizing Point 137 near Coudehard, and Points 262 (North), 252 and 262 (South) astride Mont Ormel on the main Chambois-Vimoutiers road.[3] With this in mind, the Zgorzelski and 1st Armoured Regimental Battlegroups were also ordered to advance on the 18th, and by 2300 hours they were blocking the Trun-Vimoutiers road and holding the high ground on either side of Ecorches, filling the gap between their compatriots at les Champeaux and the Canadians near Neauphe-sur-Dives. The Divisional Operational Report speaks of the Polish Battlegroups being involved in 'heavy fighting with enemy infantry and anti-tank guns'— presumably those of KG Rauch and/or the remants of the 85th Division—and of Allied air attacks preventing the 1st Armoured Regiment from capturing its objective of Bourdon. Between crossing the Dives on the 16th and last light on the 18th, the Polish Division suffered a further seventy-two killed and 119 wounded.

In view of these penetrations on his right flank, Meyer, from his Command Post immediately north of Nécy, ordered a further withdrawal. The basic combat elements were required to fight on—KGs Wünsche and Krause were to move back to Bierre, while Olboeter leap-frogged further east to Roc; but all non-essential and supply units were told to evacuate the Pocket completely. The 7th and 8th Batteries of the 3rd SS SS Panzer Artillery Battalion pulled out, leaving just the 9th Battery, as did the 12th SS Flak Battalion and 14th SS Flak Company of the 26th Regiment. Similarly, the Divisional Signals Battalion was told to withdraw. But not all these units reached safety—SS Major Fend's 12th SS Flak Battalion ran into trouble during its attempted move out of the Pocket. It had to fight its way through Canadian troops after being blocked by a horse-drawn artillery column. Retreating German infantrymen and paratroopers tried to hitch lifts on its vehicles and the situation quickly became chaotic with the road under fire from tanks, artillery and fighter-bombers. Only isolated groups managed to escape.

The scene near Trun was described graphically by one Allied artillery observer:

The floor of the valley was seen to be alive. . . . men marching, cycling and running, columns of horse-drawn transport, motor transport, and as the sun got up, so more targets came to light. . . . It was a gunner's paradise and everybody took advantage of it. . . . Away on our left was the famous killing ground, and all day the roar of Typhoons went on and fresh columns of smoke obscured the horizon. . . . We could just see one short section of the Argentan-Trun road, some 200 yards in all, on which sector at one time was crowded the whole miniature picture of an army in rout. First a squad of men running, being overtaken by men on bicycles, followed by a limber at a gallop, and the whole being overtaken by a Panther tank crowded with men and doing well up to 30 mph, all with the main idea of getting away as fast as they could.[4]

Allied aircraft flew 3,057 attack sorties on the 18th.[5]

Meyer's few remaining men, together with KG Rauch, still tried to maintain some semblance of a defence line facing north. Rauch was between Neauphe-sur-Dives and the river south of Trun, Krause was south of the river astride the Trun-Argentan road, while Olboeter's SS Grenadiers with two Tigers, two Panthers, five Flakpanzers and two assault guns were around Roc and Bierre. It is not clear whether the Tigers were from the 101st SS Heavy Panzer Battalion but it seems likely. At about 2000 hours a few members of the Divisional Escort Company, a Flakpanzer and two assault howitzers joined the group north of Roc.

Meyer's own Headquarters was fortunate in its initial moves and got back first to a new location at Bierre and then to la Londe where it maintained contact with Krause and Olboeter by liaison officer but had no communications with Rauch; nor was it in touch with any higher formation and so had no information about the overall situation. If it had, it would no doubt have been surprised to learn that its basic partner in I SS Panzer Corps, the 1st SS Panzer Division, was in the process of taking up a position on its left flank around Nécy, Pier-refitte and Ronai, with parts of the 1st SS Reconnaissance Battalion at Habloville. Knittel had orders to find and defend a route by which the LAH could escape. After two weeks the remnants of the proud twin Divisions were together again.

Perhaps the most surprising event on the 18th was the reappearance, as already mentioned, of Waldmüller with an HJ Replacement Battalion at St Gervais, only 8km north-east of Trun. It had been manned with personnel from the 4th SS (Polizei) Division and Waldmüller was trying to get through to rejoin the HJ via Trun. Since this was now impossible, the commander of the 21st Panzer Division, Major General Feuchtinger, ordered him to take up a position in the forest just south of St Gervais.

The situation deteriorated rapidly during the night 18th–19th. Unknown to anyone in the Hitlerjugend, the 21st Panzer Division's Reconnaissance Battalion had withdrawn from the Bois St André and elements of the British 4th Armoured Brigade and 53rd Infantry Division were therefore able to advance virtually unchecked into the gap created and secure the high ground south of Nécy. Max Wünsche's Command Group, including Hanreich, the commander of the 12th SS Panzerjäger Battalion, and what was left of the Divisional Escort Company mounted on six Flakpanzers, ran into enemy troops during its attempted move back during the night from Fourches to Bierre and was shot up; the Regimental doctor was wounded, Hanreich captured and the group scattered. Rather than risk further movement in daylight, Wünsche, his Adjutant, SS Captain Isecke, the Regimental Orderly officer, SS Second Lieutenant Freitag, and the wounded doctor camouflaged their two vehicles and took cover, but during the afternoon of the 19th British soldiers discovered the vehicles and took them away. The group was left with no option but to walk.

What happened next was bizarre. At around midday on the 19th, Lieutenant General Elfeldt, the commander of LXXXIV Corps, arrived at Kurt Meyer's Command Post at la Londe. He had nothing left to command and since the Headquarters of I SS Panzer Corps was now outside the Pocket, Meyer subordinated himself to him. By chance General Hausser's Seventh Army Tactical Headquarters was close by in a quarry at Villedieu-lès-Bailleul and Elfeldt and Meyer decided to report

there for orders. They walked and ran, having to take cover
from artillery fire as they did so. On arrival they found not
only Paul Hausser but Teddy Wisch of the Leibstandarte. Also
present was Hausser's Chief of Staff, von Gersdorff, along with
Lieutenant Colonel von Kluge and Major Heinz Guderian, the
Chiefs of Staff of Panzer Group Eberbach and the 116th Panzer Division respectively. Von Gersdorff had come from
Chambois with the news that the counter-attack from the
north-east by II SS Panzer Corps could not take place until the
following day. The problems of preparing and re-equipping
exhausted troops, who had themselves only just escaped from
the Pocket, Allied air strikes and the surprise presence of the
Polish Battlegroups so far to the east, precluded any chance of
an earlier attack.

The situation had of course changed radically since Model's
original orders issued twenty-four hours previously and
Hausser now ordered a breakout during the night 19th–20th,
hopefully timed to link up with the counter-attack from outside the Pocket by elements of the 2nd and 9th SS Panzer
Divisions (II SS Panzer Corps). Hausser's orders were as follows: 3rd Parachute Division, currently between Montabard
and Villedieu-les-Bailleul was to attempt to pass silently
through the St Lambert-sur-Dives sector; it was to be followed
by the remnants of the HJ less its vehicles which, with the few
remaining tanks of the HJ, were to join a KG of the LAH and
cross the Dives halfway between St Lambert and Chambois at
Moissy. This route was soon to earn for itself the unforgettable
title 'The Corridor of Death'! The LAH KG comprised: Wisch
and the remains of the Divisional staff, Schiller with his 1st SS
Panzer-Grenadier Regimental staff and some three companies
of SS Grenadiers, parts of the 2nd, 5th, 6th, 7th and 8th SS
Panzer Companies, the 3rd SS Reconnaissance Company, the
staff of the LAH SS Artillery Regiment with the 1st and 2nd
Battalions and 8th and 9th Batteries of the 3rd, and the 4th SS
Flak Battery.[6] A second Leibstandarte KG, consisting of a few
Panthers, some StuGs of the 1st Sturmgeschütz Company and
a scratch force of SS Panzer-Grenadiers from the 1st Regiment,
was to attempt a crossing 1200m to the south-east of Trun, at
Magny, where a deeply embanked road would give some pro-

tection against air attack. There was also a third LAH KG, probably under Ullerich, comprising some tanks and a few StuGs, elements of Sandig's 1st and 3rd (SPW) SS Panzer-Grenadiers, the 3rd SS Pioneer Company and the remnants of the 1st SS Flak Battalion, which assembled to the south-west of Chambois.[7] It was hoped that the majority of the other survivors in the Pocket would follow these Waffen SS spearheads to safety. In the midst of such chaos it seems incredible that such a plan could be formulated, but it was reported to Army Group 'B' by radio with a request that II SS Panzer Corps launch its counter-attack early on the 20th in the general direction of Trun.

On their way back to the HJ Command Post, Meyer and Elfeldt met Air Force General Meindl, commander II Parachute Corps, together with the commander of the 3rd Parachute Division, Lieutenant General Schimpf. The plan was discussed and Meyer agreed to attach two Tigers to the paratroopers, who would move in four separate Regimental groups totalling about 2,000 men. The gunners would fire their last rounds before blowing up their guns and joining the escape columns.

Final orders for the HJ withdrawal were issued shortly after Meyer's return to his Command Post—KG Krause was to lead the way and KG Olboeter to bring up the rear. SS Major Drexler, commander 12th SS Panzer Artillery Regiment, was told to try to extract as many vehicles as possible by following the LAH in its planned breakout at Moissy.

Meanwhile the trap was closing—albeit slowly. General Simonds issued further orders at 1100 hours on the 19th. The 2nd Infantry Division was to take over the northern part of the 3rd Infantry's area of responsibility along the Dives so that the latter could 'strengthen its line and close all escape routes.' The 4th Armoured Division was to cover the river from Trun to exclusive Moissy, while the Poles would be responsible from Moissy to Chambois and Point 262 (South). The 2nd Canadian Armoured Brigade was to reinforce George Kitching's Division north of the Dives.

Despite these clear orders, action on the ground did not reflect the urgency of the situation. Indeed, as will be seen, no

Canadian or Polish infantry were moved on to the critical
parts of the Dives river itself and the Allied failure to produce
sufficient infantry at the right places was to prove a major
blunder. To make matters worse, the three tank and two infantry units of Kitching's 4th Armoured Brigade remained idle all
day to the north-east of Trun. At Simond's insistence, and
against Kitching's wishes, they were held there as a potential
exploitation force for the expected pursuit to the Seine. It was
not until the evening that they were told to move towards
Vimoutiers.

The only significant Canadian action on the 19th had already started before the Corps commander's new orders were
issued. At 0635 hours the tanks of C Squadron of the South
Albertas, with a weak company of Argylls of Canada and a
troop of four 17 pdr SP anti-tank guns, mounted their attack
on St Lambert. After six hours fighting only half the village
had been secured and despite being reinforced by two more
weak infantry companies and eight more anti-tank guns later
in the day, the Canadians could still not clear the southern
part of the village;[8] so they dug in, and made their famous
stand against repeated German counter-attacks which earned
the South Alberta commander, Major David Currie, a Victoria
Cross—the only one awarded to a Canadian in the Normandy
campaign. In the meantime, A Squadron of the same Regiment took up a position on the Trun-St Lambert road and B
Squadron moved to Point 124, 2km east of St Lambert, with
the intention of linking up with the Poles. Neither squadron
had any supporting infantry with it, making the task of blocking German escape routes difficult by day and impossible at
night. Indeed, within sixty hours B Squadron would have lost
fourteen of its nineteen tanks to escaping German infantry.

It was the Poles who finally tried to 'put the cork in the
bottle.' In accordance with Maczek's orders the Zgorzelski Battlegroup secured Point 137, near Coudehard, by midday and
the 24th Lancers then moved south towards Frénée. At about
the same time the 1st Polish Armoured Regiment with the 9th
Infantry Battalion and a company of anti-tank guns, advanced
towards the main Chambois-Vimoutier road at Points 262
(North) and 252, 5km north-east of Chambois. This road was

being used by the Germans as their main escape route and, when the leading Polish tanks arrived there just before 1600 hours, they found it crowded with vehicles, horse-drawn transport and two Panther tanks—one being towed by the other. In a short, violent action the Panthers were knocked out and everything in sight destroyed. Then, while one infantry company and some anti-tank guns occupied Coudehard Boisjos, 700m to the north-west, the Shermans and the rest of the infantry and anti-tank guns took up positions on Point 262 (North)—the Chambois-Vimoutiers road was completely blocked with knocked out vehicles and the bodies of dead men and horses.

By 1030 hours the Koszutski Battlegroup in the les Champeaux area had been resupplied and soon after midday it too set off for Point 262 (North). By 1700 hours it had established positions on the north and east sides of the feature. But whilst Point 262 (North) and Coudehard Boisjos became a Polish stronghold, no one occupied Point 262 (South).

The position on Point 262 (North) is often referred to as 'Mont Ormel', after the nearby hamlet, but the Poles nicknamed it 'Maczuga' (The Mace), after the shape of its contours. From its summit they could enjoy spectacular views over much of the Falaise Pocket—but spectacular views are one thing and controlling the surrounding countryside is quite another. Point 262 (South) and its foothills obscured observation to the south-east and the steepness of the ground, woods and hedgerows made control of the ground to the west and south-west with direct fire weapons difficult by day and impossible at night—and it was through this Coudehard area and Point 137 on the west side of Mont Ormel that many of the Germans (particularly of the LAH and HJ) emerging from the St Lambert and Moissy crossings would inevitably pass. Fortunately for them this large force of over eighty tanks, some twenty anti-tank guns and 1500 infantrymen remained on Maczuga within a perimeter of less than two square kilometres, controlling its immediate environment but little else. Nevertheless it remained a major, if not *the* major, impediment to the German retreat.

Since the Poles on Maczuga were physically cut off from

their Divisional and Brigade commanders—General Maczek's
Divisional Headquarters was 8km away to the north-west on
Point 259 and Colonel Majewski's 10th Armoured Brigade
Headquarters at Bourdon, 3km to the west—the senior unit
commander, Lieutenant Colonel Szydlowski, took command.
Another serious problem was that the force, now behind German lines, was cut off from its supplies; but despite 'strong
representations made to [II] Corps HQ on behalf of GOC
Polish Armoured Division' by the British No 4 Liaison Unit,
the answer came back that no aerial resupply could be arranged before the 21st.[9]

By 1900 hours the Shermans of the Polish 24th Lancers had
advanced to a blocking position 1500m north-east of
Chambois, where they linked up with the 10th Mounted Rifles
Armoured Reconnaissance Regiment and two M-10 anti-tank
companies which had in the meantime reached the area of
Point 113, 1km north of Chambois. The most dramatic move
on the 19th, however, came at 1930 hours when the Polish
10th Dragoons (motorized infantry battalion), after moving
south from Point 137, entered Chambois and shortly afterwards linked up with the 2nd Battalion of the American 359th
Infantry Regiment.

The noose it seemed had been drawn tight. But not so! At
the highest level there was a serious lack of coordination, both
between the two wings of the Allied armies and within Simonds's II Corps and, as already mentioned, at the tactical
level there were no Allied troops physically blocking the 5km
of river between Magny and Moissy (a stretch which could be
waded in certain places by men on their feet) and the vehicle
crossings at Magny, St Lambert and Moissy, although heavily
interdicted by indirect fire, were still open.

This unsatisfactory situation was further exacerbated when
part of the French 2nd Armoured Division which had advanced to Frénée and the Chambois-Vimoutiers road by early
evening on the 19th, was withdrawn south of the Dives as
darkness fell. Its commander's eyes were now firmly set on a
much more attractive prize—Paris! The region north and
north-east of Chambois was therefore far from sealed and the
trap was by no means closed.

It is important to understand that by now much of the 1st and 12th SS Panzer Divisions, and even parts of the 101st SS Heavy Panzer Battalion, were already outside the Falaise Pocket. Firm details of LAH units are unavailable but of the HJ it is known that the following were well east of the Dives: Mohnke with the staff of his 26th Regiment and elements of most of his Regimental units, as well as Siebken and the core personnel of his 2nd Battalion; Milius with the same from the 25th Regiment, the command elements of his 2nd and 3rd Battalions and, as we have already heard, a new 1st Battalion under Waldmüller; Bremer and Müller with core parts of the 12th SS Reconnaissance and Pioneer Battalions respectively; all Panzer crews without tanks; all repair and supply units; and one 37mm Flak and two 150mm artillery batteries.[10] It is likely that most of the supply and repair units of the LAH had also escaped.

The Allied Expeditionary Air Force flew 2,535 sorties on this day[11] but thereafter the near impossibility of identifying specific ground targets, caused the air effort to be switched further east to the Seine and its approaches. In his report for the day, General Crerar wrote:

> This powerful weapon in support of the Army will consti-
> tute a deterrent to ground operations rather than the stimu-
> lant of which it is potentially capable.

The 3rd German Parachute Division started out on its bid for freedom at 2230 hours on 19th August. Shortly after this General Schimpf was wounded during a brush with tanks and the Corps commander, General Meindl, took command.

20TH TO 22ND AUGUST—BREAKOUT

By midnight 19th–20th August Kurt Meyer and General Elfeldt had received no word from the 3rd Division paratroop-ers—the vanguard had in fact crossed the Dives north of St Lambert but was out of touch. As it was obviously essential to try to cross the tiny river before daylight, Elfeldt and Meyer decided to proceed anyway at 0200 hours. The leading group comprised about fifty men, all on their feet, and included Elfeldt, Kurt Meyer, Hubert Meyer and Bernhard Krause.

By first light the point of the column had only reached the vicinity of Aubry-en-Exmes, 2km west of Chambois, and was still 2km short of the Dives, which Meyer later described as about 2m deep and 3–4m wide. It was in this area that the HJ commander went 'missing'; in the *History of the 12th SS Panzer Division* his Chief of Staff described how he personally:

> Spotted his commander on a Panzer IV near a barn. . . . he ran towards the Panzer and barely managed to climb on as it began to move. He noticed a man in camouflage uniform on the Panzer's skirt. It turned out he was dead. . . . the Oberführer [Kurt Meyer] sat on the front, next to the turret. . . . He was glad his men were in the vicinity. [They] quickly jumped from the moving Panzer and ran back to their infantry group.[12]

In an extraordinary coincidence the author came across what appears to be exactly the same incident described by SS Second Lieutenant Gerhard Stiller of the 7th SS Panzer Company LAH, in the History of the Leibstandarte:

> Just before we were to move out, a voice called to us: 'Hey! You've got a dead man hanging on your tank!' There was no time to bury him so we laid him on the rear of the Panzer and took off. . . . When we were even with a group of farm buildings known as Aubry-en-Exmes we. . . . saw our Panzers ahead. . . . An officer with a large bandage on his head tried to pull himself onto our Panzer by grabbing the belt of our dead gunner. He didn't make it.[13]

Readers will recall that Kurt Meyer had a bandaged head. Althoug the accounts differ slightly, it would appear that, unknown to Stiller, he had two very famous officers riding his tank at this point. Stiller was severely wounded in the face by shrapnel a short time later, but his Mk IV was one of the few tanks to cross the Dives (he did not remember where or how) and reach safety.

When the two Meyers eventually managed to rejoin Krause and his Grenadiers they discovered General Elfeldt and his Staff had gone on ahead—only to be captured by the Polish 10th Mounted Rifles whose commanding officer, Major

Maciejowski, was killed by a sniper during this fighting. Out of five Corps commanders in the Pocket, Elfeldt was the only one not to escape. Twelve of the divisional commanders managed to get out to fight another day.

Conscious of heavy fighting in St Lambert, Panzermeyer and his group, which now numbered about 200, crossed the Dives near the Château Quantité, 1000m to the north-west of the church. The Château was being used as a German casualty collecting point but there were so many wounded that scores had been left lying out in the open. Numerous stray individuals tried to join the group during the exhausting march but Meyer would allow only those with weapons to do so. Everywhere they looked lay the dead, animal and human, covered with swarms of flies. But what sickened the SS officers most was the sight of German soldiers waving white rags attached to sticks, waiting to surrender.

In their efforts to evade capture Meyer's group was often forced to split up; Meyer described the journey in his usual melodramatic way:

> I jump from cover to cover with pistol in hand. . . . We dash eastwards between the two tanks like a shot from a gun. . . . I cannot go on, the sweat burns my eyes, the head wound reopens. . . . Machine gun fire flies around our ears. Tears are running down Michel's [his driver]face as he fails to make me move quickly enough. He encourages me like a mother does a child. Repeatedly I hear, 'Commander come! Only a few hundred meters to go, please Commander, come!'[14]

Many writers say Meyer was led out of the pocket by a French guide but he makes no mention of it himself and nor does his Chief of Staff. When Point 262 (South) was finally reached and found to be free of enemy, only the two Meyers, Krause, an SS Second Lieutenant Kölln, Michel and about eight men were present. After a short rest they continued their march and eventually, in the late afternoon, ran into troops of the 116th Panzer Division who took them to the Divisional Command Post at le Mesnil-Hubert, 6km further east. Once more the commander of 12th SS had survived.

On the Allied side there were few significant moves on the
20th. The order to the Canadian 4th Armoured Brigade to
move towards Vimoutiers was cancelled early in the morning
and Kitching's 4th Armoured Division was rather belatedly
reinforced by the 9th Infantry Brigade for use in the Trun-
Moissy sector. A Polish plan to expand their Mont Ormel bastion by seizing Point 262 (South) was cancelled in view of the
strong German attacks on their perimeter (which will be described later), and attempts to get urgently needed supplies
through to the beleaguered garrison failed with severe losses.

The fighting Meyer had heard in St Lambert was between
the men of the 2nd Panzer Division trying to force their way
across the Dives and Major Currie's Canadians. Although the
latter held the northern part of village, General von Lüttwitz's
Grenadiers managed to hold open the road through the southern part, near the church, for some six hours. Von Lüttwitz
had this to say about it:

> By noon I had managed to reach St Lambert myself, and
> from the church in the town I directed the evacuation of my
> men. The crossing of the bridge over the Dives was a partic-
> ularly ghastly affair. Men, horses, vehicles and other equip-
> ment that had been shot up while making the crossing had
> crashed from the bridge into the deep ravine of the Dives
> and lay there jumbled together in gruesome heaps.
> Throughout the afternoon enemy tanks tried to break
> through again into St Lambert from Trun, while other tanks
> kept the road leading north-east from St Lambert under
> constant fire.[15]

One group of four Mk IVs from the 2nd SS Panzer Battalion
HJ, together with three Jagdpanzer IVs, reached the edge of
the pocket in the region of Moissy at about 1000 hours but
were forced back by tank and anti-tank fire—probably Polish.
Two tanks were lost, one with a gearbox failure being blown
up by its own crew. SS Senior Sergeant Willie Kretzschmar of
the 5th SS Panzer Company described what happened:

> After darkness had fallen we set out for the final breakout.
> Grenadiers of our Division and several paratroopers were at

the point. The Panzers and Jagdpanzers followed and at some distance behind came soldiers of our Division and the Army who did not want to be taken prisoner. There may have been 2,000 to 3,000 men following us. . . . We came under infantry fire, we were right in front of the enemy positions. Our Panzers fired. . . . and drove at high speed through the enemy lines. All Panzers made it undamaged. The infantry losses are not known. Regretfully, during the further march that night, crossing unknown terrain, we had to leave one Panzer after another, one got stuck in the mire, another toppled into a ditch, a third got hung up on a tree stump. In the early morning our widely dispersed group reached. . . . Panzer IVs of Das Reich [2nd SS Panzer] Division assembled for relief action.[16]

KG Olboeter's breakout was as dramatic as Meyer's. It was led by two Panthers and two Tigers, followed by the few remaining members of the Divisional Escort Company riding on five Flakpanzers and the SS Panzer-Grenadiers with some surviving SPWs. Between four and six Mk IVs joined the KG at some stage and a member of the Escort Company reported, many years later, that a company of paratroopers also joined them soon after they started out. He said the tanks knocked out seven or eight enemy tanks during clashes with Canadians and Poles for the loss of one Panther—the one in which he himself was travelling. He survived unhurt. By 1500 hours the KG, in concert with an attack by General Meindl's 3rd Paratroopers, had secured the Coudehard crossroads just to the north-west of Point 262 (North), thus opening the Coudehard to Boisjos road. The Poles on Maczuga were now in some difficulties themselves. They had been under fairly intense artillery and mortar fire ever since their arrival there 24 hours before, but they were now being attacked from inside the pocket by the forces of Meindl and Olboeter, and from outside by the 2nd SS Panzer Division DR.

The main attack from outside the pocket had started at 0400 hours and was launched by parts of the 9th SS Panzer Division on the north side of the Vimoutiers-Trun road and by more substantial elements of 2nd SS Panzer Division, including twenty-one tanks, on the south side. We need only concern ourselves with 2nd SS.

Der Führer SS Panzer-Grenadier Regiment, which comprised only two weak battalions of no more than 120 men each, was supported by six tanks. It advanced via Champosoult towards Coudehard, whilst the similarly reduced Deutschland SS Panzer-Grenadier Regiment, also with tank support, moved to the east of Mont Ormel. By 1500 hours one battalion of Der Führer had captured the road fork 1000m north-west of Coudehard, opening up the Champosoult-Boisjos road and linking up with the Meindl-Olboeter force coming up from the south. In one incident five Shermans of the Polish 1st Armoured Regiment on Maczuga were picked off in as many minutes by a single Panther firing from Point 239, 1500m to the north. The Polish situation was in fact worsening by the hour as they were unable to evacuate wounded or prisoners, and ammunition and food were running low.

By 1700 hours the Germans had broken into the northern part of the Maczuga perimeter and it was 1900 hours before they were expelled for the loss of three Mk IVs;[17] but reports that every Polish officer on Mont Ormel was either killed or wounded (there were some 100 of them) are without foundation.

In the meantime, at about 1530 hours, the SS Panzer-Grenadier Regiment Deutschland had managed to open up another escape route on the east side of Vimoutiers-Chambois road through Survie and St Pierre-la-Rivière. It was in an attempt to reach this easterly life-line that the second LAH KG, already described, and probably commanded by Ullerich, struggled against the Poles and Americans in the Chambois sector during the following thirty-six hours. The seriousness of this threat caused the Poles to reinforce their motorized infantry in Chambois with tanks of the 24th Lancers.

Returning to the escape stories—SS Major Kuhlmann, the acting commander of the 1st SS Panzer Regiment LAH, started his breakout with Hans Gruhle, Peiper's Adjutant, in his Panther and accompanied by a command group SPW. Both vehicles were knocked out and Kuhlmann wounded, but he still managed to lead a large group of men to safety. Heinrich

Heimann, the commander of the Leibstandarte's StuG Battalion, was less lucky—he was killed in unknown circumstances on the same day, almost certainly in the Magny area after encountering Canadian troops. Teddy Wisch, the Leibstandarte commander, had been severely wounded in both legs by shell fire even before the breakout began but was evacuated along the 'Corridor of Death' in the SPW of his artillery commander, Franz Steineck. General Hausser began by accompanying the 3rd Parachute Division spearhead on foot, transferred to a small Panzer KG south of Mont Ormel, was seriously wounded by mortar fire, and was eventually brought out in an SPW of the Hitlerjugend 5th SS Panzer Artillery Battery. And the final story of the Falaise pocket must be that of Max Wünsche. We left him with two officers of his staff and his wounded medical officer. They hid up all day on the 20th, soaked to the skin, cold and reduced to eating beets to curb their hunger. That night they continued their journey but ran into an enemy outpost—the doctor was captured and Wünsche wounded in the calf. They were still 5 or 6km south of the Dives in the Fôret de Gouffern near Bailleul. The British 29th Armoured Brigade was all around them![18] Repeated encounters with the enemy led to SS Captain Isecke becoming separated and captured on the 24th. Wünsche and Freitag eventually found a German vehicle in full working order and managed to drive through St Lambert quite openly. They were able to do this because many Canadians were also driving around in captured German vehicles; but their luck did not last and they too were captured on the 24th as they slept in the sun under the cover of some bushes, waiting for darkness.

Many more German soldiers and vehicles got out during the night of the 20th and at 0700 hours on the 21st General Meindl and his rearguard paratroopers reached the safety of the 2nd SS Panzer Division lines.

Early on the same day the Polish Armoured Reconnaissance Regiment tried to link up with the main force on Maczuga but was fired on by friendly forces and withdrew after two of its Cromwells were damaged. The last German attack against the Poles on Maczuga came at 1100 hours from the west. It was again repelled but by then their Armoured Regiments were

almost out of 75mm ammunition, many of the tanks immobilized due to lack of fuel and their infantry exhausted and short
of ammunition, food and water.[19] At 1330 hours they heard
the sound of more tanks approaching and feared the worst. It
turned out to be the Canadian Grenadier Guards bringing
relief. They had begun their advance at 0800 hours and lost
four tanks on the way whilst claiming to have knocked out two
Panthers, a Mk IV and two SP guns. The Canadian War Diary
records:

> The picture at 262 was the grimmest the Regiment has so
> far come up against. The Poles had had no supplies for
> three days; they had several hundred wounded who had not
> been evacuated; about 700 prisoners lay loosely guarded in a
> field, the road was blocked by burned out vehicles, both our
> own and the enemy's. Unburied dead and parts of them
> were strewn about by the score. . . . The Poles cried with
> joy when we arrived and from what they said I doubt if they
> will ever forget this day and the help we gave them.

The Poles lost 351 men killed and wounded and eleven
Shermans during the bitter fighting on Maczuga. In view of
this and the many other valuable contributions made by the
1st Polish Armoured Division before the final German surrender, it is surprising that its representatives were not asked to
participate in the post-war Victory Parade in London.

Michael Carver, whose 4th British Armoured Brigade was
now attached to Simonds's Canadian Corps, described how 44
RTR and 2 KRRC were given the task of 'liquidating the last
pocket of resistance south of Trun' in the afternoon of the
21st:

> They advanced into a mass of dying horses, abandoned ve-
> hicles and dead and dying Germans. They took 3000 pris-
> oners and had great difficulty in putting an end to our own
> artillery fire, which was concentrated into this area from all
> sides.
>   Carnage is the only word to describe it. It was a revolting
> sight, and the stench was indescribable. One was struck with
> intense pity for the inhabitants of these small villages and

farms. For days they had suffered the full weight of Allied air and artillery bombardment, had then been swamped by hordes of retreating Germans and now they were surrounded by scenes of acute horror. One small village had 400 dead horses in it. All one could do was to turn the Germans on to burying their own dead and all the cattle and horses they could. . . . For ever after, Normandy and Camembert cheese would be linked in the memory. . . . with the sight and smell of dead cattle and the sordid litter of the battlefield.[20]

The same afternoon the 2nd SS Panzer Division was ordered to withdraw to the east and by 2000 hours the tanks of the British Columbia Regiment were on Point 262 (South) and those of the 1st Hussars reached the northern outskirts of Chambois—the gap was finally closed and the last battle of Normandy was over.

The 21st Army Group's 2nd Operational Research Section carried out an intensive investigation of the area marked by the towns and villages of Pierrefitte-Argentan-Chambois-Vimoutiers-Trun-Pierrefitte, and called 'The Shambles' in its official report.[21] It found 3,043 German vehicles—187 tanks and SP guns, 252 artillery pieces, 157 light armoured vehicles, 1,778 trucks and 669 'cars'; the heaviest concentrations were to the south and south-west of St Lambert and 112 of the tanks and SP guns were burnt out. Eighty-two of the tanks and SP guns were examined in detail—they included twelve Tigers (three Mk IIs), twenty-two Panthers and twenty-two Mk IVs. Only three Panthers and two Mk IVs had been knocked out by ground fire and two Mk IVs by air delivered rockets—the rest had been destroyed or abandoned by their crews.

In the period 1st to 23rd August the First Canadian Army suffered 12,659 casualties; of these, 7,415 were Canadian, 3,870 were British and 1,374 were Polish.[22] Another casualty was Major General Kitching, the commander of the 4th Canadian Armoured Division, who was sacked by General Crerar on the day the battle ended.

The Hitlerjugend Division lost forty-five men killed and 248 wounded during the period 15th–22nd August. Another 655 were missing—most of them almost certainly taken prisoner.[23] According to Hubert Meyer, 387 of the missing were from the Artillery and Werfer units and he surmises that most of them became prisoners when they tried to get their heavy vehicles out of the Pocket along the congested roads. Comparable figures are not available for the Leibstandarte, but it is known that only fourteen members of the Corps Tiger Battalion were killed or wounded in the same period.

Almost every book written about the Normandy campaign reports that the Leibstandarte had only 'weak infantry elements', and the Hitlerjugend only 300 men left after their withdrawal from the Falaise Pocket. These statements are usually based on a Fifth Panzer Army report to Army Group 'B' dated 21st August. But as Hubert Meyer says in his *History of the 12th SS Panzer Division*:

> Based on that information, mistaken conclusions regarding the losses in the Falaise encirclement have been drawn. It is completely useless as a basis for such considerations.[24]

Meyer concludes that the Fifth Army figures must refer to those units which had broken out of the Pocket and were ready for combat. This author agrees. Taking the junior partner first: on 22nd August the Hitlerjugend numbered approximately 12,500 officers and men, 60% of its authorised strength, of which 2,500 were in the administrative units.[25] Hubert Meyer gives an exact casualty figure of 8,626 for the period 6th June to 10th September[26] (when the HJ returned to Germany) but admits that not all records are complete. He estimates total losses as 'almost 9,000'.

In the case of the Leibstandarte, the German administrative authorities compiled a total of 3,901 casualties for the period 6th June to 30th September, but according to the History of the Division this figure 'is woefully incomplete' and the authors suggest a figure of 'at least 5,000' as more reasonable.[27] That would still leave some 17,000 survivors! What is certainly true is that by 23rd August both Divisions were virtually without tanks, Jagdpanzers, SPWs and artillery pieces and had ceased to exist as fighting formations. They had, however, distinguished themselves greatly and the Hitlerjugend had probably done more than any other German Division in the battle of Normandy to frustrate Allied intentions. The major adversary of I SS Panzer Corps was the Canadian Army; it suffered 18,444 casualties in the period from D-Day to 23rd August.[28] Just one of its Battalions, The Regina Rifles, lost 926 men (224 killed, 688 wounded and fourteen missing)[29]—its strength on 6th June was 845.

23RD TO 25TH AUGUST—POSTSCRIPT

Although we have concluded that nearly 30,000 members of the 1st and 12th SS Panzer Divisions survived to cross the Dives river, we have also made it clear that by 21st August neither Division existed as a coherent fighting formation. It is true that some elements, particularly those which had been withdrawn before mid-August, continued to resist until the 25th, but it is not worth trying to describe their actions in any detail. Suffice it to say that parts of the Leibstandarte's Sturmgeschütz Battalion and 1st SS Reconnaissance Company (which had been left behind in Belgium in early July) fought west of the Seine, as did Bremer's HJ Reconnaissance Battalion and a significant KG under SS Colonel Mohnke, which included parts of both Waldmüller's and Siebken's SS Panzer-Grenadier Battalions and some StuGs and Flak companies from the LAH. Details of their actions are sketchy and unreliable, although Bremer received Oak Leaves to his Knight's Cross for his actions. I SS Panzer Corps Leibstandarte, as defined in this book, no longer existed and our story of its actions in Normandy is ended.

NOTES

1. 10th Mounted Rifles War Diary 18 Aug 44. **2.** Major Currie's citation for the Victoria Cross. **3.** 1st Polish Armd Div Op Report. **4.** Bellfield & Essame, *The Battle for Normandy*, p. 209. **5.** AEAF Ops Summary No. 212 dated 19 Aug 44. **6.** Lehmann & Tiemann, *The Leibstandarte IV/I*, pp. 211 and 214. **7.** Ibid., p. 214. **8.** Major Currie's citation for the Victoria Cross. **9.** No. 4 Liaison Unit War Diary, 19 Aug 44. **10.** Meyer, Hubert, *The History of the 12th SS Panzer Regiment Hitlerjugend*, p. 194. **11.** AEAF Ops Summary No. 213 dated 20 Aug 44. **12.** Meyer, Hubert, op. cit., p. 198. **13.** Lehmann & Tiemann, op. cit., p. 217. **14.** Meyer, Kurt, *Grenadiers*, p. 171. **15.** Interview with Milton Shulman Apr 46. **16.** Meyer, Hubert, op. cit., p. 200. **17.** Stanislaw Grabowski (veteran) to author 29 Aug 96. **18.** 29 Armd Bde War Diary, 20 Aug 44. **19.** Polish veterans to author 18 Aug 96. **20.** Carver, *Second to None*, p. 133. **21.** Report by No. 2 Operational Research Sect with 21st Army Gp, Pt I, Chap 3, (PRO WO 106/4348). **22.** Stacey, *The Official History of the Canadian Army in the Second World War, Vol III, The Victory Campaign*, p. 271. **23.** Meyer, Hubert, op. cit., p. 203. **24.** Ibid., p. 206. **25.** Ibid., p. 204. **26.** Ibid., p. 222. **27.** Lehmann & Tiemann, op. cit., p. 228. **28.** Stacey, op. cit., p. 271. **29.** Regina Rifles War Diary.

Epilogue

Incredible though it may seem, by 16th December 1944 the 1st and 12th SS Panzer Divisions had been brought up to strength, reorganised and re-equipped, and stood ready to lead Hitler's last great offensive in the west, through the Ardennes region of Belgium. The campaign, which became known as the Battle of the Bulge, was a costly disaster; but within a month of its end the Leibstandarte and Hitlerjugend had again been rebuilt and sent to Hungary to help stem the Soviet tide sweeping in from the east.

Both Divisions ended the war in Lower Austria and by the 8th of May 1945 they had, once more, been virtually destroyed. The survivors were held in various camps until early 1946—in some cases in recently emptied Nazi concentration camps. Inevitably the Waffen-SS men complained that they were being branded as war criminals without justification. They failed to appreciate that they were seen as part of a diabolical machine which had been responsible for nearly six years of war in Europe and millions of deaths; and that following the discovery of the Death Camps, *anyone* who wore SS runes was indeed seen by most Allied soldiers as a barbarian and deserving to be treated as such. The Allied authorities certainly had no intention of according to members of the Waffen-SS the honours and courtesies applicable to normal prisoners of war and this was bitterly resented by men who claimed they had never been anything more than combat soldiers.

Some well known members of the original I SS Panzer Corps had of course been killed after Normandy. Amongst them Knights Cross holder Arnold Jürgensen in the Ardennes, and 'Papa' Krause, mortally wounded on 19th February during Operation SOUTH WIND in Hungary. Others died away from the battlefield—a retreating Hitlerjugend column, led by Erich Olboeter, was ambushed by members of the Belgian resistance during the night 1st September. Olboeter's legs were blown off and he died in hospital in Charleville. His fellow Knight's Cross holder, Hans Waldmüller was similarly ambushed and killed in the Ardennes on 8th September as the HJ withdrew back to Germany.

Of the survivors, most members of the Corps were released from captivity in early 1946, but this was not the case with many of the major characters in our particular Odyssey. Sepp Dietrich was eventually paroled in October 1955, tried before a West German court in 1957 for his part in the 'Night of the Long Knives' and sentenced to eighteen months in prison. He died in April 1966 and was given a hero's funeral in Ludwigsberg by his 'boys'.

Kurt Meyer, who not surprisingly had been awarded Swords to his Knight's Cross for his performance in the Normandy campaign, was captured by Belgian partisans on 6th September in the village of Durnal, 15km to the south of Namur. As mentioned in Chapter X, he was tried as a war criminal in December 1945, sentenced to death, reprieved and eventually served over five years in Dorchester prison in New Brunswick, Canada, before being transferred to a British military prison in Werl, West Germany. He made no secret of the fact that he was still a committed Nazi and idolized Hitler. Meyer was released in 1954 and worked for the Andreas Brewery in Hagen. By 1956 he had become a principal speaker for HIAG—the 'Society for the mutual help of members of the former Waffen-SS' in its battle to obtain war pensions for its members, and the following year his book *Grenadiers* was published. He suffered three mild strokes in 1961 before dying of a heart attack on his birthday in the same year. He was just fifty-

one. His funeral was attended by over 5,000 veterans and ad-
mirers.

Wilhelm Mohnke is still alive, living in Barsbüttel near
Hamburg. After commanding the Leibstandarte in the Ardennes offensive he returned to Berlin to head the Führer's
Chancellery Guard. He was captured by the Russians in May
1945 and, after release in 1955, he worked as a dealer in small
trucks and trailers.

One of the best known veterans, Jochen Peiper, was the last
to be released from prison. Shortly after the end of the war he
was branded 'GI enemy Number One' and, following a controversial US Military trial held in the former concentration
camp at Dachau in 1946, he was sentenced to death for what
became known as the 'Malmédy Massacre'. In this incident
eighty-four American, most of whom had already surrendered, died at the hands of Peiper's men. He was released on
parole in December 1956 and after working for Porsche and as
a Volkswagen agent, he eventually retired to Traves in France
in 1972. He died during a fire bomb attack on his home on
Bastille Day, 1976 and was, as the History of the Leibstandarte
puts it, 'Der letzte Gefallene'—the last of the fallen. No one
was ever brought to justice for his death.

Over forty I SS Panzer Corps veterans were condemned to
death by hanging for war crimes but only two of the sentences
were ever carried out—on Siebken and Schnabel, at Hameln in
January 1949. All the others were reprieved and eventually
paroled. But even then some like Georg Preuss, who had been
awarded the Knight's Cross in 1945, met with tragic ends—he
died a recluse and destitute near Luneberg Heath in 1990,
without family or friends, electricity or even running water.

Gerd Bremer was imprisoned by the French for war crimes.
He was released in 1948 and died in 1989 after building and
managing a bungalow holiday park at Denia-las Rotas in
Spain. His counterpart in the LAH, Gustav Knittel, was sentenced to life imprisonment for atrocities committed in
Belgium during the Battle of the Bulge. He was released in the
early 1950s and died in 1976.

Survivors of the Normandy campaign who were not
branded as war criminals included Teddy Wisch who, after

recovering from his wounds, returned to his father's farm in Norderstedt and took up cattle breeding. He died in January 1995 aged nearly 88. Max Wünsche also died in 1995 after managing an industrial plant in Wuppertal. Rudolf Sandig became a director of an insurance company. He was wearing a miniature Knight's Cross (minus its Swastika) in his lapel when the author met him in 1982. He died in Weyhe-Leeste near Bremen in 1994.

Max Hansen became an SS Colonel in February 1945. After the war he and his wife ran a cleaning shop in Niebuell but he spent his last three or four years as little more than a living corpse—'his brain and soul already being in Valhalla' as a comrade put it.

Hubert Meyer, at 84, is still active. Apart from writing his remarkable History of the Hitlerjugend Division, he attended a British Command and Staff College battlefield tour of Normandy in 1974 and was apparently able to make a valuable contribution to the discussions and reminiscences. At the time of writing, he is currently helping to make a video about the HJ's actions in the December 1944 Ardennes campaign.

The officers and men of the Leibstandarte and Hitlerjugend Divisions were indeed extraordinary men—considered heroes and revered by some, judged as criminals and reviled by others. Not all of them acted bravely—there are plenty of examples of terrified youngsters surrendering to Allied soldiers. But they can as a whole be equated to the men of Caesar's finest Legions and to Napoleon's Old Guard. They have also been compared to Ghengis Khan's scourging hordes and Attila's invading Huns! But whatever else they were, they were remarkable soldiers—the like of which we may never see again.

And now we must ask ourselves what made them as they were? And here we face a number of contradictions. That they were motivated by what turned out to be a thoroughly evil system did not prevent them from being fine leaders and soldiers, and the fact that they came almost entirely from Christian homes and schools did not prevent them from often acting brutally and without mercy. But then they did not believe that war was a 'game' to be played by 'rules'; it was instead a contest which had to be won. The other contestants were seen as inferior and therefore it was unthinkable that the opposition could or should be allowed to win.

Despite flawed strategic direction from the Supreme Command (Hitler), which often placed the soldiers of the LAH and HJ in almost impossible situations, at the tactical level their officers usually managed to select the vital ground on which the soldiers had a reasonable chance of performing well. And despite the short and often inadequate training which many of the soldiers received before being committed to battle, their motivation, discipline, natural instincts as soldiers and intense loyalty to each other, enabled them to achieve remarkable results. The combined effect of skilled officers and senior NCOs and brave, dedicated soldiers made for an extremely formidable military machine. Wounds were to be borne with pride and never used as a reason to leave the field of battle; mercy was seen as a sign of weakness and was normally neither offered nor expected.

The willingness of the members of the Waffen-SS to go on fighting when it was clear that the war was lost can only be a source of wonder to today's generation. However, their experiences in the East undoubtedly added to their resolve to protect their homeland for as long as possible and at whatever cost.

The fact that these men were part of an elite organisation which was stamped with their charismatic leader's own name was an important influence on their outlook. But attractive uniforms, fine weapons, abundant quantities of meaningful medals worn even in battle to single out the proven brave, a strong emphasis on comradeship—these were all factors which played a part in making these men unique. Perhaps, though, the most significant thing which singled out the men of these Divisions was their obvious pride in being soldiers. It is strange that in post-war years the former Allies have spent so much time criticizing each other's performances in WWII but admiring that of their enemy—particularly the Waffen-SS. At the end of the day it has to be said that the soldiers of the I SS Panzer Corps excelled in what is still, in some circles, called 'The Art of War'.

Appendix I

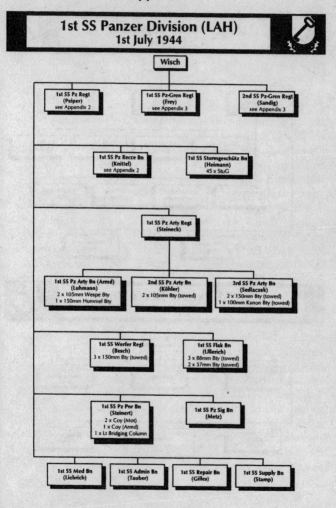

1st SS Panzer Division (LAH)
1st July 1944

Wisch

1st SS Pz Regt
(Peiper)
see Appendix 2

1st SS Pz-Gren Regt
(Frey)
see Appendix 3

2nd SS Pz-Gren Regt
(Sandig)
see Appendix 3

1st SS Pz Recce Bn
(Knittel)
see Appendix 2

1st SS Sturmgeschütz Bn
(Heimann)
45 x StuG

1st SS Pz Arty Regt
(Steineck)

1st SS Pz Arty Bn (Armd)
(Luhmann)
2 x 105mm Wespe Bty
1 x 150mm Hummel Bty

2nd SS Pz Arty Bn
(Köhler)
2 x 105mm Bty (towed)

3rd SS Pz Arty Bn
(Sedlaczek)
2 x 150mm Bty (towed)
1 x 100mm Kanon Bty (towed)

1st SS Werfer Regt
(Besch)
3 x 150mm Bty (towed)

1st SS Flak Bn
(Ullerich)
3 x 88mm Bty (towed)
2 x 37mm Bty (towed)

1st SS Pz Pnr Bn
(Steinert)
2 x Coy (Mot)
1 x Coy (Armd)
1 x Lt Bridging Column

1st SS Pz Sig Bn
(Metz)

1st SS Med Bn
(Liebrich)

1st SS Admin Bn
(Tauber)

1st SS Repair Bn
(Gilles)

1st SS Supply Bn
(Stamp)

Appendix II

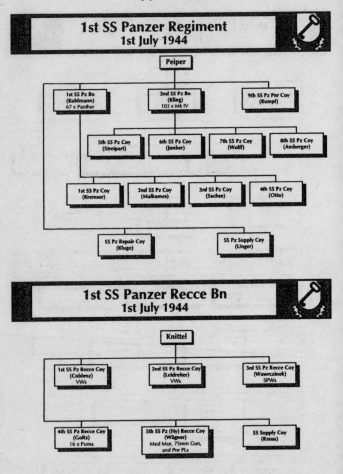

1st SS Panzer Regiment
1st July 1944

Peiper

1st SS Pz Bn
(Kuhlmann)
67 x Panther

2nd SS Pz Bn
(Kling)
103 x Mk IV

9th SS Pz Pnr Coy
(Rumpf)

5th SS Pz Coy
(Streipart)

6th SS Pz Coy
(Junker)

7th SS Pz Coy
(Wolff)

8th SS Pz Coy
(Amberger)

1st SS Pz Coy
(Kremser)

2nd SS Pz Coy
(Malkomes)

3rd SS Pz Coy
(Sachse)

4th SS Pz Coy
(Otto)

SS Pz Repair Coy
(Kluge)

SS Pz Supply Coy
(Unger)

1st SS Panzer Recce Bn
1st July 1944

Knittel

1st SS Pz Recce Coy
(Coblenz)
VWs

2nd SS Pz Recce Coy
(Leidreiter)
VWs

3rd SS Pz Recce Coy
(Wawrczinek)
SPWs

4th SS Pz Recce Coy
(Goltz)
16 x Puma

5th SS Pz (Hy) Recce Coy
(Wagner)
Med Mor, 75mm Gun,
and Pnr PLs

SS Supply Coy
(Reuss)

Appendix III

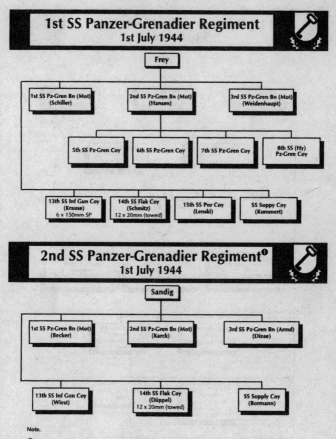

1st SS Panzer-Grenadier Regiment
1st July 1944

Frey

- 1st SS Pz-Gren Bn (Mot) (Schiller)
- 2nd SS Pz-Gren Bn (Mot) (Hansen)
  - 5th SS Pz-Gren Coy
  - 6th SS Pz-Gren Coy
  - 7th SS Pz-Gren Coy
  - 8th SS (Hy) Pz-Gren Coy
- 3rd SS Pz-Gren Bn (Mot) (Weidenhaupt)

- 13th SS Inf Gun Coy (Krause) 6 x 150mm SP
- 14th SS Flak Coy (Schmitz) 12 x 20mm (towed)
- 15th SS Pnr Coy (Lenski)
- SS Suppy Coy (Kummert)

2nd SS Panzer-Grenadier Regiment ❶
1st July 1944

Sandig

- 1st SS Pz-Gren Bn (Mot) (Becker)
- 2nd SS Pz-Gren Bn (Mot) (Karck)
- 3rd SS Pz-Gren Bn (Armd) (Dinse)

- 13th SS Inf Gun Coy (Wiest)
- 14th SS Flak Coy (Düppel) 12 x 20mm (towed)
- SS Supply Coy (Bormann)

Note.

❶ No Pnr Coy.

Appendix IV

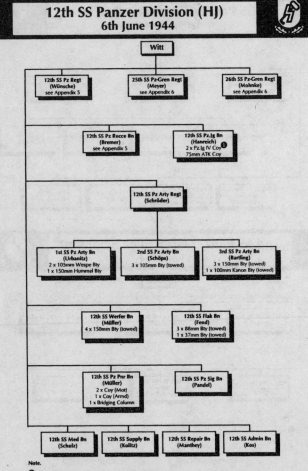

12th SS Panzer Division (HJ)
6th June 1944

Witt

12th SS Pz Regt
(Wünsche)
see Appendix 5

25th SS Pz-Gren Regt
(Meyer)
see Appendix 6

26th SS Pz-Gren Regt
(Mohnke)
see Appendix 6

12th SS Pz Recce Bn
(Bremer)
see Appendix 5

12th SS Pz.Jg Bn
(Hanreich)
2 x Pz.Jg IV Coy ❶
75mm ATK Coy

12th SS Pz Arty Regt
(Schröder)

1st SS Pz Arty Bn
(Urbanitz)
2 x 105mm Wespe Bty
1 x 150mm Hummel Bty

2nd SS Pz Arty Bn
(Schöps)
3 x 105mm Bty (towed)

3rd SS Pz Arty Bn
(Bartling)
3 x 150mm Bty (towed)
1 x 100mm Kanon Bty (towed)

12th SS Werfer Bn
(Müller)
4 x 150mm Bty (towed)

12th SS Flak Bn
(Fend)
3 x 88mm Bty (towed)
1 x 37mm Bty (towed)

12th SS Pz Pnr Bn
(Müller)
2 x Coy (Mot)
1 x Coy (Armd)
1 x Bridging Column

12th SS Pz Sig Bn
(Pandel)

12th SS Med Bn
(Schulz)

12th SS Supply Bn
(Kolitz)

12th SS Repair Bn
(Manthey)

12th SS Admin Bn
(Kos)

Note.

❶ These companies were not operational until mid-July.

Appendix V

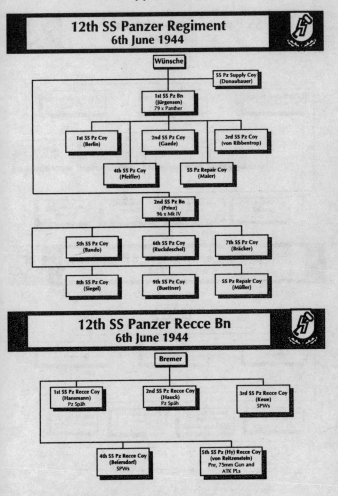

12th SS Panzer Regiment
6th June 1944

Wünsche

SS Pz Supply Coy
(Donaubauer)

1st SS Pz Bn
(Jürgensen)
79 x Panther

1st SS Pz Coy
(Berlin)

2nd SS Pz Coy
(Gaede)

3rd SS Pz Coy
(von Ribbentrop)

4th SS Pz Coy
(Pfeiffer)

SS Pz Repair Coy
(Maier)

2nd SS Pz Bn
(Prinz)
96 x Mk IV

5th SS Pz Coy
(Bando)

6th SS Pz Coy
(Ruckdeschel)

7th SS Pz Coy
(Bräcker)

8th SS Pz Coy
(Siegel)

9th SS Pz Coy
(Buettner)

SS Pz Repair Coy
(Müller)

12th SS Panzer Recce Bn
6th June 1944

Bremer

1st SS Pz Recce Coy
(Hansmann)
Pz Späh

2nd SS Pz Recce Coy
(Hauck)
Pz Späh

3rd SS Pz Recce Coy
(Keue)
SPWs

4th SS Pz Recce Coy
(Beiersdorf)
SPWs

5th SS Pz (Hy) Recce Coy
(von Reitzenstein)
Pnr, 75mm Gun and
ATK Pls

Appendix VI

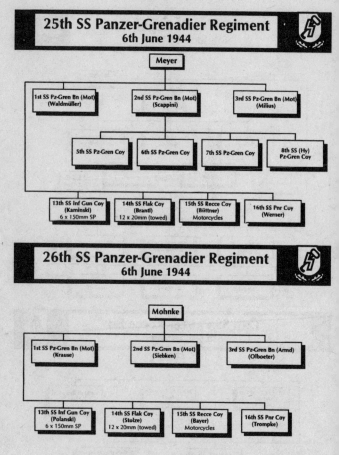

25th SS Panzer-Grenadier Regiment
6th June 1944

Meyer

1st SS Pz-Gren Bn (Mot)
(Waldmüller)

2nd SS Pz-Gren Bn (Mot)
(Scappini)

3rd SS Pz-Gren Bn (Mot)
(Milius)

5th SS Pz-Gren Coy

6th SS Pz-Gren Coy

7th SS Pz-Gren Coy

8th SS (Hy)
Pz-Gren Coy

13th SS Inf Gun Coy
(Kaminski)
6 x 150mm SP

14th SS Flak Coy
(Brantl)
12 x 20mm (towed)

15th SS Recce Coy
(Büttner)
Motorcycles

16th SS Pnr Coy
(Werner)

26th SS Panzer-Grenadier Regiment
6th June 1944

Mohnke

1st SS Pz-Gren Bn (Mot)
(Krause)

2nd SS Pz-Gren Bn (Mot)
(Siebken)

3rd SS Pz-Gren Bn (Armd)
(Olboeter)

13th SS Inf Gun Coy
(Polanski)
6 x 150mm SP

14th SS Flak Coy
(Stolze)
12 x 20mm (towed)

15th SS Recce Coy
(Bayer)
Motorcycles

16th SS Pnr Coy
(Trompke)

Appendix VII

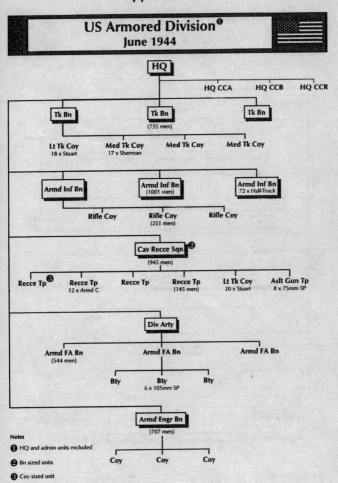

US Armored Division[1]
June 1944

HQ

HQ CCA   HQ CCB   HQ CCR

Tk Bn   Tk Bn   Tk Bn
                (735 men)

Lt Tk Coy   Med Tk Coy   Med Tk Coy   Med Tk Coy
18 x Stuart   17 x Sherman

Armd Inf Bn   Armd Inf Bn   Armd Inf Bn
                (1001 men)   72 x Half-Track

Rifle Coy   Rifle Coy   Rifle Coy
                (251 men)

Cav Recce Sqn[2]
(945 men)

Recce Tp[3]   Recce Tp   Recce Tp   Recce Tp   Lt Tk Coy   Aslt Gun Tp
                12 x Armd C   (145 men)   20 x Stuart   8 x 75mm SP

Div Arty

Armd FA Bn   Armd FA Bn   Armd FA Bn
(544 men)

                Bty   Bty   Bty
                          6 x 105mm SP

Armd Engr Bn
(707 men)

Coy   Coy   Coy

Notes

[1] HQ and admin units excluded

[2] Bn sized units

[3] Coy sized unit

Appendix VIII

British/Canadian/Polish Armoured Division[1] June 1944

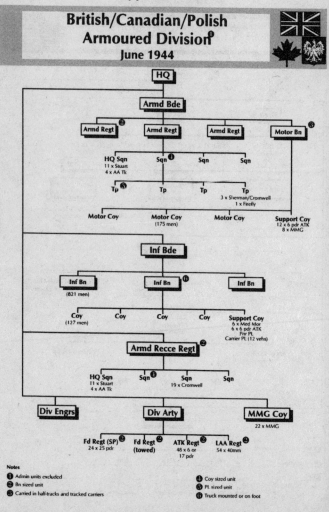

HQ

Armd Bde

Armd Regt[2] **Armd Regt** **Armd Regt** **Motor Bn[3]**

HQ Sqn Sqn[1] Sqn Sqn
11 x Stuart
4 x AA Tk

Tp[5] Tp Tp Tp
3 x Sherman/Cromwell
1 x Firefly

Motor Coy | Motor Coy (175 men) | Motor Coy | Support Coy 12 x 6 pdr ATK 8 x MMG

Inf Bde

Inf Bn (821 men) | **Inf Bn[6]** | **Inf Bn**

Coy (127 men) | Coy | Coy | Coy | Support Coy 6 x Med Mor 6 x 6 pdr ATK Pnr PL Carrier PL (12 vehs)

Armd Recce Regt[2]

HQ Sqn Sqn[1] Sqn Sqn
11 x Stuart   19 x Cromwell
4 x AA Tk

Div Engrs | **Div Arty** | **MMG Coy** 22 x MMG

Fd Regt (SP)[2] | Fd Regt[2] | ATK Regt[2] | LAA Regt[2]
24 x 25 pdr | (towed) | 48 x 6 or | 54 x 40mm
                         17 pdr

Notes

[1] Admin units excluded
[2] Bn sized unit
[3] Carried in half-tracks and tracked carriers
[4] Coy sized unit
[5] Pl sized unit
[6] Truck mounted or on foot

Appendix IX

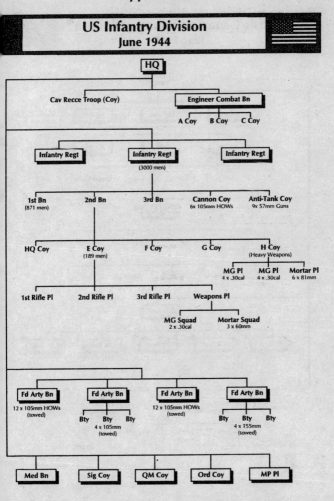

US Infantry Division
June 1944

HQ

Cav Recce Troop (Coy)

Engineer Combat Bn

A Coy   B Coy   C Coy

Infantry Regt

Infantry Regt
(3000 men)

Infantry Regt

1st Bn
(871 men)

2nd Bn

3rd Bn

Cannon Coy
6x 105mm HOWs

Anti-Tank Coy
9x 57mm Guns

HQ Coy

E Coy
(189 men)

F Coy

G Coy

H Coy
(Heavy Weapons)

MG Pl
4 x .30cal

MG Pl
4 x .30cal

Mortar Pl
6 x 81mm

1st Rifle Pl

2nd Rifle Pl

3rd Rifle Pl

Weapons Pl

MG Squad
2 x .30cal

Mortar Squad
3 x 60mm

Fd Arty Bn
12 x 105mm HOWs
(towed)

Fd Arty Bn

Bty   Bty   Bty
4 x 105mm
(towed)

Fd Arty Bn
12 x 105mm HOWs
(towed)

Fd Arty Bn

Bty   Bty   Bty
4 x 155mm
(towed)

Med Bn

Sig Coy

QM Coy

Ord Coy

MP Pl

Appendix X

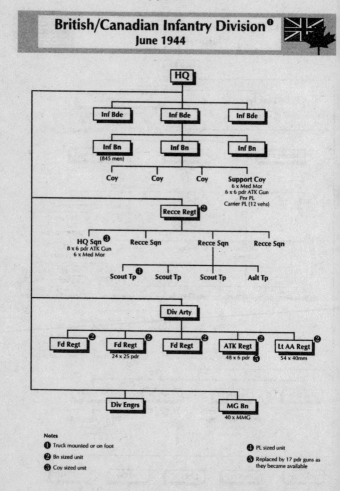

British/Canadian Infantry Division [1]
June 1944

```
                                HQ

        Inf Bde          Inf Bde          Inf Bde

        Inf Bn           Inf Bn           Inf Bn
        (845 men)

   Coy     Coy     Coy    Support Coy
                          6 x Med Mor
                          6 x 6 pdr ATK Gun
                          Pnr PL
                          Carrier PL (12 vehs)

                     Recce Regt [2]

   HQ Sqn [3]      Recce Sqn     Recce Sqn     Recce Sqn
   8 x 6 pdr ATK Gun
   6 x Med Mor

          Scout Tp [1]  Scout Tp  Scout Tp  Aslt Tp

                      Div Arty

   Fd Regt [2]  Fd Regt [2]  Fd Regt [2]  ATK Regt [2]  Lt AA Regt [2]
                24 x 25 pdr               48 x 6 pdr [5]  54 x 40mm

              Div Engrs              MG Bn
                                     40 x MMG
```

Notes

1. Truck mounted or on foot

2. Bn sized unit

3. Coy sized unit

4. PL sized unit

5. Replaced by 17 pdr guns as they became available

Appendix XI

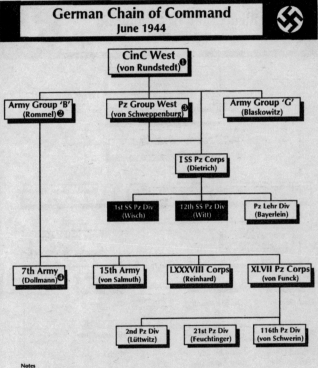

German Chain of Command
June 1944

CinC West (von Rundstedt) ❶

- **Army Group 'B'** (Rommel) ❷
- **Pz Group West** (von Schweppenburg) ❸
- **Army Group 'G'** (Blaskowitz)

I SS Pz Corps (Dietrich)

- **1st SS Pz Div** (Wisch)
- **12th SS Pz Div** (Witt)
- **Pz Lehr Div** (Bayerlein)

- **7th Army** (Dollmann) ❹
- **15th Army** (von Salmuth)
- **LXXXVIII Corps** (Reinhard)
- **XLVII Pz Corps** (von Funck)

- **2nd Pz Div** (Lüttwitz)
- **21st Pz Div** (Feuchtinger)
- **116th Pz Div** (von Schwerin)

Notes

❶ Succeeded by von Kluge on 2nd July, who was replaced by Model on 17th August.

❷ When Rommel was injured on 17th July his Army Group was commanded directly by CinC West.

❸ Succeeded by Eberbach on 2nd July.

❹ Succeeded by Hausser on 28th June.

Appendix XII

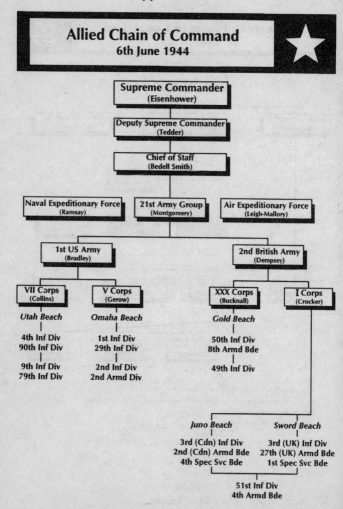

Allied Chain of Command
6th June 1944

Supreme Commander
(Eisenhower)

Deputy Supreme Commander
(Tedder)

Chief of Staff
(Bedell Smith)

| Naval Expeditionary Force (Ramsay) | 21st Army Group (Montgomery) | Air Expeditionary Force (Leigh-Mallory) |

1st US Army
(Bradley)

2nd British Army
(Dempsey)

| VII Corps (Collins) | V Corps (Gerow) | XXX Corps (Bucknall) | I Corps (Crocker) |

Utah Beach

4th Inf Div
90th Inf Div

9th Inf Div
79th Inf Div

Omaha Beach

1st Inf Div
29th Inf Div

2nd Inf Div
2nd Armd Div

Gold Beach

50th Inf Div
8th Armd Bde

49th Inf Div

Juno Beach

3rd (Cdn) Inf Div
2nd (Cdn) Armd Bde
4th Spec Svc Bde

Sword Beach

3rd (UK) Inf Div
27th (UK) Armd Bde
1st Spec Svc Bde

51st Inf Div
4th Armd Bde

Appendix XIII

Guide to Abbreviations and German Words

AA	Anti-Aircraft
AEAF	Allied Expeditionary Air Force
Armd	Armoured
Atk	Anti-Tank
Bde	Brigade
Bn	Battalion
Bty	Battery
Cdn	Canadian
CinC	Commander in Chief
Coy	Company
Cpl	Corporal
D-Day	Day of Attack
Div	Division
DR	Das Reich
Engr	Engineer
Flak	Anti-Aircraft
GI	General Infantryman
Heer	Army
H-Hour	time of an attack
HJ	Hitlerjugend
Hy	Heavy
Inf	Infantry
IWM	Imperial War Museum
Jagdpanzer (JgPz)	hunter tank
Kampfgruppe (KG)	Battlegroup
LAA	Light Anti-Aircraft
LAH	Leibstandarte Adolf Hitler
Lt	Light
Med	Medical
med	medium
Meldung	Status Report

MG	Machine-Gun
Mk	Mark
MMG	Medium Machine-Gun
Mor	Mortar
Mot	Motorized
NCO	Non Commissioned Officer
'O' Group	meeting where commander gives orders
OKW	HQ of German Armed Forces
Op	Operational/Operation
OR	Other Rank
pdr	pounder
PIAT	Projector Infantry Anti-Tank
Pl	Platoon
Pnr	Pioneer (engineer)
PRO	Public Record Office
Pz	Panzer
Pz-Gren	Panzer-Grenadier (armoured infantry)
PzJg	Panzerjäger (tank hunter)
R & R	Rest & Recuperation
Recce	Reconnaissance
Regt	Regiment
SA	Sturmabteilung (Storm Detachment)
SHAEF	Supreme Headquarters Allied Expeditionary Force
SP	self-propelled
SPW	German half track
Sqn	Squadron
SS-VT	Special Purpose Troops
StuG	armoured assault gun
Sturmgeschütz	armoured assault gun
T-Div	Totenkopf Division
Tk	Tank
Tp	Troop
Tpt	Transport
vehs	vehicles
Werfer	mortar
WW II	World War Two (Second World War)
Wehrmacht	German Armed Forces

Bibliography

It will be clear from the text that, as well as the books quoted below, the main sources of information concerning the Allies used in the compilation of this book have been personal interviews and the War Diaries, Logs and After Action Reports of the formations and units involved. With one exception, the relevant War Diary or After Action Report of every American, British and Canadian formation and unit mentioned has been consulted for the day in question—the exception is the British 53rd Infantry Division, which was unavailable since it was in 'conversation'. American After Action Reports were obtained from the National Archives of the United States of America; British and Canadian War Diaries and Royal Air Force and Royal Canadian Air Force squadron records were studied in the British Public Record Office at Kew. Other useful documents were provided by the British Army Historical Branch, Ministry of Defence, London. Crown copyright is reproduced with the permission of the Controller of Her Majesty's Stationery Office. The Operational Report of the 1st Polish Armoured Division and the Histories, Chronicles and War Diaries of various individual units were made available through the Polish Institute and Sikorski Museum in London.

In building up the German side of the picture, the author made maximum use of the Histories of the 1st and 12th SS Panzer Divisions, and the Radio and Telephone Logs and Daily Reports of Headquarters Army Group 'B' and Seventh Army, which were obtained from the US National Archives. Further valuable information was obtained from strength returns held by the Bundesarchiv, Germany and from interviews carried out after the war on behalf of the US Army Historical Branch. The records of these interviews are also held in the US National Archives and in one case in the British Imperial War

. Museum. Information on German Panzer strengths originated in the Bundesarchiv Germany (Reference RH 10).

Books consulted, and in some cases quoted, were:

Belchem, David, *Victory in Normandy*, Chatto & Windus Ltd, 1981.

Belfield, Eversley & Essame, H., *The Battle for Normandy*, Batsford Ltd, 1965.

Bennett, Ralph, *Ultra in the West, The Normandy Campaign, 1944–45*, Charles Scribner's Sons, New York.

Blumenson, Martin, *The United States Army in World War II: Breakout and Pursuit*, (Washington, DC: US Army Center for Military History, 1961).

Bradley, Omar, *A Soldier's Story*, London, 1952.

Bryant, Sir Arthur, *The Great Duke*, Collins, 1971.

Carver, Lt Col R.M.P, *Second to None, The Royal Scots Greys, 1919–1945*, Messrs McCorquodale & Co Ltd, 1954.

Carver, Michael, *Out of Step*, Hutchinson, 1989.

Carell, Paul, *Invasion—They're coming!*, George G. Harrap & Co Ltd, 1962.

Cassidy, G. L., *Warpath. The Story of the Algonquin Regiment, 1939–1945*, The Ryerson Press, Toronto, 1948.

Copp, Terry, & Vogel, Robert, *Maple Leaf Route: Falaise*, Maple Leaf Route, Ontario, 1983.

Delaforce, Patrick, *The Polar Bears*, Alan Sutton Publishing Ltd, 1995.

D'Este, Carlo, *Decision in Normandy*, HarperCollins, 1983.

Dugdale & Wood, *Complete Orders of Battle of the Waffen-SS in Normandy*, Vol I, Books International, 1997.

Eisenhower, David, *Eisenhower at War 1943–1945*, Random House, 1986.

Eisenhower, Dwight, *Crusade in Europe*, New York, 1948.

Ellis, Chris, *Tanks of World War 2*, Octopus Books Ltd, 1981.

Ellis, L, *Victory in the West, Vol I, The Battle of Normandy*, H M Stationery Office, 1962.

Featherston, Alwyn, *Saving the Breakout*, Presido Press, USA, 1993.

Forty, George, *Desert Rats at War*, Ian Allan, London, 1977.

Foster, Tony, *Meeting of Generals*, Methuen, Canada, 1986.

Hamilton, Nigel, *Monty Master of the Battlefield 1942–1944*, Hamish Hamilton, 1983.

Hart Dyke, Trevor, *Normandy to Arnhem*, 4th Bn Yorkshire Volunteers, 1966.

Hastings, Max, *Overlord, D-Day and the Battle for Normandy 1944*, Michael Joseph, 1984.

Hastings, R. *The Rifle Brigade 1939–1945*, Gale & Polden, 1950.

Hewitt, Robert, *Workhorse of the Western Front*, Washington Infantry Journal Press, 1946.

Hogg, Ian, *The Guns of World War II*, Macdonald & Jane's, 1976.

How, Major J. J. MC, *Hill 112—Cornerstone of the Normandy Campaign*, William Kimber & Co Ltd, 1984.

Irving, David, *The Trail of the Fox*, London and New York, 1977.

Keeble, Lewis, *Worm's Eye View—The Recollections of Lewis Keeble*, Appx C to 'Battlefield Tour, 1st/4th KOYLI in the NW Europe Campaign' by Geoffrey Barker-Harland.

Keegan, John, *Six Armies in Normandy*, Jonathan Cape, 1982.

Lefèvre, Eric, *Panzers in Normandy, Then and Now*, 'After the Battle' Magazine, 1983.

Lehmann, Rudolf, *The Leibstandarte Parts I, II and III*, J. J. Fedorowicz Publishing Inc, Manitoba, Canada, 1987, 1988, 1990.

Lehmann, Rudolf & Tiemann, Ralf, *The Leibstandarte IV/I*, J. J. Fedorowicz Publishing Inc, Manitoba, Canada, 1993.

Lindsay and Johnson, *History of the 7th Armoured Division 1943–45*, unpublished, 1945, Author's possession.

Lucas, James, *Das Reich*, Cassell, 1991.

Lucas, James & Barker, James, *The Killing Ground*, B. T. Batsford, 1978.

Luck, Hans von, *Panzer Commander*, Praeger, New York, 1989.

Maczek, Stanislaw, *Avec Mes Blindés*, Presses de la Cité, Paris.

Martin, H. G., *The History of the 15th Scottish Division 1939–1945*, William Blackwood & Sons Ltd, 1948.

Messenger, Charles, *Hitler's Gladiator*, Brassey's, 1988.

Meyer, Hubert, *History of the 12th SS Panzer Division Hitler-*

jugend, J. J. Fedorowicz Publishing Inc, Manitoba, Canada, 1994.

Meyer, Kurt, *Grenadiers*, J. J. Fedorowicz Publishing Inc, Manitoba, Canada, 1994.

Montgomery, B. L, *Memoirs of Field Marshal the Viscount Montgomery*, HarperCollins, 1958.

Neillands, Robin, *The Desert Rats*, Weidenfeld and Nicolson, London.

Nicolson, N, *Alex*, Weidenfeld & Nicolson, 1973.

Ritgen, Helmut, *Die Geschichte der Panzer Lehr Division im Western 1944–1945*, Motorbuch Verlag, Stuttgart, 1979.

Sayer, Ian and Botting, Douglas, *Hitler's Last General*, Bantam Press 1989.

Shulman, Milton, *Defeat in the West*, Masquerade, 1995. *Spearhead in the West, The Third Armored Division 1941–45*, Turner Publishing Co, USA.

Stacey, C. P. Col, *Official History of the Canadian Army in the Second World War, Vol III, The Victory Campaign*, Queen's Printer, Ottawa, Canada, 1960.

Vannoy, Allyn R. and Karamales, Jay, *Against The Panzers*, McFarland & Co, 1996.

Verney, G. L., *The Desert Rats*, Greenhill Books, 1990.

Wilmot, Chester, *The Struggle for Europe*, HarperCollins, 1952.

Every effort has been made to obtain permission to quote from letters and from specific books. In some cases the authors are known to have passed away or could not be contacted, and in others publishing companies have ceased to exist or failed to reply to letters.

Index

PLACES